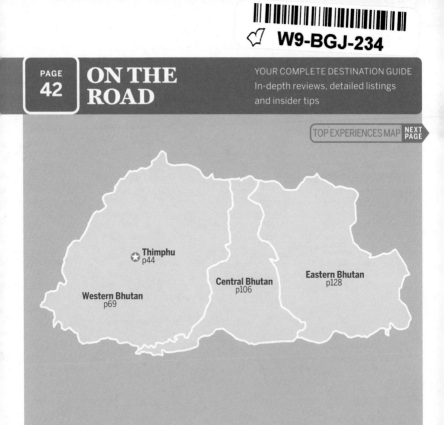

PAGE 42
ON THE ROAD

YOUR COMPLETE DESTINATION GUIDE
In-depth reviews, detailed listings and insider tips

TOP EXPERIENCES MAP | NEXT PAGE

⭐ **Thimphu**
p44

Central Bhutan
p106

Eastern Bhutan
p128

Western Bhutan
p69

PAGE 253
SURVIVAL GUIDE

YOUR AT-A-GLANCE REFERENCE
How to get around, get a room, stay safe, say hello

THIS EDITION WRITTEN AND RESEARCHED BY

Bradley Mayhew,
Lindsay Brown, Anirban Mahapatra

›Bhutan

Thimphu Valley
Hillside monasteries and
wonderful hiking trails (p64)

Thimphu
Crafts, museums and a fine
weekend market (p44)

Jhomolhari Trek
Bhutan's finest
mountain scenery (p153)

Wagye La

Gala

Masagang (7165m)
Teri Gang (7300m)

Gangchhenta (6840m)
Laya

Tsenda Kang (7100m)

Jelekangphu Gang (7300m)
Zonpghu Gang (Table Mountain) (7100m)

Kangphu Gang (7212m)
Melunghi Gang (7000m)

Thanza
Kangri (7239m)

Chozo
Thaga

Gieu Gang (7200m)
GASA

Lingzhi

Gasa
Tsachhu

Jichu Drake (6989m)
Jangothang

Damji

WANGDUE PHODRANG

Jhomolhari (7314m)
JHOMOLHARI TREK
Tashithang

Phari
Thangthangka
THIMPHU
PUNAKHA

Shing Karap
Dodina
Dawakha

Tseshinang

PARO
Dechenchholing
Punakha

Gunyitsawa
THIMPHU VALLEY
Khuruthang
Chhuzomsa

Nobding
Zelela

Yatung
Taktshang Goemba
Thimphu
Hongtsho
Lobesa
Tashila
Sephu

Cheli La (3810m)
Paro
Dochu La (3140m)
Wangdue Phodrang
Gangte Goemba
Pele La
Chende Chorte

Kyichu Lhakhang
Isuna
Simtokha Dzong
PHOBJIKHA VALLEY

HAA
Haa
Chhuzom
Chhukha
Genekha
TSIRANG

Dobji Dzong
Chapcha
Dagana
Sankosh
Damphu

SAMTSE
Bunakha
DAGANA

Sibsu
Tsimasham
Chhukha
Lamidranga
SARPANG

Dorokha
Dungna
Dagapela

Chengmari
CHHUKHA
Gedu
Jumbja

Samtse
Sarpang

Rinchending
Tala

Phuentsholing
Sinchula

Kalikhola

**Tiger's Nest
(Taktshang Goemba)**
Bhutan's most spectacular
sacred site (p82)

Wangdue Phodrang
Refreshingly unrestored
and strategic dzong (p95)

INDIA
(ASSAM)

Kyichu Lhakhang
Beautiful 1300-year-old
temple (p80)

Paro
Excellent dzong and the
National Museum (p72)

Punakha Dzong
Bhutan's most beautiful
monastic fortress (p91)

Bumthang
Sacred sites and cultural
heartland (p112)

Trashigang
Launchpad to Bhutan's
wild east (p137)

Phobjikha Valley
Premier hiking and
crane-spotting location (p98)

Trongsa
Commanding dzong with
a fine museum (p109)

CHINA
TIBET

Lhodrak

Chura
Gang
(6500m)

Gokthong La

Toktu
Zampa

Kizum

Mesithang

Jakar

BUMTHANG

tang La
425m)

Zungney

Gyetsa

rongsa

Ura

Kurxi Chhu

Dungkhar

LHUENTSE

Lhuentse

Tangmachu

Singye Dzong

Bomdeling

TRASHI
YANGTSE

Trashi
Yangtse

Tshenkarla

Shali

Tsona

INDIA
(ARUNACHAL
PRADESH)

enga
bten

Zhemgang

RONGSA

ZHEMGANG

Gelephu

Royal Manas
National
Park

Autsho

Thrumshing La
(3750m)

Sengor

Namling

Ligmethang

Chali

Panbang

Duksum

Drametse
Goemba

Yadi

Chazam

Rangjung

Radi

Sherichhu

Kanglung

Bartsam

Mongar

Pemagatshel

Yongla

Manas Chhu

Nganglam

Narphung La

Phongme

Sakteng

Trashigang

Rongthong

Merak

Khaling

Airstrip

Wamrong

Riserboo

Deothang

Samdrup
Jongkhar

SAMDRUP
JONGKHAR

Bhangtar

INDIA
(ARUNACHAL
PRADESH)

Dhansiri

TRASHIGANG

ELEVATION

6000m
5000m
3000m
2000m
1000m
500m
200m
100m
0

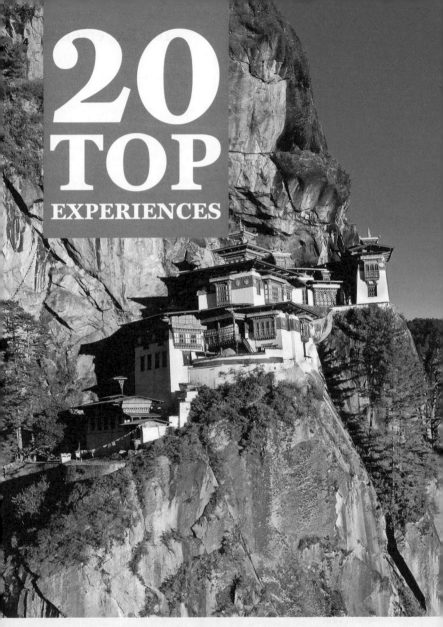

Tiger's Nest (Taktshang Goemba)

1 Bhutan's most famous monastery, Tiger's Nest (Taktshang Goemba; p82), is one of its most venerated religious sites. Legend says that Guru Rinpoche flew to this site on the back of a tigress to subdue a local demon; afterwards, he meditated here for three months. This beautiful building clings to the sheer cliffs soaring above a whispering pine forest. The steep walk to the monastery is well worthwhile, providing tantalising glimpses of the monastery, views of the Paro valley and splashes of red-blossom rhododendrons.

GAVIN GOUGH

2 Most of the dzongs and goembas have annual festivals featuring mesmerising dance dramas. The largest of these festivals is the tsechu – with dances in honour of Guru Rinpoche. The dances are performed by monks and lay people dressed in colourful costumes, and the dancers take on aspects of wrathful and compassionate deities, heroes, demons and animals. During the dances, *atsara* (clowns) mimic the dancers and perform comic routines and even harass the audience for money in exchange for a blessing with the wooden phallus they carry!
Tsechu at Wangdue Phodrang Dzong

Mountain Treks

3 Bhutan's treks (p147) are physically demanding but hugely rewarding. They generally reach high altitudes and take you through remote regions. You will be expertly guided during your trek, negotiating suspension bridges, snow or leeches! Thankfully, your pack will be carried by ponies. Trekking takes you beyond the roads and the reach of many aspects of modernisation, and meeting traditionally dressed locals will be a highlight of the experience. Above the forests, these hardy farmers tend their crops and animals according to century-old traditions. Jhomolhari trek

NICHOLAS REUSS

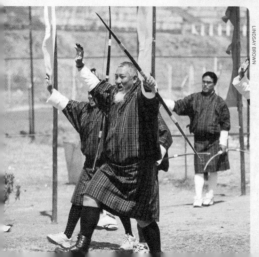
LINDSAY BROWN

Archery

4 Bhutan's national sport of archery (*datse;* p213) is exhilarating and entertaining to watch, with competitions held across the country throughout the year. There are two classes of competition: one for the traditional bamboo bows and another for the space-age carbon-fibre bows that propel arrows at astonishing speeds. The targets seem impossibly tiny and the distance immense and yet the target is hit quite regularly. Narrow misses, competitive banter, ritual singing and dancing accompany the whoosh of arrows and hoots of delight as the competition heats up.
Archery tournament, Thimphu

Buddhist Painting

5 The best place to see Buddhist murals and frescoes is inside the dzongs, goembas and lhakhangs (p228). Stories are told, mandalas mesmerise and major figures are represented, including the Guardians of the Four Directions, Sakyamuni Buddha and Guru Rinpoche. Another common and typically Bhutanese subject depicts the Four Friends *(Thuenpa puen shi)*, which illustrates the concept and harmony of teamwork and mutual respect between an elephant, monkey, rabbit and bird. Thimphu is the best place to to see and purchase traditional and contemporary painting.

Punakha Dzong

6 Superbly situated where two rivers converge, Punakha Dzong (p91) is postcard perfect and serenely monastic. Built by the Zhabdrung in 1637, Punakha Dzong is the winter home of the Je Khenpo and is the venue for the coronation of kings of Bhutan. Visit in spring to see the famous jacaranda trees splash lilac flowers down the whitewashed walls and red-robed monks wandering on a sea of purple petals. The fortress-thick walls are cold and silent one moment and then warmed with the echoes of giggles in another as a horde of young monks head off for a meal.

ANTONY GIBLIN

7

Traditional Textiles

7 Hand-woven and embroidered textiles are generally recognised as Bhutan's premier handicraft (p229). Centuries of tradition have honed the techniques of textile dyeing, weaving and stitching. Most of the weavers are women and it is a rare home in Bhutan that does not 'clunk' to the sound of a loom. In addition to the Textile Museum in Thimphu, there are small shops throughout the country – particularly in Bumthang and in the far east – selling vibrant fabrics that make a colourful souvenir.

Village Life

8 Rural Bhutan is never far away – terraced rice paddies and cornfields abut the rapidly growing, but still quite small, urban centres. Traditional homes dot the country-side, resplendent with drying chillies and decorations such as the 'thunderbolt', or good ol' phallus, a symbol of 'awareness' that never fails to attract the eye of the traveller. Life in the country still revolves around crop cycles and seasons, but electricity, satellite television and mobile phones have connected rural Bhutanese to the rest of the globe virtually overnight. House in the Paro valley

JOHNNY HAGLUND

SALLY DILLON

Gross National Happiness

9 Gross National Happiness (GNH) has become Bhutan's philosophical banner and a gift to a world grappling with materialistic 'growth economics'. Based on core Buddhist and human values, this measurable index is a counterpoint to the economist's Gross National Product. It is also a revolutionary philosophy that places real value on things such as cultural heritage, health, education, good governance, ecological diversity and individual well-being. Importantly, it sees economic growth not as an end but rather as a means of achieving more important ends.

Bumthang

10 The valleys comprising Bumthang (p112) make up the cultural heartland of Bhutan and are ideal for day hikes to monasteries. Bumthang's ancient monasteries and temples figure prominently in Bhutan's early development as well as in the foundation of the unique aspects of Bhutanese Buddhism. Witness the imprint of Guru Rinpoche, hoist Pema Lingpa's 25kg chain mail, and stare into the churning waters of Membartsho, where Pema Lingpa uncovered hidden treasures.
Monks at Tamshing Goemba

GAVIN GOUGH

Rinpung Dzong & National Museum

11 Paro's Rinpung Dzong (p73) is a hulking example of the fortresslike dzong architecture that glowers protectively over the valley and town. The colourful Paro tsechu is held here in spring; the festival culminates with a *thondrol* (huge religious picture) depicting Guru Rinpoche being unfurled. Above the dzong is an old, round watchtower, the Ta Dzong, now converted into the excellent National Museum, which has an informative and eclectic collection. Walk down from the dzong to go shopping for arts and crafts along Paro's colourful shopping strip.

Souvenir Shopping

12

Bhutan's pride in its handicrafts is on show at the schools of Zorig Chusum (Thirteen Arts) and the numerous handicraft shops. Many items have a utilitarian or religious use such as bamboo baskets, brass butter lamps or the exquisite wooden bowls, hand-turned from intricately patterned burlwood. Silk, cotton, wool and even yak hair is spun, dyed, woven and stitched into cloth and traditional garments. The artistic tradition can be seen in the intricate *thangkhas* (religious pictures). Bhutanese stamps will thrill collectors. Decorations for sale, Thimphu weekend market

Trongsa Dzong & the Tower of Trongsa Museum

13 Sprawling down a ridge towards an ominous gorge, Trongsa Dzong (p110) sits in a central position in Bhutan's geography and in its recent history. Both the first and second kings ruled the country from this strategic position. Inside is a labyrinth of many levels, narrow corridors and courtyards. Overlooking the dzong, the Tower of Trongsa Museum is housed in the two-winged watchtower. This excellent museum is dedicated to the history of the dzong and the royal Wangchuck dynasty and has exhibits ranging from personal effects of the royals to Buddhist statues.

ANTONY GIBLIN

Thimphu Weekend Market

14 Thimphu's bustling weekend market (p48) is the biggest and brightest in the country. The food section is an olfactory overload with dried fish competing with soft cheese, betel nut and dried chilli to assault your nostrils. Curly fern fronds *(nakey)* and red rice are just some of the exotic offerings. Cross the fast-flowing Wang Chhu on the traditional cantilever footbridge to get to the handicraft and textile stalls where you can barter for 'antiques', rolls of prayer flags, reams of material or even a human thigh-bone trumpet.
Prayer wheels for sale, Thimphu weekend market

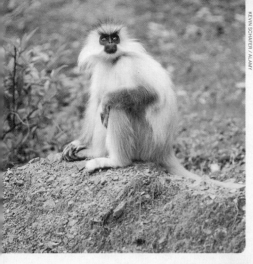

Wonderful Wildlife

15 Bhutan has the largest proportion of land designated as protected areas in the world. Its 65% forest and mountain cover comprises a suite of varying habitats and an amazing diversity of plants and creatures (p246). Bird-watchers flock to the monsoon-soaked evergreen forests of southern Bhutan, where hundreds of species can be spotted from the road. Here, you may also spot a troupe of playful golden langurs. The endangered black-necked crane overwinters in central and eastern Bhutan and the reliably returning cranes of Phobjikha are justifiably renowned.

Golden langur

Wild & Woolly Yaks

16 Woolly yaks are kept by nomadic farmers who take their charges to the high pastures during summer, returning them to lower altitudes in winter. In spring and autumn you will see free-ranging herds grazing the road verges near the mountain passes such as Pele La and Yotong La. Don't be tempted to get up close, however. Instead, reach for the telephoto lens. These are not dairy cows but irascible yaks and they know how to use those sharp horns!

Kyichu Lhakhang

17 Kyichu Lhakhang (p80) is one of Bhutan's oldest, most venerated and most beautiful temples and it sits just a short distance from the town of Paro. The oldest temple in this twin-temple complex is believed to have been built in AD 659 by King Songtsen Gampo of Tibet. A human-powered pulley-and-rope system turns prayer wheels and a treasured 7th-century statue of Jowo Sakyamuni sits in the sanctuary. Easy day walks can be commenced in the vicinity of this serene lhakhang.

Wangdue Phodrang

18 Arriving from the west you will cross a long bridge over the swift-flowing Punak Tsang Chhu and peer up to the imposing ramparts of the Wangdue Phodrang Dzong (p96) above. Strategically positioned on a steep spur at the confluence of two rivers, this dzong shared significance with Paro and Trongsa in the country's formative years. The delightful shanty-town of wooden shops leading towards the dzong selling everything under the sun, is ear-marked for resettlement, but the immense dzong is steadfastly staying put.

Wangdue Phodrang Dzong

Thimphu Valley

19 Thimphu (p44) delights, with its museums and cultural attractions, including the Trashi Chhoe Dzong, which celebrates its popular tsechu in autumn. The relatively broad valley of Bhutan's capital also provides many out-of-town sights and worthwhile distractions. There are several good walks not far from the capital, taking in a handful of perfectly positioned monasteries with excellent views down the valley. And just west of the centre at Motithang Takin Preserve is your best bet for spotting Bhutan's extraordinary national animal.

Phajoding Goemba, Thimphu valley

Forests & Blooms

20 Although the mysterious and ethereal high-altitude blue poppy is the national flower and the cypress is the national tree, no plant is more emblematic of Bhutan than the rhododendron. In spring, splashes of red, pink and white rival the multicoloured prayer flags at the high passes from Cheli La to Thrumshing La. Famous for its forest cover, Bhutan will delight the amateur botanist with its sheer variety of flora and shades of green (p243). Long forest drives are inevitable, so remember to stop the car and smell the flowers.

Flowering fields, Bumthang

welcome to
Bhutan

Bhutan, the Land of the Thunder Dragon, is no ordinary place. It is a Himalayan kingdom replete with myths and legends, where the best of traditional culture thrives and the latest global developments are enthusiastically embraced.

Low Volume, High Value Tourism

Tourism in Bhutan is unique and the Bhutanese pride themselves on a sustainable, eco-friendly approach in line with the country's popular philosophy of Gross National Happiness. Firstly, to bust a myth: there is *no* limit to the number of tourists. Visitors famously have to pay a minimum tariff of US$200 per day (rising to US$250 in 2012), making it appear as one of the world's most expensive countries to visit. However, this fee is all-inclusive – accommodation, food, transport and an official guide are all provided. Not only that, but your local guide will reveal the country's amazing landscape and Buddhist heritage, and will also introduce you to the everyday charms of the Bhutanese. You don't have to travel in a large group and you can arrange your own itinerary. What you won't find in Bhutan is crowded backpacker-style independent travel. This is Nepal for the jet set.

Surprising Bhutan

Bhutan holds many surprises. This is a country where buying cigarettes is illegal, where the rice is red and where chillies aren't just a seasoning but the main ingredient. It's also a deeply Buddhist land, where schoolkids wear the *gho* and *kira* (traditional male and female clothing, respectively) where giant protective penises are painted beside the entrance to many houses, and where Gross National Happiness is deemed more important than Gross National Product. And while it visibly maintains its Buddhist traditions, Bhutan is not a museum nor is it a nation of otherworldly ascetics shunning the rest of the world. You will find the Bhutanese well-educated, fun loving and vibrant.

Shangri La?

So why spend your money to come here? First off there is the amazing mountainous landscape, where snowcapped peaks rise out of primeval forests in every shade of green. Taking up prime positions in this landscape are the fantastic monasteries and incredible fortresslike dzongs. The unique Buddhist architecture embodies the traditional Buddhist culture and sets the scene for spectacular religious dance festivals. Then there are the textiles and handicrafts, outrageous archery competitions, spectacular trekking trails and stunning flora and fauna. All this sets Bhutan aside as the last remaining great Himalayan kingdom.

When you do visit Bhutan, you will become one of the few who have experienced the charm and magic of one of the world's most enigmatic countries – the 'last Shangri La' – and you'll be playing your part in this medieval kingdom's efforts to join the modern world, while steadfastly maintaining its distinct and remarkable cultural identity.

need to know

Currency
» Ngultrum (Nu)

Language
» Dzongkha

When to Go?

Jomolhari Base Camp
GO May-Oct

Punakha
GO Feb-Apr, Oct-Dec

Paro/Thimphu
GO Mar-Jun, Sep-Nov

Trashi Yangtse
GO Oct-Apr

Phuentsholing
GO Nov-Feb

Warm to hot summers, mild winters
Warm to hot summers, cold winters
Mild summers, cold winters
Polar Climate

High Season
(Mar-Apr, Sep-Nov)

» The weather is best in spring and autumn. Book flights well in advance; accommodation options are limited.

» Himalayan views are best in October, while rhododendron blooms peak in March and April.

Shoulder
(May, Dec-Feb)

» Bhutan no longer has seasonal tariffs so the main benefit of travelling outside high season will be fewer tourists.

» The weather is still good, though it can be cold in December and January.

Low Season
(June-Aug)

» Monsoon rains and leeches put an end to most treks, although high-altitude flowers are at their peak.

Set Your Budget

Fixed daily rate

» All tourists must pay US$200 per person per day (US$250 a day from 2012), with a US$40/30 surcharge per person for those in a group of one/two. This covers accommodation, transport in Bhutan, guide, food and entry fees (see also p26).

» Possible extra charges include hot-stone baths, cultural shows, horse riding, rafting and tips.

» Children under 12 are exempt from royalty component (US$65).

Budget

» Only Indian tourists and foreign residents are able to set their own travel budgets.

» Budget hotel: US$20-30

» Restaurant meal in Thimphu: US$5-10

High End

» Luxury hotel: US$250-1300 above the daily US$200 tariff

Money

» Tours are prepaid so you'll only need pocket money for drinks, souvenirs, laundry and tips; for this, bring cash.

Visas

» Visas are arranged by your tour company and issued on arrival only to those on a prepaid all-inclusive tour; see p263.

Mobile Phones

» As long as your phone is unlocked you can buy a B-Mobile SIM card for both local and international use and top it up with prepaid cards.

Driving/ Transport

» Your tour includes transport so you will have your own car, minivan or bus, depending on group size.

Websites

» **Bhutan 360** (www .bhutan-360.com) Introduction to travel in Bhutan.

» **Bhutan Travel Portal** (www.bhutan travelportal.com) Travel information.

» **Druk Air** (www .drukair.com.bt) National airline.

» **Kuensel** (www .kuenselonline.com) National newspaper.

» **National Portal of Bhutan** (www .bhutan.gov.bt) Official government site.

» **Tourism Council of Bhutan** (www.tourism .gov.bt) Approved tour operators and travel regulations.

Exchange Rates

Australia	A$1	Nu 44
Canada	C$1	Nu 43
Euro zone	€1	Nu 62
India	Rs1	Nu 1
Japan	Y100	Nu 55
UK	£1	Nu 70
USA	US$1	Nu 44

For current exchange rates see www.xe.com.

Important Numbers

Country Code	☎975
International Access Code	☎00
Ambulance	☎112
Fire	☎110
Police	☎113

Arriving in Bhutan

» **Paro** or **Phuentsholing**: Your guide and driver will meet you at Paro airport or the land border at Phuentsholing and whisk you away on your tour.

Don't Leave Home Without...

» A compact umbrella and/or good raincoat – for any region, at any time of the year.

» Hat, sunscreen, lip balm and sunglasses.

» Earplugs (Bhutanese dogs sleep all day and bark all night).

» Trekking poles (useful for steep hikes to dzongs and temples).

» Swimming costume for communal hot-stone baths and hot springs.

» A flashlight for unexpected power cuts and for the interiors of dark temples and monasteries.

» Motion-sickness medication for the long and winding roads.

» Slip-on shoes – useful for visiting chapels and monasteries.

if you like...

Fitting in Like a Local

Bhutanese culture is very accepting of visitors, especially if you make the effort to fit in. When visiting a monastery or festival don't just watch, join in!

Get a *gho* (or a *kira*) Locals love it when a *chilip* (foreigner) wears Bhutanese national dress, especially during a holiday or festival (p62)

Watch an archery tournament There's nothing more Bhutanese than the good-humoured banter of a *datse* (archery) or *khuru* (lawn darts) game (p53)

Hang some prayer flags Impress your guide and earn some good karma by buying some prayer flags and hanging them at a mountain pass such as Dochu La (p89)

Hang out at Benez Bar There's no better place to strike up a conversation with switched-on Bhutanese than at Thimphu's Benez Bar (p61)

Sample some local snacks Try the jellied cow skin, dried yak cheese and fresh betel nut at the Paro weekend market (p76)

High-Altitude Treks

The best way to experience Bhutan is without doubt on foot, especially if you can combine a trek with a festival and the highlights of Paro and Thimphu. Come in October and November for mountain views and March for rhododendron blooms.

Druk Path The walk between Paro and Thimphu takes in high-altitude lakes and remote hermitages (p148)

Jhomolhari trek Combines some of Bhutan's best high-mountain scenery, with remote villages, high passes and yak pastures (p153)

Laya to Gasa Perhaps the best combination of scenery and culture, with a visit to the unique people of remote Laya (p159)

Bumthang Cultural Trek A fine short walk that takes you through magical forest (p166)

Snowman Trek One of the world's ultimate treks, and the country's most expensive (p171)

Pampering Yourself

Bhutan's top-end travel is anything but tough. Über-luxury resorts such as Amankora and Uma guarantee six-star treatment, with supremely decadent restaurants and muscle-melting spas.

Hot-Stone Bath Stone, wood and hot water combine to provide the quintessential Bhutanese experience, available at most tourist hotels (p255)

Termalinca Spa Not quite the Promised Land but the milk and honey body wrap comes close enough; nonguests are welcome here (p57)

Uma Paro Massage, complimentary yoga and Ayurvedic oil treatments, all featuring Como-brand bath products (p77)

Zhiwa Ling The Menlha (Medicine Buddha) spa here offers a tasty red rice or lemongrass body polish (p77)

Taj Tashi Choose your mood – invigorating masala spice rub or relaxing coconut skin softener? (p55)

>> Local men dressed in traditional *ghos* (p62)

GAVIN GOUGH

Wildlife & Wildflowers

Bhutan is a paradise for botanists and birders, with some of the loveliest and best-protected forests in the Himalaya. Mountain goats and langur are easily spotted; Red Pandas are more commonly seen in their bottled form.

Phobjikha valley Winter (end of October to mid-February) offers guaranteed sightings of one of over 300 black-necked cranes (p101)

Dochu La One of the best places to wander through a magical forest of pink, white and yellow rhododendron blooms (March and April; p89)

Motithang Takin Preserve, Thimphu Get up close to Bhutan's odd-looking and endearing national animal, said to have inspired the legend of the golden fleece (p53)

Merak & Sakten Yeti-spotting is just one of the activities on offer in this fascinating and newly opened corner of remote eastern Bhutan (p140 and p177)

Day Walks

Sometimes it's just nice to get out, off the bus and hike to a hillside monastery or temple. Lose the crowds and meet monks, villagers and fellow pilgrims.

Tango & Cheri Goembas Excellent excursion from Thimphu to two of Bhutan's most historic monasteries, with longer hikes possible (p66)

Taktshang, Paro Valley If the two-hour hike up to the Tiger's Nest isn't enough, you can continue up to a handful of little-visited temples and cliffside viewpoints (p82)

Thowadrak A full day's hike up to a remote hermitage and meditation complex (p125)

Sacred Sites

Protector deities, spirits and saints lurk behind every pass, river junction and lake in Bhutan. These pilgrim spots are imbued with sacred significance and hold a key to understanding how Bhutanese see their world.

Taktshang (Tiger's Nest) Bhutan's most famous and revered site, tied on to the cliff face by little more than the hairs of angels (p82)

Gom Kora Pilgrims flock to this remote eastern chorten for its collection of rock footprints, relics and bizarre sin tests (p141)

Changangkha Lhakhang, Thimphu Always bustling with mothers and their babies seeking a blessing from the red-faced protector Tamdrin (p53)

Membartsho The serene and sacred 'burning lake', where Pema Lingpa found treasures and performed miracles (p124)

NICHOLAS REUSS

» Fresco prepared for the protection of Ogyen Chholing Palace (p125), Bumthang

Hidden Gems

Bhutan's big shows are its dzongs and festivals but don't overlook the charm of the country's smaller, less visited monasteries and temples. The following charming sites are well worth the detour.

Juneydrak, Haa The Haa valley is a great place to get off the beaten track and this timeless hermitage is its highlight (p88)

Kila Nunnery Perched just below the Cheli La, Kila is an hour's walk and about two centuries off the main highway (p87)

Dumtse Lhakhang, Paro Pilgrim paths wind upwards at this snail-shell-shaped chapel past some of the country's best medieval murals (p76)

Tago Lhakhang, Bondey A charming and easily missed 15th-century chapel inside a chorten, just south of Paro (p85)

Festivals

Many people time their entire trip around one of Bhutan's colourful tsechus, or dance festivals. Expect swirling mask dances, playful clowns, spectacular costumes, and superb photo opportunities. Bring extra camera batteries. For some background on tsechus, see p231.

Paro tsechu Popular with groups and with good reason; perhaps too popular for many people's taste (p19)

Ura Yakchoe A quieter rural alternative, though the dates are notoriously changeable. Camping is a good idea here (p20)

Punakha Domchoe One of Bhutan's most unusual festivals re-enacts an ancient battle; held in February or March (p94)

Kurjey tsechu Brave the monsoon rain and avoid the tourists, plus you can hit the nearby Nimalung tsechu at the same time (p20)

Arts & Crafts

Bhutan's arts and crafts vary from sacred murals to bamboo bows. For high religious art visit the dzongs and monasteries but for handicrafts try the following fascinating workshops.

National Institute for Zorig Chusum Watch students perfect the 13 traditional arts and crafts (p48 and p143)

Jungshi Traditional Paper Factory Watch the whole paper-making process; yes, it really does grow on trees! (p54)

Textile Academy This impressive new complex showcases Bhutan's most impressive art (p49)

Tshenden Incense Factory, Bondey Breathe in the fragrance of juniper, sandalwood and high-altitude herbs at this family-run workshop (p85)

Khoma village, Lhuentse Every household has a loom in this remote centre of 'brocade-style' weaving excellence (p135)

Yathra workshops, Zungney Shop for hand-woven woollen blankets at these roadside looms on the drive to Bumthang (p112)

month by month

Top Events

19

1 **Thimphu tsechu,** September/October

2 **Paro tsechu,** March/April

3 **Punakha Domchoe,** February/March

4 **Ura Yakchoe,** April/May

5 **Jampey Lhakhang Drup,** October

February

The mercury stays low in Paro in February, dropping to an average of around 0°C, but things are warmer in the lower elevations of Punakha and the east.

Punakha Domchoe

The balmy Punakha valley hosts this unique event, whose highlight is a dramatic re-creation of a 17th-century battle featuring hundreds of costumed *pazaps* (warriors). A three-day tsechu then follows. The festival follows the lunar calendar, so it can fall in March. See p94.

Chorten Kora

Thousands of pilgrims from eastern Bhutan and Arunachal Pradesh circumambulate this stupa during two festivals set two weeks apart. Unlike monastic festivals, this celebration feels more like a local fair. The main festival is from the 13th to 15th of the first lunar month, so can fall in March.

Losar

Bhutanese mark their New Year by painting their houses, visiting the local monastery and throwing epic archery and darts tournaments. The event follows the lunar Bhutanese calendar and there are lots of regional variations so it can happen anytime between mid-January and mid-March.

March

Spring, from March to May, is an excellent time to visit Bhutan, for both touring and trekking. There are fewer mountain views but the magnificent rhododendrons are in bloom and birdlife is abundant.

Gom Kora

Hundreds of people travel to this chorten in the east of the country for a night of celebrations and ritual circumambulations of the sacred stupa. The fair takes place between the 8th and 10th of the second lunar month, so it can fall in April.

April

April is the second single most popular month to visit Bhutan. The Paro tsechu is a big draw and trekking is good. Fresh asparagus and fried *nakey* (fern fronds) are a welcome addition to hotel buffets.

Paro Tsechu

This very popular festival features four days of *cham* (ritual religious dance) followed by the pre-dawn unfurling of a giant *thangka* (painted or embroidered religious picture) depicting the eight manifestations of Guru Rinpoche. The first day's ceremonies are in Paro Dzong, before the action moves outside. The festival can also fall in March.

Trekking

Warm weather and continued rhododendron blooms at higher elevations make this a fine time to trek but there's less chance of blue skies at the top of the mountain. Bring some rain gear just in case.

May

The end of spring brings warm and dusty weather, with rain and cloud increasing towards the end of the month. The lighter crowds and good weather still make it a good month to visit.

Ura Yakchoe
A small-town vibe marks this three-day festival featuring processions, dances and plenty of local moonshine. The only problem is that the dates are notoriously unreliable. The festival can fall in April but is only fixed for sure a few weeks in advance.

Monk Processions
On the first day of the fourth lunar month, the entire monk body moves from Punakha to their summer residence in Thimphu. The procession includes the Je Khenpo (Chief Abbot) and several sacred relics, and local people line up along the route for a blessing.

June/July

Monsoon clouds start to obscure views and can cancel flights at Paro airport. As the rains intensify, roads are sometimes washed away and leeches rear their ugly heads. The spectacular wildflowers at this time of year in the high valleys are a botanist's dream.

Nimalung Tsechu
Bumthang is the place to visit in the fifth lunar month. Nimalung Goemba has a three-day festival starting on the 8th day, with the final day coinciding with the nearby Kurjey tsechu. Dates can fall in July.

Kurjey Tsechu
Monks from Trongsa Monastery perform religious dances for this one-day festival in Bumthang. The date also marks the birthday of Guru Rinpoche, which is celebrated by prayer ceremonies across Bhutan.

Monsoon Madness
The summer monsoon (June to September) dominates Bhutan, which receives more rainfall than any other Himalayan region. Powerful rains are common, especially at night and during the peak month of July but the lush foliage and fresh produce (wild mushrooms, mangoes and avocados) go some way to compensate.

September

The first half of the month is still rainy but by the end of the month the monsoon has washed the Himalayan skies clear and several big festivals coincide with the beginning of the main tourist season.

Thimphu Tsechu
Crowds can be thick during the four days of spectacular monk dancing in Tashi Choe Dzong (over 3000 tourists attend each year). The event can also fall in October. The preceding three-day *dromchoe* festivities (celebrating the defeat of the Tibetans in the 17th century) are generally open to Bhutanese only.

Wangdue Tsechu
This festival on the 8th to the 10th of the eighth lunar month overlaps with the Thimphu tsechu so many groups combine a visit to both. Three days of dancing culminate in the unfurling of a giant *thangka*.

Haa Tsechu
Sleepy Haa only truly wakes up during this festival. Monk dances are held on the 8th and 9th days of the eighth lunar month in the courtyard of the Lhakhang Kharpo, before the final day's action moves to nearby Wangchulo Dzong.

Tamshing Phala Choepa
The Bumthang valley offers a double shot of festivals in the eighth lunar month. From the 9th to 11th you can enjoy dances at Tamshing Goemba, before relocating three days later to nearby Thangbi Goemba for a further three days of festivities. Both festivals can fall in October.

October

October is the single most popular month to visit Bhutan. Temperatures are warm, mountain views are clear and tour groups are everywhere.

★★ Jampey Lhakhang Drup

Cham dances and bonfires commemorate the establishment of this 7th-century temple. The first evening features a famous midnight 'naked fire dance'. The fun lasts from the 15th to 18th of the ninth lunar month, so it can fall in November. The four-day Jakar tsechu occurs a week before.

★★ Prakhar Tsechu

This three-day festival at Prakhar Monastery in the Chumey valley shares the same dates as the Jampey Lhakhang Drup so you can easily double up.

Trekking Heaven

Trekking is superb everywhere in Bhutan in October and this is when most tour companies operate their treks. Nights can be cold at high elevations but the views of snowy peaks such as 7314m Jhomolhari are superb.

November

Still a good month weather-wise, though pack a jumper for the evenings. Several smaller festivals offer a good alternative to the over-visited Paro and Thimphu tsechus.

◉ Black-Necked Crane Festival

This modern festival in Phobjikha is held on 11 November. Local children perform dances in crane costumes in the courtyard of Gangte Goemba to celebrate the winter return of more than 300 black-necked cranes.

★★ Mongar Tsechu

Mongar offers a smaller more intimate festival experience, with more opportunities for photography and cultural interaction. It occurs on the 7th to the 10th of the 10th lunar month, so it can fall in December.

★★ Ngang Lhakhang Shey

If you don't mind sleeping in tents, you can easily combine the delightful three-day Bumthang Cultural Trek with this three-day festival at the Ngang Lhakhang (Swan Temple). The festival can also fall in December.

December

December marks the beginning of winter, with possible snow at higher elevations, though it's not a bad time for touring western Bhutan. The high passes to Haa and the east may be temporarily snowbound. Get a hotel with a heater.

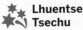
★★ Lhuentse Tsechu

Very few tourists make it to this remote monastic festival, way out in the extreme northeast of the country. The festival can also fall in January.

★★ Trongsa Tsechu

This is one of the oldest and least-visited festivals in the country. Three days of dancing run from the 9th to the 11th of the 11th lunar month, so it can fall in January. The final day features the hanging of a giant *thondrol* (a special occasion *thangka*).

★★ Nomad's Festival

Highlanders from as far away as Laya and Sakten attended 2009's inaugural nomad's festival in the Bumthang valley, bringing offerings for sale such as local products including *khoma* hats from Laya and *zaktoe* fermented cheese from Sakten. Reports were mixed but if it takes off it could prove an interesting addition to the festival scene.

itineraries

Whether you've got six days or 60, these itineraries provide a starting point for the trip of a lifetime. Want more inspiration? Head online to lonelyplanet .com/thorntree to chat with other travellers.

Four Days
A Long Weekend in Paro & Thimphu

If you have limited time or money, you can get a good impression of Bhutan in just four days by concentrating on Thimphu and Paro. Count on two full days in picturesque **Paro**, visiting Paro Dzong and the National Museum. On the second day, hike up to the dramatic Tiger's Nest at **Taktshang Goemba** and visit lovely Kyichu Lhakhang. After lunch make the three-hour drive to Thimphu, stopping at the charming **Tamchhog Lhakhang** en route.

On day three you could squeeze in a long day trip over the Dochu La to **Punakha Dzong**, the most beautiful in the country. In March, budget an hour to walk through the gorgeous rhododendron forests above the **Dochu La** pass. On the way back to Thimphu, pop into the nearby **Chimi Lhakhang**, the temple of the 'Divine Madman'.

Day four is in **Thimphu**. Go to the weekend market and visit **Cheri or Tango Goembas** in the upper Thimphu valley. If handicrafts are your thing, hit the Textile Museum and National Institute of Zorig Chusum. Late in the afternoon drive back to Paro; most flights depart early in the morning.

Seven Days
Haa to Punakha

❭ If you're thinking about a four-day trip, consider a seven-day trip. It's not that much more money and, really, when are you next going to be in Bhutan? A week gives you more time to get a feel for Bhutanese culture and enables you to get off the beaten track in either the Haa or Phobjikha valleys, while still seeing the major dzongs and monasteries of western Bhutan.

With the extra days you can definitely add an overnight trip over the mountains to **Punakha** and nearby **Wangdue Phodrang**, staying in either of these towns. This way you'll have time to make the 1½-hour return hike to the nearby **Khamsum Yuelley Namgyal Chorten**, as well as visit Chimi Lhakhang.

To get off the beaten track, add on an overnight trip to the **Haa valley**, on the road that links Paro to Thimphu. The road goes over the highest motorable pass in Bhutan, the Cheli La, and it's worth the couple of hours hiking to visit Kila Nunnery. Arrive in Haa at lunchtime, and spend an afternoon and maybe the next morning exploring the Juneydrak Hermitage and **Chhundu Lhakhang**, before continuing on to **Thimphu**.

Figure on two full days in **Paro**, including visits to Taktshang Goemba, Kyichu Lhakhang and Drukyel Dzong in the Paro valley, and a full day (or two) in Thimphu. See the previous itinerary for more on what to see in Paro and Thimphu. A few tips: try to be in Thimphu on a Saturday or Sunday to see the weekend market and avoid Paro on Monday, when the National Museum is closed. If you're lucky, you may be able to catch a weekend archery tournament, most likely in Thimphu.

If you don't visit Haa, you might be able to add on a day trip to the **Phobjikha valley**, especially worthwhile in winter (November to February) when the valley's black-necked cranes are roosting.

At some point during your trip ask your guide to arrange a Bhutanese hot-stone bath, available in most tourist hotels (for a charge).

10 Days to Two Weeks
To Bumthang

❭ A 10-day itinerary should allow you two or three days in **Bumthang**, with overnight stops in Paro, Thimphu and Wangdue Phodrang and short stops in Punakha and Trongsa as you drive through. Even better, 14 days will let you see the same places in more depth and at a much more relaxed pace. You could then also include the two-day Bumthang Cultural Trek before you have to turn back to Paro.

Follow the previous four-day itinerary. From Thimphu, a night in the **Phobjikha valley** will give you a chance to see Gangte Goemba and also view the rare and endangered black-necked cranes. If you like to explore places on foot, set aside an extra half-day's hiking in Phobjikha.

From Phobjikha it's a day's drive over the Pele La to the superb dzong and museum at **Trongsa** and on to Jakar in Bumthang. Leave early, as there's lots to see en route, including the Nepali-style **Chendebji Chorten**, which is a good place for a picnic.

If you have two full days in Bumthang, spend one day doing a loop in the **Chokhor valley**, taking in the Jampey Lhakhang, Kurjey Lhakhang and Tamshing Goemba. Day two here should be spent exploring the **Tang valley**, visiting the Burning Lake at Membartsho and the interesting Ogyen Chholing Museum near Mesithang. If you have time, overnight in the Ogyen Chholing Guest House and hike back via the rural village of Gamling.

The Bumthang valley is another good place for some hiking so budget half a day to stretch your legs after a week's driving. From Jakar it's a two-day drive back to Paro, so spend a night at **Wangdue Phodrang** and visit its earthy dzong.

If you intend to visit India in conjunction with Bhutan, consider driving from Thimphu or Paro to **Phuentsholing** instead of flying, which will add a day to the itinerary. From here you are only a few hours from Darjeeling, Kalimpong and Sikkim, as well as the airport at Bagdogra, which has frequent flights to Delhi and Kolkata (Calcutta).

Two to Three Weeks
Eastern Explorations

〉 It takes *at least* two weeks to make a trip out to the little-visited far east but you're guaranteed to leave the tour groups behind. There's certainly a *loooot* of driving involved (up to five hours a day in eastern Bhutan) but then getting there is half the fun! With this itinerary you avoid the long drive back to Paro by exiting Bhutan at Samdrup Jongkhar. You do need to arrange an Indian visa before you arrive in Bhutan though. This is a particularly good trip if you're interested in traditional weaving.

Follow the earlier itineraries from Paro as far as Bumthang, from where you can see the highlights of the east in five or six days. From Bumthang, day one takes you on a dramatic drive over the **Thrumshing La** and Bhutan's wildest road to **Mongar**. Stay here for two nights and make a scenic day trip up to remote **Lhuentse**, pausing to visit the dzong, and hike 45 minutes up to the traditional weaving village of **Khoma**.

Day three takes you on to funky **Trashigang**, with a two-or three-hour detour along the way to **Drametse Goemba**, Bhutan's most important Nyingma monastery. Accommodation standards here are not as good as western Bhutan so bring a sense of humour as well as bug spray.

Figure on two nights at Trashigang, with another great day excursion to **Trashi Yangtse**, with stops en route at the pilgrimage site of **Gom Kora**, the old Trashi Yangtse dzong and the Nepali-style Chorten Kora. March and April bring two important pilgrimage festivals to this region. The National Institute for Zorig Chusum is worth a visit to see Bhutan's national crafts, if you haven't seen the Thimphu version.

From Trashigang it's a six-hour winding drive down to the plains at steamy **Samdrup Jongkhar**; stop to check out the traditional weaving at the National Handloom Development Centre in **Khaling**. From Samdrup Jongkhar, take a three-hour taxi ride to Guwahati then fly to Kolkata, Delhi or Bangkok, or take the overnight train to West Bengal for Darjeeling and the Nepal border.

Booking Your Trip

Fixed Daily Rates

The daily tariff for tourists is US$200 (US$250 from 2012) per person per day. The rate is now the same for high and low season.

Groups of one/two people pay an additional surcharge of US$40/30 per person.

Tariff Discounts

Children up to 12 years are exempt from the US$65 government royalty, which is a component of the US$200 daily tariff.

Full-time students aged under 25, with valid identity cards, get a 25% discount if booking directly with a Bhutanese tour operator.

Discounts are offered on the royalty (not the daily tariff) for longer-stay visitors – 50% (ie US$32.50) from the ninth night and 100% after the 15th night.

Tourists are allowed a royalty-free night (ie US$65 discount) if overnighting in the border towns of Phuentsholing, Samdrup Jongkhar or Gelephu.

Despite its image as an exclusive, remote destination, Bhutan is not a difficult place to visit. There is no limit to the number of tourists who can enter and there are no restrictions on group size. You can easily organise a journey as a group of friends or even as a solo traveller. Unlike most countries, however, government regulations require foreign visitors to travel with a prepaid and pre-planned itinerary organised through a Bhutanese tour company, at a minimum daily rate.

You can simply join a group tour or arrange a custom-made program with a Bhutanese operator. Generally there is a great deal of freedom as to where you can go and what you can do. The one thing you can't do is travel without a guide.

Travel regulations look set to change, though. The government plans to triple 2009 visitor numbers to 100,000 per year by 2012. Plans to overhaul the fixed daily tariff were mooted in 2010, but in the end it was decided to raise the tariff to US$250 from 2012. Don't expect backpacker travel within Bhutan any time soon.

When to Book

Bhutanese tour operators generally need a minimum of one month to arrange the logistics, including bank transfers, visa and booking Druk Air tickets. Pinning down your itinerary and tour price may take several weeks of emailing before that. If you're timing your trip to coincide with a popular festival you will need to start several months beforehand to book Druk Air flights and secure accommodation.

Booking a Tour

Your visit to Bhutan must be arranged through an officially approved tour operator, either directly or through an overseas agent. By dealing through an overseas agent you will avoid complicated payment procedures and also have a home-based contact in case of queries or special needs but you'll pay more for your trip. If you deal directly with a Bhutanese tour operator you will have lots of scope to individualise your itinerary but you'll have to spend time exchanging emails and organising an international bank transfer.

Just because you are paying a high tariff, don't imagine you'll have Bhutan to yourself. During the high season, tourist hotels, the major dzongs and festivals hum with tour groups, especially in Paro. For a more exclusive experience you'll have to head to the lesser-visited monasteries in Haa and central Bhutan, choose the shoulder season or head out to eastern Bhutan.

If you're not used to travelling on an organised tour, we suggest you break up your itinerary with the occasional hike, bike ride or visit to a remote monastery to give you that independent travel vibe.

Which Tour Company?

There are more than 200 licensed tour companies in Bhutan, ranging from one-person operations to large organisations with fleets of vehicles and their own hotel facilities. For a list of companies, see p28.

Large companies such as Norbu Bhutan, Etho Metho, BTCL, Yangphel, International Treks and Tours, Rainbow and Gangri have more clout to obtain reservations in hotels (some of which they own) and on Druk Air but they are focused on groups and so may have less time to answer individual enquiries.

One Bhutanese hotelier suggested that the following companies would be large enough to handle overseas queries, but still small enough that the owner would pay personal attention to your program: Bhutan Mountain Holiday, Bhutan Mandala, Sakten, Thunder Dragon, Windhorse and Yodsel. Other companies known for their personal attention and quality service are Bhutan Travel Bureau, Chhundu, Lhomen, Namsey and Yu Druk.

If you wish to go trekking, consider one of the companies that specialises in this activity (see p147).

All operators in Bhutan are subject to government regulations that specify services, standards and rates, and tour funds are held by the Bhutanese government and only released to the operator at the end of the tour, so you have safeguards no matter which company you choose. In the event of a problem with your Bhutanese tour company, the **Tourism Council of Bhutan** (TCB; ☏02-323251; www.tourism.gov.bt) can provide advice and assistance.

Daily Tariff

Bhutan's tourism mantra is 'high value, low impact'. Although there is no restriction on visitor numbers, there is a minimum daily tariff fixed by the government, which is the same whether you stay in hotels or camp on a trek. Of this daily tariff, US$65 goes to the government as a 'royalty'.

The costs seem steep at first, but when you factor in what that gets you – accommodation, food, private transport, guides, entry fees, permits, a fully organised trek etc – it's not a bad deal. The personal service can be remarkable. For our solo treks we had a staff of six, plus six horses!

Solo travellers and couples can easily travel in Bhutan, though you will pay a surcharge. In fact, the most common group size visiting Bhutan is two people.

Because of the daily tariff there's little difference in price between agencies. A few travel agencies will offer some discount to people who book with them directly, effectively passing on to you the commission they pay to international companies. Another advantage to booking with a local agent is that with no commission to pay, the agent has more funds to allocate to better accommodation. If you book through an Indian or Nepalese agent you may find the Bhutanese agent has less funds to book you in a better hotel, since a commission is going to the agent abroad.

The daily tariff doesn't include luxury accommodation, for which you will have to pay a surcharge, which amounts to paying the bulk of the normal hotel rate.

Some agents include visa fees, drinks and perhaps a cultural show in the daily tariff, while most charge separately for this. Activities such as rafting and mountain biking entail additional fees (see p255).

Special Categories

Diplomats A 25% discount on the rates applies to diplomats from foreign embassies or missions accredited to Bhutan.

Group Leaders A discount of 50% is given to one person in a group of 11 to 15 people. A free trip is allowed for one member per group exceeding 15 people.

Travel Agents Established tour companies intending to put Bhutan into their programs may apply for a discounted familiarisation tour. This requires both a pretrip and a post-trip briefing.

Payment Procedure

If you have arranged your trip directly with a tour operator in Bhutan, you must make payment directly to the Tourism Council of Bhutan (TCB) in Bhutan, not to the Bhutanese agent. Tours must be fully paid for in advance in order to get visa authorisation. For information on how visas are arranged, see p263.

The most straightforward and efficient procedure is to make a US-dollar transfer through Citibank in New York. Transfers into this account are monitored by TCB and credited to the agent in Bhutan. Transfers should be made to **Citibank** (111 Wall St, 19th fl, New York City, NY 10043), to the account of **Bhutan National Bank** (ABA No 0210-0008-9, account No 36023474, Swift Code Citius 33, Chips Routing No 008). The name of the tour operator should be stated as the 'beneficiary'.

Note that you are paying an agency of the Bhutanese government, not the tour operator directly; therefore you have more protection against default on the part of the tour company.

Delays & Cancellation

There is no daily tariff for days of delay in your arrival or departure due to weather conditions, Druk Air problems or roadblocks. In cases of delayed departure, tour operators will simply charge the actual expenses for accommodation, food, transport and any other services required.

Each agency has its own cancellation policy so check the fine print with your agency. There is no refund if you have to cut a trip short once in Bhutan. Travel insurance is a very worthwhile investment, given that you must make full payment up front.

Bhutanese Tour Operators

The following list includes a selection of the largest companies. For a complete list, see the websites of the **Tourism Council of Bhutan** (www.tourism.gov.bt) and the **Association of Bhutanese Tour Operators** (ABTO; www.abto.org.bt):

All Bhutan Connection
(☎02-327012; www.abc.com.bt)

Bhutan Journeys
(☎02-333890; www.bhutanjourneys.com)

Bhutan Mandala Tours and Treks
(☎02-323676; www.bhutanmandala.com)

Bhutan Men-Lha Adventures
(☎02-321555; www.trekkingbhutan.com)

Bhutan Mountain Holiday
(☎02-320115; www.bhutanmountainholiday.com)

Bhutan Tourism Corporation Limited
(BTCL; ☎02-324045; www.kingdomofbhutan.com)

Bhutan Travel Bureau
(☎02-332105; www.btb.com.bt)

Bhutan Travel Service
(☎02-325785; www.bhutantravel.com.bt)

Bhutan Your Way
(☎17641224; www.bhutanyourway.com)

Boonserm Travels
(☎02-322257; www.welcome2bhutan.com)

Bridge to Bhutan
(☎02-331766; www.bridgetobhutan.com)

Chhundu Travels and Tours
(☎02-322592; www.chhundu.com.bt)

INDIAN TRAVELLERS

Indian nationals are categorised differently from other international tourists. Indians do not require a visa and may pay local rates for food, transportation and accommodation. They may travel independently throughout most of Bhutan, though a special permit is required. For more details, see p264.

Dragon Trekkers and Tours
(☎02-323599; www.dragontrekkers.com)

Etho Metho Tours and Treks
(☎02-323162; www.bhutanethometho.com)

Gangri Tours and Trekking
(☎02-323556; www.gangri.com)

International Treks and Tours
(☎02-326847; www.intrekasia.com/bhutan.htm,
www.intrektour.com)

Jojo's Adventure Tours
(☎02-333940; www.jojos.com.bt)

Keys to Bhutan
(☎02-327232;www.keystobhutan.com)

Lhomen Tours and Trekking
(☎02-324148; www.lhomen.com.bt)

Lingkor Tours and Treks
(☎02-323417; www.lingkor.com)

Namsey Adventure
(☎02-325616; namsay@druknet.bt)

Nirvana Expeditions
(☎02-328875; www.nirvanaexpeditions.com)

Norbu Bhutan Travel (☎02-336319;
www.triptobhutan.com, www.visitbhutan.com)

Rainbow Tours and Treks
(☎02-323270; rainbow@druknet.bt)

Raven Tours and Treks
(☎02-326062; www.raventoursnadtreks.com)

Sakten Tours and Treks
(☎02-325567; www.bhutanhimalayas.com)

Snow Leopard Trekking Co
(☎02-321822; www.snowleopardtreks.com)

Snow White Treks and Tours
(☎02-323028; www.snowwhitetours.com.bt)

Thoesam Tours and Trekking
(☎02-365101; www.thoesam.com.bt)

Thunder Dragon Treks
(☎02-321999; www.thunderdragontreks.com)

Village Tours and Treks
(☎02-334325; www.villagetoursandtreks.com)

White Tara Tours and Treks
(☎02-333224; wtara@druknet.net.bt)

Windhorse Tours
(☎02-326026; www.windhorsetours.com)

Yangphel Adventure Travel
(☎02-323293; www.yangphel.com)

Yu Druk Tours and Treks
(☎02-323461; www.yudruk.com)

Tours From Abroad

Many overseas travel agencies and adventure travel companies offer trips to Bhutan, though few are real specialists. In addition to removing the hassle of transferring money, they will also arrange your tickets on Druk Air. Most group tours to Bhutan fly to Paro together, often collecting their tickets at the check-in counter in Bangkok, Delhi or Kathmandu.

Australia

Intrepid Travel
(☎1300 364 512; www.intrepidtravel.com.au)

Peregrine Adventures (☎03-8601 4444;
www.peregrineadventures.com)

World Expeditions
(☎1300 720 000; www.worldexpeditions.com.au)

Continental Europe

Explorator
(France; ☎01-53 45 85 85; www.explorator.fr)

Hauser Exkursionen (Germany;
☎089-235 0060; www.hauser-exkursionen.de)

Horizons Nouveaux (Switzerland;
☎027-771 7171; www.horizonsnouveaux.com)

Snow Leopard Adventures (Netherlands;
☎070-388 3261; www.snowleopard.nl)

UK

Abercombie & Kent
(☎0845-618 2200; www.abercrombiekent.co.uk)

Audley Travel
(☎01993-838300; www.audleytravel.com)

Blue Poppy Tours & Treks
(☎0207-700 3084; www.bluepoppybhutan.com)

Exodus (☎0870-240 5550; www.exodus.co.uk)

Explore Worldwide
(☎0845-013 1537; www.explore.co.uk)

KE Adventure Travel
(☎17687-73966; www.keadventure.com)

Mountain Kingdoms
(☎01453-844400; www.mountainkingdoms.com)

World Expeditions
(☎0208-545 9030; www.worldexpeditions.co.uk)

USA & Canada

Above the Clouds
(☎802-482 4848; www.aboveclouds.com)

Adventure Center
(✆800-228 8747; www.adventurecenter.com)

Asian Pacific Adventures (✆800-825 1680; www.asianpacificadventures.com)

Bhutan Travel
(✆800-950 9908; www.bhutantravel.com)

Dhenzang Travel
(✆813-785 7154; www.adventuresinbhutan.com)

Far Fung Places
(✆415-386 8306; www.farfungplaces.com)

Geographic Expeditions
(✆800-777 8183; www.geoex.com)

Journeys International
(✆800-255 8735; www.journeys.travel)

Mountain Travel Sobek
(✆888-831 7526; www.mtsobek.com)

Wilderness Travel
(✆800-368 2794; www.wildernesstravel.com)

Planning Your Trek

Trek Length
Short trek Three or four days
Average trek One week
Long trek Three weeks or more

Best Short Trek
Bumthang Cultural Trek A beautiful trek featuring a 500m climb to Phephe La.

Best Long Trek
Snowman Trek Gruelling, expensive (US$4280) and treacherous, this route is a brutal way to earn your trekking stripes.

Best Trek to Spot the Summits
Jhomolhari Trek Takes you within an arm's reach of Jhomolhari and Jichu Drakye, two of Bhutan's most beautiful summits.

Best Cultural Trek
Laya-Gasa Trek Experience the unusual culture of the Layap people in a village at 3700m.

Most Popular Trek
Druk Path Trek Atmospheric monasteries and breathtaking alpine scenery converge on this route between Paro and Thimphu.

Best New Trek
Merak-Sakten Trek Passes through isolated valleys in eastern Bhutan; blaze it before the rest of the world comes calling.

So you thought dzongs, tsechus and a vibrant Himalayan culture were the only aspects of Bhutan you could write home about? Well, think again. Being a country where nearly three-quarters of the terrain still thrives as virgin wilderness, the real charm of Bhutan lies in its remote backwoods. Composed of a smattering of rugged mountain folds, snowy passes, icy summits, pristine forests, turquoise lakes, rolling meadows, remote villages and a healthy sprinkling of exotic wildlife, this is perhaps one of the world's best preserved (and least explored) landscapes. And the best way to experience the untamed natural beauty of this wonderland is by walking one of the many treks that cut into its magical depths. Set aside a few days for a walk in these wilds, and you are bound to return home a happier person.

When to Go
The first thing to consider while planning your trek is weather. The second half of October provides the best window for trekking in Bhutan; mid-April comes a close second. However, both these periods fall within high tourist seasons, when flights are booked out and hotel rooms at a premium, so book well in advance. The popular trekking routes also see a steep rise in human traffic during these periods. No matter when you trek, you are likely to have sporadic – and sometimes heavy – rain.

Bhutan's Best Treks

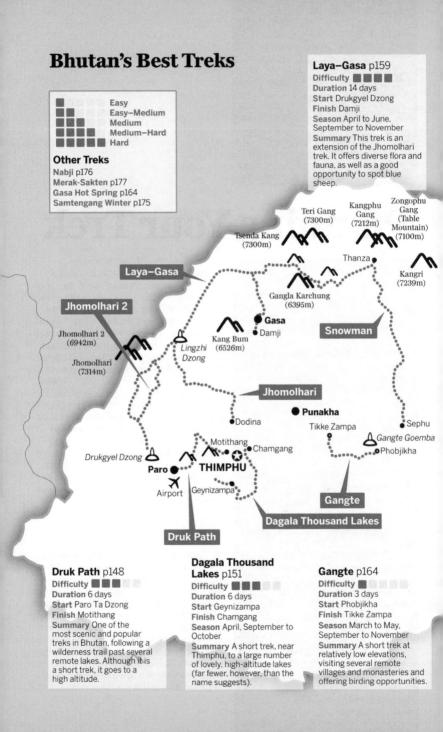

	Easy
	Easy–Medium
	Medium
	Medium–Hard
	Hard

Other Treks
Nabji p176
Merak-Sakten p177
Gasa Hot Spring p164
Samtengang Winter p175

Laya–Gasa p159
Difficulty ■ ■ ■ ■
Duration 14 days
Start Drukgyel Dzong
Finish Damji
Season April to June, September to November
Summary This trek is an extension of the Jhomolhari trek. It offers diverse flora and fauna, as well as a good opportunity to spot blue sheep.

Teri Gang (7300m)
Kangphu Gang (7212m)
Zongophu Gang (Table Mountain) (7100m)
Tsenda Kang (7300m)
Thanza
Kangri (7239m)
Gangla Karchung (6395m)

Laya–Gasa

Jhomolhari 2

Jhomolhari 2 (6942m)
Jhomolhari (7314m)

Gasa
Damji
Kang Bum (6526m)
Lingzhi Dzong

Snowman

Jhomolhari

Dodina
● Punakha
Tikke Zampa
● Sephu
Gangte Goemba
Phobjikha

Motithang
Chamgang
Drukgyel Dzong
Paro ●
Airport
Geynizampa
THIMPHU

Gangte

Dagala Thousand Lakes

Druk Path

Druk Path p148
Difficulty ■ ■ ■
Duration 6 days
Start Paro Ta Dzong
Finish Motithang
Summary One of the most scenic and popular treks in Bhutan, following a wilderness trail past several remote lakes. Although it is a short trek, it goes to a high altitude.

Dagala Thousand Lakes p151
Difficulty ■ ■ ■
Duration 6 days
Start Geynizampa
Finish Chamgang
Season April, September to October
Summary A short trek, near Thimphu, to a large number of lovely, high-altitude lakes (far fewer, however, than the name suggests).

Gangte p164
Difficulty ■
Duration 3 days
Start Phobjikha
Finish Tikke Zampa
Season March to May, September to November
Summary A short trek at relatively low elevations, visiting several remote villages and monasteries and offering birding opportunities.

Snowman p171
Difficulty ■■■■■
Duration 25 days
Start Drukgyel Dzong
Finish Sephu
Season September to October
Summary The Snowman trek travels to the remote Lunana district and is a difficult trek. Fewer than half the people who attempt this trek finish it, either because of problems with altitude or heavy snowfall.

Duer Hot Spring p167
Difficulty ■■■
Duration 8 days
Start/Finish Duer
Season March to April, September to November
Summary This trek is the old expedition route to Gangkhar Puensum, the world's highest unclimbed peak. It includes a day at the hot springs.

Bumthang Cultural p166
Difficulty ■■
Duration 3 days
Start Thangbi Goemba
Finish Kizum
Season March to May, September to November
Summary This trek is so named because the opportunities to visit villages and lhakhangs are greater than on most other treks in Bhutan.

Gangkhar Puensum (7541m)

Hot Springs

Duer Hot Spring

Bumthang Cultural

Chorten Kora

Duer

Thangbi Goemba

Kizum

Jakar

Trashi Yangtse

Rodang La

Jhomolhari p153
Difficulty ■■■■
Duration 9 days
Start Drukgyel Dzong
Finish Dodina
Season April to June, September to November
Summary Bhutan's most popular trek offers spectacular views of the 7314m-high Jhomolhari from a high camp at Jangothang.

Jhomolhari 2 p157
Difficulty ■■■
Duration 8 days
Start/Finish Drukgyel Dzong
Season April to June, September to November
Summary The shorter and earlier version of the main Jhomolhari trek goes to the Jhomolhari base camp at Jangothang, returning the same or an alternate route.

Rodang La p168
Difficulty ■■■■
Duration 10 days
Start Thangbi Goemba
Finish Trashi Yangtse
Season October to November
Summary This trek across eastern Bhutan is tough and involves a tremendously long, steep descent. The logistics are complicated and horses are often difficult to obtain for the final four days of the trek.

Best Times

» **October–November** The best overall season, with vivid blue skies common and dazzling views. The bright sun makes for pleasant daytime temperatures upward of 20°C, falling to around 5°C at night. Mornings are crisp and clear. Clouds tend to build up after 1pm, but typically disappear at night to reveal spectacular starry skies.

» **March–May** Affords warmer weather and suits those who fancy rhododendrons and other exotic Himalayan flora. However, there is a higher chance of rain, and high passes can be snowed under, especially through March.

Avoid

» **June–August** This is when the monsoons descend on Bhutan in all their fury, and it can sometimes rain for days on end. Mudslides are common, trails get dangerously wet and slippery, and there's an army of bloodthirsty leeches wiggling along the way.

» **September** Alpine wildflowers are in bloom, but the mud remains deep and soggy due to rain. Mountain views are generally blocked out by passing clouds, barring the odd sunny morning.

Booking Your Trek

Government rules dictate that all treks in Bhutan must be arranged as full-fledged camping trips booked through a tour operator. This is essential, since most routes pass through uninhabited and undeveloped forest areas, and parties must therefore be self-sufficient in terms of provisions, personnel and equipment.

It's also mandatory for trekkers to be escorted by a licensed guide registered with the Tourism Council of Bhutan (TCB). Guides in Bhutan come with varied levels of

work experience, and a seasoned trek leader is often hard to find. If you're trekking in the high season, ask your tour operator to arrange for a knowledgeable guide well in advance.

All operators in Bhutan are subject to government regulations specifying services, standards and rates. So there's little room for variation, and you are quite safe no matter who you choose. The biggest trek operators are Yangphel, International Treks & Tours, Yu Druk, Lhomen and Namsey. See p28 for a full list of recommended operators.

Trekking in Bhutan also involves obtaining a slew of permits for entering national parks, walking through protected areas and engaging in activities such as fishing. Brief your tour operator about your plans, so that these permits can be duly obtained.

What to Pack

Trekking gear is not widely available in Bhutan, so bring all personal equipment with you. While packing for the trek, limit your baggage to 15kg. Each pack animal carries 30kg, and it's expected that one animal will carry the luggage of two trekkers.

Your trek operator will provide two-person tents with foam mattresses, eating utensils, kitchen equipment, a kitchen tent and a toilet tent. Sleeping bags are not provided, so bring your own. Regulations specify that the operator should provide a first-aid kit and a pressure bag (portable altitude chamber) for high-altitude treks.

Schedule Changes

Despite all the planning and advance arrangements involved, itineraries can often be disrupted by several unforeseen factors.

SOMETHING DIFFERENT

In 2009 a pilot project was carried out by the government to study the viability of lodge-based treks in Bhutan, where trekkers could go easy on excess camping equipment such as tents or cooking gear, and could use facilities and amenities in villages along the way.

Two routes, from Duer in Bumthang to the Duer hot springs (p167), and from Gangte in Phobjikha valley to Rubisa, were identified. Guesthouses with toilets and showers were planned at campsites, with the idea of having local villagers provide services such as food, porterage, guiding and the staging of cultural shows, generating revenue for sustainable community development. Last heard, the initiative had been extended to cover two new treks recently commissioned by the government: the Nabji trail (p176) in central Bhutan and the Merak–Sakten trek (p177) in eastern Bhutan.

Clothing

- ☐ down- or fibre-filled jacket
- ☐ jumper or pile jacket
- ☐ hiking shorts or skirt
- ☐ waterproof jacket, poncho or umbrella
- ☐ hiking pants
- ☐ quick-drying T-shirts or blouses
- ☐ long-sleeved shirt
- ☐ underwear
- ☐ sun hat
- ☐ swimwear (optional)

Footwear

- ☐ trekking or running shoes (properly broken-in)
- ☐ camp shoes, thongs or sandals
- ☐ socks (polypropylene)

Other Equipment

- ☐ backpack
- ☐ sleeping bag (down-filled for high-altitude treks)
- ☐ water bottle (preferably metal)

- ☐ torch (flashlight), batteries & bulbs

Miscellaneous Items

- ☐ toiletries
- ☐ toilet paper & cigarette lighter
- ☐ multi-function pocket knife
- ☐ sunscreen (SPF 30+)
- ☐ towel
- ☐ laundry soap
- ☐ medical & first-aid kit
- ☐ pre-moistened towelettes & hand sanitiser
- ☐ sewing kit
- ☐ bandanna
- ☐ goggles or sunglasses, and spare spectacles
- ☐ sunscreen for lips
- ☐ binoculars
- ☐ books
- ☐ pen & notebook
- ☐ duffel bag with a padlock, a few stuff sacks and lots of plastic bags
- ☐ another duffel bag or suitcase to leave your city clothes in

Photography Equipment

- ☐ camera & lenses
- ☐ chamois cleaning strips
- ☐ plenty of film or memory cards
- ☐ spare camera batteries
- ☐ solar battery charger (optional)
- ☐ waterproof camera bag
- ☐ polarising filter
- ☐ tripod (optional)

For Treks Above 4000m

- ☐ insulated pants
- ☐ nylon windbreaker
- ☐ nylon wind pants
- ☐ long underwear
- ☐ woollen hat or balaclava
- ☐ gloves
- ☐ gaiters
- ☐ mountain trekking boots (properly broken-in)
- ☐ socks (wool)
- ☐ socks (light cotton) to wear under wool socks
- ☐ down booties (optional)

Unexpected showers can make trails slippery, snow can block out tracks, horses can fail to appear on schedule, or horse drivers may consider the trail too dangerous for their animals. These happen more frequently than you might imagine. Be prepared to take any disappointment in your stride.

On the Trail

Trail Conditions

Difficulty-wise, a trek in Bhutan ranges from a vigorous ramble up the hillside to a punishing slog through harsh terrain. They are physically demanding due to their lengths and drastic changes in elevation. The average daily gain is about 500m spread over 8km to 12km, with an odd 1000m ascent thrown in. There's a lot of side-hill climbing on steep slopes, which means more up-and-down climbing around vertical cliffs, avalanche tracks and side canyons. Campsites are sometimes spaced out over long distances, requiring you to walk seven to nine hours in a day. Other days, however, may involve just three or four hours of brisk walking.

Many treks follow ancient trade routes that fell into disuse once roads were built. Some of these trails, especially in eastern Bhutan, have seen scant maintenance for several decades, and route conditions are thus often difficult to predict. It's always possible to encounter snow, especially on high passes. The terrain is amazingly rocky, and you might often have to traverse long stretches of round river rocks, which is hard on your feet. Trails are often extremely muddy, and diversions are quite common.

Guides & Camp Staff

For a small group, a trekking party typically contains a guide, a cook, a helper and a horseman with his animals. The guide takes important decisions, and often teams up with the cook to handle the logistics. Larger groups are accompanied by a 'trek organiser' who oversees sundry campsite activities, packers to manage and streamline porterage and a couple of 'waiters' who serve food and handle kitchen duties. English names, not Dzongkha, are used for the various job titles.

Accommodation

You will sleep in a tent, with foam pads placed on the floor as a mattress. All your gear goes into the tent with you at night. Guides and helpers have their own tents as well, so you don't need to camp near villages for their sake and can comfortably move on to campsites in remote areas or at higher elevations. In some places, there is a facility that the Bhutanese call a 'community hall'. This is a stone building that the staff can use for cooking and shelter and may be available for trekkers to use as a dining room or emergency shelter.

Food

The food on a Bhutan trek is pampering, to say the least. Most cooks are adept at tossing together a reasonable variety of Western and Asian dishes, and they often add interesting local touches such as cheese sauces. You can rely entirely on camp meals, which are quite elaborate, and your cook can look after any special dietary requirements if given advance notice. All rations are carried from the start of the trek, and food is cooked over stoves fuelled by bottled gas.

READ UP

For a comprehensive lowdown on Bhutan's mountain trails as well as a sea of information on the flora, fauna, environment and geology of the region, pick up the excellent handbook by Bart Jordans, titled *Bhutan: A Trekker's Guide* (Nu 1300). Also look at www.greathimalayatrail.com.

Breakfast at camp comprises cornflakes or porridge, served with coffee or tea. Midday meals are usually prepared and packed beforehand, and consist of fried rice or noodles, chapatis and a potato dish. It is normally accompanied by tea from a large flask. For dinner, you'll likely be served red or white rice, chapatis, lentil soup and vegetables. Fresh meat may be served on the first two nights, and canned fruit cocktails are often thrown in for dessert. Pig out.

Pack Animals

In the absence of porters, pack horses (and at higher elevations, yaks) form the lifeline of treks in Bhutan. They carry all personal and common trekking gear, plus rations, allowing you to trek with nothing but a daypack. Contractors arrange for animals at the starting point, and their owners accompany them on the trek to arrange their loads and ensure their overall wellbeing. The ancient *dolam* system in Bhutan allocates specific grazing grounds to each village. For this reason, pack animals don't cross *dzongkhag* boundaries. Messages are sent ahead so that replacement animals are (with any luck) waiting at the boundary.

Health & Safety

Trekking in Bhutan involves trudging over innumerable ascents and descents, which gets more strenuous with altitude gain. Train intensively before coming. Walk up and down hills or inclines as much as possible. Try carrying a backpack to increase the strength training associated with walking or jogging. If you are too busy to hike over weekends, try riding a bicycle, jogging or training intensively with exercise machines (such as Stairmasters).

People aged over 45 often worry about altitude and potential heart problems. Relax. There's no evidence that altitude is likely to bring on previously undiagnosed heart disease. If you can exercise to your maximum at home, you should not have an increased risk while trekking. However, if you have a known heart disease and your exercise is already limited by symptoms at low altitude, consult an experienced doctor before committing yourself to a trek.

For general advice on medical issues see p272. For information on high altitudes and acclimatisation, see p276.

AILMENT	SYMPTOMS
Trekkers' knee	Pain generally comes from mild trauma repeated thousands of times on the descent. Anti-inflammatory pills are helpful, as are ski poles or a walking stick.
Blisters	Blisters can usually be avoided by careful attention to your feet. Immediately investigate any sore spot on your foot, and apply some protection over the affected area. When the bubble breaks, infection can develop. Wash the area and keep it clean. If swelling and redness develop, you should take antibiotics.
Snow blindness	This is a temporary, painful condition resulting from sunburn of the clear surface of the eye (the cornea). The treatment is simply to try to relieve the pain. Cold cloths held against the outside of the eyelids can bring relief. Antibiotic eye drops are not necessary and anaesthetic drops should be avoided as they slow the healing and make the eyes vulnerable to other injuries.

Losing Your Way

Since you are escorted by a licensed guide familiar with the lie of the land, it's unlikely that you'll get lost in the hills. However, this has happened to trekkers in the past, so tread with caution. Never stray from your group, and keep an eye out for signs while you trek. Watch for the lug-sole footprints of other trekkers or for arrows carved into the trail or marked on rocks by guides. Hoof prints and dung of pack animals can confirm that you are on track. On a major trekking route, the trail is usually well defined, although there may be a few confusing short cuts. If you find yourself descending when the trail should be going up, if the trail vanishes, or if you suddenly find yourself alone ahead of the rest of your party, *stop and wait for the other trekkers and guides to catch up.* If you noticed a trail junction some distance back, retrace your steps to try to find where you went wrong.

Rescue

Trekking entails a certain amount of risk, and there's always a possibility of courting illness or injury. However, *do not panic,* as it only makes things worse. Assess the incident with a clear mind before taking a decision, without jumping to conclusions. Suspected broken bones may only be bruises, a fever may subside overnight, and a dazed person may wake up and be all right in a few hours. In most areas, horses or yaks will be available to help ferry a sick or injured trekker.

Sometimes, however, the seriousness of the situation may call for immediate evacuation. In this case, the only option is to request a helicopter, since land evacuation may be near impossible. Fortunately, this is a reasonably simple process, but once you ask for a helicopter, you will be charged upward of US$1500, depending on weather conditions, your exact location and the number of rescue attempts made by the chopper. Rescue helicopters come from Indian Air Force bases in Hasimara or Bagdogra airport, after a request – sent out by the guide to the tour operator – reaches the Indian forces through TCB and the Royal Bhutan Army. It's an efficient chain of communication and a helicopter is usually dispatched within a day.

TOPOGRAPHIC MAPS

Good quality maps of Bhutan are extremely difficult to obtain. The entire country has been mapped by the Survey of India at 1:50,000, but these are restricted documents, as are a related series of topographic maps produced by the Survey of Bhutan. Another series is the 1:200,000 Russian Military Topographic set which takes 10 sheets to cover Bhutan, but its text is in Russian.

In cooperation with an Austrian project, TCB produced large-scale contour maps of the Jhomolhari and Dagala Thousand Lakes treks based on the Survey of Bhutan series. These are the best (although not entirely accurate) trekking references available, and can be purchased from the TCB office in Thimphu for Nu 300 each.

SUMMIT SAGA

While they may not physically measure up to the legendary 8000m-high peaks in other Himalayan countries, the mountains of Bhutan are ruggedly beautiful. Jhomolhari was a famous landmark for early Everest expeditions. On the approach march for the 1921 British Everest Expedition, George Leigh Mallory described it as 'astounding and magnificent', but said he felt 'cold and rather horrified' towards the mountain. It was climbed from Tibet in 1937 by F Spencer Chapman and Passang Lama, and again in 1970 by a joint Indo-Bhutanese team.

Michael Ward and Dr Frederic Jackson made an extensive survey of Bhutan's mountains in 1964–5. Climbing several peaks of around 5500m, they categorised the Bhutan Himalaya as a defined group of mountains. Climbers were allowed in for a short period from 1983 to 1994. A Bhutanese team scaled Thurigang (4900m), north of Thimphu, in 1983. Jichu Drakye was attempted thrice before being climbed in 1988 by an expedition led by Doug Scott. In 1985 Japanese expeditions climbed Gangri (7239m), Kari Jang, Kang Bum (6526m) and Masang Gang (7165m). Gangkhar Puensum (7541m) still remains the highest unclimbed peak in the world after unsuccessful attempts by Japanese and British teams in the 1980s. Climbing peaks above 6000m was subsequently prohibited in Bhutan, owing to religious beliefs and reservations of villagers residing near them.

Bhutan Telecom (www.telecom.net.bt) also provides satellite phones using the Thuraya system, which allows direct dialling from anywhere in the country, even on a trek. Some tour operators rent satellite phones to trekkers, though the charges are steep.

Responsible Trekking

Trekking exerts great pressure on nature, and you should take special care when trekking to help preserve the fragile ecology. The following tips are common sense, but they are also mandated by the government, and you (or your guide) could be fined for violating them.

Fires

» Campfires are prohibited and you should decline the offer if your staff suggest one. Bring enough warm clothing and you won't need to stand around one. It's a real dilemma, though, if the packers build a fire, or if one is struck as part of a 'cultural show' in a village.

» Since 1996, cooking meals over a fire has been prohibited by law, and staff are required to carry a supply of fuel. However, it's a hard rule to enforce, and animal herders sometimes violate the code and cook their own meals over wood.

» Burning garbage is offensive to deities, especially within sight of a sacred mountain such as Jhomolhari.

Rubbish

» What's carried in can also be carried out. Don't overlook easily forgotten items such as silver paper, cigarette butts and plastic wrappers, including those left behind by others. They weigh little and can be stored in a dedicated rubbish bag.

» Sanitary napkins, tampons and condoms cause serious damage to the environment if they are not carried out of a trek.

Human Waste Disposal

» Contamination of water sources by human faeces can lead to the transmission of hepatitis, typhoid and intestinal parasites, and poses severe health risks to trekkers as well as local residents and wildlife. A toilet tent will be set up at each camp.

» Where there is no toilet tent, consider burying your waste. Dig a hole 15cm deep and at least 100m from any watercourse. Consider carrying a trowel for this purpose. Cover the waste with soil and a rock. Use toilet paper sparingly, and burn it or bury it with the waste. In snow, dig down to the soil or your waste will be exposed when the snow melts.

Washing

» Detergents and toothpaste, even biodegradable ones, pollute watercourses. For personal washing, use biodegradable soap and a basin at least 50m away from any watercourse. Widely dispersing the waste water allows the soil to filter it fully before it makes it back to the watercourse.

Erosion

» Hillsides and mountain slopes are prone to erosion. Sticking to existing tracks and avoiding short cuts helps to prevent it. If you blaze a new trail straight down a slope it will turn into a watercourse with the next rainfall and soil loss and scarring will result.

» Sometimes a track passes right through a mud patch. Walking through the mud preserves the trail while walking around the edge will increase the size of the patch.

» Avoid removing or disturbing plants that keep the topsoil in place.

Wildlife Conservation

» Be aware that in some places, animals found in huts are likely to be protected native animals rather than non-indigenous vermin.

» Do not leave food scraps behind, thereby avoiding attracting wildlife to the camp.

» Disturbing or feeding wildlife or destroying their natural habitat threatens their wellbeing.

Cultural Conservation

» Thoughtful travellers respect the culture and traditions of local village, camp staff and horse drivers.

» Giving sweets, money, medicines or gifts to local people, particularly children, encourages begging.

» Buying local household items or religious artefacts from villagers could deprive them of family heirlooms or precious relics and utensils that are difficult to replace. It could also be considered disrespectful.

regions at a glance

Which region of Bhutan you decide to visit will most likely depend on how much time you can afford to spend here. The vast majority of visitors quite naturally focus on the west and Thimphu. With its excellent tourist infrastructure, fantastic sights and spectacular festivals, it allows you to see the most of Bhutan in the shortest amount of time.

Central Bhutan on the other hand sees fewer tourists and is a quieter, dreamier collection of alpine valleys and important monasteries. The winding roads east are for adventurers, weaving researchers and yeti hunters. It offers warmer, wetter and wilder climes, tougher travel and, some would say, the 'real' Bhutan, untouched by group tourism or even much of the modern age.

Thimphu

Shopping ✓✓
Museums ✓✓
Modern Bhutan ✓✓✓

Shopping
It's not just that Thimphu has the best handicraft shops in the country (it does), it's also the best place to actually see the products being made, from traditional paper and incense factories to local silversmiths and weaving workshops.

Museums
The best general museums are not in Thimphu (try Paro and Trongsa for that) but for specialised interests such as Bhutanese medicine, traditional country life and the country's rich textile tradition, this is the place.

Modern Bhutan
There's nowhere better than the capital for the daily cultural collisions that sum up Bhutan's inherent quirkiness. Monks with mobiles and lamas with laptops are a daily sight here and this is also the place to hit the town with trendy, hoodied Bhutanese clubbers.

p44

Western Bhutan

Architecture ✓✓✓
Trekking ✓✓✓
Scenic Views ✓✓

Architecture
If you only visit two towns in Bhutan, make them Paro and Punakha. The west is blessed with not only the country's loveliest dzong (Punakha), but also its loveliest lhakhang (Kyichu Lhakhang) and the most dramatic monastery (Takt-shang). These are the big sights that you simply have to see.

Trekking
From awesome Jhomolhari to the remote land of Laya and the popular trails of the Druk Path, Bhutan's most popular trek, the west offers you the opportunity to combine the best of the cultural sights with a walk in the mountains.

Scenic Views
In October or November, a trip to the Dochu La, with its view of Himalayan peaks framed by chortens and prayer flags, is a literal high-point, rivalled only perhaps by views of Jhomolhari from the upper Paro valley.

p69

Central Bhutan

Architecture ✓✓
Hiking ✓✓
Sacred Sights ✓✓✓

Architecture
The heartland of central Bhutan is Bumthang, a delightful collection of Swiss-style valleys sprinkled with golden-roofed chapels, remote red-walled goembas and sacred temples, including the fabulous 1500-year-old Jampey Lhakhang.

Hiking
Bumthang offers the best day hikes through bamboo forest and yak meadows, past chortens to remote monasteries. The delightful Bumthang Cultural trek goes through moss-covered forests, while the villages of Ura and Shingkhar are great for strolls.

Sacred Sights
The line separating fact and fiction can be fuzzy in Bhutan. Stand where Guru Rinpoche wrestled a snowlion, run your hand over meditation caves etched with the body prints of saints and peer into a lake full of treasure visible only to the virtuous. It's a sacred landscape.

p106

Eastern Bhutan

Off the Beaten Track ✓✓
Dramatic Drives ✓✓✓
Handicrafts ✓✓

Off the Beaten Track
Bhutan's wild east is for the hardy. Long, winding drives on rough roads ending in simple accommodation is the norm here. Life is more rural and led at a slower pace. And you'll likely have it to yourself. Just don't come during the monsoon...

Dramatic Drives
Roads in the east regularly inch along sheer cliff faces on a ledge not wide enough for two vehicles. Throw in dense fog and a monsoon downpour and you can expect a thrilling, chilling drive. The variety of landscapes is equally impressive, from the heights of Thrumshing La and the lush Himalayan foothills down to the subtropical.

Handicrafts
Eastern Bhutan is the heartland of the country's rich weaving traditions. Enthusiasts can wander the village looms of Khoma and find out which natural dye comes from insect secretions at Khaling.

p128

Look out for these icons:

 TOP CHOICE Our author's recommendation

A green or sustainable option

FREE No payment required

See the Index for a full list of destinations covered in this book.

On the Road

Thimphu

♪02 / POP 100,000 / ELEV 2320M

Best Places to Stay

» Hotel Jumolhari (p55)
» Hotel Kisa (p55)
» Taj Tashi (p55)
» Hotel Migmar (p55)

Best Places to Eat

» Seasons Restaurant (p60)
» Chula (p59)
» Zone (p59)
» Ambient Café (p59)

Why Go?

As the 50-year-old capital of one of the world's un-usual countries, Thimphu has a youthful exuberance that constantly challenges the country's natural conservatism. The resulting juxtapositions of old and new are an es-sential part of its charm. Crimson-robed monks, Indian labourers, government ministers clad in *ghos* and *kiras* (traditional dress) and camera-wielding tourists all share the pot-holed pavements, and nobody, it seems, is in a hurry. Thimphu is as close as Bhutan gets to being urban, but never feels more than a friendly over-sized village.

For the visitor Thimphu offers the best opportunity to briefly break away from the tour itinerary. As a big town, it offers espresso bars and Thai restaurants beside pro-tector shrines and hillside hermitage retreats. Finding a balance between monasteries and museums – the old and the new – is the key to getting the most out of this intriguing city.

When to Go

Dochu La and the colourful and dramatic Thimphu tse-chu make September to November the peak season, when flight and accommodation bookings can be tight.

There's not really a bad time to visit the city, though low clouds and rain frequently obscure the hillsides between June and September.

Saturday is a good day to be in the city throughout the year, with archery tournaments, expanded opening hours at the dzong, the weekend market and the liveliest night-life, though some sights and all government offices are closed.

☉ Sights

Trashi Chhoe Dzong DZONG

(Map p46; ⏱5-6pm Mon-Fri, 8am-6pm Sat & Sun, to 5pm in winter) This splendid dzong, north of the city on the west bank of the Wang Chhu, seems to fit seamlessly into the valley, lending the city both regal splendour and monastic weight. The dzong was the site of the lavish formal coronation of the fifth king in 2008 and hosts the city's biggest annual bash, the colourful tsechu festivities.

The building you see is actually not the original Thimphu dzong. In 1216 Lama Gyalwa Lhanangpa built Dho-Ngen Dzong (Blue Stone Dzong) on the hill above Thimphu where Dechen Phodrang now stands. A few years later Lama Phajo Drukgom Shigpo, who brought the Drukpa Kagyu lineage to Bhutan, took over the dzong. In

◎ 0 ▬▬▬▬▬ 1 km
Ⓝ 0 ▬▬▬▬▬ 0.5 miles

To Tango Goemba/
Cheri Goemba
(7km)

LANGJO

ZILUNGKHA

Chhophel Lam

Dechen Lam

❶ Trashi Chhoe Dzong

SANGAYGANG

❺ National Institute for Zorig Chusum

Gaden Lam

Desi Lam

❻ Motithang Takin Preserve

Chhubar Chhu

MOTITHANG

Changangkha Lhakhang

Norzin Lam

Chang Lam

❼ Sevina Lam

❷ Weekend Market

❹ Benez Bar

Coronation Park

Clocktower Square

Rabten Lam

Doebum Lam

Thimphu

❶ Savour the serenity of the imposing yet peaceful **Trashi Chhoe Dzong** (p45)

❷ Shop for incense and amulets in the bustling **weekend market** (p48)

❸ Climb through whispering pines to the peaceful solitude of **Tango Goemba** or **Cheri Goemba** (p66)

❹ Bend your elbow at a friendly bar, such as **Benez Bar** (p61), and chat over *momo*s (dumplings)

❺ Marvel at the skill and artistry of Bhutanese arts and crafts at the **National Institute for Zorig Chusum** (p48)

❻ Spot the seriously odd-looking takins at **Motithang Takin Preserve** (p53)

❼ Join the pilgrims at colourful **Changangkha Lhakhang** (p53), Thimphu's liveliest temple

1641 the Zhabdrung acquired the dzong from the descendants of Lama Phajo and renamed it Trashi Chhoe Dzong (Fortress of the Glorious Religion). He arranged to house both monks and civil officials in the dzong, but it was too small so he built another dzong lower down in the valley for the civil officials. The 13th Druk Desi, Chhogyel Sherab Wangchuck (1744–63), later enlarged Trashi Chhoe Dzong so that it could again accommodate both civil officials and monks.

The original upper dzong was destroyed by fire in 1771 and was abandoned in favour of the lower dzong, which was expanded. That dzong itself suffered a fire in 1866, and twice again since then. The five-storey *utse* (central tower) was damaged in the 1897 earthquake and rebuilt in 1902.

When he moved the capital to Thimphu in 1962, King Jigme Dorji Wangchuck began a five-year project to renovate and enlarge the dzong. The royal architect performed the repairs without touching the *utse*, Lhakhang Sarpa or any other of its chapels at the centre. Other than these structures, the entire dzong was rebuilt in traditional fashion, without nails or architectural plans. The dzong once housed the National Assembly and now houses the secretariat, the throne room and offices of the king and the ministries of home affairs and finance.

For more on the structure of a dzong see p235; the illustration is based on this dzong.

Visiting the Dzong

The whitewashed two-storey outer structure has three-storey towers at the four corners projecting out over the walls and capped by red-and-gold, triple-tiered roofs.

There are two main entrances on its eastern side. The southern entrance leads to the administrative section (off-limits to visitors), while the northern leads to the monastic quarter, the summer residence of the *dratshang* (central monk body).

Entering the dzong from the northeast entrance you are greeted by the four guardian kings, while the steps are flanked by images of Drukpa Kunley, Thangtong Gyelpo and Togden Pajo with consort. Upon entering the **dochey** (courtyard) it's hard not to be impressed by the splendid proportions of the architecture, the enclosed silence broken only by the flight of pigeons, the shuffle of feet and the whirr of prayer wheels. A large *utse* separates the northern monastic courtyard and its Lhakhang Sarpa (New Temple) from the southern administrative courtyard. The northern **assembly hall** houses a large statue of Sakyamuni (the historical Buddha) and the thrones of the current king, past king and Je Khenpo. Look to the ceiling for fine painted mandalas.

It is sometimes possible to enter the **utse**. If you're allowed in, look for the 3rd-floor funeral chorten of the 69th Je Khenpo, where pilgrims receive the blessing of betel nut from his nut container. If this seems weird, head next door to visit the toilet of the Zhabdrung in his former living room.

Northeast of the dzong is an excellent example of a traditional cantilever bridge. To the southeast is the unassuming residence of the current king, while across the river you can see the impressive SAARC building, which houses the National Assembly and hosted the major 2010 SAARC conference. The small Neykhang Lhakhang, west of the dzong, houses the local protective deities Gyenyen Jagpa Melen and Dorji Daktshen and so is off-limits to visitors. The large and newly built open-air courtyard on the north side of the dzong now hosts the dances of the annual tsechu festival (see p231 and p55). The dzong's huge Sangay Tsokhorsum Thondrol (a painted/embroidered religious picture) is unfurled here at the climax of September's tsechu.

Weekend Market   MARKET

(Map p50; ☺Sat & Sun) The weekend market is crammed into a set of stalls on both banks of the Wang Chhu, just north of Changlimithang Stadium. Vendors from throughout the region arrive on Thursday and Friday, setting up evening stalls in Norzin Lam, and remain until Sunday night. The most interesting selection is upstairs.

Wander around and you'll find a pungent collection of dried fish, strips of fatty pork and balls of datse (home-made soft cheese). During the winter you can even pick up a leg of yak (with the hoof still attached). The **incense area** is one of the most interesting sections, full of deliciously pungent raw ingredients, as well as pink cubes of saffron that look like dice but are used to flavour the holy water given to pilgrims in all lhakhangs. The special bags of mixed grains and grasses are for throwing in the air during religious rituals.

One of the most popular sections sells *doma* (areca nut wrapped in betel leaf to chew; Indian name *paan*) kits (Nu 5 for four pieces) complete with *paney* (banana leaf) and *tsune* (lime). The bricks of tea provide the main ingredient for *suja* (butter tea), whereas the locally made yeast patties are used to brew *chang* (barley beer).

Depending on the season, look out for banana pods, jackfruit and the curly fern fronds known as *nakey*. The cereals section has red rice and tsampa, the ground roasted barley beloved by highland Bhutanese and Tibetans.

Across the newly constructed cantilever footbridge, known as the Kundeyling Baazam, on the west bank, is a collection of clothing stalls as well as a **handicraft market**. Products include wooden bowls, mala beads, printing blocks, amulets, yak tails and prayer wheels, some of which are made in Nepal. There are some gems amid the junk. Bargaining is very much in order; your guide can advise you on the quality of your intended purchase.

National Institute for Zorig Chusum
ART SCHOOL

(Map p46; ☎322302; izc@druknet.bt; Pedzoe Lam; ☺9am-noon & 1-3.30pm Mon-Fri, 9am-noon Sat) This institute, commonly known as 'the painting school', operates four- to six-year courses that provide instruction in Bhutan's 13 traditional arts. Students specialise in painting (furniture, *thangkas* – painted religious pictures, usually on canvas), woodcarving (masks, statues, bowls), embroidery (hangings, boots, clothes) or statue-making (clay).

Most tour operators include a visit to the school in their sightseeing program. Though large groups of visitors can disrupt the classes, the craft demonstrations are a photographers' dream and it's hard not to be impressed at the skill and discipline of the young students.

There are several handicraft shops nearby.

National Memorial Chorten   CHORTEN

(Map p46; Chorten Lam) This large Tibetan-style chorten is one of the most visible religious structures in Thimphu, and for many Bhutanese it is the focus of their daily worship. It was built in 1974 as a memorial to the third king, Jigme Dorji Wangchuck (1928–1972).

The whitewashed chorten is decorated with richly painted annexes facing the cardinal directions, and features elaborate mandalas, statues and a shrine dedicated to the popular king. Four stone snowlions guard the corners. See p239 for more on the symbolism of chorten architecture.

Throughout the day people circumambulate the chorten, whirl the large red prayer wheels and pray at a small shrine inside the gate. Particularly charming is the timeless collection of old timers hauling away at room-size giant prayer wheels beside the main entrance. Early morning is particularly tranquil as elderly people shuffle in, and spruced-up kids on their way to school whiz in and out to pay homage.

Most of the major attractions will already be included in your itinerary. Here are a few suggestions if your itinerary includes some free time in Thimphu.

24 Hours

After your hotel breakfast head down to the weekend market and explore the traditional produce stalls before crossing the atmospheric cantilever bridge to the souvenir stalls on the east bank of the Wang Chhu. If the market isn't on, check the **Changlimithang Archery Ground** for any activity or drop into the **Textile Museum**, **Painting School** (National Institute for Zorig Chusum) or **VAST** (Voluntary Artists Studio Thimphu) to watch artisans at work or track down that unique souvenir. Visit the **Mid Point** or **Musk** restaurants for a light lunch or the trendy **Art Café** for coffee and cake. Round off the afternoon by checking out the numerous shopping centres for handicrafts, books or Bhutan's extravagant postage stamps. As beer o'clock approaches, head towards **Benez Bar** or the **Zone**. After-dinner entertainment can be found in one of the many discos or a late-night haunt such as the **Om Bar**.

Folk Heritage Museum MUSEUM
(Phelchey Toenkhym; Map p46; ☎327133; Pedzoe Lam; SAARC national/adult Nu 25/150; ☺9.30am-1pm & 2-4.30pm Mon-Fri, 10am-1pm Sat & Sun) This restored three-storey, rammed-earth and timber building replicates a traditional farmhouse and is furnished as it would have been about a century ago. A guided tour of this almost-living museum is included in the admission and provides an interesting glimpse into traditional Bhutanese life. Details that jump out include the traditional noodle press, the leopardskin bags and Brokpa yak-hair 'spider' hats.

National Library LIBRARY, MUSEUM
(Map p46; ☎333301; www.library.gov.bt; Pedzoe Lam; ☺9am-1pm & 2-5pm Mon-Fri) West of the golf course, the National Library was established in 1967 to preserve ancient Dzongkha and Tibetan texts. For tourists it's of interest mainly as a fine example of traditional Bhutanese architecture, but it's also a good resource for books about Bhutan.

Traditional books and historic manuscripts are kept on the top floor and include texts from the famous Tibetan printing presses of Derge and Narthang. Scriptures from all religious schools are represented, including the Bön tradition. Most of the books are Tibetan-style, printed or written on long strips of handmade paper stacked between pieces of wood and wrapped in silken cloth. Other displays include some great historic photos, a copy of a letter sent from the Druk *desi* (secular ruler) to British army officer and surveyor Samuel Turner

in 1783, and carved wooden blocks used for printing books and prayer flags.

National Institute of Traditional Medicine MUSEUM, CLINIC
(Map p46; ☎324647; Serzhong Lam; admission Nu 100; ☺9am-1pm & 2-5pm Mon-Fri) Established in 1978, this interesting government facility researches, prepares and dispenses traditional herbal and other medicines. The small museum details ingredients that range from herbs and minerals to animal parts, precious metals and gems. The institute collects medicinal plants from remote corners of the Bhutanese Himalaya such as Lingzhi, Laya and Lunana and then distributes pills, tablets, ointments and medicinal teas to regional health-care units around the country.

Of particular interest is *yartsa goenbub* (cordyceps), the high-altitude cure-all 'Himalayan Viagra' that is actually a worm that has been killed and mummified by fungal spores. The curious worm-root sells for between US$600 and US$5000 per kilogram in China.

If you're feeling under the weather, the on-site clinic will tell you if your wind, bile and phlegm are in balance and prescribe appropriate medicines or treatments, all free of charge. *Lasgang* root is said to do wonders for a sore throat; we're not quite sure about the elephant's gallstone. For more on traditional Bhutanese medicine see p211.

Textile Museum MUSEUM
(Map p46; ☎321516; Norzin Lam; SAARC national/adult Nu 25/150; ☺9am-4pm Mon-Sat) Thimphu's Textile Museum is worth a visit

Zorig Lam
Phenday Lam
Samten Lam
Doendrup Lam
Jangchhub Lam
Jangchhub Lam
Jangchhub Lam
Dolbum Lam
Norzin Lam
Dremton Lam
Druk Air
Wogzin Lam
Chorten Lam
Doebum Lam

Bank of Bhutan
(Main Branch)
Bhutan
National
Bank
Hong Kong
Market
Norling
Medical
Bhutan Thailand
Friendship Park
Druk
PNB
Bank
India Bhutan
Friendship
Hospital

0   200 m
0   0.1 miles

Weekend Market ⊙

Kuendeying Bazaam

🏨 19

Chhogyel Lam

Dechen Lam

Kunday Lam

🍴 29

⛴ 5

☆ 56

🍴 39
🍴 46
💲 37
🔒 57 🍴 38
🍴 35
🍴 44

Namdag Lam

Khuju Lam ⊙ 3

Chang Lam

Changlimithang Stadium

Gatoen Lam
🍴 28
🍴 50

🏨 24

Coronation Park

Ⓟ

Chhogyel Lam

Chhogyel Lam

Wang Chhu

🏨 14

⊙ 4

🍴 41

⊙ 1

🍴 47

Clocktower Square

🏨 6

🏨 7 🛍 52

Chang Lam

🏨 8 🏨 11

🏨 18

Norzin Lam

Ⓟ

Coronation Park

⊙ **Changlimithang Archery Ground**

Dechen Lam

⊙ 2

🚕 *Taxi Stand*

🚌 *Bus Station*

to learn a bit more about Bhutan's living national art of weaving. The ground floor focuses on *cham* costumes, while the upper floor introduces the major weaving techniques, styles of local dress and type of textiles made by women and men. There is usually a small group of weavers working their looms inside the shop, which features work from the renowned weaving centre of Lhuentse in northeastern Bhutan. Each item is labelled with the name of the weaver, at prices ranging from Nu 1500 to 25,000.

In 2011 the museum will move across the road to the impressive new **Royal Textile Academy** (www.royaltextileacademy .org), a work in progress that will eventually house a weaving school, conservation centre, shop and cafe.

Changlimithang Stadium & Archery Ground
STADIUM

(Map p50; Choegyel Lam) The national stadium occupies the site of the 1885 battle that helped establish the political supremacy of Ugyen Wangchuck, Bhutan's first king. It was also the location of the 2008 coronation celebrations. You might catch the occasional football match here, but the next-door archery ground is much more fun. It's worth checking to see if there's an archery tournament going on: whether it's traditional bamboo or high-tech carbon-fibre bows, the skill, camaraderie and good-humoured ribbing are always entertaining. Traditional songs and victory dances are all part of the fun (see p214). Archers often practise here in the mornings.

Voluntary Artists Studio Thimphu
GALLERY

(VAST; Map p50; ✆325664; www.vast-bhutan.org; Chang Lam) The impressive Voluntary Artists Studio Thimphu in Clocktower Sq is the capital's main centre for artists. The goal of the studio is to promote both traditional and contemporary works of Bhutanese art, to provide vocational training for young artists and to act as a creative meeting place for artists. It's a great place to plug into the Thimphu art scene and chat with artists. Art by the students and instructors is sold here. The studio location may well change, so check the website.

Motithang Takin Preserve
ZOO

(off Map p46; Sangaygang) A short distance up the road to the telecom tower is a trail leading to a large fenced area that was originally established as a minizoo. Some years ago the king decided that such a facility was not in keeping with Bhutan's environmental and religious convictions, and it was disbanded. The animals were released into the wild, but the takins, Bhutan's national animal, were so tame that they wandered around the streets of Thimphu looking for food, and the only solution was to put them back into captivity. It's worthwhile taking the time to see these oddball mammals, which look a bit like a cross between a gnu and a bison. The best time to see them is early morning when they gather near the fence to feed. For more about this curious creature, see p247. There are also a few barking deer around.

Changangkha Lhakhang
TEMPLE

(Map p46; Sevina Lam) This popular fortress-like temple perched on a ridge above central Thimphu regularly hums with pilgrim

BHUTAN, THE BOOK

At the National Library, be sure to check out the copy of the world's largest published book. Aptly entitled *Bhutan*, and weighing in at 68kg and over 2m tall, this heavyweight tome could crush any coffee table. Its huge illustrated pages are turned one page per month. Details on the book and how to buy a copy (US$15,000 for a full-sized edition, US$100 for the smaller version) can be found at www.friendlyplanet.org. You can also see a copy of the book close up in the library of the Uma Paro hotel (p77).

activity. It was established in the 12th century on a site chosen by Lama Phajo Drukgom Shigpo, who came from Ralung in Tibet. Parents traditionally come here to get auspicious names for their newborns or blessings for their young children from the protector deity Tamdrin (to the left in the grilled inner sanctum, next to Chenresig). Don't leave without taking in the excellent view from the back *kora* (pilgrim path), with its lovely black and gold prayer wheels.

Zilukha Nunnery
NUNNERY

(Map p46; Gadem Lam) After visiting the telecom tower, take Gaden Lam for great views of Thimphu and Trashi Chhoe Dzong. Just above the road is this modern nunnery, which is also called Drubthob Goemba. The site has links to Thangtong Gyelpo, and there's an interesting enclosed chorten in the main courtyard.

Dechen Phodrang
MONASTERY

(Map p46; Gaden Lam) At the end of Gaden Lam is Dechen Phodrang, the site of Thimphu's original 12th-century dzong. Since 1971 it has housed the state monastic school, where a team of 15 teachers provides an eight-year course to more than 450 students. The 12th-century paintings in the goemba's Guru Lhakhang have been restored, and the upper floor features a large figure of Zhabdrung Ngawang Namgyal as well as a *goenkhang* (chapel dedicated to protective deities).

Zangto Pelri Lhakhang
TEMPLE

(Map p50) This private chapel, built in the 1990s by Dasho Aku Tongmi, a musician who composed Bhutan's national anthem, is

CRAFTY THIMPHU WORKSHOPS

If you are into your arts and crafts, ask your tour company to arrange a visit to the following workshops and traditional factories in Thimphu.

Jungshi Handmade Paper Factory (Map p50; ☑323431; www.gawaling.com; Khuju Lam; ⊗8.30am-5pm, Mon-Sat) This small factory produces traditional Bhutanese paper handmade from the daphne bush. You can see the whole paper-making process, from soaking and boiling to sorting, crushing, pulping, layering, pressing and drying. Products for sale include lovely decorated paper (Nu 150 to Nu 350 per sheet), as well as cards, notebooks, lampshades and calendars. *Jungshi* means 'natural'.

Nado Poizokhang Incense Factory (Map p46; ☑323107; www.nadopoizokhang.com; Changangkha; ⊗9am-5pm Mon-Fri) Easily Thimphu's sweetest-smelling excursion, this traditional workshop churns out between 5000 and 10,000 sticks of handmade incense every month. You can learn about the various ingredients (juniper, cloves, cardamom, sal wood) and see the production process at the main workshop just above the Changangkha Lhakhang, or just browse for the final product at the **showroom** on Rabten Lam. Incense packets ranges from Nu 75 for a cinnamon fragrance to Nu 300 for extra sandalwood.

Goldsmiths Workshop (Map p50; ⊗9am-1pm & 2-5pm Mon-Fri) This government workshop behind the bus station is a bit rough and ready, but it's a good place to see copper and silver chasing and the production of everything from fine jewellery to large monastery pieces like *torana*s (arches found over statues) and finials. Artists mount smaller pieces in pine resin to make them easier to work on.

---

southwest of the weekend market. It's beside the older Mani Dungkhar Lhakhang and is a replica of Guru Rinpoche's celestial abode. Inside is an array of large 4m-high statues, including several Guru Rinpoches. Look for the elephant skull in a box – reputedly unearthed while digging the foundations.

Buddha Viewpoint   MONUMENT
(off Map p46) Even unfinished, the huge 50m tall steel statue of Buddha Dordenma commands the entry to the Thimphu valley. The huge three-storey throne will eventually hold several chapels, while the body itself is filled with 125,000 smaller statues of Buddha. The statue was made in China (of course), cut into pieces and then shipped and trucked in from Phuentsholing (we would love to have seen the faces of the local farmers as the super-sized features of the Buddha drove by!). See www .dordenma.org for more details on the impressive construction. The drive or bike up the paved road to the Changri Kuensel Phodrang site is worth it for the great views of Thimphu alone.

🏃 Activities

You will probably be too busy sightseeing, trekking or shopping to swim, cycle or go rock climbing, but these activities are available if you want them.

There are two tennis courts, squash courts and a basketball court at the north end of Changlimithang Stadium and a public swimming pool at the Sports Complex.

Royal Thimphu Golf Club   GOLF
(Map p46; ☑325429; www.golfbhutan.com; Chhophel Lam; green fees US$40, club hire per day US$20; ⊗8am-5pm Tue-Sun) The Royal Thimphu Golf Club has a delightful nine-hole course beautifully situated above Trashi Chhoe Dzong. Resident Indian Brigadier General TV Jaganathan got permission from King Jigme Dorji Wangchuck to construct a few holes in the late 1960s, and the course was formally inaugurated in 1971. How often do you get to tee off in sight of a Bhutanese dzong and have to dodge chorten hazards?

Schoolboy caddies are available for Nu 200 to Nu 300. You don't need to make an appointment to play, but you may have to wait to tee off on weekends. The clubhouse canteen (closed Monday) has decent food and fine views of the greens.

Bhutan Bicycle Club   MOUNTAIN BIKING
(Map p50; ☑321905; www.bhutanmtb.com; Clock-tower Sq) Local company Yudruk Tours runs this club, which organises rides and rents mountain bikes (US$30 per day, including helmet). The club can arrange to have you

and the bike transported to the start of several rides (see p255 for more details).

Vertical Bhutan
CLIMBING

(☎322966; www.verticalbhutan.com) Bhutan's only rock-climbing club, Vertical Bhutan, gathers most weekends to climb on the Nose Rock, a rock face high above the southwest part of Thimphu. There are several fixed routes with names such as 'Wedding Present' and 'Reach and Preach'. Contact the club secretary for the climbing schedule.

Deer Park Thimphu
MEDITATION

(Map p46; www.deerparkthimphu.org; Nazhoen Pelri Youth Development Centre) For those whose pursuits tend towards the spiritual more than the physical, this small centre offers Tuesday evening meditation classes, short weekend retreats and Buddhist discussions for adults and children, as well as Friday-night movie night. See the website for a schedule.

✸ Festivals & Events

Thimphu really comes alive during the annual *domchoe* and tsechu festivities, held consecutively over eight to 10 days in September/October, corresponding to the eighth lunar month in the Bhutanese calendar. Many businesses are closed during the main dates.

🛏 Sleeping

If you are on a normal tourist visa, you will be booked into one of the comfortable midrange hotels unless you have paid a premium for a top-end hotel (shown here as luxury hotels). If you are an Indian national or are working in Bhutan on a project, you have the option to choose a more moderately priced hotel; these are reviewed towards the end of this section.

TOP CHOICE Hotel Jumolhari
HOTEL $$

(Map p50; ☎322747; www.hoteljumolhari.com; Wogzin Lam; s/d Nu 2940/3360, deluxe Nu 3675/4095; @🖥) This centrally located hotel bills itself as a boutique hotel and boasts a classy ambience and stylish decor. The rooms are tasteful, carpeted and comfortable; there is a health club with free sauna and steam room, and an excellent restaurant serving good Indian dishes, among others. All in all a good choice without needing to pay an extra surcharge for a top-end hotel.

Namgay Heritage Hotel
HOTEL $$$

(Map p50; ☎337113; www.nhh.bt; s/d Nu 3200/3700, deluxe Nu 5000/5500; @🖥) At the tiptop end of the tourist class is this excellent new place, a short walk from the centre. Rooms are comfortable with good beds and stylish Buddhist motifs, though some rooms suffer from slow drains. Pluses include a good Bhutanese restaurant and free sauna, steam room and gym. Visiting lamas should splash out on the suite, which comes with its own meditation throne.

Hotel Kisa
HOTEL $$$

(Map p50; ☎336495; www.hotelkisa.com; Chang Lam; r Nu 3500-5000; 🖥) The Kisa has quickly become one of best-regarded hotels in town. It's central and stylish, with 35 very comfortable rooms and one of the best hotel restaurants in town. This is at the top end of the tourist class and recommended.

Hotel Migmar
HOTEL $$

(☎338901; www.hotelmigmar.bt; Thimphu Expressway, Olakha; s/d Nu 2850/3500, deluxe Nu 3500/4000; 🖥🏊) Opened in 2010, the Migmar is also at the top end of the tourist class, featuring 27 spacious luxurious rooms with excellent facilities like hair dryer and safe. The location out of town in the southern suburbs is quiet, as long as you request a room away from the expressway. The swimming pool is a bit of a white elephant.

Taj Tashi
LUXURY HOTEL $$$

(Map p50; ☎336699; www.tajhotels.com; Samten Lam; r/ste from US$385/575; @🖥) The striking dzonglike architecture of the five-star Taj is a great introduction to the understated but stylish luxury inside. The cool

---

THE BEST VIEW IN TOWN

One of the best views of the Thimphu valley comes from the prayer-flag-strewn hillside just below the **telecommunications tower** (2685m), high above the town in an area known as Sangaygang. The lovely half-hour walk to Wangditse Goemba (p66) starts from here, as do several hiking, running and mountain-biking trails (see the map at the site). The access road attracts fitness fans after work and becomes a lovers' lane after dark. Be careful not to photograph the telecommunications installation or the Bhutan TV broadcasting tower.

START CLOCKTOWER SQUARE
FINISH CHANGLIMITH-ANG ARCHERY FIELD
DISTANCE 3KM
DURATION TWO TO THREE HOURS

Walking Tour
Downtown Thimphu

❯ Start at ❶ **Clocktower Square**, the town's real centre and a great place to sit and take in the city. Head north along Wogzin Lam, past such interesting shops as ❷ **Dawa Norbu Religious Shop** (for *ghos*, prayer flags and cloth) and ❸ **Gasep Sangay Wangdi Tsongkhang** (a monks' outfitters), before reaching the ❹ **traffic circle** with the arm-snapping police. Continue uphill to the ❺ **Swiss Bakery**, whose time-warp decor hasn't changed since opening day in 1970, when expats travelled for days to get cold plastic-wrapped hamburgers.

From here, head west up the footpath to spin the giant prayer wheel of the timeless ❻ **Droma Lhakhang**. The eye-catching ❼ **Thai Pavilion** next door makes much more sense when you realise it marks the Thailand-Bhutan Friendship Park.

Head back downhill and swing north along Doibum Lam. Just by the Seasons Restaurant, take a quick look at ❽ **Samphel Traditional Furniture**, selling painted chests and Tantric drums, before squeezing down the vegetable market alley of Hong Kong Market. Turn left up Norzin Lam and after 50m you'll pass the ❾ **Sephab Gyeltsen Tsongkhang**, with its excellent range of traditional cloth, silks and Tibetan-style carpets. The shop also sells prayer flags but don't get the long white *mani pa* – these are bought for the dead. The ❿ **Handicrafts Emporium** and ⓫ **National Textile Museum** are both worthwhile detours before popping into the opulent lobby of the ⓬ **Taj Tashi**.

Head east down Samten Lam to Chang Lam and then down Dungkhar Lam, passing local-style Chhodon Restaurant. Pop into the ⓭ **Zangto Pelri Lhakhang** to spin the giant prayer wheel of the Mani Dung-khor Lhakhang and then continue down to the ⓮ **Weekend Market**. Finally, head south along Chhogyel Lam, past the traditional district courthouse to ⓯ **Changlimithang Archery Field**, checking for signs of life.

modern bar and outdoor terrace are both great places for a sophisticated drink. The five deluxe rooms with balcony (US$415) are a good choice and come with a sun deck and day bed, though the balconies could do with more privacy. Corner rooms are also popular for the fine views. The sporty will enjoy the top-end gym and indoor pool; couples will like the candle-lit aromatherapy oil massage, followed by a rose petal bath and a bottle of champagne.

Bhutan Suites
HOTEL, APARTMENTS **$$**
(Map p46; ☎333377; www.bhutansuites.com; Changangkha; s/d Nu 2900/3500; @☎) Business travellers and tourists alike are sure to appreciate the separate sitting room, underfloor heating and mini-kitchens here, plus the sweeping private balcony views over Thimphu. The location is more convenient for visiting government ministries than having dinner in town, but you can order room service from the good vegetarian restaurant. A steam bath and sauna is planned.

Wangchuk Hotel
HOTEL **$$**
(Map p50; ☎323532; www.wangchukhotel.com; Chang Lam; s/d incl breakfast Nu 1900/2500; @☎) This hotel overlooks the stadium and is a favourite of many expatriates. The wood-panelled, carpeted rooms are spacious, light and comfortable, so don't be put off by the gloomy lobby. The restaurant has a good reputation.

Druk Hotel
HOTEL **$$**
(Map p50; ☎322966; www.drukhotels.com; Wogzin Lam; s/d Nu 3000/3500, deluxe Nu 4000/4500; @☎) This hotel was for a long time the best in Thimphu but has enjoyed a lower profile over recent years. It is in the centre of town, overlooking Clocktower Sq and boasts a bar, a restaurant noted for its Indian food, a 24-hour business centre and a health club with a gym, sauna and steam bath. Recent renovations have freshened up the standard rooms, though you can expect room rates to rise.

Hotel Phuntsho Pelri
HOTEL **$$**
(Map p50; ☎334970; phuetshopelri@druknet .bt; Phenday Lam; s/d/apt from Nu 2000/2500/4000; @☎) This bright, modern and central place has rooms set around a central inner courtyard, with polished floorboards, thicker-than-usual mattresses, and tea and coffee facilities. The businessy vibe is tempered by the bar and Turkish-style spa.

NOT YOUR AVERAGE TOURIST SIGHT

Thimphu is apparently the world's only capital without traffic lights. A set was installed a few years back, but residents complained in classic Bhutanese fashion that it was too impersonal, which is why the beloved white-gloved police continue to direct the increasing traffic with the balletic grace of someone doing a 1980s robot dance. As well as being a classic Bhutanese anachronism, it may well be the city's most photographed spectacle.

Amankora
LUXURY HOTEL **$$$**
(Map p46; ☎8272333; www.amanresorts.com; Thori Lam; s/d incl full board US$1300/1400; @☎) On the 'less is more' theme comes this five-star resort on the forested fringes of town. Amankora looks like a mini dzong, its stone-paved passageways inspiring hushed tones in the reverential guests. Inside the open-plan rooms, plenty of wood and tan-coloured textiles mellow the monastery asceticism. The traditional *bukhari* wood heaters are a nice touch but were also the cause of a fire that burned down the dining hall in 2010. As with other Amankoras hotels, there is a luxurious spa, and airport transfers and meals are included in the tariff.

Termalinca
LUXURY HOTEL **$$$**
(Map p65; ☎351490; www.termalinca.com; Babesa; r/ste US$350/450; @) Thimphu's latest luxury choice is actually 7km from Thimphu, outside the valley on the banks of the Wang Chhu, just below the main road to Paro. The 30 rooms are spacious, sleek and stylish, with cool open-plan bathrooms and unexpected Chinese furniture. Sadly there are no balconies, so spend your time instead at the lovely riverside bar or the impressive slate-and-pine yoga room/gym/spa. The turn-off to the resort is by a large white chorten. The resort is owned by the eldest wife of the fourth king.

Hotel Riverview
HOTEL **$$**
(Map p50; ☎325029; hotelriverview@druknet.bt; Dechen Lam; s/d/ste from Nu 2600/3000/4500; @☎) On the east bank of the Wang Chhu is this hefty and somewhat dated group place.

All of the spacious rooms have a balcony with fine views (which are slightly better from the upper floors). The architecture certainly isn't charming and it's a little inconvenient for exploring the town, but many people like the quiet location and there's a restaurant and business centre here.

Jambayang Resort GUESTHOUSE, APARTMENTS $$
(Map p50; 322349; www.jambayangresort.com.bt; Dechen Lam; s/d from Nu 2500/3000, apt Nu 2700; @) High above the Wang Chhu on the east bank is the old-fashioned but charming Jambayang Resort. The sprawling, creaking guesthouse has 18 comfortable (but not luxurious) rooms, many with balcony and excellent views, and four private apartments with kitchens. Many Bhutanese recommend the restaurant here, with its great views over Thimphu.

Yeedzin Guest House GUESTHOUSE $$
(Map p50; 325702; yeedzin@druknet.bt; Jangchhub Lam; s/d/ste Nu 1500/1800/2000; @⊛) This modest but quiet and friendly guesthouse overlooks central Thimphu and oozes old-world charm. It's popular with local NGO staff and consultants, who like the five suites, each with a kitchen. The cosy ground floor restaurant is warmed by an open fire, and the resident weavers add a homey touch, even if the weedy courtyard could do with some care.

Hotel Dragon Roots HOTEL $$
(Map p50; 323256; droots@druknet.bt; Wogzin Lam; s/d Nu 2400/2900; ⊛) The old-fashioned and somewhat noisy rooms at the oddly named Dragon Roots are cosy enough but definitely at the lower end of the tourist spectrum. The pink and lime colour scheme doesn't exactly scream cool. There is a large restaurant with plenty of vegetarian options.

Hotel Druk Sherig HOTEL $$
(Map p50; 322598; fax 322714; Wogzin Lam; s/d Nu 2600/2800) This former guesthouse was under renovation during our last visit but should reopen soon as a solid midrange option with a very central location.

Hotel Pedling HOTEL $$
(Map p50; 325714; pedling@druknet.bt; Doendrup Lam; s/d Nu 1600/2000, deluxe Nu 2200/3000; @) The old-fashioned Hotel Pedling is showing its age these days and certainly isn't a luxury option. But you can't beat the location, and the staff are very friendly. The hotel is owned by Gangte Monastery and often gets visiting Buddhist groups.

Motithang Hotel HOTEL $$
(Map p50; 322435; www.motithang.com; Thori Lam; s/d Nu 2000/2500, deluxe Nu 3000/3800; @⊛) Looking a century older than its 1990s heritage, the rustic, wood-panelled Motithang is far from the centre, in the peaceful suburb of Motithang – not far from the residence of the King's Grandmother. The 15 old-fashioned rooms are all mothballs and 1970s headboards, but it's oddly appealing, perhaps because the creaking corridors were once the residence of the former prime minister. The old-school lounge has a wood fire in winter.

Hotel Galingkha HOTEL $$
(Map p50; 328126; Doendrup Lam; s/d from Nu 2500/3000; ⊛) This central three-star place overlooking the southern traffic circle was extensively remodelled in 2010. Expect nice decor, teak flooring and a ground-floor restaurant. There are plans to create a chain of Galingkhas across Bhutan.

Shambala Executive Apartments
APARTMENTS $$
(Map p46; 17110722; kesang011@gmail.com; Thori Lam; apt per month Nu 25,000) These spacious two-bedroom, two-bathroom, fully furnished, fully serviced apartments boast polished floorboards, wood panelling and other nice touches. Nightly rates for short-term guests are available on request.

The following local budget hotels are not as comfortable as the tourist hotels but they're all quite adequate.

Hotel Zey Zang LOCAL $
(Map p50; 334707; Norzin Lam; s/d Nu 600/700) Characterless but clean and comfortable.

Hotel Tandin LOCAL $
(Map p50; 322380; Norzin Lam; s/d/tr Nu 600/700/900) The rooms are plain and not immune to noise, but the bathrooms are clean and it has a good Bhutanese/Indian restaurant.

Hotel Yoedzer LOCAL $
(Map p50; 324007; mendrell@druknet.bt; City Centre Complex, Wogzin Lam; d Nu 600-1200) Rooms are a bit rundown, with thin mattresses and hot water in the mornings only, but they are essentially clean and it's very central. The restaurant's shepherd's pie (special order) has attracted a small local appreciation society.

R Penjor Lodge
LOCAL **$**
(Map p50; ☎325578; Norzin Lam; s/d Nu 750/1000) Upstairs from Ambient Café and run by the same people, the good-value rooms are clean and each come with a bathroom.

Hotel Singye
LOCAL **$**
(Map p50; ☎333229; hotelsingyethimphu@yahoo.com; Norzin Lam; r Nu 1000-2000) A good, clean and fresh central option but you'll need to haggle to get a decent rate.

✖ Eating
Thimphu is the one place in Bhutan where you can break out of the same-same-but-different hotel buffets and track down some authentic local tastes.

CLOCKTOWER SQUARE & AROUND
Plums Café
BHUTANESE, CONTINENTAL **$$**
(Map p50; ☎324307; Chorten Lam; mains Nu 60-120; ⊙lunch & dinner Mon-Sat) This cosy popular restaurant above the main junction is an ideal place to try *ema datse* (chillis with cheese), *shamu datse* (mushrooms and cheese) or some fried *nakey* (ferns), washed down with good apple pie. Come early and grab a window seat and you'll get prime views of the police directing traffic below you.

Chula
INDIAN **$$**
(Map p50; ☎336275; Wogzin Lam; mains Nu 80-180; ⊙Mon-Sat) Chula gets our vote as the best Indian food in town. The chicken karai, tikka masala, and fresh paneer tikka are all great, as are the good-value set lunch thalis (Nu 180). The restaurant is set to move to the Druk Punjab Bank plaza.

Ambient Café
CAFE **$$**
(Map p50; coffees Nu 50-90, mains Nu 150; ⊙9am-9pm; 🛜) A central, bright and well-run place, popular with expats, offering free wi-fi, good strong coffee, home-made cakes and daily lunch specials such as Bumthang cheese paninis. The kitchen is closed on Monday.

Khamsa Coffee
CAFE **$**
(Map p50; Changlam Plaza, Chang Lam; snacks Nu 25-65; ⊙10am-7pm; 🛜) The coffee's not quite as good in this upstairs modern coffee shop but it's a quiet haven, with clean Japanese-style decor, and there are treats like waffles with ice cream.

Zone
WESTERN **$$**
(Map p50; ☎331441; mains Nu 110-215; ⊙11am-10pm, bar until 11pm Wed-Mon) The burgers in this expat favourite are just as they should be – big and sloppy – plus there's house-made ice cream, pizza and fish and chips. The outdoor pub-style seats are a great place to read the paper over an Illy coffee and a home-made donut, or come for an evening beer.

Bhutan Kitchen
BHUTANESE **$$**
(Map p50; ☎331919; Gatoen Lam; mains Nu 100-300; ⊙lunch & dinner) This elegant restaurant showcases Bhutanese cuisine in a spacious but warm setting that features traditional seating and a showcase kitchen. It was designed with tour groups in mind, so you can dive into the *ema datse* (chillies and cheese) and other local dishes without calling for the fire brigade. Get things going with a shot of *arra* – the local firewater.

Hotel Jumolhari
INDIAN **$$**
(Map p50; ☎322747; www.hoteljumolhari.com; Wogzin Lam; mains Nu 50-150; ⊙breakfast, lunch & dinner) This delightful restaurant in one of Thimphu's most appealing hotels is notable for its delicious tandoori and curries, delicate naans, cold beer and relaxed atmosphere.

Mid Point Restaurant
BHUTANESE, INDIAN **$**
(Map p50; ☎321269; Wogzin Lam; mains Nu 55-100; ⊙lunch & dinner Mon-Sat) This simple spot is a favourite of many Bhutanese for its generous dishes, particularly *dosas* and other South Indian cuisine, at very reasonable prices. The fish curry is excellent, as is the *hogey* (cabbage, carrot and chilli) salad. The outdoor seats are one of the few places in town for alfresco dining.

Musk Restaurant
BHUTANESE **$**
(Map p50; ☎323388; Clocktower Sq; mains Nu 80-130, set meals Nu 140-180; ⊙9am-10pm Tue-Sun) This local hang-out on the main Clocktower Sq is a great spot to join the locals who sit outside to shoot the breeze and puff surreptitiously on their cigarettes. The menu consists mostly of Bhutanese dishes, but there are also a few Thai and Indian dishes, plus roast chicken and sizzlers. Our beef *dhop dhop* was very tasty, even if we're not quite sure what it was. The place also functions as a bar on the weekends, which is perhaps why the dessert plate features both aniseed and paracetamol tablets.

Lower Norzin Lam is lined with cheap hotels frequented by Indian tourists, all offering simple and inexpensive vegetarian Indian food at lunch and dinner for between

Nu 30 and Nu 70; try the **Hotel New Grand** (Map p50; mains Nu 60-120) or **Hotel Ghasel** (Map p50; mains Nu 70-130) for their good South Indian vegetarian dishes; and the **NT Hotel** (Map p50; mains Nu 40-120) for its inexpensive curries and liquid Tuesday special.

OTHER LOCATIONS

TOP CHOICE Seasons Restaurant ITALIAN $$
(Map p50; ☑327413; Doendrup Lam; small pizzas Nu 180-300 ◷9.30am-9pm Wed-Mon) This deservedly popular restaurant specialises in excellent pizzas but also offers daily specials, excellent desserts and great salads, including walnut and pear, and haloumi with *fattoush* (Middle Eastern cheese with toasted bread). The alfresco dining area overlooking bustling Hong Kong Market is the perfect place to enjoy a Red Panda beer. A small pizza is enough for one, or two if added to a salad.

Art Café CAFE $$
(Map p50; Doebum Lam; cakes & soups Nu 90-130; ◷9am-7pm Tue-Sun; ☎) Smart, bright and cosy best describe this expat favourite. Decent coffee and wicked cakes (try the banoffee pie or cheesecakes) will have you coming again and again, and the small mains selection – hearty soups, pasta, burgers – make for an ideal light lunch.

Baan Thai THAI $$
(Map p50; ☑339966; 4th fl, Karma Kangzang Bldg, Norzin Lam; mains Nu 100-220; ◷lunch & dinner Wed-Mon) The excellent Thai food here is authentically spicy, so ask for tourist levels unless you want a serious sweat. The bubbly Thai owner can offer recommendations, or try the delicious *tom kha ghai* (chicken coconut soup) and *som tam* (green papaya salad), perfectly favoured with lime and fish sauce.

Zombala BHUTANESE $
(Map p50; Doendrup Lam; momos Nu 35; ◷lunch & dinner Mon-Sat) Any local Thimphupa will tell you the best *momos* in town are at Zombala's, a cheap and cheerful local dive near Hong Kong Market. Choose between beef or cheese and expect to fight for a seat.

Cypress Hotel NEPALI $$
(Map p50; ☑334453; FCB Bldg, Norzin Lam; set veg/nonveg meals Nu 120/180) An unpretentious but charming family-run place serving delicious Nepali food (the *shahi paneer* – paneer cheese in mildly spiced gravy – is recommended), with a popular Friday night *thali* (set meal) of eight dishes.

Karma's Coffee CAFE $$
(Map p50; Tashi Rabten Bldg, Phendey Lam; coffees Nu 50-90, food specials Nu 160-180; ◷10am-10pm; ☎) A cosy US-style coffeehouse with the full range of espresso drinks (hot, iced or frapped), comfy seating, plenty to read, delicious brownies and daily food specials, and there's even a smoking room out the back.

Chhodon Restaurant BHUTANESE $
(Map p50; ☑323679; Dungkhar Lam; mains Nu 70-100; ◷Mon-Sat) If you really fancy going local, this family restaurant in an old traditional house is known for the city's best spicy ribs (*tsim* or *tsidro*). Order these with some *shikam* (dried beef with chillis), rice and *suja* (butter tea) for a totally authentic Bhutanese meal.

Jichu Drakey Bakery BAKERY $
(Map p50; Doebum Lam; pastries from Nu 20; ◷7.30am-9pm) Stroll up the hill for pretty good takeaway cakes and pastries (there are no tables). The apple pie and strudel are our favourites.

Big Bakery BAKERY $
(Map p46; ◷9am-7pm Mon-Fri, 10am-5pm Sat & Sun) This Japanese-assisted project trains young Bhutanese with a learning disability as bakers. It's worth your support, especially as all that this involves is popping in for a cup of coffee and a croissant.

Rice Bowl CHINESE $
(Map p50; ☑333844; Centre Mall, Norzin Lam; mains Nu 80-100; ◷lunch & dinner Mon-Sat) Excellent chilli pork, Sichuan chicken and crispy shredded lamb are made to be shared, though the service is slow. If you get tired of waiting, head downstairs to the cheaper and friendlier Chopsticks Restaurant.

Terdzor Hotel INDIAN $
(Map p50; Norzin Lam; mains Nu 40-120) Excellent Nepali (Friday) and Punjabi (Saturday) vegetarian buffets.

Lingshay's Restaurant WESTERN $$
(Map p50; ☑336081; Changlam Sq; mains Nu 190; ◷Tue-Sun) Changlam Sq is lined with half a dozen good restaurants. This bright and breezy option is perfect for a light lunch, with daily specials, burgers, pancakes, grilled sandwiches and real coffee.

Other fine options in Changlam Sq:

Kar Gyal INDIAN $$
(Map p50; ☑336037; mains Nu 100-150; ◷Mon-Sat) Good for curries.

Khamsa Oriental CHINESE **$$**
(Map p50; 335655; mains Nu 70-220)

Sangay's Place WESTERN **$$**
(Map p50; mains Nu 80-250; Wed-Mon) Ambitious food and outdoor seating.

SELF-CATERING
For fresh produce, remember the busy weekend market and the street stalls in Hong Kong Market.

Sharyang Enterprise SUPERMARKET
(Map p50; Changlam Plaza; 10am-8pm Tue-Sat, noon-8pm Sun) Also known as 'Wangdi's Supermarket' and offering perhaps Thimphu's best selection of foodstuffs, much of it imported from Thailand.

Tashi Supermarket SUPERMARKET
(Map p50; Clocktower Sq; 8am-7.30pm) Decent range of imported and local groceries, with a convenient central location.

Sharchhogpa Grocery SUPERMARKET
(Map p46; Norzin Lam; 7am-9pm) Friendly grocery shop with cereals, bread and plenty of packaged foodstuffs.

🍷 Drinking & Entertainment
Good places for coffee include Art Café, Ambient Café, Khamsa Coffee and Karma's Coffee, which are listed under Eating (p59).

Thimphu has lots of corner-shop bars, but only a handful could be recommended for outsiders looking for more than a game of *carom* (finger snooker) and a swig of cheap whisky. As well as the hotel bars, there are numerous small bars throughout the town. Alcohol won't be served until after 1pm, and bars are closed on Tuesday, the national dry day. Bars close at 11pm weekdays and midnight on Friday and Saturday.

Entertainment is patchy, but you can always persuade your guide to take you to a local *drayang* bar: members of the audience request songs at Nu 100 each, which are then sung in traditional style by locals or the resident group. There is sometimes a small cover charge. Places change all the time so ask your guide for his favourite.

For a small town there's a fair bit of competition and lots of turnover in the club scene so you'll have to ask around for the latest places. Discos don't really kick off much before midnight. Depending on the night and the time you rock up, a cover charge of about Nu 200 may be asked of men. Nightclubs and discos generally close at midnight weekdays and at 2am Friday and Saturday.

Benez Bar PUB
(Map p50; Gatoen Lam; 11am-11pm Wed-Mon) Thimphu's friendly neighbourhood pub is a lively and inviting place with a cosy back bar that is popular with locals and expats, especially on Fridays. Pop in for a pint of draft Red Panda and you could end up sharing a drink with a minister or visiting diplomat. In addition to main courses there are excellent bar snacks such as *momos*, samosas and fried cheese balls.

Om Bar BAR
(Map p50; www.changkhang.com; Jojo's Shopping Complex, Chang Lam; 5pm til late Wed-Mon) A popular place for young locals and a good late-night option, as it's next to two clubs. It's on the 2nd floor of the shopping complex; the entrance is on the north side.

Khuju Luyang CULTURAL PERFORMANCE
(Map p46; 328649; khujuluyang@druknet.bt; Gongphel Lam; performance per group Nu 3500-5000) This troupe of 30 performs a popular hour-long selection of religious, regional and folk songs and dances, including *cham* masked dances and songs from Laya and Sakten, accompanied by live music on the zither, flute, fiddle and *dranyen* (lute). It's stagey but enjoyable and worth it, especially if you haven't timed your trip with a major festival.

Royal Academy of Performing Arts
CULTURAL PERFORMANCE
(Map p46; 322569; Chhophel Lam; 8.45am-4.30pm Mon-Fri) The home of the Royal Dance Troupe works to preserve Bhutan's folk-dancing heritage and trains professional dancers who perform several of the dances at the Thimphu tsechu. With advance notice they will provide a one-hour performance for visitors, or ask your guide if there's a practice session you could attend.

Tashi Nemcha Theatre CULTURAL PERFORMANCE
(Map p50; 336874) A more relaxed atmosphere prevails at this theatre near the Zangto Pelri Lhakhang, home to the Lha-Yee Performing Arts troupe. The studio can provide a Bhutanese meal and an evening of classical and folk music around a bonfire.

Luger Cinema CINEMA
(Map p50; 322317; Norzin Lam) This usually crowded and always uncomfortable cinema screens Hindi and Bhutanese movies as well as the occasional ancient English/ foreign-language movie.

GETTING A *GHO*

Getting your very own *gho* (traditional cloak for men) in Bhutan is an excellent idea, whether you intend to hang it on the wall or, even better, wear to a festival or event in Bhutan. Many shops in Thimphu's shopping complexes, including the souvenir shops, sell off-the-rack *gho*s as well as *kiras* (traditional dress for women).

According to Chimmi at **Sephub Gyeltsen Tsongkhang** (Map p50; Norzin Lam; ⊗8am-9pm), one of Thimphu's best cloth stores, ready-made *gho*s cost from Nu 1000 for cotton, Nu 1500 for wool or Nu 2000 for silk varieties, with hand-woven cloth costing as much as Nu 6000. For a better fit, Chimmi recommends taking a couple of days to get a tailor-made item. Bhutanese-style cloth made in India ranges from Nu 250 to Nu 350 per metre; most people will need 3.5m of cloth. As for which tailor, Chimmi says it doesn't matter ('all the stitches work'). Don't forget you'll also need to invest in a *kera* (belt; Nu 250), a white *lhagey* (inner liner; Nu 200) and some *omso* (socks).

Once you have your *gho*, you'll need some help learning how to wear it. The tricky bit comes when hoisting the robe up and folding the pleats at the back. You'll also need some instruction on storing the *gho*, which involves folding the pleats origami-style so it hangs properly on your return. It's a great souvenir and a guaranteed winner at fancy dress parties.

Recommended nightclubs:

Club Ace   NIGHTCLUB
(Map p46; Phenday Lam; ⊗9pm-midnight Wed, to 2am Fri & Sat) Popular place just outside the centre.

Hive   NIGHTCLUB
(Map p50; Chang Lam; ⊗11pm-2am Wed, Fri & Sat) Big, bold and popular, with the Boomerang Club next door.

Space 34/Dept of Sound   NIGHTCLUB
(Map p50; Jojo's Shopping Complex, Chang Lam; ⊗10pm-2am Wed, Fri & Sat) Cosy and thumping and conveniently next to Om Bar. Alternatively try the downstairs **Rumours**.

Splash   NIGHTCLUB
(Map p50; Peling Complex, Doendrup Lam; ⊗9pm-midnight Wed, to 2am Fri & Sat) Underground disco, lounge and bar. Find it on Facebook.

🔒 Shopping

Thimphu has a plethora of general shops containing everything from prayer flags to canned fish. To provide even more variety, some corner shops also sell hard liquor by the glass and their sign may read 'shop-cum-bar' or the all-encompassing 'general-cum-bar-shop'.

Many 'local' tourist items are actually made in India or Nepal, but there are lots of interesting Bhutanese products, especially textiles, baskets, jewellery, incense, books, Dragon Kingdom T-shirts, *atsara* (clown masks) and religious items. Local products also include Tsheringma safflower- and gooseberry-flavoured herbal teas and the organic lemon grass oil and sprays made by **Bio Bhutan** (www.biobhutan.com). Don't neglect the handicraft section at the weekend market, where you can put your bargaining prowess to the test.

Gagyel Lhundrup Weaving Centre

CLOTHING
(Map p46; Changzamtog; ⊗9am-5pm Mon-Fri) This private centre at the south end of Thimphu produces hand-woven textiles on site and has a selection of cloth and ready-made garments for sale. This is one of the few places where you can watch weavers at work. A finely embroidered *kira* can take a year to make and cost over US$1000; cheaper ones start at US$40.

DSB Books   BOOKSTORE

(Map p50; www.bhutanbooks.com; Chang Lam) This place has probably Thimphu's best selection of coffee-table and other books on Buddhism, Bhutan and the region. Its prices are reasonable, especially for Indian editions, which are cheaper than overseas editions. It's on the ground floor of Jojo's Shopping Complex; enter from the lane behind Chang Lam.

National Handicrafts Emporium

HANDICRAFTS
(Map p50; www.coloursofbhutan.com; Norzin Lam; ⊗9am-1pm & 2-6pm) This large emporium run by the government has fixed prices and is on many itineraries. It closes an hour earlier November to February.

Lungta Handicraft HANDICRAFTS
(Map p50; www.lungtahandicraft.com; Chang Lam; ☺8.30am-8.30pm) The best buys here are the larger items like bamboo boxes, carpets, metal ewers, even antique saddles and monastic trumpets, but expect to pay US$250 for a good piece. The antiques all have stamped seals from the National Commission, which mean they are safe to take through customs. Like many shops, they can arrange pricey but convenient DHL shipping.

Tsering Dolkar Handicrafts HANDICRAFTS
(Map p50; Shop 36, Norzin Lam) Unlike many Thimphu craft shops, this one stocks mostly Bhutanese crafts, and is strong on jewellery. Visa cards accepted.

Choki Handicrafts HANDICRAFTS
(Map p46; www.chokischool.com; Pedzoe Lam) Near the National Institute for Zorig Chusum, Choki sells masks, *thangkas*, paintings and painted lama tables called *choektse*. Many products come from the affiliated Choki Traditional Art School (see p66).

Yarkay Central Building HANDICRAFTS
(Map p50; Norzin Lam) If you prefer to keep the legwork to a minimum, this shopping complex has several craft stores under one roof, including Druk Handicrafts, Kelzong Handicrafts and Kurtoe Handicrafts.

Sangay Arts & Crafts HANDICRAFTS
(Map p46; Pedzoe Lam) You can purchase works by students of the National Institute for Zorig Chusum at this nearby shop, run by a former student.

Philatelic Bureau STAMPS
(Map p50; Dremton Lam) This tiny back room at the post office offers the best souvenir sheets of Bhutanese stamps. Also for collectors, a tiny stall on the ground floor of Hotel Tandin has a small selection of postcards and unusual stamps. Several of the souvenir shops also sell stamps.

Pekhang Bookshop MAGAZINES
(Map p50; Norzin Lam) Next to the Luger Cinema, this stationary shop is good for magazines and newspapers.

Bhutan Archery Shop ARCHERY
(Map p50; Gatoen Lam) Catering to the large community of Bhutanese archers, this store specialises in US-made Hoyt brand bows that cost from US$600 to US$1300. Arrows are the steel-tipped Easton brand,

which sell for Nu 550 to Nu 720. Traditional bamboo bows are usually home-made, but bamboo arrows can often be picked up at the weekend market.

Norling Audio MUSIC
(Map p50; Norling Centre, Norzin Lam) CDs and tapes of Bhutanese and Bollywood songs are available here for Nu 200 to Nu 400.

Sachok Enterprise OUTDOOR GEAR
(Map p50; Centre Mall, Norzin Lam) If you are missing a piece of gear for your trek, this place has both real and fake brand-name gear, and the owner is honest about what's what.

Camp Outdoor OUTDOOR GEAR
(Map p50; Changlam Plaza) The Chinese-made King Camp brand here isn't top-notch, but there are useful items like water bottles, socks and gaiters, plus imported hiking shoes.

ℹ Information

Internet Access
There are a dozen or so internet cafes spread around town, all charging Nu 50 to Nu 90 per hour. Most hotels have rudimentary business centres with internet access, charging considerably more.

AP Cyber Café (Map p46; Norzin Lam; ☺9am-8pm; 🛜) Hidden on the 1st floor.

Gems Business Centre (Map p50; City Centre Complex, Wogzin Lam; ☺9am-9pm) Near Hotel Yoedzer.

Jigme Dorje Wangchuck Public Library (Map p46; Norzin Lam; ☺12.30-6.30pm Mon-Fri, 11am-3pm Sat) This tiny place feels like a British village library and has a dog-eared collection of books on Buddhism and Bhutan, as well as internet access.

Maps
City maps (Nu 100) are available in bookshops and handicraft shops.

Survey of Bhutan (Map p46; Rm 35, National Land Commission, Motithang) Sells good satellite maps of Bhutan (Nu 400), plus 1:50,000 topo maps of much of the country (some off-limits), and tourist maps of Paro, Bumthang and Thimphu. The 1:12,000 *Thimphu Centre Map* shows ministries, government offices and religious buildings and is available around town.

Medical Services
Pharmacies can supply medications, including over-the-counter antibiotics. Consider also the clinic at the National Institute of Traditional Medicine (see p49).

City Pharmacy (☎321382; City Centre Complex, Wogzin Lam; ⊗8.30am-9pm Mon-Sat, 10am-9pm Sun) Near Hotel Yoedzer, the pharmacy also sells veterinarian supplies, so get help choosing your drugs...

India Bhutan Friendship Hospital (Map p50; ☎322485; Chorten Lam)

Jigme Dorji Wangchuck National Referral Hospital (Map p46; ☎322496; Gongphel Lam) Bhutan's best hospital.

Norling Medical (Map p50; Norling Centre, Norzin Lam) Pharmacy on the ground floor of the plaza.

Money

Most hotels can change money at government rates, although they usually have a limited supply of cash.

Bank of Bhutan (Map p50; Norzin Lam; ⊗9am-1pm Mon-Fri, to 11am Sat) This main branch tends to be busy. There's a smaller branch on nearby Wogzin Lam.

Bhutan Forex (Map p50; Room 24, 1st fl, Changlam Plaza; ⊗9am-7pm Mon-Sat) Changes cash US dollars at the bank rate, with no commission, and keeps longer hours than the banks.

Bhutan National Bank (Map p50; Chang Lam; ⊗9am-4pm Mon-Fri, to 11am Sat) In the same building as the main post office, it's the easiest and best place to change cash, but not euro travellers cheques.

Druk PNB Bank (Map p50; ⊗9am-1.15pm & 2-4pm Mon-Fri, 9am-noon Sat) This new bank should soon have an ATM that accepts Visa and MasterCard.

TBank (Map p50; Norzin Lam; ⊗9am-1pm & 2-4pm Mon-Fri, 9am-noon Sat) This new bank opposite the Taj Tashi Hotel changes cash and travellers cheques.

Post

Many hotels and shops sell stamps; it is safe to simply drop cards and letters into post boxes here.

DHL (Map p46; sangay_wangmo@dhl.com; 19-13 Thori Lam)

Post office (Map p50; Chang Lam; ⊗9am-5pm Mon-Fri, 10am-1pm Sat) Well-organised, with a postcard and philatelic shop.

❶ Getting There & Away

The long-distance bus station (Map p46) is below the east end of the bridge (*zampa*) at the southern end of town. (Even the bus depot has a prayer wheel in the courtyard and names its bus companies after the eight auspicious symbols!). There are over two dozen daily buses (so-called 'vomit comets') to Phuentsholing (Nu 81 to Nu 111; Coaster Nu 192), plus two daily to Paro (Nu 55), one to Haa (Nu 103), and weekly departures to longer-distance destinations (see p270 for more details).

Shared taxis depart just outside the station for Phuentsholing (Nu 500 per seat), Paro (Nu 100 to Nu 150) and Wangdue Phodrang (Nu 200).

❶ Getting Around

If you are on a normal tourist visa, you will have a car/minibus, driver and guide available throughout your stay in Bhutan. Most shops and points of interest are within easy walking distance of Thimphu's major hotels so it's easy to pop out for a drink or a round of shopping on foot.

Although usually well signposted, very few locals, including taxi drivers, actually know and use street names; landmarks and building names will serve you better when asking for or giving directions.

TO/FROM THE AIRPORT You can book a taxi outside Paro airport at a fixed rate of Nu 800 to Thimphu. A taxi to the airport from Thimphu's bus station can cost half this. It is 53km from the airport to Thimphu; the journey takes less than two hours.

If your tour operator has not arranged transport for your departing flight, the most reliable way is to have your hotel arrange a vehicle. If you have an early-morning flight from Paro (and most are), it's best to spend the night in Paro.

TAXI Most of Thimphu's taxis are tiny Maruti minivans with meters that the drivers rarely use. Taxi drivers have a habit of charging foreigners, including Indians, as much as they can – one of Bhutan's few rip-offs. A short ride around town costs around Nu 50 to 60 or you can hire a taxi for the day for about Nu 500. The taxi stand on Chang Lam has shared taxis that shuttle across the valley when full.

AROUND THIMPHU

North of Thimphu

As you travel up the east side of the Wang Chhu, you'll pass the impressive SAARC building (National Assembly) and banquet hall. On the opposite side of the river you may catch a glimpse of Samtenling Palace, the cottage that is the king's residence.

Six kilometres north of Thimphu centre is the suburb of Taba, where you can stay at the atmospheric **Wangchuk Resort Taba** (Map p46; ☎365262; www.wangchukhotel.com; off Dechen Lam; s/d from Nu 2300/2500). The resort is associated with the Wangchuk Hotel in town and has a restful, pine-forest location, hot-stone baths, antique museum and a private goemba built on the ruins of a former palace; perfect for meditation. There are great valley views from the balconied rooms.

The large **Dechenchoeling Palace** is some distance north of the dzong. It was built in 1952 and is the official residence of the king's grandmother so is off-limits to visitors. North of the palace is the Royal Body Guard (RBG) facility.

DAY WALKS AROUND THIMPHU

In addition to the short walks to Tango Goemba and Cheri Goemba (p66), there are several good day walks to monasteries and lookout points around Thimphu. *Mild and Mad Day Hikes Around Thimphu* by Piet van der Poel & Rogier Gruys details 27 hikes, as well as numerous alternatives and side trips. You can download the text and hiking maps from www.bhutan-trails.org/index.html. As the title suggests, the hikes range from easy walks to the 25km Thimphu to Paro 'Punishment Trail'. It is important to remember that many of these hikes pass meditation cells near monasteries, so don't shout, disturb them or knock on the door to ask for directions.

Wangditse Goemba

A flat and easy 30-minute walk with great views of Trashi Chhoe Dzong takes you from the Sangaygang telecom tower to Wangditse Goemba, which was founded in 1750 by the attendants of Bhutan's eighth *desi*, Druk Rabgye, and renovated in 2001. The inner chapel houses eight chortens and a two-story statue of Sakyamuni Buddha. There are views north towards Samtenling Palace, home to the current (fifth) king, and the Dhey and Dorje Drak meditation retreats on the hillside above. From Wangditse you can descend steeply southeast, veering right to Zilukha Nunnery, or you can descend even more steeply northeast to Dechen Phodrang.

Drolay Goemba

It's a two- to three-hour round trip from the parking lot below Tango Goemba to Drolay Goemba at 3400m. The walk offers amazing views of the Thimphu valley and you can combine it with a visit to Tango Goemba.

Thadranang Goemba

Another strenuous two-hour uphill hike leads to Thadranang Goemba (3270m). Start at the Yangchenphug High School and climb steeply up the ridge through a blue-pine forest.

Lungchuzekha Goemba

Perhaps the best easy walk in the area is the three- to four-hour round trip from Dochu La to Lungchuzekha Goemba. It affords excellent views of the Bhutan Himalaya and

---

PANGRI ZAMPA

North of Dechencholeing is **Pangri Zampa**, two imposing whitewashed buildings beside a grove of huge cypress trees. Founded in the early 16th century, Zhabdrung Ngawang Namgyal lived here after he arrived in 1616 because this temple appeared in the vision that directed him from Tibet to Bhutan. The complex is a centre for traditional astrology, and the well-respected head astrologer was entrusted to divine the auspicious date for the king's coronation in 2008. Next door is a popular archery ground.

The nearby **Dechenphu Lhakhang** is home to Gyenyen, the valley's protective deity, and so is off-limits to tourists.

If you're interested in arts and crafts, arrange to pay a visit to the **Choki Traditional Art School** (✆380219; www.choki school.com), which trains disadvantaged kids in traditional arts of painting, sculp-

ture and carving. It's in the nearby village of Kabesa, 10km north of Thimphu.

TANGO GOEMBA & CHERI GOEMBA

The excursion to Tango and/or Cheri goembas at the head of the valley is an excellent one, but there's nowhere to eat nearby so bring a water bottle and a packed lunch.

Continuing up the valley from Pangri Zampa, the road crosses to the east side of the Wang Chhu at Begana, near a huge and very photogenic gold-painted **rock painting** of Guru Rinpoche. Just past the bridge are some 'self-arisen' rock images of a fish and mongoose. A sign requests visitors to 'refrain from indulging in uproarious acts'. Look for the Nepalese-style chorten sitting on the ridge above Begana. Soon you'll see the white buildings of Cheri Goemba on the hillside in the distance.

A few kilometres beyond Begana, 12km from Thimphu, a road branches right and you can return via the same route or descend to Trashigang Goemba and Hongtsho. From the 108 chortens the trail gradually climbs into red, white and pink rhododendron forest for 1½ hours with some steep sections, before branching left to Longchuzekha Goemba and right to Trashigang (see below). Combine the hike with dawn views from Dochu La for a great half-day excursion or do it after a morning visit to Punakha.

Phajoding Goemba

It is a 5km walk uphill from upper Motithang to Phajoding Goemba (3950m), a large monastic complex with 10 lhakhangs and 15 monastic residences, many of them used for extended meditation retreats. Togden Pajo, a yogi from Tibet, founded the site in the 13th century, though most of the buildings were constructed in 1748 through the efforts of Shakya Rinchen, the ninth Je Khenpo, whose image is the central figure in the main Khangzang Lhakhang here. The monastic school is housed in the Jampa Lhakhang and offers a more secluded environment than the Dechen Phodrang School in Thimphu. In 2010 the **World Monuments Fund** (www.wmf.org) added Phajoding to its list of global sites under threat.

From Phajoding you can ascend another 300m to Thuji Drak Goemba. This is the last day of the Druk Path Trek (see p148) in reverse.

Talakha Goemba

This 15th-century goemba (3080m) offers spectacular views of the Bhutan Himalaya and Thimphu valley. You can drive part way and then set out on foot, or visit it on the last day of the Thousand Lakes trek (see p151). From the small goemba you could make a strenuous six- to nine-hour hike up to 4280m Talakha peak.

Trashigang Goemba

It's two hours from the hillside below Hongtsho to Trashigang Goemba (3200m). This goemba, built in 1786 by the 12th Je Khenpo, is an important meditation centre, and there are numerous pilgrim guesthouses here. In addition to about 16 monks, there are a few *anims* (Buddhist nuns). Inside the lhakhang are statues of the several Je Khenpos who meditated here.

climbs a short distance to a parking lot. The trail to **Tango Goemba** is a climb of 280m and takes about half an hour if you follow the steeper shortcut, or about an hour if you take the longer, more gradual trail. Lama Gyalwa Lhanampa founded the site in the 12th century, and the 'divine madman', Lama Drukpa Kunley (see p92), built the present building in the 15th century. In 1616 Zhabdrung Ngawang Namgyal visited Tango Goemba and meditated in a nearby cave for three years. The head lama, a descendent of Lama Drukpa Kunley, presented the goemba to the Zhabdrung, who carved a sandalwood statue of Chenresig, which he installed in the monastery. Because of its connections to the Zhabdrung, Tango is a popular place to visit during the memorial of his death in April or May, known as the Zhabdrung Kuchoe.

The picturesque three-storey tower and surrounding buildings were built in the 18th century by the eighth *desi*, Druk Rabgye, and Zhabdrung Jigme Chhogyel added the golden roof in the 19th century. Tango currently functions as a university of Buddhist studies for 280 monks and is the residence of Gyalse Rinpoche, an important young *trulku* (reincarnated lama) who is recognised as the seventh reincarnation of the highly respected fourth *desi,* Gyalse Tenzin Rabgye (the founder of Taktshang Goemba).

There are several chapels to visit, including the 3rd-floor *zimchung* (living quarters) of the fourth *desi*, where you can receive a blessing from his walking stick. Tango gets its name (it translates to 'horse head') from the natural shape of the rock outcrop. If you leave the site down the short cut path, you can visit the meditation cave of the Zhabdrung (Tandin Ney) perched on this outcrop.

A short distance beyond the turn-off to Tango Goemba, the road ends at Dodina (elevation 2600m) and the entry to Wangchuk National Park. A walk of about 45 minutes leads to **Cheri Goemba** (Cheri Dorji Dhen), Bhutan's first monastery. The trail starts by crossing a lovely covered bridge that spans the Wang Chhu (a fine picnic spot), and then climbs steeply to the monastery, where you can normally spot tame *jaru* (mountain goats). Zhabdrung Ngawang Namgyal built this goemba in 1620 and established the first monk body here. His father's ashes were interred in a richly decorated silver chorten inside the upper goemba after the body was smuggled here from Tibet.

The next-door *goenkhang* features the two protector deities of Cheri and Tango. From here it's a steep climb (pilgrims aim to do it without pausing) to the Demon-Subjugating Monastery, built into the cliff where the Zhabdrung overcame the local demons.

Cheri is still an important place for meditation retreats, with 30 or so monks here for the standard three years, three months and three days.

South of Thimphu

A road leads uphill from Babesa to the **Royal Botanical Garden** (SAARC national/ adult Nu 30/50) at Serbithang, which was inaugurated in 1999 and has a weedy collection of 500 species of plants. It's a favourite weekend picnic spot of Thimphu residents.

From the garden's far viewpoint you can see across the valley to the **Gangchen Nyezergang Lhakhang**, an ancient lhakhang that was rebuilt and reconsecrated in 2001 under the sponsorship of current prime minister, Lyonpo Jigme Thinley.

SIMTOKHA DZONG

Simtokha is about 5km south of Thimphu on the old road to Paro and Phuentsholing. The junction with the road to eastern Bhutan is just before Simtokha.

Officially known as Sangak Zabdhon Phodrang (Palace of the Profound Meaning of Secret Mantras), **Simtokha Dzong** was built in 1629 by Zhabdrung Ngawang Namgyal. It is often said to be the first dzong built in Bhutan. In fact, there were

dzongs in Bhutan as early as 1153, but this was the first dzong built by the Zhabdrung, was the first structure to incorporate both monastic and administrative facilities, and is the oldest dzong to have survived as a complete structure. There are currently 148 monks here. Just above the dzong is the important Institute for Language and Culture Studies.

During its construction Simtokha Dzong was attacked by an alliance of Tibetans and five Bhutanese lamas from rival Buddhist schools who were opposed to the Zhabdrung's rule. The attack was repelled and the leader of the coalition, Palden Lama, was killed. In 1630 the Tibetans again attacked and took control of the dzong. The Zhabdrung regained control when the main building caught fire and the roof collapsed, killing the invaders. Descriptions of the original Simtokha Dzong were provided by the two Portuguese Jesuit priests who visited here in 1629 on their way to Tibet.

Expansion and restoration of the dzong was performed by the third Druk Desi, Mingyur Tenpa, in the 1670s. It has been enlarged and restored many times since, most recently by a team of Japanese architects.

The site is said to guard a demon that had vanished into the rock nearby, hence the name Simtokha, from *simmo* (demoness) and *do* (stone). The site is also, of course, a vitally strategic location from which to protect the Thimphu valley and entryway to the Dochu La and eastern Bhutan. The dzong is about 60m square, and the only gate is on the south side (though the original gate was on the west side.)

The **utse** is three storeys high, and behind the usual prayer wheels around the outside there is a line of more than 300 fine slate carvings depicting saints and philosophers. The large central figure in the central lhakhang is of Sakyamuni, flanked by the eight Bodhisattvas. The dark murals inside this lhakhang are some of the oldest and most beautiful in Bhutan. In the **western chapel** are statues of Chenresig, green and white Taras, and an early painting of Zhabdrung Ngawang Namgyal, which was cleaned in 1995 but is still cracked. Check out the tigers' tails and guns hanging from the pillars in the eastern *goenkhang*. The **protector chapel** is dedicated to the protectors of Bhutan, Yeshe Goenpo (Mahakala) and Pelden Lhamo.

Western Bhutan

Best Places to Stay

» Gangtey Palace (p77)
» Dewachen Hotel (p99)
» Kichu Resort (p97)

Best Places to Eat

» Sonam Trophel
Restaurant (p79)
» Bukhari Restaurant (p79)
» Phuenzhi Diner (p95)

Why Go?

Whether you arrive by air at the lovely Paro valley or by road at tropical Phuentsholing, your first impression of Bhutan is one of stepping into a world that you had only hoped existed. Vertical prayer flags flutter in the breeze and men dressed in a traditional *gho* (tunic) and Argyle socks stroll past yellow-roofed shrines and wooden slate-roofed houses. It soon becomes clear that you have arrived somewhere quite special.

The West is the region of Bhutan that most tourists see and for good reason. It's the heartland of the Drukpa people and is home to the only airport, the capital, the most popular festivals and the largest, oldest and most spectacular dzongs (monastic forts) in the kingdom. Throw in the country's most popular treks, lots of scope to get off the beaten track and minimal driving times and the appeal is obvious. Whether it's the beginning of your trip or the only part of Bhutan that you have time to see, it's a spectacular introduction to a magical land.

When to Go

September to November are great months to visit Bhutan. You'll get great weather, clear mountain views from Dochu La and dramatic festivals at Thimphu and Wangdue Phodrang. Black-necked cranes arrive in the Phobjikha valley in late October and early November. March and April are also popular, with the Paro tsechu a major draw, as lovely spring rhododendron blooms carpet the hillsides.

Western Bhutan Highlights

1 Visit the beautiful dzong at **Punakha** (p91), the capital of Bhutan from the 17th to the 19th centuries

2 Take a crash course in Bhutanese culture and history at Paro's **National Museum** (p73)

3 Spot black-necked cranes or do some great hiking in the remote, glacial **Phobjikha valley** (p98)

4 Hike uphill to the dramatic cliff-hanging **Tiger's Nest** (Taktshang Goemba; p82), Bhutan's most famous sight

5 Make the pilgrimage to the **Kyichu Lhakhang** (p80), one of Bhutan's oldest and most beautiful temples

6 Explore remote monasteries and timeless hermitages in the little-visited **Haa valley** (p87)

7 Be blessed with a 10-inch penis, if only for a day, at **Chimi Lhakhang** (p91), the monastery of the Divine Madman!

CHINA
TIBET

Wagye La

Masang Gang (7165m)
(5475m)
Ya La

(5090m)

Teri Gang (7300m)

Tsenda Gang (7100m)

Jejekangphu Gang (7100m)

Kangphu Gang (7212m)

Zongophu Gang (Table Mountain) (7100m)

Melunghi Gang (7000m)

Mon La Karchung

(6965m)

Fogtsherkhagi Chhu

Tsomo La

Gangla Karchung La

Keche La

Chozo

Thanza

Raphstreng Tsho

Kangri (7239m)

Laya

Army Post

Bahitung Chhu

Koina Chhu

Thaga

Jeze La

Gangkhar Puensum (7541m)

Bari La

Loju La

Mo Chhu

Gasa
Gasa Tsachhu

GASA

Rinchen Zoe La

ang um 5526m)

Damji

Si Chhu

WANGDUE

PHODRANG

Tashithang

PUNAKHA

Yak Chhu

Thampe La

Thampe Chhu

Rimchhu

Pho Chhu

Dawakha

Tamshing Goemba

Dodina

Mo Chhu

Tseshinang

Nikka Chhu

To Jakar (2km)

Dechenchoeling

❶ Punakha

Black

Zelela

Nobding

Pele La (3420m)

Longte

Sephu

Trongsa

Chimi Lhakhang ❼

Tikke Zampa

Gangte Goemba

Rukubji

Yotong La

THIMPHU

Lobesa

Chhuzomsa

Phobjikha

❸ Phobjikha Valley

Kuenga Rabten

Wangdue Phodrang

Tsele La

Mountains

Wachi Chhu

Zhemgang

lamseling

Tashila

Shobe La

Kisana Chhu

Hara Chhu

Buri Chhu

Wangdi Chhu

Kharibje

Talakha Peak (4280m)

Gingkam Chhu

Genekha

Tingtibi

Puna Tsang Chhu

Lana Chhu

TSIRANG

Gong Khola

Tsimasham

DAGANA

Dagana

Sankosh

Chhuka

Dagsa Chhu

Damphu

Lamidranga

Dagapela

Sarbjang Khola

Tala

Puna Tsang Chhu

Sarpang

Gelephu

Raigye Chhu

Sinchula

INDIA

PARO DZONGKHAG

With our passage through the bridge, behold a curious transformation. For just as Alice, when she walked through the looking-glass, found herself in a new and whimsical world, so we, when we crossed the Pa-chhu, found ourselves, as though caught up on some magic time machine fitted fantastically with a reverse, flung back across the centuries into the feudalism of a mediaeval age.

Earl of Ronaldshay, Lands of the Thunderbolt (1923)

The Paro valley is without doubt one of the loveliest in Bhutan. Willow trees and apple orchards line many of the roads, whitewashed farmhouses and temples complement the green terraced fields and forested hills rise on either side to create a beautiful, organic and peaceful whole.

The fertile land, clement climate and network of trade routes from Tibet have combined to make the people of Paro better off than elsewhere in Bhutan. For most of the 19th century, Paro held the seat of government and was the commercial, cultural and political centre of the country.

Several treks begin in or near Paro. The Druk Path trek climbs over the eastern valley wall, crossing a 4200m pass before descending to Thimphu. The Jhomolhari, Laya-Gasa and Snowman treks all lead west from Drukgyel Dzong on to Jhomolhari base camp and the spectacular alpine regions of Gasa and Laya beyond (for more on these regions, see p147).

Paro

⏹08 / ELEV 2280M

The charming small town of Paro lies on the banks of the Paro (or Pa) Chhu, just a short distance northwest of the imposing

Paro, Thimphu & Punakha Valleys

Paro Dzong. The main street, only built in 1985, is lined with colourfully painted wooden shop fronts and restaurants, though these are under threat as a rapidly expanding multistorey concrete extension takes root to the side. Paro is one of the nicest Bhutanese towns to explore and is worth an hour or two's stroll at the end of a day of sightseeing.

◉ Sights

Paro (Rinpung) Dzong   DZONG
(Map p74; ⊙9am-5pm) The Paro Dzong is one of Bhutan's most impressive and well-known dzongs, and perhaps the finest example of Bhutanese architecture you'll see. The massive buttressed walls that tower over the town are visible throughout the valley.

The dzong's correct name, Rinchen Pung Dzong (usually shortened to Rinpung Dzong), means 'fortress on a heap of jewels'. In 1644 Zhabdrung Ngawang Namgyal ordered the construction of the dzong on the foundation of a monastery built by Guru Rinpoche. The fort was used on numerous occasions to defend the Paro valley from invasions by Tibet. The British political officer John Claude White reported that in 1905 there were old catapults for throwing great stones stored in the rafters of the dzong's veranda.

The dzong survived the 1897 earthquake but was severely damaged by fire in 1907. It was formerly the meeting hall for the National Assembly and now, like most dzongs, houses both the monastic body and district government offices, including the local courts.

An interesting sidenote: scenes from Bernardo Bertolucci's 1995 film *Little Buddha* were filmed here.

Visiting the Dzong
The dzong is built on a steep hillside, and the front courtyard of the administrative section is 6m higher than the courtyard of the monastic portion. The road to the National Museum branches down to the dzong's northeastern entrance, which leads into the *dochey* (courtyard) on the 3rd storey. The *utse* (central tower) inside the *dochey* is five storeys tall and was built in the time of the first *penlop* (governor) of Paro in 1649. To the east of the *utse* is another small lhakhang dedicated to Chuchizhey, an 11-headed manifestation of Chenresig. The richly carved wood, painted in gold, black and ochres, and the towering whitewashed walls reinforce the sense of established power and wealth.

> **ⓘ WEEKEND IN PARO**
>
> When planning your itinerary remember that Sunday is a good day to visit the Paro market but that the excellent National Museum is closed Sunday and Monday. A weekend visit covers all the bases.

A stairway leads down to the monastic quarter, which houses about 200 monks. The *kunre,* which functions as the monks' classroom, is in the southeast corner (to the left). Look under the vestibule covers for the mural of the 'mystic spiral', a uniquely Bhutanese variation on the mandala. The large *dukhang* (prayer hall) opposite has lovely exterior murals depicting the life of Tibet's poet-saint Milarepa. The first day of the spring **Paro tsechu** is held in this courtyard, which fills to bursting point. The views from the far windows are superb.

Outside the dzong, to the northeast of the entrance, is a stone-paved area where masked dancers perform the main dances of the tsechu. A *thondrol* (huge *thangka,* painted or embroidered religious picture) of Guru Rinpoche, more than 18m square, is unfurled shortly after dawn on the final day of the tsechu – you can see the huge rail upon which it is hung. It was commissioned in the 18th century by the eighth *desi* (secular ruler of Bhutan, also known as *druk desi*), Chhogyel Sherab Wangchuck.

Below the dzong, a traditional wooden covered bridge called **Nyamai Zam** (Map p74) spans the Paro Chhu. This is a reconstruction of the original bridge, which was washed away in a flood in 1969. Earlier versions of this bridge were removed in time of war to protect the dzong. The most picturesque pictures of Paro Dzong are taken from the west bank of the river, just downstream from the bridge.

The dzong courtyard is open daily but on weekends the offices are deserted and most chapels are closed.

National Museum   MUSEUM
(Gyelyong Damtenkhang; Map p74; ☎271257; www.nationalmuseum.gov.bt; locals/SAARC nationals/adult Nu 10/50/200, monks, nuns & children under 10 free; ⊙9am-4.30pm Tue-Sat, closed national holidays) At the top of the hill above Paro Dzong is an old watchtower

Paro

Paro

WESTERN BHUTAN PARO

that was renovated in 1968 to house the National Museum. The unusual round building is said to be in the shape of a conch shell, with 2.5m-thick walls; it was completed in 1656 and was originally the *ta dzong* (watchtower) of Paro Dzong, which lies undefended below. An underground tunnel is said to lead from the watchtower to the water supply below.

The route through the museum ensures that you walk clockwise around the central images. Cameras are not allowed inside the museum itself but you can photograph the grounds. The museum is an attraction for locals as well as tourists and you may be accompanied by groups of school children on an outing.

The 4th floor kicks off with a description of early history that perfectly illustrates how magic and science are inseparable in Bhutan. Early stone implements are described as the weapons of the *naga* (snake) spirits; early rock carvings and inscriptions are labelled as 'self-created'.

The 5th floor has an impressive collection of *thangkas,* both ancient and modern,

depicting all of Bhutan's important saints and teachers. The Namse Lhakhang has a collection of religious statues and stone carvings. The 6th floor reveals the eclecticism of Bhutan's philatelic collection, including some stamps that you can listen to on a record player.

At the end of the gallery, a doorway leads to the Tshozhing Lhakhang, the Temple of the Tree of Wisdom, a complex four-sided carving depicting the history of Buddhism, with its schools and lineages. The four branches represent the Sakya (with images of Sakyamuni), Nyingma (Guru Rinpoche), Gelug (Atisha, Tsongkhapa and Nagarjuna) and Drukpa Kagyu (Marpa, Milarepa, Naropa and Tilopa) lineages. Clean your shoes on the yak-hair squares when entering the temple and walk clockwise around the room.

The lower-floor galleries highlight teapots, clothes, musical instruments, stuffed animals (the gharial in particular looks like it's been run over by a truck), plus religious ritual objects and a display of ancient weapons and shields, many captured during various Tibetan invasions. Look out for the excellent shield made from the hide of a rhino, saddle made from the skin of a stingray and hat made from the scales of a fish! The worrisome cracks in the walls are the result of an earthquake in 2009.

Driving to the museum involves a 4km loop into the Dop Shari Valley. After visiting, you can walk down a path from the museum to the dzong and back to the town, enjoying good views of the valley and of the Ugyen Pelri Palace.

Ugyen Pelri Thang   PALACE
The secluded wooded compound of the Ugyen Pelri Palace was built by the Paro *penlop,* Tshering Penjor, in the early 1900s and is now a residence of the queen mother, thus closed to the public. It is designed after Guru Rinpoche's celestial paradise, Zangto Pelri, and is a beautiful example of Bhutanese architecture. For views from the palace from above, head to the dzong.

On the road beside Ugyen Pelri Palace are five square **chortens** that were built in memory of the first king of Bhutan, Ugyen Wangchuck.

Chhoeten Lhakhang   TEMPLE
The tower-like Chhoeten Lhakhang is southeast of the town square. The caretaker may allow you to visit the upstairs chapel, which features a central Jowo Sakyamuni, with Guru Rinpoche and Chenresig to the side.

WORTH A TRIP

HIKING TO ZURI DZONG

A great way to end a visit to the National Museum is with a hike along the forested hillside to **Zuri Dzong** and then down to the Uma resort, where your vehicle can pick you up. En route you'll pass **Gönsaka Lhakhang** (Map p74), a neglected but charming place that actually predates Paro Dzong. Don't miss the meditation cave here. The views down over the valley and dzong are wonderful. Zuri Dzong was built in 1352 and is well protected by double walls. It is home to the valley's local protector gods. The trail at the back of the dzong is easy to miss; stay high past a cave and collection of prayer flags before dropping down. Budget two hours for the trip.

Druk Choeding   TEMPLE
Also known as Tshongdoe Naktshang, the quiet and peaceful Druk Choeding is the town temple. It was built in 1525 by Ngawang Chhogyel (1465–1540), one of the prince-abbots of Ralung in Tibet and an ancestor of the Zhabdrung Ngawang Namgyal. The main statue is of a seated Jampa (future Buddha). Also present are the local protectors Gyenyen, Jichu Drakey and Hong Gyelri, surrounded by a fearsome collection of old Bhutanese shields and weapons.

Dumtse Lhakhang   TEMPLE
To the west of the road leading to Paro Museum is Dumtse Lhakhang, an unusual chorten-like temple that was built in 1433 (some sources say 1421) by the iron-bridge builder Thangtong Gyalpo (see the boxed text, p86). The temple was built to subdue a demoness and so is chained firmly to the ground. Its three floors represent hell, earth and heaven, and hold some of the finest murals in Bhutan. It's essential to bring a good torch. Your travel agency will need to have Dumtse listed on your permits so mention you'd like to stop here in advance.

Beyond Dumtse Lhakhang, to the east of the road, the tiny privately maintained **Puna Lhakhang** is said to date from the 7th century.

Paro Sunday Market   MARKET
Paro's weekly vegetable market isn't very large but it has a more traditional feel than Thimphu's weekend market and is a fine introduction to some of Bhutan's unique local products. You'll see strings of *chugo* (dried yak cheese), either white (boiled in milk and dried in the sun) or brown (smoked). The fruit that looks like an orange egg is actually fresh husky betel nut, imported from India. The jars of pink paste contain lime, which is ingested with the betel nut. There are also exotic-looking ferns, powdered juniper incense, squares of dried jellied cow skin known as *khoo* (a local snack!) and slabs of *datse,* the cheese used in almost every Bhutanese dish. The market is busiest between 6.30am and 10am.

After visiting the market check out the weekend action in the archery ground to the southeast.

🛏 Sleeping
Paro's better accommodation options are in resort-style hotels scattered around the valley, not in the town itself. The closest options to town are on the hillside west of

Paro, in a suburb known as Geptey, which offers great views over the valley.

Most hotels increase their rates significantly during the spring Paro tsechu, when every hotel and even many local farmhouses are full to bursting point. Some hotels stage dance performances around a campfire when there are enough guests to warrant it.

TOP CHOICE Gangtey Palace
BOUTIQUE **$$**

(Map p74; ☎271301; www.gangteypalace.net; s/d Nu 2300/2700, deluxe s/d Nu 3000/3500; @) This 19th-century, traditional Bhutanese courtyard-style building was once the residence of the *penlop* of Paro and it oozes musty historical charm. The spacious deluxe rooms in the main tower come with creaking wooden staircases and a few antique pieces but the standard rooms are also pleasant and have garden views. Ask staff to show you the murals in the main tower's altar room. The views from the restaurant balcony are also great and there's a cosy bar. This is one place where you want to arrive early in order to savour the atmosphere.

Olathang Hotel
BOUTIQUE **$$**

(Map p74; ☎271304; ohotel@druknet.bt; s/d Nu 2000/2500, cottage s/d Nu 2500/3000, deluxe cottage s/d Nu 3000/3500, ste from Nu 3250; @) This grand dzong-like hotel was built in 1974 for guests invited to the coronation of the fourth king and, though getting on a bit, it still maintains a whiff of grandeur. The main building rooms are set around a lovely interior courtyard; the peaceful standard cottages share a lounge, so are particularly good for families and small groups; and the private deluxe cottages are better for couples. Always bustling with groups, it's now managed by the Bhutan Tourism Corporation Limited (BTCL) so smaller companies often have trouble securing rooms.

TOP CHOICE Uma Paro
LUXURY HOTEL **$$$**

(Map p74; ☎271597; www.uma.paro.como.bz; superior/deluxe r US$275/375, ste US$595, villa US$900-1500; ☒) Kudos goes to the Uma for tastefully combining traditional Bhutanese architecture with top-of-the-line facilities to create the best hotel in town. Highlights are the excellent restaurant and spa, with a gym, heated indoor lap pool and plenty of pampering available, as well as a herbal hot-stone bath. Deluxe rooms are the best choice, offering balconies with a view. Activities include complimentary yoga and Bhutanese archery lessons on the grounds. While here, check out arguably the world's biggest book (see p53), on display in the library. During the Paro tsechu the hotel requires a minimum stay of five nights.

Zhiwa Ling
LUXURY HOTEL **$$$**

(Map p81; ☎271277; www.zhiwaling.com; Satsam Chorten; s/d incl breakfast from US$230/250) This impressive luxury place, 8km from Paro, consists of an echoing, central lodge surrounded by a collection of stern-looking stone towers. Nice antiques, plush leather sofas and a spa (Thai, Shiatsu and Swedish massage) temper the austerity, and there's even a temple on the 2nd floor, built with 400-year-old pillars from Gangte Monastery. Most rooms have a balcony and the royal suite even comes with its own altar room. Oddly, they manufacture fishing flies here for export to the US.

Amankora
LUXURY HOTEL **$$$**

(Map p81; ☎272333; www.amanresorts.com; s/d full board US$1300/1400; @) 'Designer dzong' is the architectural theme here, with the half-dozen sleek rammed-earth buildings calling to mind an elite campus at one of the world's coolest universities. The rooms benefit from calming natural woods and home-spun fabrics, a sexy open-plan bathroom and traditional Bhutanese *bukhari* (stoves). The spa has a wide range of muscle-melting treatments and there's an intimate restaurant and reading room. It's certainly sleek and stylish but it's hard to justify the price tag (the tax alone is US$210 a night!). The resort is in a pine forest near Balakha village, about 14km from Paro, not far from Drukgyel Dzong. The nightly tariff here is about equal to Bhutan's annual per capita income.

Tenzinling Resort
HOTEL **$$**

(Map p81; ☎272503; www.tenzinling.com.bt; Lango; s/d Nu 2500/2800, ste Nu 3500; ☎) Quiet, rural and stylish, this excellent new complex above Lango village, 6km from Paro, is a more affordable option and an excellent choice. The spacious wood-floored rooms come with balconies and there's a decent bar.

Nak-Sel Boutique Hotel and Spa
LUXURY HOTEL **$$$**

(☎272991; nak-sel@druknet.bt; Ngoba; r superior/luxury US$100/150, ste US$200-300, discounts of 25% possible) Luxury at tourist prices is what this opulent new resort promises. Built by Rainbow Tours on a similar plan to the Zhiwa Ling, there are plans for a cafe, bakery and spa, with deluxe rooms in the main building and five self-contained cottages with spacious rooms, underfloor heating and balconies. Expect standards comparable to Zhiwa Ling and Uma. It's 3km up a secluded side valley at the edge of the forest.

Janka Resort
HOTEL $$

(Map p81; ☎272352; www.jankaresort.com; Nemjo; s/d Nu 2200/2800, deluxe s/d Nu 3500/4000; @) There's a rural feel at this good resort, 2.5km from Paro, yet it's still close to town. The 19 standard rooms frame the courtyard, with five stylish deluxe rooms in the main building. The resort has a huge prayer wheel and staff can arrange for guests to visit the chapel in the owners attached farmhouse. Look for the archery ground just by the turnoff.

Ugyen Phendeyling Resort
HOTEL $$

(Map p81; ☎272017; www.upresortparo.com; s/d Nu 1750/2500, ste Nu 3500; @) This quiet, comfortable place with simple concrete cottages is particularly popular with Buddhist groups. It's run by local Rinpoche Ugyen Dorji, who offers his next-door chapel for guest meditation. Hiking trails behind the property lead to the hillside Dosu Lhakhang, rebuilt in 2009 after a forest fire. The hotel is at the end of a bumpy tractor trail.

Dhey Kyed Resort
HOTEL $$

(Map p81; ☎271744; www.dheykyedresort.bt; Chelupang; s/d from Nu 1450/1990) The views over the terraced valley are what sold us on this collection of ochre-coloured buildings, as well as the proximity to local hiking trails. The rooms with balconies are not plush but there's a family-run vibe. It can be windy here.

Tashi Namgay Resort
HOTEL $$

(Map p74; ☎272319; www.tnr.bt; Damsebu; s/d Nu 2500/2800, deluxe Nu 3000/3500, lodge 3500/4000; ☎) This well-run and popular new place on the west bank is directly across the river from the airport. Deluxe riverside rooms are spacious and decorated with Tibetan carpets; standard rooms are in a block above the main building. The four budget rooms (single/double Nu 800/1000) are a bargain if not booked by guides.

Haven Resort
LUXURY $$$

(Map p74; ☎270999; www.haven-bhutan.com; Dop Shari; r low/high season US$250/400) The latest in Paro's line of über-luxury boutique resorts is this Thai-built place in the quiet Dop Shari valley. Expect the standouts to include the Thai cuisine and the luxury spa. Branches are planned in Punakha and Bumthang.

Tiger Nest Resort
HOTEL $$

(Map p81; ☎271310; www.tigernest.bt; cottage s/d Nu 1500/1700, deluxe s/d from Nu 2500/2800) Just past the turn-off to Taktshang in the upper valley, this recently renovated resort, 9km from Paro, offers rare views of Taktshang Goemba and, on clear days, the snow-capped peak of Jhomolhari. It has simple but cosy rooms in twin cottages or deluxe rooms in the main block.

Pelri Cottages
COTTAGES $$

(Map p74; ☎272473; www.pelricottages.com; r Nu 2200-2500, ste Nu 3500) On a hill above the Olathang Hotel, the Pelri is a low-key collection of cottages in a former apple orchard. More old-school than luxurious, the clean wood-clad rooms are decorated with Tibetan carpets to give a cosy feel and the small wooden balconies are pleasant.

Dechen Hill Resort
HOTEL $$

(Map p74; ☎271392; dchncot@druknet.bt; Geptey; r old s/d from Nu 1450/1750) This hotel, in a secluded area below the road and 2km from the centre, is a favourite with expats and has some of the best Indian food in the valley. It's not flash but renovations are planned.

Hotel Jor-Yang'z
HOTEL $

(Map p74; ☎271747; www.joryangzhotel.com.bt; Geptey; s/d from Nu 1000/1250; @) Next door to and similar to Dechen Hill, this friendly modern place has good staff, excellent food and some nice balcony seating, though rooms vary quite a bit. It's named after the owners' two children.

Sonam Trophel Hotel
HOTEL $$

(Map p74; ☎274444; www.sonamtrophelhotel .com; s/d Nu 1800/2200, deluxe s/d Nu 2500/2800; ☎) If you want to be based in the town, this neat and comfortable lodge straddles the local and tourist markets. It doesn't have the peace of the valley resorts but it does allow you to grab a local beer in town, if you can put up with a little extra street noise.

Hotel Jigmeling
LOCAL $

(Map p74; ☎271444; jighotel@hotmail.com; s/d Nu 1100/1300) Of the five nearly identical local hotels in Paro town that are popular with Indian tourists, the Jigmeling is probably the best, with quite stylish rooms, porch and balcony seating and also a nice restaurant-bar.

Hotel Peljorling   LOCAL **$**
(Map p74; ☎271365; s/d Nu 350/650) Operated by the same group as the Peljorling in Phuentsholing, this basic but central four-room local-style hotel has thin mattresses but en-suite bathrooms and a good restaurant that serves a mean breakfast beans on toast!

Your agent may book in one of a dozen other decent tourist hotels in the valley, including the following:

Khangkhu Resort   HOTEL **$$**
(Map p74; ☎272393; www.khangkhuresort. com; Khangkhu; s/d Nu 2000/2200, ste s/d Nu 3500/4200) New place southwest of Paro lacks intimacy but rooms are well equipped and come with good private balcony seating.

Kichu Resort   HOTEL **$$**
(Map p81; ☎271468; www.intrektour.com; r Nu 2700, ste Nu 4500) A large complex 5km from Paro, past the Kyichu Lhakhang and popular with trekking groups and Indian tourists, though rooms could do with some freshening up.

Rema Resort   HOTEL **$$**
(Map p74; ☎240082; remaresort2010@gmail .com; r Nu 1250; ☎) It's a new place, 1km from Paro, surrounded by farmhouses on the quieter north side of valley, with nice panoramas from the restaurant and cottages.

Rinchenling Lodge   HOTEL **$$**
(Map p81; ☎271111; nawangd@druknet.bt; s/d Nu 2000/2300, deluxe s/d Nu 2700/3000; ☎) Homey, unpretentious place set in apple and plum orchards; 7km from Paro.

Valley View   HOTEL **$$**
(Map p74; ☎272541; valleyview@druknet.bt; s/d Nu 2000/2500; @) None of the pine-clad rooms here actually take advantage of the touted views but they are comfortable and there's a cosy bar and restaurant. The location is useful for Druk Path trekkers.

✖ Eating

Most tourists eat dinner in their hotels but you can request the following places for lunch.

> ### ⓘ A TASTE OF TRADTIONAL BHUTAN
>
> Most tour companies can arrange a hot stone bath and/or Bhutanese meal at a traditional farmhouse. One simple but nice traditional place in Paro is the **Tshering Farm House** (Map p74) in Dop Shari, which serves up great food and adds Artemisia herbs to its traditional-style wooden baths.

Sonam Trophel Restaurant   RESTAURANT **$$**
(Map p74; ☎271287; mains Nu 35-75, set meal Nu 350) Upstairs, Sonam has excellent home-style Bhutanese cooking adapted to foreign tastes and is popular with small groups. The *momos* (dumplings), boneless chicken, ginger potatoes and pumpkin curry (in summer-only) are all excellent. No MSG is used here.

Bukhari Restaurant   RESTAURANT **$$$**
(Map p74; ☎271597; Uma Paro hotel; mains Nu 1200, set meal Nu 2500) The sophisticated semicircular-shaped restaurant at the Uma is considered the best in the valley. The menu changes every three days; when we visited it included a fresh and tasty pomelo, pomegranate and fennel salad, and a sinful treacle tart for dessert, as well as set Bhutanese or Indian meals.

Chharo Restaurant   RESTAURANT **$**
(Map p74; ☎272642; mains Nu 60-100) This pleasant tourist restaurant (*chharo* means friendship) has a good range of Indian, Chinese and Bhutanese dishes and can prepare Bumthang-style buckwheat pancakes and noodles with some advance warning.

Tshernoyoen's Café   CAFE **$**
(Map p74; coffee Nu 50; ☒10am-9pm Tue-Sun; ☎) Paro's first real cafe serves up reviving espresso and fine carrot cake in a relaxed environment. It's a good place to take a break, read the papers and recaffeinate.

These other similar group-orientated places (not many locals here) are recommended.

Yue-Ling Restaurant   RESTAURANT **$**
(Map p74; ☎272802) Good reliable place with fine naan breads.

Chharo and Dho Restaurant   RESTAURANT **$**
(Map p74; ☎272802) Offers some fine set meals.

🛍 Shopping

There are numerous handicraft shops in town offering everything from stamps to jewellery and most take credit cards.

Chencho Handicrafts HANDICRAFTS
(Map p74) Chencho has probably the most interesting selection of local handicrafts, particularly strong on weavings and embroidery; it has a dozen weavers working on site.

Made in Bhutan HANDICRAFTS
(Map p74) This slick operation has some expensive pieces like silver amulets and lutes, alongside cheaper souvenirs, rare stamps and postcards.

Handicrafts Emporium HANDICRAFTS
(Map p74; www.coloursofbhutan.com; ⊙9am-1pm & 2-6pm) This government-run emporium, on the main street, has books and modern souvenirs at tourist prices.

Vajrayana Art Gallery GALLERY
(Map p74; chhidorj@hotmail.com) Vajrayana Art Gallery features art by self-taught Bhutanese artist Chimmi Dorje, who incorporates Buddhist themes such as prayer flags and mandala motifs into his abstract art. The gallery is often closed out of high season.

ℹ Information

Internet Access

Bhutan Nest (Map p74; ☎272689; per min Nu 3; ⊙9am-9pm) Also rents mountain bikes for US$30 per day, plus trekking equipment.

WORTH A TRIP

TRADITIONAL SHOPS

Paro has several interesting traditional shops that are aimed squarely at locals rather than tourists. They have no fixed hours. **Dophu Dolma General Shop** (Map p74) and **Lama Tshering Dorji General Shop** (Map p74), both marked by a line of prayer wheels, are monks' supply shops that sell prayer flags, incense, statuary, butter lamps, trumpets and nonreligious items like *khuru* darts and bamboo arrows. On the main street, the **Zhayden Nagtsho Traditional Boot Unit** (Map p74) is the place for a pair of traditional handmade Bhutanese boots, retailing for around US$60.

Netlink Internet Café (Map p74; per min Nu 1.5; ⊙9am-8.30pm)

Medical Services

Kuen Phuen Medical Shop (Map p74) Stocks basic medical supplies; opposite Made in Bhutan.

Hospital (Map p74; ☎271571) On a hill to the west of town, they accept visitors in an emergency.

Money

Bank of Bhutan (Map p74; ⊙9am-1pm Mon-Fri, 9am-noon Sat)

Bhutan National Bank (Map p74; ⊙9am-4pm Mon-Fri, 9-11am Sat)

Post

Post Office (Map p74; ⊙9am-5pm Mon-Fri, 8.30am-12.30pm Sat)

ℹ Getting There & Away

Paro airport is 7km south of Paro town and 53km from Thimphu. See p267 for details of the Druk Air office in Paro.

A shared taxi to Thimphu costs Nu 150 per seat or Nu 400 to Nu 600 per minivan; to Phuentsholing it costs Nu 400 to Nu 500 per seat. Daily Coaster buses to Thimphu and Phuentsholing leave from Dhug and Metho Transport at the northwest end of town.

Around Paro

UPPER PARO VALLEY

Though the Paro valley extends west all the way to the peaks on the Tibetan border, the road only goes as far as Drukgyel Dzong, 11km beyond Paro. En route it passes half a dozen resorts, some lovely rural scenery and some of Bhutan's most famous sights. Beyond the dzong, a side valley leads to the Tremo La, the 5000m pass that was once an important trade route to Tibet and also the route of several Tibetan invasions.

KYICHU LHAKHANG

A short drive from Paro is this lhakhang (Map p81), one of Bhutan's oldest and most beautiful temples. The temple is popularly believed to have been built in 659 by King Songtsen Gampo of Tibet, to pin down the left foot of a giant ogress who was thwarting the establishment of Buddhism into Tibet (see the boxed text, p83). Additional buildings and a golden roof were constructed in 1839 by the *penlop* of Paro and the 25th Je Khenpo.

WESTERN BHUTAN AROUND PARO

Upper Paro Valley

◉ Sights

1 Choedu Goemba	A1
2 Dranjo Goemba	C3
3 Drukgyel Dzong	A1
4 Kuenga Choeling Goemba	C3
5 Kyichu Lhakhang	C3
6 Machig-phu Lhakhang	B1
7 Sanga Choekor Shedra	C2
8 Satsam Chorten	B2
9 Shama Lhakhang	B1
10 Taktshang Goemba	B1
11 Tingchok Goemba	C3
12 Tsendo Girkha Goemba	C3
13 Urgyen Tshemo Lhakhang	B1
14 Yosel Choekhorling	C1
15 Zangto Pelri Lhakhang	B1

🛏 Sleeping

16 Amankora	A1
17 Dhey Kyed Resort	C3
18 Janka Resort	C3
19 Kichu Resort	B3
20 Rinchenling Lodge	B2
21 Tenzinling Resort	B3
22 Tiger Nest Resort	B2
23 Ugyen Phendeyling Resort	B2
24 Zhiwa Ling	B2

🍴 Eating

25 Cafeteria	B1
26 Yak Herder Restaurant	B2

As you enter the intimate inner courtyard you'll see a mural to the right of the doorway of King Gesar of Ling, the popular Tibetan warrior-king, whose epic poem is said to be the world's longest. Outside the courtyard, a band of pilgrims almost as old as the temple itself toil away on ropes and pulleys that are rigged up to turn prayer wheels.

The third king's wife, Ashi Kesang Wangchuck, sponsored the construction of the

Guru Lhakhang in 1968. It contains a 5m-high statue of Guru Rinpoche and another of Kurukulla (Red Tara), holding a bow and arrow made of flowers. To the right of Guru Rinpoche is a chorten containing the ashes of Dilgo Khyentse Rinpoche, the revered Nyingma Buddhist master and spiritual teacher of the queen mother, who passed away in 1992, and was cremated nearby. There is a statue of him here, as well as

TAKE A HIKE

There are several options if you're interested in a day hiking the Paro valley. Southeast of Kyichu Lhakhang in the direction of Paro are the hilltop **Tingchok (Dinche) Goemba** (Map p81) and **Dranjo Goemba** (Map p81), home to Tserim, the Goddess of Wealth, both of which can provide an excuse for a short hike. From here you could walk back to Paro via the Olathang Hotel. More ambitious is the cardio day hike up from the hospital to Gorena Lhakhang, high on the ridge behind the Olathang Hotel.

some old photos of the fourth king's grandmother and the first king of Bhutan. In the corner of the lhakhang is a pile of iron links forged by the famous bridge builder Thangtong Gyalpo (see p86). The ornately carved wooden pillars are superb.

The inner hall of the main **Jowo Lhakhang** conceals the valley's greatest treasure, an original 7th-century statue of Jowo Sakyamuni, said to have been cast at the same time as the famous statue in Lhasa. In front of the statue you can feel the grooves that generations of prostrators have worn into the wooden floor. King Songtsen Gampo himself lurks up in the upper left niche. The main door is superbly gilded. The former quarters of Dilgo Khyentse to the left are closed to visitors.

Further north, outside the temple and up a side road by the huge Zhiwa Ling hotel, is the site where Dilgo Khyentse was cremated in 1991. His reincarnation lives in the complex, which is generally closed to visitors. The small and inconspicuous **Satsam Chorten** (Map p81) by the turn-off once marked no-mans-land between two rival *penlop*s (governors). The dirt road that leads from Satsam Chorten back to Paro is an excellent option for mountain bikers.

SANGA CHOEKOR SHEDRA

At night you'll see the Sanga Choekor shedra (Map p81) spotlit up high on the top of a hill on the north side of the valley. The *shedra*, a Buddhist college, is home to 130 monks and is worth a visit mainly for the fine views from the switchbacking drive up. Look for the stuffed bear in the main entryway. On the way back down pop into the small and charming **Kuenga Choeling Goemba** (Map p81), where monks can show you the walking path down to nearby **Tsendo Girkha Goemba** (Map p81).

Sanga Choekor is 12km up the unpaved north bank road. Mountain bikers could cycle up this road, then cross the footbridge to Kyichu Lhakhang.

TAKTSHANG GOEMBA

The Taktshang Goemba (which translates as Tiger's Nest Monastery; Map p81) is the most famous of Bhutan's monasteries, miraculously perched on the side of a sheer cliff 900m above the floor of Paro valley, where the only sounds are the murmurs of wind and water and the creaking of the prayer wheels. It is said that Guru Rinpoche flew to the site of the monastery on the back of a tigress (a manifestation of his consort Yeshe Tsogyal) to subdue the local demon, Singey Samdrup. He then meditated in a cave here for three months.

The site has long been recognised as a *ney*, or holy place. Milarepa is said to have meditated here, Thangtong Gyalpo revealed a *terma* (treasure text) here and Zhabdrung Ngawang Namgyal visited in 1646. Pilgrims from all over Bhutan come to the site. The *penlop* of Paro, Gyalse Tenzin Rabgye, built the primary lhakhang in 1692 around the Dubkhang (also called the Pelphu), the holy cave in which Guru Rinpoche meditated.

On 19 April 1998 a fire (which some rumour was arson, to disguise a theft) destroyed the main structure of Taktshang and all its contents. It had suffered a previous fire and had been repaired in 1951. Reconstruction started in April 2000 at a cost of 130 million ngultrum and the rebuilt site was reconsecrated in the presence of the king in 2005. Tradition says that the original building was anchored to the cliff-face by the hairs of *khandroma* (dakinis, or female celestial beings), who transported the building materials up onto the cliff on their backs. The renovation team had only a cable lift for assistance.

The paved road to the Taktshang parking lot branches right, 8km north of Paro, and climbs 3km past a white chorten and a small lhakhang to the trailhead at 2600m.

The Hike

The only way up to the Tiger's Nest is to walk, ride a horse or fly up there on the back of a magic tiger (the latter generally reserved for Tantric magicians). The 1¾ hour hike is a central part of any tourist itinerary and is unmissable for the spectacular views. It's also a good warm-up hike if you are going trekking. If the full hike sounds a bit tough you can walk (or ride horses) for the first hour to the 'caféteria', a wooden teahouse-restaurant, which offers a good view of the monastery. If you require horses (Nu 500/800 to the caféteria/monastery), be sure to mention this to your guide in advance. Wear a hat and bring water.

The walking trail climbs through blue pines to a series of three water-powered prayer wheels, then switchbacks steeply up the ridge, where a sign exhorts you to 'Walk to Guru's glory! For here in this kingdom rules an unparalled benevolent king!' If you have just flown into Paro, walk slowly because you are likely to feel the altitude.

Once you reach the ridge there are excellent views across the valley and southwest towards Drukgyel Dzong. After a climb of about one hour and a gain of 300m you will reach a small chorten and some prayer flags on the ridge. Be watchful here as the trail crosses an archery ground. It's then a short walk to the caféteria (2940m), where you can savour the impressive view of the monastery over a well-deserved cup of tea. The BTCL-run **cafeteria** (☎1760 1682; buffet Nu 360; ☼noon-3pm) also serves full vegetarian meals; if you arrange your schedule accordingly, you can have a simple breakfast or full lunch here.

The trail continues up for another 30 minutes to a spring and the basic monastery guesthouse. A **cave** and plaque marks the birthplace of a previous Je Khenpo; his former residence is just up the hill. A short walk further along the main trail brings you to a spectacular **lookout** at 3140m that puts you eyeball to eyeball with the monastery, which looks like it is growing out of the rocks.

From this vantage point Taktshang seems almost close enough to touch, but it's on the far side of a deep valley about 150m away. The trail curves past a charming chapel of butter lamps and descends to a waterfall by the **Singye Pelphu Lhakhang** (Snow Lion Cave), a meditation retreat associated with Guru Rinpoche's consort Yeshe Tshogyel and jammed dramatically into a rock crevice, before climbing back up to the monastery entrance.

The Monastery

Tourists can enter the **monastery** (☼8am-1pm & 2-5pm daily Oct-Mar, until 6pm Apr-Sep), as long as your guide has arranged the standard permit in advance. Bags and cameras have to be deposited at the entrance where you must register with the army.

As you enter the complex you pass underneath images of the Rigsum Goempo (Jampelyang, Chenresig and Chana Dorje). Look to the right for the relic stone; Bhutanese stand on the starting line, close their eyes and try to put their thumb into a small hole in the rock as a form of karmic test.

SUBDUING THE DEMONESS

When the Tibetan king Songtsen Gampo married the Chinese princess Wencheng in 641, her dowry included the Jowo Sakyamuni, a priceless Indian statue of the Buddha as a small boy. As the statue was transported through Lhasa, it became stuck in the mud and no-one could move it. The princess divined that the obstruction was being caused by a huge supine demoness, lying on her back with her navel over a lake where Lhasa's main temple, the Jokhang, now stands.

In 659 the king decided to build 108 temples in a single day to pin the ogress to the earth forever and, as a by-product, convert the Tibetan people to Buddhism. Temples were constructed at her shoulders and hips, which corresponded to the four districts of central Tibet, and her knees and elbows, which were in the provinces. The hands and feet lay in the borderlands of Tibet, and several temples were built in Bhutan to pin down the troublesome left leg.

The best known of these temples are Kyichu Lhakhang in Paro, which holds the left foot, and Jampa Lhakhang in Bumthang, which pins the left knee. Other lesser-known temples have been destroyed, but it is believed that, among others, Konchogsum Lhakhang in Bumthang, Khaine Lhakhang south of Lhuentse, and two temples in Haa may have been part of this ambitious project.

Most groups then visit the **Dubkhang**, or Pelphu Lhakhang, the cave where Guru Rinpoche meditated for three months. Outside the cave is a statue of Dorje Drolo, the manifestation the Guru assumed to fly to Taktshang on a tigress. The inner cave is sealed off behind a spectacularly gilded door. Murals of Guru Tshengye, the eight manifestations of Guru Rinpoche, decorate the walls. Behind you, sitting above the inside of the main entrance is a mural of Thangtong Gyalpo holding his iron chains.

From here ascend to the **Guru Sungjem Lhakhang**, which has a central image of Pema Jungme, another of the eight manifestations of Guru Rinpoche. This statue replaced a famous 'talking' image that was lost in the 1998 fire. Various demonic animal-headed deities and manifestations of the deity Phurba decorate the walls, while outside is an image of the protector Tseringma riding a snow lion.

The next chapel on the left has connections to Dorje Phagmo, with a rock image of the goddess' crown hidden in a recessed hole in the floor. The inner chorten belongs to Langchen Pelgye Tsengay, a 9th-century disciple of Guru Rinpoche, who meditated in the cave. Behind the chorten is a holy spring.

Further on inside the complex, to the left, is the Drole Lhakhang where the monks hand out *sungke* (blessed threads), while to the right is the **Guru Tsengye Lhakhang**, which features an image of the monastery's 17th-century founder, Gyelse Tenzin Rabgay. Ask a monk to show you the trap door! Further up is a butter lamp chapel (light one for a donation of Nu 20). You can also peer into the original Tiger's Nest cave just above the chapel but it's too dangerous to climb down into.

After visiting the Tiger's Nest and re-ascending to the previous viewpoint, it is possible to take a signed side trail uphill for 15 minutes to the **Machig-phu Lhakhang** (Map p81), where Bhutanese pilgrims come to pray for children. Head to the cave behind the chapel and select the image of the Tibetan saint Machig Labdron on the right (for a baby girl), or the penis print on the cave wall to the left (for a boy). The main statues inside the chapel are of Machig (see also p88) and her husband Padampa Sangye.

Taktshang Hiking

Instead of returning to the parking lot the way you came you can make an adventurous two to three hour hike to higher chapels before descending steeply to the parking lot. Just to the side of the Machig-phu Lhakhang a trail climbs a couple of perilous log ladders and then branches right for 15 minutes to the Ugyen Tshemo Lhakhang, or left up to the **Zangto Pelri Lhakhang** (Map p81), named after Guru Rinpoche's heavenly paradise and perched on a crag with great views from the back down to the Tiger's Nest. Roll the dice inside the chapel to double your chances of conceiving more kids. From here the trail descends past a charming holy spring (behind a wooden door) and down to the monastery guesthouse mentioned earlier.

The **Ugyen Tshemo Lhakhang** (Map p81) has an unusual set of four exterior protectors. Inside is a 3-D mandala and some charred statues rescued from a fire 50 years ago. If you're keen you can continue up to the Yosel Choekhorling (Yoselgang; Map p81) before returning.

From the Ugyen Tshemo Lhakhang, descend steeply down the valley for 15 minutes to a right turnoff, past a chorten to the cliff-face **Shama Lhakhang**, just next to Taktshang but inaccessible from there. Look out for *jaru* (mountain goats) here.

Back at the junction, trails drop steeply for 45 minutes down to the three water prayer wheels just before the car park. Figure on six hours for the entire hike up to Taktshang and down this alternative route. The descent is best not attempted in wet weather.

✖ Eating

Yak Herder Restaurant RESTAURANT **$$**
(☑1711 1142; fixed lunch Nu 300) If you don't have a packed lunch, your guide can reserve lunch at this cosy place with traditional seating below Taktshang.

DRUKGYEL DZONG

At the end of the road, 14km from Paro, stand the ruins of **Drukgyel Dzong** (Map p81; ⊘8am-5pm). This dzong was built in 1649 by Zhabdrung Ngawang Namgyal in a location chosen for its control of the route to Tibet. The dzong was named '*Druk*' (Bhutan) '*gyel*' (victory) to commemorate the victory of Bhutan over Tibetan invaders in 1644. One of the features of the dzong was a false entrance that lured the returning Tibetan invaders into an enclosed courtyard during a second attack in 1648.

The dzong sits at the point where the trail from Tibet via the Tremo La enters the Paro valley. Once the Tibetan invasions ceased, this became a major trade route, with Bhutanese rice being transported to the Tibetan town of Phari Dzong in barter for salt and bricks of tea. Trekking groups have largely replaced the trade caravans and you'll likely see mule men here packing up their loads at the start or end of the Jhomolhari trek.

The building was used as an administrative centre until 1951, when a fire caused by a butter lamp destroyed it. You can still see the charred beams lodged in the ruined walls. There have been a few attempts at renovation, but all that has been accomplished is the installation of some props to keep the roof of the five-storey main structure from collapsing.

As you walk up to the dzong you'll pass a small chapel on the left, a chorten on the right and then the remains of the large towers and the walled tunnel that was used to obtain water from the stream below during a long siege. There's not much left to the dzong except the front courtyard and *ta dzongs* (watchtowers) behind.

Back in the village you can take a nice stroll up to the small **Choedu Goemba**, which houses a statue of the local protector, Gyeb Dole.

The road to the dzong passes Jetshaphu village, several army camps and the Amankora resort. On a clear day (most likely in October or November) there are fine views of Jhomolhari's snowy cone from this stretch, which makes for a great bike ride.

Southeast of Paro

Twin roads leads south from Paro to Bondey, where roads head west to Haa and southeast to the confluence at Chhuzom, 24km from Paro and 18km from Bondey.

PARO TO BONDEY
6KM

The west-bank road south of Paro passes above the airport and Khangkhu village to Bondey, which straddles the Paro Chhu to the southeast of the airport. A couple of turnouts offer great views of planes taking off or landing at the airport.

Beyond the turn-off to the Cheli La is the 400-year-old **Bondey Lhakhang** (Map p74), on the west bank of the river. On the east side of the Paro Chhu, beside the main road near the Bondey Zam, is the charm-ing and unusually-shaped **Tago (Walnut) Lhakhang** (Map p74), founded by Thangtong Gyalpo. A circular chapel occupies the upper floor; ask for the key at the next-door Tharpala General Shop if the caretaker is not around. A 15-minute uphill hike above Tago is the small **Pelri Goemba**, a rare Nyingmapa-school chapel that was reduced in size after an unwise dispute with the dominant Kagyu school. A road to the monastery is under construction.

CHELI LA

If you don't have time to visit the Haa valley, the 35km drive up to the 3810m Cheli La makes an interesting day excursion from Paro and is an excellent jumping-off point for day walks to Kila Nunnery. On a clear day there are views of Jhomolhari from the pass, as well as down to the Haa valley.

For details of the drive over the pass to the Haa valley, see p87.

Paro to Thimphu
53KM

Figure on two hours driving from Paro to Thimphu, longer if you stop en route.

BONDEY TO CHHUZOM
18KM / 30 MINS

If you're coming from the airport you'll first reach the settlement of Bondey, where there are some lovely old traditional Bhutanese houses and chapels (see above).

Just 1km from Bondey is the family-run **Tshenden Incense Factory** (☎271352; ☺Mon-Sat) where you can see the boiling, dyeing and drying processes, if your guide rings in advance. Two kilometres further on at Shaba are two cliff-face sites. A short hiking trail near the army camp leads to Drak Ngagpo (Black Cliff) hermitage, while a little further on a rough road heads up to **Drak Kharpo** (White Cliff), a cliffside monastery where Guru Rinpoche meditated for several months. At Isuna, 12km from Bondey and 8km from Chhuzom, the road crosses a bridge to the south bank of the Paro Chhu.

About 5km before Chhuzom, the road passes **Tamchhog Lhakhang**, a private temple across the river owned by the descendants of the famous Tibetan bridge-builder Thangtong Gyalpo. The traditional iron bridge here was reconstructed in 2005 using some of Thangtong's original chain links from Duksum in eastern Bhutan. A

THE IRON-BRIDGE BUILDER

Thangtong Gyalpo (1385–1464) was a wonder-working Tibetan saint and engineer who is believed to be the first to use heavy iron chains in the construction of suspension bridges. He built 108 bridges throughout Tibet and Bhutan, earning himself the nickname *Lama Chakzampa* (the Iron Bridge Lama).

In 1433 he came to Bhutan, originally in search of iron ore, and built eight bridges in places as far removed as Paro and Trashigang. You can see some of the original iron links at the Paro Museum and at Kyichu Lhakhang in the Paro valley. Sadly, the only surviving Thangtong Gyalpo bridge, at Duksum on the road to Trashi Yangtse in eastern Bhutan, was washed away in 2004.

This medieval Renaissance man didn't rest on his engineering laurels. Among his other achievements was the composition of many folk songs, still sung today by people as they thresh wheat or pound mud for house construction, and the invention of Tibetan *lhamo* opera. He was also an important *terton* (discoverer of *terma*) of the Nyingma lineage and attained the title Drubthob (Great Magician), and in Paro he built the marvellous chorten-shaped Dumtse Lhakhang. His descendants still maintain the nearby Tamchhog Goemba Lhakhang.

Statues of Thangtong Gyalpo depict him as a stocky shirtless figure with a beard, curly hair and topknot, holding a link of chains.

small cave above the bridge supposedly marks Thangtong's iron mine, as well as the mouth of the snake-shaped hillside that the chapel is built on.

You can almost feel the clocks slowing down as you step into the 600-year-old temple. A 100-year old mandarin tree dominates the courtyard. The lovely murals have been darkened by centuries of yak-butter lamps. A *kora* (circumambulation) path in the main chapel leads around central murals of Thangtong Gyalpo and his son Dewa Tsangpo. The doorway of the upper floor *goenkhang* (protector chapel) is framed by rows of skulls and a hornbill beak and is dedicated to the local protector Maza Damsum. It's a magical place to visit.

Chhuzom, better known as 'the Confluence' is at the juncture of the Paro Chhu and the Wang Chhu (*chhu* means 'river', *zom* means 'to join'). Because Bhutanese tradition regards such a joining of rivers as inauspicious, there are three **chortens** here to ward away the evil spells of the area. Each chorten is in a different style – Bhutanese, Tibetan and Nepali.

Chhuzom is also a major road junction, with roads leading southwest to Haa (79km), south to the border town of Phuentsholing (141km) and northeast to Thimphu (31km). A checkpoint here keeps track of vehicle movements and local farmers sit by the side of the road selling vegetables, apples and dried cheese.

CHHUZOM TO THIMPHU
3KM / 1 HOUR

As the road ascends the Wang Chhu valley, the hillsides become surprisingly barren. Three kilometres past Chhuzom a rough, unpaved side road leads to Geynikha (Geynizampa) and the start of the Dagala Thousand Lakes trek (see p151).

After turnoffs to Kharibje and the former hydro plant at Khasadrapchhu, the valley widens at the small village of **Namseling**. Above the road are numerous apple orchards. Much of the fruit is exported, particularly to Bangladesh. In the autumn people sell apples and mushrooms from makeshift stalls at the side of the road. Just below a white chorten is the luxury new Termalinca resort (p57).

The Thimphu 'expressway' drops off the road towards the valley floor and enters Thimphu from the south. A second, older road travels via Babesa and Simtokha, enabling you to visit the Simtokha Dzong or bypass Thimphu completely on the way to Punakha.

HAA DZONGKHAG

The isolated Haa valley lies southwest of the Paro valley, hidden behind the high ridge of the Cheli La. Despite easy access to Tibet, the remote valley has always been off the major trade routes and continues to be on the fringes of tourism. The valley is the ancestral home of the Dorji family, to which the queen grandmother, Ashi Kesang Wangchuck, belongs.

Less than 3% of visitors to Bhutan make it to Haa, but it's a picturesque valley that is ideal for mountain biking and hiking, and there is real scope here for getting off the beaten track. There are at least a dozen monasteries in the valley. Perhaps the best way to visit is to spend a day cycling to the nearby sights.

There are two roads into Haa. One climbs from Paro, crossing the 3810m Cheli La. The other diverges from the Thimphu–Phuentsholing road at Chhuzom and travels south, high above the Wang Chhu, before swinging into the Haa valley.

Paro to Haa Via Cheli La

68KM / 2½ HOURS

From the turn-off at Bondey, south of Paro, it's 2½ hours to Haa over the high Cheli La on the highest motorable road in Bhutan. As you start to climb, a side road branches left for 2km to **Dzongdrakha Goemba**, where four chapels and a large white Nepali-style chorten perch dramatically on a cliff ledge. The site is one of several where

Guru Rinpoche suppressed local demons and is worth the detour.

As you drive up to the pass, look for the roadside *drub chuu* (spring) with rock paintings of Guru Rinpoche and his two wives. About 20km from the turnoff to Dzongdrakha is an easily-missed turnout (and possible picnic spot) where a hiking trail leads to Kila Nunnery (see the boxed text).

When you finally crest the Cheli La, join the Bhutanese in a hearty cry of *'lha-gey lu!'* (May the gods be victorious!). A sign says the elevation of the pass is 3988m, but it's really more like 3810m. If it's raining in Paro, it's likely snowing here, even as late as the end of April. During the clear skies of October and November you can take hiking trails up the mountain ridge for 1½ hours to spectacular mountain views towards Jhomolhari.

As you make the steep switchbacking 26km descent from the pass to Haa, you'll soon see the golden roof of the Haa Dzong below you.

Haa

☑08 / ELEV 2670M

The town of Haa sprawls along the Haa Chhu and forms two distinct areas. Much of the southern town is occupied by the Indian Military Training Team (IMTRAT) camp (complete with a golf course that has sand 'greens') and a Bhutanese army training camp. Near here is the dzong and monastery. The central bazaar to the north has the main shops and local restaurants and is the site for a planned new town.

The three hills to the south of town are named after the Rigsum Goempo, the trinity of Chenresig, Chana Dorje and Jampelyang; they also represent the valley's three protector deities.

The scenic road to the north continues past the Talung valley and Chhundu Lhakhang, and ends at Damthang, 15km from Haa town. It would be prudent to turn around before you reach the gates of the large Bhutanese army installation.

◉ Sights

Wangchulo Dzong   DZONG

Haa's Wangchulo Dzong is one of Bhutan's newest, built in 1915 to replace a smaller structure. It is inside the Indian army compound (an impressive chorten marks the entrance) and so houses several army offices and a rations shop.

Haa Dratshang
MONASTERY

The 150-strong monk body is housed not in the dzong but in the Haa Dratshang, also known as the Lhakhang Kharpo (White Chapel), at the southern entrance to town. An annual **tsechu** is held in the large courtyard on the eighth and ninth day of the eighth lunar month, before a large *thangka* is displayed on the 10th day at Wangchulo Dzong. A 10-minute walk behind the *dratshang* is the grey Lhakhang Nagpo (Black Chapel), from where trails lead to Shek Drak.

Shek Drak
CHAPEL

A short excursion up the valley behind the Haa Dratshang is Shek Drak, a tiny retreat centre perched on the hillside. Take the side road just south of the Haa Dratshang, by Domcho village, and continue halfway (3.5km) up the hillside towards Takchu Goemba. From here, a 10-minute walk climbs to the small and charming chapel attended by a single lama and two monks.

🛏 Sleeping & Eating

Risum Resort
HOTEL $$

(📞375350; risum_77@yahoo.com; s/d Nu 1500/1700) Good accommodation is available here in cosy, pine-clad rooms with clean hot-water bathrooms, heaters and, on the upper floors, balconies. An excellent photo album in the restaurant has information on trips to outlying monasteries, including Wantsa Goemba, a short walk behind the resort. The hotel is located on the east side of the road, between the two sections of town.

Hotel Lhayul
RESTAURANT $

(📞375251; mains Nu 70-85) This is a decent place for lunch, with comfy sofas and a bar. There are also simple, overpriced rooms, with four better suites (single/double Nu 950/1100, suite Nu 1400). It's in the central bazaar area of town.

Around the Haa Valley

JUNEYDRAK

About 1km north of Haa, by the Two Sisters Hotel and the hospital and just before the main bridge, a 4WD track branches east 1km to Katsho village, from where you can take a lovely hike to **Juneydrak hermitage** (also known as Juneydrag). The cliffside retreat contains a footprint of Machig Labdrom (1055–1132), the female Tibetan Tantric practitioner who perfected the *chöd* ritual, whereby one visualises one's own dismemberment in an act of 'ego annihilation'.

From the village a trail follows the stream past a *mani* wall to a two-legged archway chorten (known as a *khonying*). Cross the bridge and ascend the trail through a charming rhododendron forest. At a red sign in Dzongkha, take the trail to the left and climb up to a chorten that marks the entry to the hermitage. A sign here asks visitors not to disturb the hermits so don't try to enter the lhakhang. In case you needed persuading, a green-faced demon guards the entryway.

From here, a set of exposed log ladders ascend the cliff and the trail curves round the exposed bluff. Don't attempt this if you are afraid of heights or if it's raining. The trail curves around to **Katsho Goemba**, which has fine views down to Katsho village. Your vehicle can meet you here.

A less strenuous alternative is to drive up to Katsho Goemba and then walk down to Juneydrak from there.

YANGTHO GOEMBA & AROUND

North of the turning to Katsho, the main road crosses to the river's south bank and passes several villages as it heads up the lovely upper Haa valley. About 5km from Haa, a side road branches right over the river past Yangthang village to several remote monasteries which offer some good exploring.

Follow the road as it swings into the side valley and you'll pass the Yangthang ceremonial ground that is still used for annual sacrifices to the local deity Chhundu. At the Makha Zampa bridge take the right branch 1.5km to **Yangtho Goemba**, up on the ridge. The monastery's charming upper chapels feature murals depicting Zangto Pelri (the paradise of Guru Rinpoche) and also the Tshomen (water deities) that are said to inhabit the pool beside a cypress tree just outside the monastery. Ask the monk to show you the excellent medieval rat trap!

Back at the bridge, the left branch takes you further up the valley for 2km to Talung village and **Tsenkha Goemba** (signposted Changkha), which is currently under renovation. Hardcore explorers can take the branch road here for 2km to curve around to Jangtey Goemba. An enticing two-day trek continues up the Talung Valley and over the Saga La to Drukyel Dzong.

CHHUNDU LHAKHANG

Three kilometres further along the main road (11km from Haa) is the delightful Chhundu Lhakhang (Getsu Lhakhang), one of several shrines dedicated to the valley's protective deity. The timeless chapel is a five-minute walk down a concrete path below Chenpa Haatey (Gechu) village, just past the Yakchu Zam bridge. Call the **caretaker** (☑7721 0520) if the temple is closed. Blue-faced Chhundu and his red-faced cousin Jowya glower in glass cabinets on either side of the main altar.

Troublesome Chhundu was banished to Haa by the Zhabdrung after an altercation with Gyenyen, Thimphu's protector. He also had a quarrel with Jichu Drakye of Paro, resulting in Paro's guardian stealing all of Haa's water – and that's why there is no rice grown in Haa. Annual sacrifices to Chhundu are still carried out in nearby Yangthang, highlighting how deeply Bhutan's roots run to its pre-Buddhist animist past.

Haa to Chhuzom

79KM

From Haa village it's 6km to Karnag (also called Karna), 2km further to Jyenkana and then 19km to Nago, with its picturesque water prayer wheels. A few kilometres further is **Bietakha**, with its small dzong (get the key from a house just below the Bhutan Power Corporation). At kilometre marker 40, shortly before the village of Gyeshina, look for the photogenic **Gurugang Goemba** just below the road.

Now high above the river, the road swings into a huge side valley, passing below the village of Susana en route to Mendegang. Near the houses and basic restaurants of **Tshongkha** is a new road leading 15 minutes uphill to Phundup Pedma Yoeling Shedra. The road traverses in and out of side valleys, passing above **Dobji Dzong**, which served as Bhutan's central prison from 1976 and is now a small religious school for 22 monks (the old prison cells are now classrooms!). Milarepa is said to have spent the night here. A hairy road leads down to the dzong via a stone quarry.

The road continues its descent into the Wang Chuu valley to join the main road at Chhuzom. From Chhuzom it's 24km (45 minutes) to Paro or 31km (one hour) to Thimphu.

Thimphu to Punakha

76KM / 2¾ HOURS

The drive from Thimphu to Punakha, along the National Hwy and over the Dochu La, leads from the cool heights of Thimphu to the balmy, lush landscapes of the Punakha valley.

THIMPHU TO THE DOCHU LA

23KM / 45 MINS

From Thimphu, the route to the east leaves the road to Paro and Phuentsholing and loops back over itself to become the east-west National Hwy. About a kilometre past the turn-off there is a good view of Simtokha Dzong (see p68). The route climbs through apple orchards and forests of blue pine to the village of **Hongtsho** (2890m), where an immigration checkpoint controls all access to eastern Bhutan. Your guide will present your restricted-area travel permit, giving you the chance to haggle for walnuts, apples and dried cheese from the roadside vendors.

High on a ridge across the valley to the south is **Trashigang Goemba** (see p67); you can take a nice half-day hike from the Dochu La to the goemba, ending at Hongtsho (see p67).

The road climbs to the **Dochu La** (3140m), marked by a large array of prayer flags and an impressive new collection of 108 chortens. On a clear day (only really likely between October and February), the pass offers a panoramic view of the Bhutan Himalaya – some groups make special pre-dawn trips up here to catch the views. The collection of chortens was built in 2005 as atonement for the loss of life caused by the flushing out of Assamese militants in southern Bhutan. Bring your own prayer flags to add to the collection.

The new **Druk Wangyal Lhakhang** to the side is well worth a visit to view its unique cartoon-style modern murals. Images include the fourth king battling rebels in the jungle, monks using a laptop and a Druk Air plane, alongside a modern history of the kingdom. It's a quintessentially Bhutanese fusion of the 21st and 15th centuries.

The hill above the chortens is covered in a lovely rhododendron forest, part of a royal botanical park. If you are here between mid-March and the end of April it's well worth taking some time to wander in the forest and take in the wonderful blooms. It is also a good area for bird-spotting. If you have more time, you can take an excellent half-day hike to Hongtsho via Lungchuzekha and Trashigang goembas – see p67 for details.

On the hill just below the pass is the **Dochu La Resort** (☎02-380404; www.dochularesort.com; s/d Nu 1600/2500), where many people break for tea (breakfast/lunch Nu 240/360). The proprietor also has a business making embroidered *thangkas* including some large *thondrols* for tsechus, and there's a small gift shop here. It's a popular overnight stop in October and November, when views are clearest.

There is a powerful binocular telescope here, a gift from the Kyoto University Alpine Club after members made the first ascent of Masang Gang (7165m) in 1985. A photograph on the wall above the telescope labels the peaks on the horizon (with different spellings and elevations from those used in this book). Gangkhar Puensum (7541m) is the highest peak that is completely inside Bhutan; Kulha Gangri (7554m) is higher, but it is on the border with Tibet. Using the telescope, it's also possible to see the distinctive shape of Gasa Dzong (see p163), a small white speck almost 50km to the north.

The area near the pass is believed to be inhabited by numerous spirits, including a cannibal demoness. Lama Drukpa Kunley, the 'Divine Madman', built Chimi Lhakhang in the Punakha valley to subdue these spirits and demons.

DOCHU LA TO METSHINA
42KM / 1½ HOURS

The vegetation changes dramatically at the pass from oak, maple and blue pine to a moist mountain forest of rhododendron, alder, cypress, hemlock and fir. There is also a large growth of daphne, a bush that is harvested for making traditional paper. The large white chorten a few kilometres below the pass was built because of the high incidence of accidents on this stretch of road.

About 11km below the pass at Lamperi is the **Royal Botanical Garden** (admission Nu 50; ⊙9am-5pm), which can give advice on hiking the ancient trail from the Dochu La down to Lunitsawa (three hours), or the full-day ridge trail from Tharana (above Hongtsho) to the Dochu La.

It's a long, winding descent past Lumitsawa to **Thinleygang**, during which the air gets warmer and the vegetation becomes increasingly tropical with the appearance of cactus, oranges and bamboo. Every November (on the first day of the 10th month), the Je Khenpo and *dratshang* (central monk body) overnight here on their two-day journey from their summer residence in Thimphu to their winter residence in Punakha.

Monasteries soon start to appear on the surrounding hills; first the striking hilltop Jakar Goemba and then Dalay and Talo goembas. The road passes a chorten that flows with *drub chhu* (holy water), said to have its source in a lake far above.

Three kilometres from Thinleygang, near Mendelgang, a short but steep drive above the main road, is the small **Dechen Hill Resort** (☎7719 0171; s/d Nu 1500/1800), a secluded and recently renovated collection of cottages, which are used mostly by birding enthusiasts.

The road continues its descent, looping in and out of a side valley, to the road junction and petrol station at **Metshina**, where the road to Punakha branches left off the National Hwy. If you are continuing the 8km to Wangdue Phodrang, stay on the main road.

METSHINA TO PUNAKHA
11KM / 30 MINS

The road to Punakha makes a switchback down past a collection of restaurants and houses at **Sopsokha**, from where you can visit the Chimi Lhakhang (discussed opposite). Beyond here, the road crosses the small Teop Rong Chhu and swings round a ridge into the valley of the Punak Tsang Chhu. The quiet tarmac road on the far side of the valley offers several mountain-biking options (see p94).

After another 2km or so, by the village of Wolakha, a road peels off to the left and climbs to the Meri Phuensom and Zangto Pelri hotels (see p94). Just above the hotels is an impressive new *anim goemba* (nunnery) and huge Nepali-style chorten, financed by the fourth king's father-in-law.

High up on the hillside, this side road continues a relentless uphill for 15km to **Talo Goemba**. You need a permit specifying Talo in order to visit the monastery. Up on the nearby ridge, the village of Norbugang reportedly has several fine lhakhangs but is closed to visitors since it is home to the family of the fourth king's four wives. A 1km side road branches off 5km before Talo to **Dalay Goemba**, a *lobdra* (monastic school) which is home to 30 students and a young *trulku* (reincarnated lama). The monastery was founded by the seventh Je Khenpo and is also known as Nalanda, after the famous Indian Buddhist university.

Back on the main road, just under 2km from the junction and 6.5km from Metshina is the new town of **Khuruthang**. All of Punakha's shops were relocated to this charmless concrete grid in 1999. There are several restaurants, local hotels and a Saturday vegetable market.

To the side of the road is the new **Khuruthang Goemba**, built by the royal grandmother and consecrated in 2005. The main Zangto Pelri Lhakhang here has excellent ceiling mandalas. The murals on the far wall depict the Zhabdrung and the various dzongs he established. The large Nepali-style chorten here was built by the Indian guru Nagi Rinchen (see p93) and is said to enshrine a speaking image of Guru Rinpoche known as Guru Sungzheme.

It's a further 3km to a middle school and small park with an excellent viewpoint over the Punakha Dzong. A kilometre further on is a parking area and the footbridge leading across the Mo Chhu to gorgeous Punakha Dzong.

CHIMI LHAKHANG

On a hillock in the centre of the valley below Metshina is the yellow-roofed Chimi Lhakhang, built in 1499 by the cousin of Lama Drukpa Kunley in his honour after he subdued the demoness of the nearby Dochu La with his 'magic thunderbolt of wisdom'. A wooden effigy of the lama's thunderbolt is preserved in the lhakhang, and childless women go to the temple to receive a *wang* (blessing or empowerment) from the saint.

It's a pleasant 20-minute walk across fields from the road at Sopsokha to the temple. The trail leads downhill across rice fields to Yoaka (which means 'in the drain') and on to the tiny settlement of Pana, which means 'field'. It then crosses an archery ground (keep your eyes peeled!) before making a short climb to Chimi Lhakhang. During the wet season, this is an especially muddy and slippery walk, one reason why a road to the temple is under construction. In characteristically bawdy fashion Kunley likened the shape of the hillock to that of a woman's breast.

There are a few monks at the temple, which is surrounded by a row of prayer wheels and some beautiful slate carvings.

You'll see the central statue of the lama and his dog Sachi, as well as statues of the Zhabdrung, Sakyamuni and Chenresig. Make a small offering and you'll be rewarded with a blessing from the lama's wooden and bone phalluses and his iron archery set. Mothers-to-be pray to a fertility goddess and then select their future baby's name from a collection of bamboo slips. The small chorten on the altar is said to have been crafted by Drukpa Kunley himself. Murals to the right of the chapel depict events from Kunley's colourful life.

The well-run **Chimi Lhakhang Cafeteria** (☎1761 2672; set meal Nu 300; ☺lunch) in Sopsokha is a great place for lunch or tea, with tables lined up against the window overlooking Yoaka and Pana villages.

Punakha & Khuruthang

♪ 02 / ELEV 1250M

Punakha sits in a sultry, fertile and beautiful valley at the junction of the Mo Chhu (Mother River) and Pho Chhu (Father River). Commanding the river junction is the gorgeous Punakha Dzong, perhaps Bhutan's most impressive building. If you are short on time, we recommend focusing your energies on Punakha rather than Wangdue Phodrang.

Punakha served as Bhutan's capital for over 300 years. The first king was crowned here in 1907 and the third king convened the Bhutan National Assembly here for the first time in 1952. In 2008 the fifth and current king underwent a secret ceremony in the dzong, receiving the royal raven crown, before proceeding to a formal coronation in Thimphu.

The low altitude of the Punakha valley allows two rice crops a year, and oranges and bananas are in abundance. Punakha also has one of the most famous festivals in the country, the springtime *domchoe*, dedicated to the protector deity Yeshe Goenpo (Mahakala).

All of Punakha's shops and facilities are in the unappealing new town of Khuruthang, 4km to the south.

⊙ Sights

Punakha Dzong
DZONG

This **dzong** (☺8am-5pm) was the second dzong to be built in Bhutan and it served as the capital and seat of government until Thimphu was promoted to the top job in

THE DIVINE MADMAN

Lama Drukpa Kunley (1455–1529) is one of Bhutan's favourite saints and a fine example of the Tibetan tradition of 'crazy wisdom'. He was born in Tibet, trained at Ralung Monastery and was a contemporary and disciple of Pema Lingpa. He travelled throughout Bhutan and Tibet as a *neljorpa* (yogi) using songs, humour and outrageous behaviour to dramatise his teachings to the common man. He felt that the stiffness of the clergy and social conventions were keeping people from learning the true teachings of Buddha.

His outrageous, often obscene, actions and sexual antics were a deliberate method of provoking people to discard their preconceptions. Tango Goemba is apparently the proud owner of a *thangka* that Kunley urinated on! He is also credited with having created Bhutan's strange animal, the takin, by sticking the head of a goat onto the body of a cow.

His sexual exploits are legendary, and the flying phalluses that you see painted on houses and hanging from rooftops are modelled on his. Kunley's numerous sexual conquests often included even the wives of his hosts and sponsors. On one occasion when he received a blessing thread to hang around his neck, he wound it around his penis instead, saying he hoped it would bring him luck with the ladies.

He spoke the following verse on one occasion when he met Pema Lingpa:

I, the madman from Kyishodruk,
Wander around from place to place;
I believe in lamas when it suits me,
I practise the Dharma in my own way.
I choose any qualities, they are all illusions,
Any gods, they are all the Emptiness of the Mind.
I use fair and foul words for Mantras; it's all the same,
My meditation practice is girls and wine;
I do whatever I feel like, strolling around in the Void,
Last time, I saw you with the Bumthang trulku;
With my great karmic background, I could approach.
Indeed it was auspicious, to meet you on my pilgrim's round!

For a biography and collection of songs, poems and bar-room anecdotes concerning Drukpa Kunley, try Keith Dowman's *The Divine Madman*.

the mid-1950s. It's arguably the most beautiful dzong in the country, especially in spring when the lilac-coloured jacaranda trees bring a lush sensuality to the dzong's characteristically towering whitewashed walls. Elaborately painted gold, red and black carved woods add to the artistic lightness of touch.

Guru Rinpoche foretold the construction of Punakha Dzong, predicting that '...a person named Namgyal will arrive at a hill that looks like an elephant'. When the Zhabdrung visited Punakha he chose the tip of the trunk of the sleeping elephant at the confluence of the Mo Chhu and Pho Chhu as the place to build a dzong.

A smaller building called Dzong Chug (Small Dzong) housed a statue of the Buddha here as early as 1326. Construction on the current dzong began in 1637 and was completed the following year, when the building was christened Pungthang Dechen Phodrang (Palace of Great Happiness). Later embellishments included the construction of a chapel to commemorate the victory over the Tibetans in 1639. The arms captured during the battle are preserved in the dzong.

The Zhabdrung established a monk body here with 600 monks from Cheri Goemba in the upper Thimphu valley and the dzong is still the winter residence of the *dratshang* (official monk body).

Punakha Dzong is 180m long and 72m wide and the *utse* is six storeys high. The gold dome on the *utse* was built in 1676 by local ruler, Gyaltsen Tenzin Rabgye. Many of the dzong's features were added between 1744 and 1763 during the reign of the 13th *desi*, Sherab Wangchuk. One item he donated was the *chenmo* (great) *thondrol,* a large *thangka* depicting the Zhabdrung that is exhibited to the public once a year during the tsechu festival. A brass roof for the dzong was a gift of the seventh Dalai Lama, Kelzang Gyatso.

Frequent fires (the latest in 1986) have damaged the dzong, as did the severe 1897 earthquake. In 1994 a glacial lake burst on the Pho Chhu, causing damage to the dzong that has since been repaired.

Visiting the Dzong

In addition to its strategic position at the river confluence, the dzong has several features to protect it against invasion. The steep wooden entry stairs are designed to be pulled up, and there is a heavy wooden door that is still closed at night.

The dzong is unusual in that it has three *docheys* instead of the usual two. The first (northern) courtyard is for administrative functions and houses a huge white chorten and bodhi tree. In the far left corner is a collection of stones and a shrine to the Tsochen, queen of the *nagas* (snake spirits), whose image is to the side. The second courtyard houses the monastic quarters and is separated from the first by the *utse*. In this courtyard there are two halls, one of which was used when Ugyen Wangchuck, later the first king, was presented with the Order of Knight Commander of the Indian Empire by John Claude White in 1905.

In the southernmost courtyard is the temple where the remains of the *terton,* Pema Lingpa, and Zhabdrung Ngawang Namgyal are preserved. The Zhabdrung died in Punakha Dzong, and his body is still preserved in the Machey Lhakhang (*machey* means 'sacred embalmed body'), which was rebuilt in 1995. The casket is sealed and may not be opened. Other than two guardian lamas, only the king and the Je Khenpo may enter this room. Both come to take blessings before they take up their offices.

At the south end is the 'hundred-pillar' assembly hall (which actually has only 54 pillars). The exceptional murals, which were commissioned by the second *druk desi*, depict the life of Buddha. The massive gold statues of the Buddha, Guru Rinpoche and the Zhabdrung date back to the mid-18th century, and there are some fine gold panels on the pillars.

Bhutan's most treasured possession is the Rangjung ('Self-Created') Kharsapani,

an image of Chenresig that is kept in the Tse Lhakhang in the *utse* of the Punakha Dzong. It was brought to Bhutan from Tibet by the Zhabdrung and features heavily in Punakha's famous *domchoe* festival (see the boxed text, p94). It is closed to the public.

After you exit the dzong from the north you can visit the *dzong chung* and get a blessing from a wish-fulfilling statue of Sakyamuni. The building marks the site of the original dzong. North of the dzong is a cremation ground, marked by a large chorten, and to the east is a royal palace.

The Upper Punakha Valley

The road up the west side of Mo Chhu valley passes several country houses owned by Bhutan's nobility, including the Phuntsho Pelri palace, a royal summer residence. The fourth king's father-in-law built many of the lhakhangs in the valley and owns several hotels, including the Damchen Resort.

Just 1km north of the dzong is the **Bhutan Souvenir Production Training Centre** (☎584664; ⊙9am-5pm), a program that offers a one-year course to train a dozen disadvantaged girls to produce handicrafts. Products include hand-woven bags, slippers, embroidered purses and tablemats, prayer-flag bookmarks and Christmas decorations. Products are well designed, prices are reasonable and it's a worthy cause.

On the left side of the road, 4.5km from Punakha, look out for the **Dho Jhaga Lama Lhakhang**, whose pretty gardens surround a huge boulder split miraculously in two. It is said that the Indian guru-magician Nagi Rinchen sent lightning and hail to split the rock to liberate his mother who was trapped inside. The chapel houses a statue of the guru (to the far right), who is recognisable by the scriptures in his top knot. Rinchen meditated in a cave across the river (behind Sona Gasa, the former palace of the third king), and so is depicted here as a long-haired *drubthob* (hermit-magician). To the far left is a statue of the local female protector, Chobdra, riding a snow lion.

In Yambesa, 7km north of Punakha, is the huge **Khamsum Yuelley Namgyal Chorten**, perched high on a hill on the opposite bank of the river. The 30m-tall chorten (also known as the Nyzergang Lhakhang) took eight years to build and was consecrated in 1999. The chorten is dedicated to the fifth king and serves to protect the country, so it is stuffed with a veritable 'Who's Who' of Bhutanese

PUNAKHA DOMCHOE

The Punakha Domchoe (or dromchoe) festival in February/March is unusual because of its dramatic recreation of a 17th-century battle scene. In 1639 a Tibetan army invaded Bhutan to seize Bhutan's most precious relic, the Rangjung Kharsapani, a self-created image of Chenresig. The Zhabdrung concocted an elaborate ceremony in which he pretended to throw the relic into the Mo Chhu, after which the disappointed Tibetans withdrew.

On the final day of the five-day Punakha Domchoe, the *thondrol,* which features an image of the Zhabdrung, is displayed. Later a group of 136 people dressed as *pazaps* (warriors) perform a dance in the main courtyard, then shout and whistle as they descend the front stairs of the dzong. Next, a procession of monks led by the Je Khenpo proceeds to the river to the accompaniment of cymbals, drums and trumpets. At the river the Je Khenpo throws a handful of oranges symbolising the Rangjung Kharsapani into the river. This is both a recreation of the Zhabdrung's trick and also an offering to the *naga (lu* in Dzongkha), the sub-surface spirits in the river. The singing and cheering warriors then carry their generals back into the dzong as firecrackers explode around them. Mask dances then celebrate the Zhabdrung's construction of the dzong.

demonography; some with raven or elephant heads, others riding snow lions or *garudas,* and most covered in flames. Look in the ground-floor stairwell for one protector riding a brown, hairy *migoi* (yeti). Go to the roof for fine views of the valley.

A bridge provides access to a sweaty 45-minute hike uphill to the chorten. Head off in the morning to avoid the subtropical heat. Ask your guide to point out the wonderfully fragrant *tingye* (flower pepper) plants that grow along the trail beside fields of chillis and beans.

The bridge is also a put-in spot for relaxing rafting and kayaking float trips down the Mo Chhu to Punakha Dzong (see p256).

Beyond the chorten, the dirt road leads up past Kabesa village and the Uma Resort to Tashithang and then Damji, the jumping-off point for treks to the Gasa hot springs (see p164) and the ending point of the Laya-Gasa trek (see p159 for details).

🏃 Activities

Punakha's mountain-bike trails offer one of the best chances to break out the fat tyres, though you'll have to bring your own bike as there's nowhere to rent locally.

A 27km loop route from Khuruthang crosses the bridge there and heads up the east side of the valley along a feeder road to Samdingkha (14km), then returns along a trail to Punakha Dzong (7.5km), finally coasting back to Khuruthang along the paved road.

A longer 40km loop starts from the new town of Bajo, just north of Wangdue Pho-

drang, and heads up the east side of the valley to Jangsabu (14km), before climbing a technical trail (some carrying required) to Olodama and Tschochagsa (9.5km). From here you can detour to Lingmukha or coast down 10km to the Aumthekha junction, across the river from Chimi Lhakhang, and then pedal back to Bajo and Wangdi.

🛏 Sleeping

Many people visit Punakha as a day trip from Thimphu or visit en route to Wangdue Phodrang, where there are several more hotels (see p97).

Thimphu's Hotel Jumolhari is renovating the old Singye Hotel above the Hotel Zangto Pelri; they should open in 2011.

TOP CHOICE Meri Puensum Resort HOTEL $$
(☑584195; www.meripuensum.com.bt; s/d Nu 1700/1900, deluxe s/d Nu 2000/2500; @) This privately run place is 6km south of Punakha, 1.2km up a side road, on a hill above the Punakha valley. It's just below the Hotel Zangto Pelri and is smaller, cosier and has much better service than it's neighbour. Rooms are in a central building and cottages that hug the steep hillside overlooking the rice terraces of the Punakha valley. The garden gazebo is a great place to breakfast or relax after a long day's touring.

Hotel Zangto Pelri HOTEL $$
(☑584125; hotzang@druknet.bt; s/d Nu 1600/2000, deluxe s/d Nu 1700/2100) Named after the paradise of Guru Rinpoche, this hotel has 45 rooms in the central building and quieter surrounding cottages (upper-floor

rooms are best). Service is lacklustre but at least most rooms have a balcony. If you stay here (or at the Meri Puensum), consider getting up at dawn and driving 8km up the paved road to Laptshaka (1900m) for a beautiful view of the mountains.

Amankora LUXURY HOTEL **$$$**
(☎584222; www.amanresorts.com; s/d full board US$925/1000) This is the smallest and most intimate of these über-luxury resorts, with only eight rooms in three buildings. The main farmhouse (now the restaurant and reading room) was the former residence of the Queen Mother and has some charming touches, including a traditional altar room. The spa reception area is in the former farmhouse kitchen and the lovely outdoor dining area is surrounded by rice fields and orchards. Park at the suspension bridge over the Mo Chhu, 6km north of Paro, and take a golf cart up to the resort (arrange this in advance). Air-con rooms available.

Uma Punakha LUXURY HOTEL **$$$**
(Kabesa) Further up the valley, 14km from Punakha, in a rural location, just north of the Khamsum Yuelley Namgyal Chorten, the new Uma branch will open in 2012 with similar facilities to the Paro flagship but on a more intimate scale, with only 12 rooms.

Damchen Resort HOTEL **$$**
(☎584354; www.damchenresort.com; s/d Nu 2000/2200, deluxe s/d from Nu 2600/2800; ❀) On the banks of the Punak Chhu, below Khuruthang, this appealing-looking riverside resort was recently rebuilt – although it has potential, it still feels a bit glum, with uninspiring decoration and no riverside seating. The proximity to Khuruthang means you can visit the town or goemba by yourself. Some deluxe rooms have nice balconies.

Hotel Y.T. HOTEL **$$**
(☎376014; hotelyt@druknet.bt; s/d Nu 1800/2200, deluxe Nu 2500) Above the road department complex in Lobesa, 1.5km from Metshina en route to Wangdue Phodrang, this friendly, slightly old-fashioned hotel has comfortable rooms and a Bhutanese-style sitting room. The friendly owner is an ex-forester, which is why the gardens are stuffed with mango, avocado and papaya trees.

✖ Eating

Phuenzhi Diner BHUTANESE **$**
(☎584145; Dungkhar Lam; set meals Nu 175-300) The 'Four Friends' is easily the best place

in Khuruthang new town, with good food (pancakes!) and equally delicious air-con. If you don't eat here, your guide will probably book lunch at one of the tourist hotels.

ℹ Information

Bank of Bhutan (Khuruthang; ⊘9am-1pm Mon-Fri, 9am-11am Sat) Changes cash and travellers cheques

WANGDUE PHODRANG DZONGKHAG

The scenic dzongkhag of Wangdue Phodrang is centred on the town and dzong of that name and stretches all the way to the Pele La and Phobjikha valley. South of Wangdi, as it is known locally, towards the southern region of Tsirang, is the giant Indian-financed Punatsangchuu hydroelectric project.

Punakha to Wangdue Phodrang

21KM / 30 MINS

It's a half-hour drive from Punakha to Wangdue Phodrang. Follow the road back to Metshina and drive 1.5km to Lobesa, following the Punak Tsang Chhu. Soon the dramatic Wangdue Phodrang Dzong comes into view, draped along the end of a ridge above the river. There is a police and immigration checkpoint before the bridge across the Punak Tsang Chhu.

The modern bridge over the Punak Tsang Chhu replaced the original 17th-century wooden cantilever structure that was washed away by floods in 1968.

Wangdue Phodrang

☎02 / ELEV 1240M

Legend says that the Zhabdrung Ngawang Namgyal met a small boy named Wangdi playing in the sand on the banks of the Punak Tsang Chhu and was moved to name his new dzong Wangdi – later Wangdue – Phodrang (Wangdi's Palace). The town is still known colloquially as Wangdi.

The small ramshackle town of white-washed clapboard shops and funky restaurants currently feels like a man awaiting execution; plans are afoot to demolish the wooden buildings and relocate the old town 4km north to Bajo new town.

WESTERN BHUTAN WANGDUE PHODRANG DZONGKHAG

for a site for the dzong, four ravens were seen flying away in four directions. This was considered an auspicious sign, representing the spreading of religion to the four points of the compass.

Wangdi is important in the history of Bhutan because in the early days it was the country's second capital. After Trongsa Dzong was established in 1644, the *penlop* of Wangdue Phodrang became the third most powerful ruler, after the *penlops* of Paro and Trongsa. The dzong's strategic position gave the *penlop* control of the routes to Trongsa, Punakha, Dagana and Thimphu.

The dzong's complex shape consists of three separate narrow courtyards that follow the contours of the hill. The buildings are refreshingly unrestored, with a wooden roof still held in place by large stones, and the occasional lost chicken wandering across the empty courtyards.

There is only one entrance, fronted by a large *darchen* (prayer pole) and reached by a road that leads downhill from the bazaar. The cacti that cover the hillside below the dzong were planted long ago to discourage invaders.

The administrative portion surrounds a large flagstone-paved *dochey* at the north end of the dzong and the *utse* divides the north and south portions of the dzong. The Guru Tshengye Thondrol, depicting Guru Rinpoche, is unfurled here each year in the early hours of the final day of the autumn **tsechu festival**. As you detour around the *utse* you can peer through arrow slits into the valley below. The main assembly hall in the far south of the dzong features a central Dusum Sangay – the past, present and future Buddhas.

Radak Neykhang   TEMPLE

Just behind the bazaar, above the dzong and by the tall cypress trees of the district court, is this timeless 17th-century temple. The temple is dedicated to an ancient warrior king and there's a collection of helmets, arrows and shields in the anteroom. Inside there are five versions of the local protector deity, as well as a statue to the far right of a *tshomen* (water spirit) who lived in the river and was an obstacle to the construction of this building.

Make an offering and roll the chapel dice and the resident monk will read your future.

Because it is on an exposed promontory overlooking the river, Wangdi is usually windy and dusty, particularly during the afternoon.

⊙ Sights

Wangdue Phodrang Dzong   DZONG

This commanding **dzong** (☯8.30am-5pm) was founded by the Zhabdrung in 1638. It sits atop a high ridge between the Punak Tsang Chhu and the Dang Chhu, clearly chosen for its commanding view of the valleys below. Legend relates another reason for choosing this spot: as people searched

🛏 Sleeping

There's not a great deal of demand for hotel rooms in Wangdi. Many travellers just make a day trip to see the dzong or stay in Punakha (30 minutes' drive away) and drive straight through to Gangte, Trongsa or Bumthang. At tsechu time in autumn, however, the town is packed and rooms are at a premium.

Punatsangchhu Cottages   HOTEL **$$**
(📞380907; www.punatsangchhucottages.com; s/d Nu 2300/2800, deluxe s/d Nu 3300/3800) Second to the Meri Puensum in Punakha, this is your best choice, below the road and next to the river, 5km from Wangdi. Modern rooms vary in size but some have nice balconies overlooking the river. The restaurant is good and the lawn is a nice place to savour a beer on a warm summer evening.

Dragon's Nest Resort   HOTEL **$$**
(📞480521; www.dragonsnesthotel.com; s/d from Nu 1800/2300, deluxe s/d Nu 2300/2800; @🛜) This trusty place is on the west side of the river, 4km below Wangdi and diagonally across from Bajo new town. The spacious rooms and lush grounds overlook the river and are safely away from the town's nocturnal canine chorus. The restaurant staff seem to be in a competition to see who can ignore the guests for the longest. Our waiter won.

Kichu Resort   HOTEL **$$**
(📞481359; intchuzomsa@druknet.bt; r Nu 2700) In Chhuzomsa, 9km east of Wangdi, this tranquil hotel has 24 well-appointed rooms in a lovely landscaped garden overlooking the rushing Dang Chhu. The son of the owners is a *rinpoche* (title given to a revered lama), so the restaurant serves only vegetarian food. Ask for a riverside balcony room and pack insect repellent against the sand flies.

Hotel Tashiling   LOCAL **$**
(📞481403; fax 481682; Dzong Lam; s/d Nu 1500/1800) This local hotel near the dzong has 16 pine-walled rooms and fragrant chillis drying on the roof. It's only worth considering for Indian tourists, who pay 50% less than the rate for foreigners. The giant fridge full of cold beers will raise spirits.

ℹ Information

Bank of Bhutan (Bajo; ⊙9am-1pm Mon-Fri, 9-11am Sat) Changes cash and travellers cheques. It's in Bajo new town, 2.5km north of Wangdue Phodrang.

National Bank of Bhutan (Bajo; ⊙9am-4pm Mon-Fri, 9-11am Sat) Changes cash and travellers cheques.

Post Office (⊙8.30am-1pm & 2-5pm Mon-Fri, 8.30am-1pm Sat) In Wangdue Phodrang old town.

Wangdue Phodrang to Pele La

61KM / 1¾ HOURS

The beautiful drive east towards the Pele La offers access to central Bhutan and the Phobjikha valley, known for its winter population of black-necked cranes. The pass itself takes you over the Black Mountains, the physical boundary between western and central Bhutan.

Leaving Wangdue Phodrang, the road traverses bare hillsides high above the Dang Chhu. The large riverside building below the road is a jail for prisoners serving life imprisonment.

By the time the road reaches **Chhuzomsa** at the confluence of the Pe Chhu and the Dang Chhu, 8km from Wangdi, it is level with the river (Chhuzomsa means 'meeting of two rivers'). Below the small village is the idyllic riverside Kichu Resort (see opposite).

Just beyond Chhuzomsa is a ropeway that climbs 1340m in 6km to Tashila. The ropeway is primarily used to carry goods up to the village and to bring logs back down the hill, but it makes two special trips daily (8am and 5pm) to carry people. Passengers sit in an open wooden box and dangle high above the trees for 45 minutes to the top. The Gangte trek (p164) passes the top of the ropeway – some tired trekkers have been known to declare an emergency and ride down from Tashila.

At **Tikke Zampa**, 4km past Chhuzomsa, the road crosses to the south bank of the Dang Chhu and begins a gradual climb to the Pele La. A further 10km and you'll see a superbly located lhakhang atop a hillock to the left. The valley gets steeper as the road climbs its edges. In many places the road has been blasted out of the cliff and hangs high above the deep forests of the valley below.

The road detours frequently into side valleys, passing the one-house village of **Kalekha** (or Khelaykha), the end of an interesting Shasi La hike from the Phobjikha valley (see p100). From here it's 12km to the village of Nobding (2640m), where the tourist-standard **Kuenphen Restaurant**

(☏442000; set lunch Nu 250-350) offers a useful lunch stop. A further 7km on is **Dungdung Nyelsa**, where the old (disused) road to the Pele-La branches off. In spring the upper hillsides here are covered with red, white and pink rhododendron blossoms. The road climbs steeply up the hillside for 5km, to the turn-off to Gangte in the Phobjikha valley.

From the turn-off, it's a final 3km through forests to the top of the **Pele La** (3420m), which is marked by a chorten and an array of prayer flags. On a clear day (which is rare in these parts) there is a view of Jhomolhari (7314m), Jichu Drakye (6989m) and Kang Bum (6526m) from a viewpoint 500m down the old road between Nobding and the Pele La. There are no mountain views from the pass itself. The Pele La marks the western border of the Singye Wangchuck (formerly the Black Mountains) National Park and is the gateway to central Bhutan.

Phobjikha Valley

☏02 / ELEV 2900M

Phobjikha is a bowl-shaped glacial valley on the western slopes of the Black Mountains, bordering the Jigme Singye Wangchuck National Park. Because of the large flock of black-necked cranes that winters here, it is one of the most important wildlife preserves in the country. In addition to the cranes there are also muntjacs (barking deer), wild boars, sambars, serows, Himalayan black bears, leopards and red foxes in the surrounding hills. The Nakey Chhu drains the marshy valley, eventually flowing into the lower reaches of the Punak Tsang Chhu.

Some people refer to this entire region as Gangte (or Gangtey), after the goemba that sits on a ridge above the valley. The three-day Gangte trek takes off from this valley (see p164).

The road to Phobjikha diverges from the main road 3km before the Pele La. It's then a 1.5km drive through forests to the Lowa La (3360m), where you may encounter a few stray yaks. After the pass the trees disappear and the scenery switches dramatically to low-lying dwarf bamboo as the road descends to Gangte village and goemba. From the goemba junction, the road switchbacks down past the turn-off to the Amankora resort to the valley floor, past extensive russet-coloured fields of potatoes. Gangte potatoes are the region's primary cash crop and one of Bhutan's important exports to India.

The valley is snowbound during the height of winter and many of the valley's 4700 residents, including the monks, shift to winter residences in Wangdue Phodrang during December and January, just as the cranes move in to take their place. The local residents are known as Gangteps and speak a dialect called Henke.

◉ Sights

Gangte Goemba   MONASTERY

Gangte Goemba enjoys the valley's prime chunk of real estate, on a forested hill overlooking the green expanse of the entire Phobjikha valley. The extensive complex consists of the central goemba, monks' quarters, a small guesthouse and outlying meditation centres.

During a visit to the Phobjikha valley, the 15th-century treasure-finder Pema Lingpa prophesied that a goemba named *gang-teng* (hill top) would be built on this site and that his teachings would spread from here. Pema Thinley, the grandson and reincarnation of Pema Lingpa, built a Nyingma temple here in 1613, and the larger goemba was built by the second reincarnation, Tenzing Legpey Dhendup. The current Gangtey *trulku* (reincarnation), Kunzang Pema Namgyal, is the ninth reincarnation of the 'body' of Pema Lingpa.

The **tshokhang** (prayer hall) is built in the Tibetan style with eight great pillars, and is one of the largest in Bhutan. The inner sanctum houses the funeral chorten of founder Tenzing Legpey Dhendup. Much of the interior and exterior woodwork of the 450-year-old goemba was replaced between 2001 and 2008 due to a beetle infestation. A three-day **tsechu** is held here from the 8th to 10th day of the eighth lunar month (September/October), with *cham* (religious dances) and the hanging of a large *thondrol* on the final day.

A nearby **shedra** offers a nine-year course in Buddhist studies. The long white building on the hill to the north of the goemba is **Kuenzang Chholing**, a *drubdey* (retreat and meditation centre for monks) that was started in 1990 by the Je Khenpo. The normal period of meditation is three years, three months and three (sometimes seven) days, during which time the monks remain inside and eat food passed in to them by another monk.

The beautiful glacial valley bowl below the goemba is peppered with villages, hiking trails, potato fields, lhakhangs and, if you time your visit right (November to mid-February), nesting pairs of black-necked cranes. It's a great place to hike and explore surrounding valleys and it's a good idea to budget an extra half-day here for that.

Your first stop should be the Royal Society for Protection of Nature's (RSPN) **Black-Necked Crane Information Centre** (☑442536; ☺5am-1pm, 2-5pm Mon-Fri, 9am-noon Sat & Sun Nov-Mar, from 9am Apr-Oct), which has informative displays about the cranes and the valley environment. You can use the centre's powerful spotting scopes and check what you see against its pamphlet, 'Field Guide to Crane Behaviour'. If the weather's iffy you can browse the library and handicraft shop, and watch videos at 10am and 3pm (Nu 100). This is also the centre of the valley's fledgling eco-tourism initiative and they can arrange local hiking guides (Nu 300), horse hire (Nu 300), an overnight stay in a local homestay or lectures on the local ecosystem.

A further 1.5km on is the village and hotels at Tabiting. Behind the Phuntsho Chholing Guest House is the small **Wangmo Hand-Woven Carpet Factory** (☑442553). Established in 1992 by a local woman, Dorji Wangmo, it has a small hall housing four weavers, who produce about 30 carpets a year.

Further on, the road becomes a rough 4WD track as it continues past Yusa village to the small **Domchoe Lhakhang**, said to be the oldest in the valley, dating to the 7th century. It's a 45-minute walk from Tabiting.

Across the valley from Tabiting is the 15th-century **Khewang Lhakhang**, which has a **tsechu** on the third day of the ninth month, when local men (not monks) do the dancing, celebrating an ancient victory over local demons.

🛏 Sleeping

Electricity lines (partly underground) will arrive in the valley in 2011, bringing heating, hot water and most likely a sprinkling of new hotels. A new hotel is already under construction at the road junction above Gangte village and Dorji Wangmo is building a six-room guesthouse next to her carpet centre. The valley can be chilly so bring warm clothes.

Phobjikha Valley

Phobjikha Valley

Dewachen Hotel HOTEL $$
(☑442550; www.hoteldewachen.com; s/d Nu 2200/2600) Owned by the Yangphel travel company, this impressive stone-and-wood building in Tabiting village is the first

choice for most travellers. The rooms are large and stylish (corner rooms are the best) and the good restaurant has floor-to-ceiling bay windows that offer great valley views. The name refers to the 'Pure Land' paradise of the Buddha Amithaba.

Gakiling Guest House   GUESTHOUSE $

(☑442540; r Nu 1550-1900) We like the traditional wooden architecture of this small place and the fact that it's the only locally owned guesthouse in the valley, just behind the Black-Necked Crane Information Centre, but there's no getting away from the fact that you'll spend most of your time listening to the next room's conversation (and worse). Don't expect to sleep past 6am. A new concrete block of rooms will offer less charm but more soundproofing. The views from the upper-storey balcony are great.

Phuntsocholing Farm House
                            GUESTHOUSE $
(☑442554; s/d Nu 1000/1500) Below the Dewachen, this large Bhutanese-style house belonging to the sister of the Gangte *trulku* was converted to a hotel in 1994. It has creaking wooden floors, traditional wall paintings, a cosy dining room and even a chapel on the 2nd floor, though the rooms themselves are pretty simple for the money, with clean shared bathrooms. If you value experience over mod-cons, this is a good opportunity to get a close-up look at the traditional architecture of rural Bhutan. Better still, arrange a local homestay.

Amankora Gangtey   LUXURY HOTEL $$$

(☑442235; www.amanresorts.com; s/d full board US$1300/1400; @ 🛜) A side road branches off 1km from just below the goemba to this top-of-the-line lodge. The eight rooms are identical to Thimphu's Amankora and the dramatic picture windows, spa massage and excellent service won't disappoint.

CHHUKHA DZONGKHAG

Unless they are making an overland crossing to or from India, most Western travellers tend to give Chhukha Dzongkhag a wide berth. For those who insist on taking the land route, the district effectively consists of the winding road that drops from the mountains through the lush tropical

---

HIKING THE PHOBJIKHA VALLEY

There's some great hiking in the valley and surprisingly for Bhutan, it's mostly flat going! The information centre has suggested the following walking routes – you should be able to get information on these and other trails there.

A good short walk is the **Gangte Nature Trail** (1½ hours), which leads downhill from the *mani* stone wall just north of the Gangte Goemba to the Khewang Lhakhang. The trail descends to Semchubara village and continues straight at the chorten into the edge of the forest, before descending to a square chorten and the lhakhang. From here you can cross over the metal bridge to the roadside local school.

You could add on a half-day hike into the valley behind Khewang Lhakhang along the **Tenkhor Yuetshe Sum Trail**, linking up the villages of Gophu, Doksina and Pangsa with Jangchu Goemba in a loop back to Khewa.

Another option is the one-hour **Kilkhorthang Trail**, from the large modern lhakhang at Kingathang across the valley to the Damchoe Lhakhang, south of Tabiting. Alternatively, drive further south from Kingathang to the lovely side valley of Lawog and explore on foot from there.

The tougher half-day **Shasi La Nature Trail** leads up the valley behind Beyta school, though the trail is easier to follow from the track behind the Amankora resort. The path leads through rhododendron forests to the village of Ramgokha, a collection of chortens at Mani Thongju and then the Shasi La pass, before descending through old-growth forest to Kalekha on the main Wangdue Phodrang road. Arrange to get picked up here and continue on to Wangdi. This is the traditional route taken by the Gangte *trulku* and local farmers when they leave the valley for the winter. A local guide would be sensible for this route.

The centre can also show you the hike from Gangte Goemba to the **Kuenzang Chholing** retreat centre and on to the **Kumbhu Lhakhang**, a protector chapel dedicated to the ancient Bon deity Sipey Gyalmo.

WATCHING THE CRANES

The marshy centre of the Phobjikha valley means it's best avoided on foot, but it's a perfect winter residence for the flock of 325 (up from 212 a decade ago) rare and endangered black-necked cranes that migrate from the Qinghai-Tibet Plateau to Bhutan in late autumn, typically between 23 and 26 October. The Bhutanese have great respect for these 'heavenly birds' (known locally as *thrung thrung kam*), and songs about the cranes are popular among village folk. In mid-February, the cranes circle Gangte Goemba and fly back across the Himalaya to their summer homes in Tibet. One of the most popular folk songs of the people of Phobjikha laments the time when the cranes leave the valley.

The best months to spot cranes are between late-October and March, with the best chance between November and January. The best times for viewing are at dawn or dusk, when all the birds in the valley congregate for the night. You can watch the birds from the centre's viewing area or from the valleyside hiking trails. Wear dull-coloured clothes, keep your distance and refrain from flash photography. For more on black-necked cranes see p250.

The RSPN initiated and sponsors the annual **Black-Necked Crane Festival** on 12 November. It's primarily an effort to instil conservation values into the people of Phobjikha, but tourists are welcome to watch the festivities, most of which are folk dances staged by school children.

foothills of southern Bhutan to Phuentsholing, a boom town on the international border; Jaigaon, its twin settlement, is on the other side. It's a dramatic road trip and it gives you a sense of geographical continuity that flying into Paro doesn't. En route, you'll pass gigantic 'Lost World' ferns that spill onto the road and dozens of silver-threaded waterfalls, cascading off high cliffs into the mist.

Most of this road is a winding and treacherous 1½-lane highway, and you may want to point out to your driver the superbly cheesy Indian signboards that bear cautionary lines such as 'Speed is the knife that kills life', 'Speed thrills but kills', and 'Impatient on Road, patient of Hospital'!

Thimphu to Phuentsholing

172KM / 5 HOURS

The downhill journey from Thimphu to Phuentsholing follows the first highway in Bhutan, built in 1962 by Dantak, the Indian border-roads organisation. It's still the most important road in the country, and is currently being widened – you'll meet road crews toiling away on several stretches. Sometime by 2012, the road should resemble a runway, and cars should be able to zip down this stretch in less than four hours. Before the original highway was completed, this journey could take up to 10 days.

The first stage of the trip is from Thimphu to Chhuzom (31km, 40 minutes). See p85 for a description of this section of the route (as travelled in the opposite direction, ie from Chhuzom to Thimphu).

CHHUZOM TO CHAPCHA

23KM / 20 MINS

The wide two-lane expressway connecting Thimphu to Chhuzom has now been extended to Chapcha, thus halving travel time. It follows the Wang Chhu valley southward; you can see the road to Haa climbing on the opposite side of the valley. Passing beneath **Dobji Dzong**, which sits atop a promontory high above the river, the road crosses the settlement of Hebji Damchu (2020m). About 4km ahead is the tiny Hotel Damchu, where the road starts climbing away from the river, making several switchbacks out of the valley.

Finally, the road crests a ridge and passes the **Chapcha Bjha** (Chapcha Rocks) as you squeeze between a vertical rock face to the left and an equally vertical sheer drop to the right. Cross the Chapcha La to reach the Dantak road construction camp at Chapcha (2450m).

CHAPCHA TO CHHUKHA

34KM / 1 HOUR

Past Chapcha, it's a vertigo-inducing journey on alternate stretches of rough, narrow road and broad, newly-metalled tarmac all the way to Phuentsholing. The road passes through several landslide zones, where the asphalt has peeled off to reveal a slushy and cratered mud-track, which is as perilous as it is hard on your posterior.

Driving out of Chapcha, you can see the dramatic **Thadra Ney Lhakhang**, built into a rock face on a cliff far above to the right. The road climbs steeply, and clears a few hair-pin bends before hitting the highest stretch of the road, above 2800m. It then switchbacks steeply down through forests to the Tachhong Zam and the immigration check-post at Tanalung. Another 10km down a forested slope is Bunakha (2270m), where the **Tourist Hotel Bunagu** (☎08-460522; set meal Nu 260) caters to travellers who have booked in advance, and boasts pleasant balcony seating and clean toilets.

From Bunakha, the road passes a lovely waterfall to the goemba of **Chhukha Rabdey**. A few kilometres further on, in the lower part of Tsimasham (formerly Chimakothi; 2210m), is the **Karma Hotel** (☎08-478221; r Nu 150), which has moved to a new site across the road where it offers hot food and renovated rooms.

The road now switchbacks down to the **Chhukha hydroelectric project**. The air gets thicker and warmer, and several side roads lead down to the massive dam site at the valley floor. Beyond the basic Deki Hotel & Bar is the **Thegchen Zam** ('strong high bridge'), which takes the road west of the Wang Chhu. This is the mid-point between Thimphu and Phuentsholing, both around 95km away.

CHHUKHA TO GEDU
38KM / 1 HOUR

The road climbs to a lookout over the Chhukha project, beyond which is the first of several roads leading to the 2007 1020MW **Tala hydroelectric project**. This road leads 8.5km to the intake structure where water is diverted into a 22km-long tunnel. From the lookout, you can see the transformers and the transmission station, and beside the distribution station is the yellow-roofed Zangto Pelri Lhakhang and the old Chhukha Dzong. The two projects meet the entire power demand of Western Bhutan, with enough surplus to export to India.

The rest of the climb is over the ridge that separates the Wang Chhu valley from the Torsa Chhu drainage. Look out for the spectacular high waterfall visible to the east across the valley. Up ahead is a short bridge over what's left of Toktokachhu Falls (Takti Chhu), much diminished after a flood brought down a collection of huge boulders.

Atop the next ridge, at 2020m, is a Dantak canteen, selling usual Indian fare such as *dosa* (paper-thin pancakes made from rice flour), and syrupy milk tea. It also has public toilets (the ones to the right are for 'officers only'). Beyond a second road to the Tala project is a road-crew camp at Makaibari ('cornfield'). Then comes Asinabari ('field of hailstones') and the small settlement of **Chasilakha** (*la kha* means 'grazing field'). About 9km before Gedu is the *shedra* of Tsatse Lhakhang.

Another climb leads to **Gedu**, a biggish highway town with several small restaurants near the road. On your way in, you'll pass the newly-incepted Gaeddu College of Business Studies, the only college under the Royal University of Bhutan to currently offer business management degrees. The institute is housed in an imposing building that previously served as the offices of the Tala hydroelectric project. The best bet for a meal in Gedu is the **Lhamu Restaurant & Bar** (☎05-272332) at the south end of town, with great Nepali-style food, cheese *momos,* and well-brewed tea. The nearby Laptshakha Lhakhang has some new murals.

Beyond Gedu, a newly-built side road leads downhill to Mirching and the Tala power station, and rejoins the Phuentsholing road just north of Rinchending. It's currently open to traffic through the daytime, but the tarmac is patchy, and for the time being at least you're better off sticking to the main highway.

GEDU TO RINCHENDING
41KM / 1¼ HOURS

A short distance from Gedu is **Jumja** village at 2050m. Around a sharp bend is the huge Jumja slide that often wipes away the road during the monsoon, holding up traffic for days on end. Passing the Kuenga Chholing Lhakhang in the village of Kamji, the road turns a corner and begins to drop like a stone all the way down to the plains.

At **Sorchen**, a road construction camp houses workers who continually repair damage from landslides. A diversion ('bye pass') was built in 2001 to provide a way around roadblocks, and a new road from Jumja to Phuentsholing via Pasakha is being readied to provide a short cut around this volatile section.

From here, it's 12km past an industrial area and an army camp to the checkpoint at Rinchending. You will pick up an entry or exit stamp here, depending on which way you're headed.

RINCHENDING TO PHUENTSHOLING
5KM / 15 MINUTES

If you are heading into Bhutan, Rinchending is the last place to invest in perishable rations such as fruit. As you proceed, the prices rise almost as quickly as does the altitude.

Below Rinchending is the small **Kharbandi Goemba**, built in 1967 by the late Royal Grandmother Ashi Phuentso Choedron, who had a winter residence here. The modern temple houses large statues of Sakyamuni, the Zhabdrung and Guru Rinpoche. In the lush grounds there are examples of eight different styles of Tibetan chortens.

Below Kharbandi, the road switchbacks down to Phuentsholing, offering spectacular views over the Torsa Chhu valley as it spills onto the plains.

Phuentsholing

♪05

The small, sweltering border town of Phuentsholing sits opposite the much larger Indian bazaar town of Jaigaon, separated by a flimsy fence and the much-photographed Bhutan Gate. It's a congested, noisy settlement bustling with hordes of traders, security personnel and migrant riff-raff. Coming from India, however, you will notice an instantaneous change in the degree of cleanliness and organisation. Unless it's absolutely necessary to halt for the night, you'll find little reason to linger in Phuentsholing apart from clearing immigration. The air here is thick with vehicular pollution, and the infrastructure quite utilitarian. Besides, it can get terribly hot and clammy in summer.

For further information on the border crossing, head to shop.lonelyplanet.com to purchase a downloadable PDF of the Northeast States chapter of Lonely Planet's *India* guidebook.

◎ Sights

Zangto Pelri Lhakhang   TEMPLE
(☺dawn-dusk) The modern Zangto Pelri Lhakhang is a replica of Guru Rinpoche's celestial abode, though we're guessing the original isn't made of concrete! There's not much to see here, but the surrounding garden is pleasant and the pilgrims spinning prayer wheels offer some photo ops.

Pungthim Dratshang   MONASTERY
(☺dawn-dusk) This newly constructed monastery stands to the north of the Zangto Pelri Lhakhang, at the site of the old vegetable market. It houses the local *rabdey* (monk community), and is a rather nonfussy building that shouldn't take much time to survey.

Crocodile Breeding Centre   ZOO
(☺dawn-dusk) Got an hour to kill? Perhaps go and snooze with the sleepy marsh muggers and gharials at the Crocodile Breeding Centre, a 10-minute walk north of the bus station. The crocs are fed every other day at noon.

🛏 Sleeping & Eating

The following hotels are all TCB-approved, and have rooms with attached bathrooms. Apart from approved hotels, Phuentsholing also has numerous small hotels with a limited number of air-con rooms, they fill up quickly with Indian businessmen and travellers. The main hotels all have good restaurants, tossing up palatable (and predictable) Indian, Bhutanese, Continental and Chinese fare.

Lhaki Hotel   HOTEL $$
(☎257111; lhakihotel@druknet.bt; Pelkhil Lam; s/d from Nu 1800/2300, ste s/d Nu 2800/4500; @) This is your best bet in town, but book in advance as most tour operators prefer to lodge their tour groups here. A new and modern hotel with air-con, it sits off a quiet lane in the upper quarters of town, and has clean and spacious rooms (with excellent loos) built around a bright and airy central hall. Other draws include a restaurant with good Indian and quasi-Chinese dishes, and a massage parlour.

Hotel Druk   HOTEL $$
(☎252426; www.drukhotels.com; Zhung Lam; s/d from Nu 3000/3500, ste Nu 7000) Recently touched up, the Druk is an oldie located in a secluded spot behind the customs and immigration office. It's spread out around a manicured lawn with garden seating, and offers comfy, tastefully furnished rooms, with hot water in the mornings and evenings. The restaurant serves decent Indian food, and there's air-con.

Phuentsholing

Hotel Namgay   HOTEL **$**
(☏252374; hotel_namgay@yahoo.com; Tharpai Lam; s/d from Nu 1100/1300, ste Nu 1950; @) Overlooking the Zangto Pelri Lhakhang, the Namgay is a step down in quality but is still pleasant, with air-con, tropical plants in the lobby and money-exchange services. The reception is manned by friendly and helpful staff, which is especially welcome after a tiring road trip.

Sinchula Hotel   HOTEL **$**
(☏252589; hotelsinchula@yahoo.com; Phuensum Lam; s/d from Nu 450/650; @) Preferred mainly by local travellers, this oldish es-

tablishment located next to an old peepul tree has clean, tiled rooms with hot-water bathrooms, air-con, a good restaurant and a rooftop terrace bar.

Hotel Peljorling   HOTEL **$**
(☏252833; Zhung Lam; s/d/tr from Nu 300/400/600, deluxe d Nu 750) Another hotel preferred by local travellers, the Peljorling has clean but basic rooms lacking air-con, which can be a put-off during summer. However, the joint scores with its excellent restaurant that tosses up delectable Continental stuff, including decent sizzlers and a 'Macdonalds Burger'.

Central Hotel
HOTEL $

(☎252172; centralhotel@druknet.bt; cnr Tharpai & Gatoen Lams; s/d Nu 450/800, ste Nu 1200) It's central, that's for sure. But that apart, there's little else that can be said about this standard-issue place with air-con. Oh, and there's plenty of noise from the streets below.

Kuenga Hotel
HOTEL $

(Map p104; ☎252293; 5-53 Gatoen Lam; s/d Nu 400/550) This one's a real cheapie, although it has been around for a long time and is thus popular among regional travellers. Only a few rooms at this mothballed place have hot water, but the lobby restaurant seems popular with locals.

🛍 Shopping

Phuentsholing has the cheapest consumer goods in Bhutan and many Bhutanese and Indians come here especially on shopping trips. It's also one of the cheapest places to have a *gho* made.

Bhimraj Stores
FABRIC

(Map p104) In the bazaar, they sell a range of cloth here from Nu200 to Nu400 per metre; you'll need about 3.5m for a *gho*.

Druk Carpet Industries
CARPETS

(☎252004; ☺9am-8pm Wed-Mon) The factory is north of the town, but this showroom is the place if you are looking to buy. An 18in x 48in carpet costs around US$450.

⭐ Entertainment

If you like Hindi movies, you'll adore the **Mig Cinema**, a melting-pot in the heart of town and the **Norgay Cinema**, near the Dhoti Chhu at the north end of town, offering several three-hour screenings daily.

For a bottle of cold Indian Fosters beer (Nu 70), park yourself on the terrace of Hotel Peljorling, with traffic crawling below, or stargaze on the roof terrace of the Sinchula Hotel. The garden bar at the **Hotel Greenville** (Jorden Lam) is a good place to get some peace and quiet.

ℹ Information

See p269 for information about visa and other formalities upon arrival in Phuentsholing for foreigners and Indian nationals. All the banks will swap Bhutanese ngultrums for Indian rupees, and vice versa. Indian rupees can be used freely in Bhutan, but in bills not exceeding Rs100.

Bank of Bhutan (Samdrup Lam; ☺9am-1pm Mon-Fri, 9-11am Sat) Changes foreign currency, including travellers cheques.

Bhutan National Bank (Samdrup Lam; ☺9am-4pm Mon-Fri, 9-11am Sat) Deals in foreign currency.

Bhutan Photo Studio (Gatoen Lam) One of several studios for instant passport photos (Nu 50 to Nu 100).

Druk PNB Bank (Zhung Lam; ☺9am-3pm Mon-Fri, 9-11am Sat) Changes money and offers limited ATM services.

DSB Books (Gechu Shopping Mall; ☺9am-9pm) Paperback novels, Indian newspapers and books on Bhutan.

GPY Cyber Café (per hr Nu50; ☺9am-9pm) Printing, photocopying and long-distance calls also possible. Behind the Gechu Shopping Mall.

Phuentsholing General Hospital (☺254825) A 50-bed hospital equipped with a modern lab, operating theatres and a casualty department.

Post Office (Samdrup Lam; ☺9am-5pm Mon-Fri, to 1pm Sat) Next to the Bank of Bhutan on a hill above town.

ℹ Getting There & Away

For details on getting to and from India see p269.

Transport companies such as Dhug, Metho, Pelyab and Sernya run morning Coaster mini-buses from the bus station to Thimphu (Nu 188, seven hours) and Paro (Nu 182, six hours), with a few weekly services to Haa (Nu 245, nine hours), Wangdue Phodrang (Nu 252, 10 hours) and Punakha (Nu 253, 10 hours). There are early-morning mini buses to Siliguri (Nu 93, four hours) but these aren't really set up for foreigners, and you would have to detour via immigration en route. Bhutan Post has one 3pm bus to Kolkata (Nu 330, 18 hours), but it might cost you an additional slipped disc or two.

Central Bhutan

Best Places to Stay

» Swiss Guest House (p117)

» Yangkhil Resort (p111)

» Chumey Nature Resort (p113)

» Jakar Village Lodge (p117)

» Gongkhar Guest House (p118)

Best Views

» Trongsa Viewpoint (p109)

» Tower of Trongsa Museum (p111)

» Jakar Dzong (p114)

» Pelseling Goemba (p116)

» Kunzangdrak Goemba (p124)

Why Go?

Central Bhutan's forested mountains and fertile valleys comprise the country's cultural heartland. The region boasts several of Bhutan's oldest and most significant temples and monasteries, great day hikes and short treks, and several spectacular festivals.

Across the 3420m-high Pele La and the Black Mountains is the large, fertile Mangde Chhu valley and the magnificent Trongsa Dzong. Commanding the junction of three major roads, Trongsa has long been the glue that holds the country together. Even today the Crown Prince must serve as the *penlop* (regional governor) of the dzong before he can rule as king.

From Trongsa, a short, steep drive over the Yotong La (3425m) leads to the four valleys of Bumthang, a magical region of saints and treasure-seekers, great demon-subduing struggles and fabulous miracles, rich with relics from the visits of Guru Rinpoche and Pema Lingpa. Because it takes a little extra time to get here, Central Bhutan sees fewer tourists than Thimphu, Paro and Punakha.

When to Go

Central Bhutan, particularly the fertile valleys of Bumthang, is a year-round destination: pleasant in summer, and ideal in spring (especially for the rhododendron displays on the mountain passes) and also in autumn. Winters can be very cold, so bring appropriate clothing and don't be surprised if snow temporarily closes the high passes.

Ideally you should time your visit to include at least one of the colourful and fascinating festivals, such as at Ura, Trongsa Dzong, Jampey Lhakhang, or Kurjey Lhakhang (see p19).

Central Bhutan Highlights

① Explore sprawling **Trongsa Dzong** (p110), a dramatic example of traditional Bhutanese architecture

② Discover the heritage of Trongsa at the **Tower of Trongsa Museum** (p111)

③ Take one of the many excellent hikes in the **Bumthang valleys** (p116)

④ Wander around the **Kurjey Lhakhang** (p121) complex, a legacy of Guru Rinpoche

⑤ Visit one of Bhutan's oldest and most significant temples at **Jampey Lhakhang** (p119)

⑥ Circumambulate **Tamshing Goemba** (p122) wearing a cloak of chainmail made by Pema Lingpa

⑦ Pause at **Chendebji Chorten** (p108): smaller than, but patterned after, Swayambhunath in Kathmandu

⑧ Detour up the Tang Valley to the 100-year-old **Ogyen Chholing Palace** (p125), now home to a superb museum and bucolic guesthouse retreat

History

Central Bhutan is believed to be the first part of Bhutan to have been inhabited, with evidence of prehistoric settlements in the Ura valley of Bumthang and the southern region of Khyeng. These and many other valleys were separate principalities ruled by independent kings. One of the most important of these kings was the 8th-century Indian Sindhu Raja of Bumthang, who was eventually converted to Buddhism by Guru Rinpoche (see p185). Bumthang continued to be a separate kingdom, ruled from Jakar, until the time of Zhabdrung Ngawang Namgyal in the 17th century.

During the rule of the first *desi* (secular ruler), Tenzin Drugyey, all of eastern Bhutan came under the control of the Drukpa government in Punakha. Chhogyel Mingyur Tenpa unified central and eastern Bhutan into eight provinces known as Shachho Khorlo Tsegay. He was then promoted to Trongsa *penlop* (governor).

Because of Trongsa Dzong's strategic position, the *penlop* exerted great influence over the entire country. It was from Trongsa that Jigme Namgyal, father of the first king, rose to power.

Bumthang retained its political importance during the rule of the first and second kings, both of whom had their principal residence at Wangdichholing Palace in Jakar. Several impressive royal residences and country estates remain in the region, including at Kuenga Rabten, Eundu Chholing and Ogyen Chholing.

TRONGSA DZONGKHAG

Wangdue Phodrang to Trongsa

129KM / 4 HOURS

The route between the windswept town of Wangdi (Wangdue Phodrang's colloquial name), in western Bhutan, and Trongsa crosses the Black Mountains over the Pele La (3420m) before entering the broad, heavily cultivated Mangde Chhu valley. See p97 for details of the drive from Wangdi to the Pele La.

PELE LA TO CHENDEBJI

27KM / 1 HOUR

From Pele La the road drops through hillsides carpeted with a strange dwarf bamboo called *cham*. This bamboo never gets large enough to harvest for any useful purpose, but when it is small it is a favourite food of yaks and horses. The area near Pele La is probably the best place in Bhutan to see yaks from the road. Be alert, though, as these great shaggy beasts are skittish and likely to run off into the forest when your vehicle approaches.

The road drops into the evergreen forests of the Longte valley, passing Kgebji village and the Tashi Choeling Restaurant below the high village of **Longte**. Nine kilometres from the pass, a new hotel and restaurant were under construction at the time of research.

Lower down into the valley the vegetation changes to multi-hued broadleaved species and bamboo. The road passes opposite **Rukubji** village, with its large school and goemba at the end of a huge alluvial fan believed to be the body of a giant snake. The houses in this village are clustered closely together, an unusual layout for Bhutan. Surrounding the village are extensive fields of mustard, potatoes, barley and wheat.

About 16km from the pass keep an eye open on the left for the roadside rock inscription and mural that was left here in 2002 for the filming of the Bhutanese movie *Travellers and Magicians*. After the Buddhist blessing come the words 'Scene 112, take 101'!

The road enters a side valley and drops to **Sephu** (2610m), next to the bridge that spans the Nikka Chhu. This is the end point of the 25-day Snowman trek that starts from Paro and passes through the remote Lunana district (see p171). You could stop briefly to examine the bamboo mats and baskets for sale here, although most of the products are functional items. The larger baskets, called *zhim,* are tied to horses' pack saddles to transport goods. Tsering's restaurant-cum-bar beside the bridge offers *momos* (dumplings), tea and a clean toilet.

The road follows the Nikka Chhu to two chortens that mark the river's confluence with the Nyala Chhu. It is then a gentle, winding descent through rhododendrons, blue pines, spruces, oaks and dwarf bamboo to the village of Chendebji, recognisable by the yellow roof of its *lhakhang* (chapel), on the far bank. This was a night halt for mule caravans travelling from Trongsa during the reign of the second king.

Two kilometres beyond Chendebji village is **Chendebji Chorten**, at a lovely spot by a river confluence. The large white chorten is patterned after Swayambhunath in Kathmandu and was built in the 19th century by Lama Shida, from Tibet, to cover the remains of an evil spirit that was killed here. The proper name of this structure is Chorten Charo Kasho; it is the westernmost monument in a 'chorten path' that was the route of early Buddhist missionaries. (The easternmost monument in this path is Chorten Kora in Trashi Yangtse.) The nearby Bhutanese-style chorten was constructed in 1982.

Just 500m past the chorten is **Chendebji Resort** (☏03-440004; r Nu 1800; breakfast/lunch/dinner set meal Nu 200/300/350), a popular lunch spot and gift shop run by the owner of the Dochu La Resort, who is a renowned artist. The pine-clad rooms have attached bathrooms, some with tubs, and beds with deep mattresses.

CHENDEBJI TO TRONGSA
41KM / 1¼ HOURS

From Chendebji Chorten the road passes a few farms, crosses a side stream and climbs again to a ridge, passing above the village of Tangsibji. The valley widens and the road turns a corner into the broad Mangde Chhu valley. The shrubs along this part of the road are edgeworthia, which is used to make paper. The brown monkeys you will probably see are rhesus macaques.

At Tashiling, next to the Tashicholing Restaurant, you'll see **Potala Lhakhang**, consecrated in late 2005 by the Je Khenpo, Bhutan's Chief Abbot. Inside is an impressive thousand-armed 9m-tall statue of Chenresig (Avalokiteshvara), the Bodhisattva of Compassion, flanked on his left by a wrathful Guru Rinpoche in his 'collective thought manifestation' with consort, and on his right by a protector deity. In 2008 the King instigated construction of a *shedra* (religious school) here.

After the road weaves in and out of side valleys for another 5km you finally get a view of Trongsa and the imposing whitewashed dzong that seems to hang in the air at the head of the valley. On the opposite side of the huge Mangde Chhu valley you can see the road that heads south to Zhemgang and Gelephu near the Indian border. A **viewpoint** next to a small chorten in the centre of the road offers a good place for a photo stop and cup of tea. The

dzong looks almost close enough to touch but it is still 14km away. The **Viewpoint Restaurant** (breakfast/lunch Nu 200/300; ◷7am-7pm) hides underneath the viewing platform. From here you can walk to the dzong on the **Mangdue Foot-Trail** (◷7am-2pm), a two-hour, steep track that winds down to a cantilevered bridge over the Mangde Chhu before ascending to the western gate of the dzong. Your driver will need to drive ahead to the dzong so that the western gate will be unlocked for your arrival.

Above the viewpoint and road, the sprawling **Viewpoint Resort** was nearing completion of construction at the time of research. Plans include 64 traditionally styled rooms, a conference centre, gym, spa and swimming pool.

To reach Trongsa, you switch back into the upper reaches of the Mangde Chhu valley, cross the raging river at the Bjee Zam checkpost, and then climb again above the north bank of the river, past a waterfall and the Yangkhil Resort, before pulling into town.

Trongsa
☏03 / ELEV 2180M

Trongsa is smack in the middle of the country, a seven-hour drive from Thimphu, and separated from both east and west by high mountain ranges. The dzong and surrounding town is perched above a gorge, with fine views of the Black Mountains to the southwest. It's a sleepy and pleasant town, lined with whitewashed shops decorated with pot plants.

The town received a large influx of Tibetan immigrants in the late 1950s and early 1960s, and Bhutanese of Tibetan descent run most shops here. The Tibetans are so well assimilated into Bhutanese society that there is almost no indication of Tibetan flavour in the town.

The main road from the west traverses above the dzong and passes the weekend vegetable market and small Thruepang Palace (closed to visitors), where the third king, Jigme Dorji Wangchuck, was born in 1928. The road then climbs to a cluster of shops and hotels that form the bazaar. A traffic circle marks the junction of the road that leads south to Gelephu. A short walk down this road offers good views of the dzong.

Trongsa

Trongsa

◉ Top Sights

🛏 Sleeping

✖ Eating

🛍 Shopping

◉ Sights

Trongsa Dzong   DZONG
This commanding dzong, high above the roaring Mangde Chhu, is perhaps the most spectacularly sited dzong in Bhutan, with a sheer drop to the south that often just disappears into cloud and mist.

Trongsa Dzong has a rich history dating back to the 16th century. The first construction on the site was carried out by Lam Ngagi Wangchuck, son of Ngawang Chhojey, who established Pangri Zampa near Thimphu (see p66). He came to Trongsa in 1541 and built a *tshamkhang* (small meditation room) after discovering self-manifested hoof-prints belonging to the horse of the protector deity Pelden Lhamo. Trongsa ('New Village' in the local dialect) gets its name from the retreats, temples and hermit residences that soon grew up around the chapel.

The rambling assemblage of buildings that comprises the dzong trails down the ridge and is connected by a succession of alley-like corridors, wide stone stairs and beautiful paved courtyards. The southernmost part of the dzong, Chorten Lhakhang, is the location of the first hermitage, built in 1543. The dzong was built in its present form in 1644 by Chhogyel Mingyur Tenpa, the official who was sent by the Zhabdrung to unify eastern Bhutan. It was then enlarged at the end of the 17th century by the *desi,* Tenzin Rabgye. Its official name is Chhoekhor Raptentse Dzong, and it is also known by its short name of Choetse Dzong.

The dzong's strategic location gave it great power over this part of the country. The only trail between eastern and western Bhutan still leads straight through Trongsa and used to run directly through the dzong itself. This gave the Trongsa *penlop* enviable control over east–west trade and the tax revenue to be derived from it. Today most visitors enter through the main eastern gate, but energetic types can hike the **Mangdue Foot-Trail** from the viewpoint (see p109) and enter the dzong via the western gate, in traditional fashion.

Trongsa Dzong is the ancestral home of Bhutan's royal family. The first two hereditary kings ruled from this dzong, and tradition still dictates that the crown prince serve as Trongsa *penlop* before acceding to the throne. When the current king became *penlop* in 2004 the yellow roof was repainted red.

The Trongsa *rabdey* (district monk body) migrates between winter (Trongsa) and summer (Bumthang) residences, just as the main *dratshang* (central monk body) does between Thimphu and Punakha.

There are 23 separate lhakhangs in the dzong, though what you get to see depends on which keys are available. The dzong was severely damaged in the 1897 earthquake, and repairs were carried out by the *penlop* of Trongsa, Jigme Namgyal, father of Bhutan's first king. Most of the existing fine decoration was designed during the rule of the first king, Ugyen Wangchuck. More recent renovations were carried out by the Austrian team that restored the nearby Tower of Trongsa museum.

The atmospheric northern **assembly hall** is still preserved as it was during Ugyen Wangchuck's reign. There is a painting of the court as it was then, and other paintings of the guardians of the four directions and the deity Phurba in the main hall. There is also a 17th-century mural depicting Swayambhunath in Nepal and another with a pictorial map of Lhasa. The main chapel to the south, the **Chorten Lhakhang**, houses the funerary chorten of the founder, Ngagi Wangchuck.

The five-day Trongsa tsechu is held in the northern courtyard in December or January.

Tower of Trongsa Museum   MUSEUM
(admission Nu 200; ⊙9am-5pm Mon-Sat Apr-May, until 4pm Nov-Mar) This watchtower, or Ta Dzong, on the hill above the dzong has been converted into the excellent Tower of Trongsa Museum by the same Austrian-financed team that renovated the wonderful Patan Museum in Nepal. The state-of-the-art displays focus on Buddhist art and the history of the monarchy, and the tour starts with an audiovisual presentation. You are then guided up several floors of displays of statuary and royal memorabilia. There are sweeping views from the top, and a cafe on the ground floor provides tea, coffee, biscuits and lunch by prior arrangement.

There are two lhakhangs inside the Ta Dzong; the Gesar Lhakhang is dedicated to the 19th-century *penlop* of Trongsa, Jigme Namgyal. Two British soldiers are said to have been kept in the dungeon here for several months during the Duar War.

Currently access is via a merit-earning slog up a steep stone stairway; however, a road and car park were under construction when we visited.

🛏 Sleeping & Eating

Yangkhil Resort   HOTEL $$
(☏521417; yangkhilresort@druknet.bt; s/d Nu 2200/2400, deluxe Nu 2700/3000; @) This resort, 1.5km west of town, is a good choice, with accommodation constructed on a terraced hill facing the dzong. Rooms are spacious and relaxing with heating, a balcony and extremely comfortable beds (but no TV). The pleasant grounds, vistas and restaurant make it a great place to relax, so arrange your itinerary to ensure an early arrival or late departure. Request one of the six view rooms in advance, as some rooms have only partial views.

Puenzhi Guest House   HOTEL $$
(☏521197; puenzhi@druknet.bt; s/d Nu 1600/2000, deluxe r Nu 2500; @) A 4km drive above the town leads to this place, run by the former governor of Trongsa. The rooms in the new wing are the best – airy and spacious with eagle-eye views from the balconies down to Ta Dazong and Trongsa Dzong. The older rooms are cosier, with smaller bathrooms and less private balconies. The restaurant balcony also offers great aerial views of Trongsa Dzong and steep foot-paths lead down to the Ta Dzong.

Hotel Shambala   LOCAL $$
(☏521171; fax 521178; s/d Nu 1300/1600) This hotel is run by the same family that owns the Norling Hotel. Rooms here are marginally fresher than the Norling's rooms, and you can also get recommended Tibetan and Bhutanese dishes here.

Norling Hotel   LOCAL $$
(☏521171; fax 521178; s/d Nu 1300/1600) This concrete hotel in the bazaar occupies a spot somewhere between a local and tourist hotel. Rooms are small and bathrooms are basic, while the food dished up in the pleasant dining room is quite good.

Oyster House   RESTAURANT $
(Map p110; ☏521413) This popular restaurant boasts a sunny balcony overlooking the main strip and a large menu featuring Indian, Bhutanese, Chinese and continental dishes. Pride of place goes to the full-size snooker table, which accounts for Oyster's popularity with Trongsa's teens.

Several small Tibetan-style 'hotels' offer hearty meals of *ema datse,* noodles, vegetables and, occasionally, meat and momos. Their basic accommodation is not usually available for foreign tourists, but the hotels can be good places to mix with locals and share a drink and a meal. These include, among others, the **Ugyen Chholing Hotel** (☏521400) and **Nidar Karsum Lodge** (☏521133). Expect to pay about Nu 80 for a meal of rice, curry and vegetables.

🛍 Shopping

Phuntsho Wangmo Bhutanese Handicraft & General Shop   HANDICRAFTS
(⊙7am-7pm) The Phuntsho shop stocks a good selection of hand-woven textiles, masks and metalwork in addition to everyday goods.

ⓘ Information

Bank of Bhutan (⊙9am-1pm Mon-Fri, to 11am Sat) You need a photocopy of the cheque to change travellers cheques here.

Post Office (⊙8.30am-5pm Mon-Fri, to 1pm Sat)

Around Trongsa

KUENGA RABTEN

The winter palace of the second king, Jigme Wangchuck, is 23km (one hour) south of Trongsa. It's an interesting drive, passing below Takse Goemba (after 17km), several huge waterfalls, and the fertile rice terraces of the lower Mangde Chhu valley. It's a good half-day or three-quarter-day trip from Trongsa and could even make for a fine bike trip if you can arrange to be picked up at Kuenga Rabten. Traffic is light and it's all downhill from Trongsa!

The palace is under the care of the National Commission for Cultural Affairs so you don't need a special permit to enter. The first storey of the U-shaped building was used to store food; the second was the residence of royal attendants and the army; and the third housed the royal quarters and the king's private chapel. Part of this floor has been converted into a library, and books from the National Library are stored here. Sandwiched between the king's and queen's quarters is the Sangye Lhakhang, with statues of Sakyamuni, the Zhabdrung and Guru Rinpoche.

A 15-minute hike uphill from the building is the **Karma Drubdey Nunnery**, which is currently being expanded by its hardworking *anim* (Buddhist nuns).

A further 25km down the valley is **Eundu Chholing**, the winter palace of the first king, Ugyen Wangchuck. From Kuenga Rabten the road drops down in huge loops, past Refey village to the river and road camp at Yourmu, and then 2km later branches up a dirt road to the palace. The building belongs to a local Dasho (noble) but is looked after by the *dzongpen* (lord of the dzong), and tourists can normally visit. The 2nd-floor *goenkhang* (chapel devoted to protective deities; men only) has a highly venerated chorten of Pema Lingpa, as well as a fabulous collection of arms and a lovely *dranyen* (lute). The entry chapel has some of the finest murals you'll see, depicting the mythical kingdoms of Zangto Pelri and Sukhavati.

BUMTHANG DZONGKHAG

The Bumthang region encompasses four major valleys: Chokhor, Tang, Ura and Chhume. Because the dzongs and the most important temples are in the large Chokhor valley, it is commonly referred to as the Bumthang valley.

There are two versions of the origin of the name Bumthang. The valley is supposed to be shaped like a *bumpa*, the vessel of holy water that is usually found on the altar of a lhakhang. *Thang* means 'field' or 'flat place'. The less respectful translation relates to the particularly beautiful women who live here – *bum* means 'girl'.

See p21 for details of the Nomad's Festival, which is held in December.

For a more detailed map of the region, see p166.

Trongsa to Jakar
68KM / 2½ HOURS

The run between Trongsa and Jakar, the main town in Bumthang, is one of the easier and more interesting drives in Bhutan because it passes numerous villages and goembas as it winds through the Chhume valley.

TRONGSA TO YOTONG LA
28KM / 1 HOUR

The road zigzags up the ridge above Trongsa, climbing steeply past the Puenzhi Guest House then the small Dorji Goemba to the head of a valley. Finally the road traverses the top of the valley to a Tibetan chorten and array of prayer flags atop the **Yotong La** (3425m). The old trade route to eastern Bhutan parallels the modern road as it crosses the pass.

YOTONG LA TO ZUNGNEY
24KM / 1 HOUR

The descent from the pass is through firs, then blue pines and bamboo. The road enters the upper part of the Chhume valley, marked by the small roadside Chuchi Lhakhang at Gaytsa. On a hill 10 minutes' walk to the north of Gaytsa is the Nyingma school **Buli Lhakhang**, built by Tukse Chhoying, the son of Dorji Lingpa (1346–1405) and recently renovated with assistance from the American Himalayan Foundation (see www.ahf-bhutan.com for details). On the ground floor is the Jowo

Lhakhang, with some impressive 12-sided pillars, or *kachens,* and on the upper floor is the Sangay (or Sangey) Lhakhang, named after images of the past, present and future Buddhas. The mural by the window depicts Dorji Lingpa. Look above the stairs to the upper story for a slate carving of the local protective deity. A few black-necked cranes winter in the fields to the northeast of the village.

The red roofs of **Tharpaling Goemba** are visible above the trees on a cliff to the northeast. Nyingma (Dzogchen) philosopher and saint Longchen Rabjampa (1308–63) founded Tharpaling as part of eight *lings* (outlying temples) and lived here for many years, fathering two children. It has several temples and houses more than 100 monks with a new *shedra* under construction. It's possible to visit the goemba by driving 10km up a rough road through bucolic countryside or by trekking over the hill from Jakar (see p116). Above Tharpaling, at about 3800m, is the white hermitage of Choedrak Goemba, which consists of two ancient chapels separated by a chorten and a sacred spring. The Thukje Lhakhang to the right has a central 1000-armed statue of Chenresig. The Lorepa Lhakhang contains a stone footprint of Guru Rinpoche and the stone skull of a *dakini* (*khandroma*, or female celestial being). Further uphill is the Zhambhala Lhakhang, named after the popular God of Wealth. Pilgrims ask for boons here at a set of circular grooves in the rock behind the lhakhang, which contains the surprisingly grand funeral chorten of Nyoshul Khen Rinpoche. Pema Lingpa revealed several *terma* (sacred texts and artefacts) near these monasteries.

Back on the main road, and less than a kilometre from the Tharpaling turn-off, a bridge crosses the Gaytsa Chhu and a signposted gravel road leads off to the **Chumey Nature Resort** (☎03-641286; www.chumey natureresort.com; s/d Nu 1875/2500, ste Nu 3500; @) a fabulous rural retreat surrounded by fields and forests with numerous walking trails. Black-necked cranes overwinter in the fields below the resort, and luxurious rooms are comfortable, cosy and private. There is an excellent bar with TV and balcony and a very good multicuisine restaurant. The resort has its own lhakhang and can cater for visitors wishing to learn about Buddhism.

The main road follows the Gaytsa Chhu gently down the valley for 2km to Domkhar. A dirt road branches south for about 900m to **Domkhar Trashi Chholing Dzong**, the summer palace of the second king. It was completed in 1937 and is a replica of Kuenga Rabten (see p112). It served for years as the residence of the grand queen mother, and is now a guesthouse for the king and so is closed to visitors. The monastic school to the south was built in 1968 by the previous reincarnation of the Karmapa, the head of the Karmapa lineage.

Beyond Domkhar village, past Hurjee, is the settlement of Chhume, with two large schools alongside more than 500m of straight road, perhaps the longest stretch of its kind in the hills of Bhutan. Speed bumps have been strategically placed to ensure that your driver does not take advantage of this to make up time!

A little further on is **Yid Ga Handicraft Shop**, and 1km beyond it, at Zungney you pass the 1.5MW Chhume mini-hydro plant, which supplies electricity to Trongsa and Bumthang. Just before Zungney a new paved road branches off to Nimalung Goemba (p114).

Stop at the two shops at the eastern end of Zungney village to watch the weavers. The speciality here is *yathra,* distinctive strips of woven woollen fabric in numerous colours and patterns (see p114). You can buy single strips of cloth or woollen jackets and blankets. Zungney Lhakhang is the small building to the west of the **Thogme Yeshe Handicraft & Yathra Production Centre** (⊙6am-8pm). Just past Zungney look out for some unusual two-storey prayer wheels.

ZUNGNEY TO JAKAR
16KM / 30 MINS

East of Zungney, **Prakhar Goemba** is visible on a promontory on the opposite side of the river. It's a delightful 10-minute walk to the three-storey goemba, which was built as a residence by Dawa Gyaltshen, a son of the famous Pema Lingpa (see the boxed text, p189). On the ground floor is a statue of Sakyamuni crafted by artists from Nepal. On the middle floor are statues of Guru Tshengay, the eight manifestations of Guru Rinpoche. The top floor contains nine small chortens and murals that are as old as the goemba. The Prakhar tsechu is held in autumn (middle of the ninth month) in the courtyard of a nearby newer building.

A stiff 20-minute walk uphill from Prakhar leads to **Nimalung Goemba**, a Nyingma monastery that was founded in 1935 by Dorling Trulku. It now houses more than 100 monks, who study here in the *shedra*. The ground-floor inner chapel contains a venerated statue of Drolma (Tara) inside an amulet. Walk behind the cabinets full of statues to see the collection of black hats used during the tsechu in the fifth month (around July). Also here are large metal boxes, one of which holds a *thondrol* (a large *thangka* – a painted or embroidered religious picture) depicting the eight manifestations of Guru Rinpoche. The upper floor is a *goenkhang*. Outside you might catch the monks playing *khuru,* a game that is part darts, part archery.

The road follows the valley down past the apple orchards of Nangar and into blue-pine forests. A new road is being built from here to Ura, bypassing Jakar. It's a short climb to the Kiki La, a crest at 2860m marked by a chorten and many prayer flags. Once over the side ridge, the road descends into the Chokhor valley.

YATHRA

Hand-spun, hand-woven wool strips with patterns specific to the Bumthang region are called *yathras*. They mostly have geometric designs, sometimes with a border. Three strips may be joined to produce a blanket or bed-cover called a *charkep*.

In earlier days *yathras* were often used as shawls or raincoats to protect against the winter cold of Bumthang. *Yathras* were once made from wool from Tibet; nowadays some of the wool is imported from New Zealand and some wool is used from nearby Australian-supported sheep-breeding projects.

Since Bhutan does not have the carpet-weaving tradition of Tibet, *yathra* pieces have often served the same function as Tibetan rugs. Today *yathras* are fashioned into *toegos*, the short jackets that women often wear over the *kira* (traditional dress) in cold weather.

Jakar

03 / ELEV 2580M

Near the foot of the Chokhor valley, Jakar (or Chakkar) is the major trading centre of the region. This will probably be your base for several days as you visit the surrounding valleys. The road from Trongsa enters Jakar from the south, passing a football field that doubles as an army helipad. A traffic circle and the 14th-century **Jakar Lhakhang** mark the centre of the town. A new airport under construction on the east bank of the Chamkhar Chhu is expected to revolutionise tourism when it is operational by early 2011.

Jakar itself is a bustling one-street town, with a goldsmith, tailors, several butchers, cafes, restaurants and handicraft stores, and it's well worth a wander. As with other towns in Bhutan, Jakar plans to shift location to a new town, just north of the Sey Lhakhang. Though the new town roads are complete, no date has been given as yet for the big move.

The main street leads east from here to a bridge over the Chamkhar Chhu. Just before you cross the bridge to leave the town, a small chorten marks the spot where a Tibetan general's head was buried after the defeat of a 17th-century Tibetan invasion force. From the bridge roads lead north to the Swiss Guest House and the east bank of the Chamkhar Chhu, and south to Mongar and eastern Bhutan.

Bumthang has some important festivals, of which the most important is the Jampey Lhakhang Drup, in the ninth month (October). The three-day Bumthang tsechu, a week earlier, features mask dancing in the dzong, while Tamshing, Ngang and Ura monasteries all have large festivals. See p20 for approximate dates.

There is a strong up-valley wind from the south every afternoon, which makes Jakar nippy in the evenings.

◉ Sights

Jakar Dzong   DZONG

(Map p115) According to legend, when the lamas assembled in about 1549 to select a site for a monastery, a big white bird rose suddenly in the air and settled on a spur of a hill. This was interpreted as an important omen, and the hill was chosen as the site for a monastery and for Jakar Dzong, which roughly translates as 'castle of the white

CENTRAL BHUTAN JAKAR

Jakar

◉ Top Sights
Jakar Dzong	A3
Wangdichholing Palace	B1

◉ Sights
1	Bumthang Brewery	C1
2	Namkhe Nyingpo Goemba	D3

⊜ Sleeping
3	Amankora	B1
4	Hotel Wangdichholing	B1
5	Jakar Village Lodge	B3
6	Kaila Guest House	B3

7	Mepham Guest House	D2
8	Mountain Lodge	A1
9	Swiss Guest House	D1

⊗ Eating
10	7-eleven Cafe	C3
11	Sunny Restaurant	D3

⊜ Shopping
12	Bumthang Handicraft Shop	C3
13	Handicrafts Emporium	A2
14	Sonam Handicrafts	C3
15	Yoser Lham Shop	C1

bird'. The Zhabdrung's great-grandfather, Ngagi Wangchuck, founded the monastery.

Jakar Dzong is in a picturesque location overlooking the Chokhor valley. The current structure was built in 1667 and has a circumference of more than 1500m. Its official name is Yuelay Namgyal Dzong, in honour of the victory over the troops of Tibetan ruler Phuntsho Namgyal. The *utse* (central tower) is unusually situated on the outside wall, so there is no way to circumambulate it. A covered passage leads from the dzong down the hill to a nearby spring – a feature

that ensured water could be obtained in the event of a long siege.

The approach to the dzong is made on foot along a stone-paved path. The entrance leads into a narrow courtyard surrounded by administrative offices. The *utse* is on the east side of the courtyard, and beyond that is the monks' quarters and the district court. At the west end of the dzong is a slightly larger courtyard surrounded by administrative offices. Behind here, outside the main dzong, is a half-round *ta dzong*, or watchtower.

Compared to other dzongs, there are relatively few woodcarvings here; most of the timber is decorated with paintings.

Even if the chapels are closed, it's a worthwhile climb for the views of the Chokhor valley from the front courtyard.

Wangdichholing Palace PALACE

(Map p115) The extensive palace of Wangdichholing was built in 1857 on the site of a battle camp of the *penlop* of Trongsa, Jigme Namgyal. It was the first palace in Bhutan that was not designed as a fortress. Namgyal's son, King Ugyen Wangchuck, the first King of Bhutan, chose it as his principal residence. The entire court moved from Wangdichholing to Kuenga Rabten (see p112) each winter in a procession that took three days. Wangdichholing was also for a time the home of the third king, before he moved the court to Punakha in 1952.

Wangdichholing was inherited by Ashi Choeki Wangchuck, an aunt of the fourth king, and the grand but rather neglected building is now used as a *lobdra* (monastic school). There are five giant prayer wheels inside square chortens just to the north. The modern whitewashed building next door is the Amankora resort.

Namkhe Nyingpo Goemba MONASTERY

(Map p115) On the hill to the east of Jakar is the Namkhe Nyingpo Goemba. This Nyingma monastery was founded in the 1970s and has more than 300 monks in residence. The new prayer hall has massive statues of Guru Rinpoche, Chenresig and Sakyamuni. If you're here between 4.30pm and 6pm check out the mass debating in the courtyard of the *shedra,* behind the main monastery, where monks reinforce their theological arguments with a stamp of the foot and a victorious slap. Don't disturb the debating with your photography.

Lamey Goemba MONASTERY

High on a hill sits Lamey Goemba, a large palace and monastery built in the 1800s as a residence for King Ugyen Wangchuck. Its design is in the palace style of the time and is similar to Wangdichholing. It is now being used by the Integrated Forest Development Project and isn't formally open to visitors.

Sleeping

Most of Bumthang's guesthouses follow a similar design, with pine-clad rooms and separate dining rooms, and the majority

---

WORTH A TRIP

WALKING THE BUMTHANG VALLEYS

There are plenty of opportunities for day hikes in the Bumthang region, many involving visits to remote goembas. If you are on a tourist visa, take advantage of the vehicle at your disposal and arrange for the driver to pick you up at the end of a walk.

From Swiss Guest House in Jakar to **Pelseling Goemba** is a favourite half-day walk, descending a different route to Tamshing Goemba in a total of about four hours' walking. The first half is all uphill (2½ hours) but is more varied than the hike to Tharpaling, through a mix of forest, meadows and villages, and you are rewarded with great views. Carry a packed lunch or flask of tea to enjoy at the monastery.

You can also walk from Lamey Goemba over the ridge to **Tharpaling Goemba** (p113), at 3500m in the Chhume valley, and meet your vehicle there. The trail branches off a logging road 1km past the goemba. The first two hours are a hard uphill slog through rhododendron and bamboo, before you finally cross a pass and descend across the bare hillsides of the Chhume valley to the Zhambhala Lhakhang, Choedrak Hermitage, and finally Tharpaling. The hike offers less in the way of views but more the feel of a pilgrimage, taking in several sacred sites. Check for ticks along this route.

A good full-day excursion is to hike up the valley from **Thangbi Goemba** (p122) to **Ngang Lhakhang** (p122). This is the first day of the Bumthang Cultural trek (p166).

A longer day hike leads from the Swiss Guest House over the ridge to **Kunzangdrak Goemba** (see p124).

The best short walk is between **Kurjey Lhakhang** (p121) and **Tamshing Goemba** (p122) via the Dozam and rock paintings of Lha Kharpo. You can also walk down the east valley road from Konchogsum Lhakhang to the Bumthang Brewery (5km) for fine views of Jakar and the Chokhor Valley.

are family run. More recently, large travel agencies and hoteliers have built impressive large hotels that provide unequalled luxury but lack the cosy guesthouse atmosphere. Most guesthouses and hotels have *bukhari*s (wood stoves) to heat the rooms. If you're cold, ask the room attendants to light the stove – they start it with a dollop of kerosene and a *whump*! The *bukhari*s heat the room quickly, but don't burn for very long.

JAKAR

The following hotels are either in Jakar town or on the outskirts.

Swiss Guest House   HOTEL $$
(Map p115; ☎631145; swissguesthouse@druknet. bt; s/d Nu 1900/1980, deluxe r Nu 3200; @) It doesn't get more bucolic than this wooden farmhouse surrounded by apple orchards on a hill overlooking the valley. In 1983 this was the first guesthouse in Bumthang, but there have been plenty of upgrades since then. Rooms in the new wing are spacious and warm, with good beds and bathrooms. The water supply to the main building is from a spring and probably the only place in South Asia advertising that you can safely drink the tap water. The bar is also one of the few places in Bhutan where you can get Red Panda beer on draught, guaranteed fresh, since it's brewed just down the road!

Jakar Village Lodge   HOTEL $$
(Map p115; ☎631242; gyeldup@druknet.bt; s/d Nu 2300/2500, deluxe Nu 2800/3000; @) Boasting some of the best food in Bumthang, this hotel situated down a narrow village lane below the dzong is run by an ex-*dzongdag* (district administrator) who will regale you with stories as you sample his assortment of teas and real freshly ground coffee. Rooms are spotless and comfortable, while the sunny terrace enjoys great views over the valley and up to the dzong. There is also secure parking.

Hotel Wangdichholing   HOTEL $$
(Map p115; ☎631369; hotelwangdichholing@ druknet.bt; s/d Nu 2100/2500; @) Owned by one of Bhutan's biggest travel agencies, this hotel is close to the Wangdichholing Palace and offers above-average accommodation. Standard rooms are almost suites with their separate sitting area heated with a *bukhari* and private balcony. The small bathrooms, however, don't carry the same

level of luxury. There is a decent multi-cuisine restaurant and a relaxing bar.

River Lodge   HOTEL $$
(☎631287; pemadawa@druknet.bt; s/d Nu 1490/ 1590; deluxe from 1790/1890; @) This popular place has a variety of rooms overlooking the valley south of town. The lodge has helpful management, a small library and a hot-stone bath (Nu 750 per person) in the laundry. The bright dining room has great valley views, good food and a warming *bukhari*. The owner also runs the Mesithang River Lodge in the Tang Valley.

Kaila Guest House   HOTEL $$
(Map p115; ☎631219; kailaguesthouse@druknet .bt; standard/deluxe r Nu 1500/1990; @) This is the closest hotel to Jakar bazaar and is frequented by NGO workers, who get a hefty discount on the cosy rooms. The owner was the cook at the Swiss Guest House for many years, so the food is very good and the friendly welcome is genuine in this unpretentious establishment. The restaurant and bar is a great place to catch up with what's happening in Bumthang as locals, tourists, officials and NGOs join in conversation with the garrulous owner.

Yu-Gharling Resort   HOTEL $$
(☎631948; yughaling@druknet.bt; r standard/de-luxe Nu 2950/3500, ste from Nu 3800; @) This new luxury option overlooking the valley is as enormous as it is luxurious. Rooms are massive and the views are spectacular. Though there are no TVs in the rooms, hotel facilities include a spacious bar with sofas and snooker tables, a gym, massage spa, and a backing Jacuzzi and hot-stone bath.

Amankora   LUXURY HOTEL $$$
(Map p115; ☎02 331333; www.amanresorts.com; s/d US$1300/1400; @) The last word in luxury in Bumthang, the dzonglike Amankora sits beside the Wangdichholing Palace in serene grounds. Rooms are spacious with king-size beds, soaring ceilings and a central, sumptuous bathtub. Rates include all meals in the multicuisine restaurant.

Mountain Lodge   HOTEL $$
(Map p115; ☎631255; mtnlodge@druknet.bt; s/d Nu 1900/2100; @) This cosy lodge has wood-panelled rooms in a large two-storey building overlooking Wangdichholing Palace. Friendly staff, tasty food and good rooms and bathrooms make this a very pleasant place to stay.

Mepham Guest House GUESTHOUSE **$$**
(Map p115; ☏631738; mephamgh@druknet.bt; standard/deluxe r Nu 1650/1760; @) This secret guesthouse belongs to the Namke Nyingpo Goemba and nestles below the monastery. The rooms are basic but comfortable, and the best have views across the valley to the dzong.

Hotel Home HOTEL **$$**
(☏631444; hotelhomebtn@yahoo.com; r Nu 2500; @) Hotel Home has simple pine-clad rooms – try and get one with a valley view – with large bathrooms that oddly face the corridor. The large dining room is made cosy with a big *bukhari*.

CHOKHOR VALLEY
The following hotels are outside Jakar bazaar in the surrounding Chokhor valley but still within easy reach of the town and with quiet rural locations.

Gongkhar Guest House HOTEL **$$**
(Map p120; ☏631288; tsheringgong@yahoo.com; s/d Nu 1755/1995, deluxe s/d Nu 3000/3500; @) This excellent hotel, 1.5km southeast of Jakar, has spacious and comfortable rooms with *bukhari*s and superclean bathrooms. There's a good view of the dzong, garden seating among amazing roses, and excellent service, and the food is among the best and most varied in the valley. The eight new deluxe rooms are exceptionally comfortable.

Lodge Rinchenling HOTEL **$$**
(Map p120; ☏631147; jampel@druknet.bt; s/d from Nu 1500/1700; @) This hotel is run by amiable Dasho Jampel Ngedup and family. It has spacious rooms with large bathrooms, and an excellent restaurant. Rooms are in buildings scattered among the apple trees, and there is an ingenious hot-stone bath set-up.

Wangdicholing Resort HOTEL **$$**
(Map p120; ☏631452; wangdicholingresort@druknet.bt; s/d Nu 1700/1800; @) This is another well-run place, on a bluff overlooking the valley to the south of town. The main building has a relaxing balcony festooned with climbing flowers. Rooms are a bit old-fashioned but spacious and comfortable.

Hotel Pelling HOTEL **$$**
(Map p120; ☏631222; www.hotelpeling.com.bt; s/d r Nu 3000/3500, ste Nu 5000; @) This lavish new hotel has very spacious rooms with big bathrooms and balconies, and exceptional valley views abound. Rooms are heated, but there are no TVs. There is a dedicated bar and a cavernous restaurant, and a hot-stone bath is available.

Leki Guest House HOTEL **$$**
(Map p120; ☏631231; lekilodge@druk net.bt; s/d Nu 1800/2500) The Leki is one of the oldest hotels in the valley and is showing its age, though 15 new rooms were under construction when we visited. The dining room is decorated with home-made weavings (for sale), and some Japanese dishes are available. Textile buffs will enjoy the traditional dyeing demonstration.

Yozerling Lodge HOTEL **$$**
(Map p120; ☏631846; yozerling@yahoo.com; s/d Nu 1700/1800; @) This typical Bumthang hotel has comfortable pine-clad rooms and an extra-large dining hall. The comfy sofas around the *bukhari* in the dining hall make for cosy pre- and post-dinner drinks.

✗ Eating
The hotels in Bumthang do a great job feeding their guests hearty local and continental food, and there's even some healthy competition among hotels in the culinary stakes. Because of the altitude, buckwheat is the crop of choice in Bumthang and buckwheat noodles and pancakes are a Bumthang speciality. The Bumthang Chhu is also famous for its trout, and despite Buddhist prohibitions on the taking of life, fish do mysteriously appear on hotel dinner plates.

There are plenty of small bars and local restaurants along Jakar's main street, the brightest and cleanest of which is **Sunny Restaurant** (Map p115; ☏631879; mains Nu 40-85; ☉7am-9pm Mon-Sat), with Bhutanese, Chinese and continental dishes.

If you're craving Western-style food head to the petite **7-eleven Cafe** (Map p115; mains Nu 35-150; ☉8am-9pm), an internet cafe where you can purchase real espresso, pizza by the slice, and scrumptious home-baked muffins. There's also Red Panda beer on tap.

🔒 Shopping
As in most towns in Bhutan, the shops in Jakar contain a hodgepodge of goods, many of which are from China. A typical shop may sell shoes, pens, nails, soap, toy cars, dried fish, prayer flags, and the ubiquitous mobile phone vouchers. Another item in good supply in Jakar is *chugo*, dried cheese. Unless you want to break your teeth, let a piece soften for a long time in your mouth before you bite into it.

Yoser Lham Shop FOOD

(Map p115; ☎631193; ⏱5am-7pm) Yoser Lham is the main outlet for the Swiss Farm enterprises. The shop sells Red Panda beer, apple juice, peach brandy and apple or honey wine, as well as soft Gouda or hard Emmenthal cheese at Nu 300 per kg. This cheese is made for eating off the block, unlike the soft Bhutanese *datse,* which is used only in sauces. Honey is usually available in July and August.

Handicrafts Emporium HANDICRAFTS

(Map p115; ☎631576; ⏱9am-6pm) This showroom of a government-supported handicraft project sells textiles, wooden bowls, tables runners and *ghos* (traditional dress for men). It's opposite the turn-off to the Amankora and Wangdichholing Palace.

Sonam Handicrafts HANDICRAFTS

(Map p115; ☎631370; ⏱9am-6pm) Sonam has pricey but nice pieces, including *chang* (barley beer) holders and ornate *gau* (amulets). Credit cards incur a surcharge of 5%.

Bumthang Handicraft Shop HANDICRAFTS

(Map p115; ⏱9am-6pm) Also in the bazaar, this shop is strong on textiles from eastern Bhutan.

ⓘ Information

Bank of Bhutan (Map p115; ☎631123; ⏱9am-1pm Mon-Fri, to 11am Sat)

Bumthang Medical Store (Map p115; ⏱8am-7pm) For medical supplies.

7-eleven Cafe (Map p115; ⏱8am-9pm; per 15 min Nu 70) Internet access.

ⓘ Getting There & Away

At the time of writing a new **domestic airport** was under construction east of the Chamkhar Chhu. It should be operating when you get there. **Metho Transport** has Coasters to Thimphu (Nu 272, 12 hours) daily except Monday, boarding at 5.30am and departing at 6am. Taxis congregate east of the Jakar Lhakhang.

Chokhor Valley

To most people the Chokhor valley *is* Bumthang and the Chokhor valley is often called the Bumthang valley or just simply Bumthang. It's possible to visit Jampey and Kurjey lhakhangs in the morning, cross the river and have a packed lunch at Do Zam, and then visit Tamshing and Konchogsum lhakhangs in the afternoon.

BUMTHANG CHEESE & CHEERS

Bumthang's famous Swiss Farm is a mature development project that was established by Fritz Maurer, one of the first Swiss to work in Bhutan. The project introduced cheese-making, brewing, farming machinery and fuel-efficient wood stoves to the valley, as well as its first tourist guesthouse. The delicious cheese from Bhutan's only commercial cheese factory is sold in the farm's **Yoser Lham Shop**. And nearby, Bhutan's best beer, **Red Panda**, is brewed in a state-of-the-art microbrewery. It's possible to tour the **Bumthang Brewery** (Map p115; admission US$3; ⏱7.30-5pm, closed Sat afternoon & Sun, also during brewing and bottling times), where you will learn about the making of Red Panda from the brewer Tshering, before sampling the end product – a hot-mash, top-fermented natural ale. Purrfect...

WESTERN SIDE OF THE VALLEY

The road that leads up the western side of the valley connects a string of interesting temples which are connected in one way or another with the visit of Guru Rinpoche to Bumthang in 746. A mountain bike would offer a great way to link up the monasteries and continue over to the east bank.

Sey (Gold) Lhakhang

Beyond the hospital north of Jakar is the Sey Lhakhang. Properly known as Lhodrak Seykhar Dratshang, this is a monastic school established in 1963. The central figure in the lhakhang is Marpa Lotsawa, a great teacher and translator of the Kagyu lineage. The chapel is open to visitors.

⌖TOP CHOICE Jampey Lhakhang

This fabulous temple is up a short side road about 1.5km past Sey Lhakhang. It is believed to have been built in the year 659 by the Tibetan king Songtsen Gampo, on the same day as Kyichu Lhakhang in Paro, in order to subdue a Tibetan demoness (see the boxed text, p83).

The temple was visited by Guru Rinpoche during his visit to Bumthang and was renovated by the Sindhu Raja after the Guru restored his life force (see p185). It has been repaired several times, and a golden

Chokhor Valley

Chokhor Valley

Sights

Sleeping

roof built over time by various *penlops* of Trongsa.

Inside the main Jampey (or Jampa) Lhakhang are three **stone steps** representing ages. The first signifies the past, the age of the Historical Buddha, Sakyamuni. This step has descended into the ground and is covered with a wooden plank. The next age is the present, and its step is level with the floor. The top step represents a new age. It is believed that when the step representing the present age sinks to ground level, the gods will become like humans and the world as it is now will end.

The central figure in the ancient inner sanctum is **Jampa**, the Buddha of the Future, with his feet on an elephant. This is the oldest part of the oldest chapel in Bhutan. The statue is protected by an iron chainmail that was made by Pema Lingpa. Look up into the alcove above the entry to see a statue of Guru Rinpoche. He sat in this alcove and meditated, leaving behind a footprint. It is said that under the lhakhang there is a lake with several *terma* (sacred texts and artefacts hidden by Guru Rinpoche).

The inner *kora* (circumambulation) path around the chapel is lined with ancient-looking murals. There are more lovely murals in the atrium. On the right side of the wooden wall divider is an image of Kimlha, the goddess of the home.

On the northern side of the courtyard is the **Kalachakra Temple** (Dus-Kyi-khorlo), added by Ugyen Wangchuck when he was *penlop*. Chimi Dorji, the administrator of Jakar Dzong, added the Guru Lhakhang, on the south side of the *dochey* (courtyard), which features statues of Guru Rinpoche, Tsepame and Chenresig. Above the entryway is the Sangay Lhakhang.

Behind the main temple are two large stone **chortens**; one is in memory of the second king's younger brother, Gongsar Dorji. Nearby is a chorten in memory of Lama Pentsen Khenpo, spiritual adviser to the first and second Bhutanese kings. The four corners of the complex are anchored by four more chortens, coloured yellow, red, white and blue.

The pile of carved *mani* stones (stones carved with the Buddhist mantra *om mani peme hum*) in the parking lot in front of the goemba is called a *thos* and represents the Guardians of the Four Directions.

Each October one of the most spectacular festivals in Bhutan, the **Jampa Lhakhang Drup**, is staged here. The festival ground and VIP viewing platform is to the left (south) of the chapel. On one evening, after the lama dances, the monastery is lit by a bonfire for a *mewang* (fertility rite, a fire blessing at a bonfire), when pilgrims jump through a burning archway. Another late-night rite is the *tercham* (fertility rite known as a treasure dance or 'naked' dance), normally performed at midnight.

Tourists need a Cultural Affairs permit to visit the lhakhang, which your travel agency will arrange for you.

Chakhar Lhakhang

Beside the main road, a short distance beyond Jampa Lhakhang, is **Chakhar (Iron Castle) Lhakhang**. Although it is easy to mistake it for a house, this is an interesting temple and worth a short visit. It is the site of the palace of the Indian king Sendha Gyab, better known as the Sindhu Raja (see p185), who first invited Guru Rinpoche to Bumthang. The original palace was made of iron, hence the name Chakhar; it was said to have been nine storeys high, holding within it all the treasures of the world.

The current building was built in the 14th century by the saint Dorji Lingpa and its correct name is Dechen Phodrang. The main statue is of Guru Rinpoche, and there are dozens of masks and black hats that are used during the Jampey Lhakhang Drup festival.

Opening hours are a bit hit and miss, and you may have to pay several visits to find the caretaker in.

TOP CHOICE Kurjey Lhakhang

This large, active and important temple complex is named after the body (*kur*) print (*jey*) of Guru Rinpoche, which is preserved in a cave inside the oldest of the three buildings that make up the temple complex. It is at the end of the paved road, 2.5km from Chakhar Lhakhang.

As you enter the complex, there are three large lhakhangs against a hillside on the right. The first temple, the **Guru Lhakhang**, is the oldest and was built in 1652 by Mingyur Tenpa (see p128) when he was *penlop* of Trongsa. Tucked just below the eaves is a figure of a snow lion with a *jachung* (also called *garuda*) above it, which represents the famous struggle between Guru Rinpoche (appearing as the *garuda*) and the local demon, Shelging Kharpo (as the snow lion).

At the entrance to the lower-floor **Sangay Lhakhang** is a small crawl-through rock passage; Bhutanese believe that in crawling through a narrow tunnel like this you will leave your sins behind. Behind the statues of the three Buddhas is a secret passageway that is said to have once led to Tharpaling.

The upper-floor **sanctuary** is the holiest in the complex, and has an image of Shelging Kharpo in a shrine just inside the door. There are a thousand small statues of Guru Rinpoche neatly lined up along the same wall, plus statues of Guru Rinpoche, Pema Lingpa and Drolma (Tara). The main statue in this sanctuary is again of Guru Rinpoche, flanked by his eight manifestations and eight chortens. Hidden behind this image is the **meditation cave**, where he left his body imprint. The far wall has paintings of Guru Rinpoche, his manifestations, his 25 disciples and various other figures connected with the Guru. The big cypress tree behind the lhakhang is said to have sprouted from the Guru's walking stick.

Ugyen Wangchuck, the first king of Bhutan, built the second temple, the **Sampa Lhundrup Lhakhang**, in 1900, when he was still *penlop* of Trongsa. On the entrance porch are paintings of the guardians of the four directions and of various local deities who were converted to Buddhism by Guru Rinpoche. The white ghostlike figure on the white horse to the top right is Shelging Kharpo. Inside the temple is a statue of Guru Rinpoche, this one 10m high, flanked again by his eight manifestations. A smaller image of the Guru sits facing the entrance.

The third building in the complex was built by Ashi Kesang Wangchuck, queen to the third king, in 1984 under the guidance of Dilgo Khyentse Rinpoche. She also had the courtyard in front of the three temples paved with stones and built a wall with 108 chortens around the whole complex. On the porch in front of the temple is a large wheel of life. At the bottom you can see a man being judged, with black and white stones representing his good and bad deeds. There's a mystic spiral mandala on the opposite wall. Interior murals illustrate various monastic rules and regulations, including the strict dress codes.

The elaborately decorated **Zangto Pelri Lhakhang**, a short distance south of the Kurjey Lhakhang compound, features a 3-D depiction of the paradise of Guru Rinpoche.

A five-minute walk up the hillside near the entrance is the **Khurjey Drupchhu**, a sacred spring where monks come to wash their socks.

The popular **Kurjey tsechu** is held in June and includes a masked dance that dramatises Guru Rinpoche's defeat of Shelging Kharpo. A large *thangka,* called Guru Tshengye Thondrol, depicting the eight manifestations of Guru Rinpoche, is unfurled in the early morning before the dances, which are performed by the monks from Trongsa.

Deothang Goemba

This little-visited but charming private monastery, just north of Kurjey Lhakhang, was founded in 1949 by Dasho Phuntsok Wangdi. The surprisingly large main hall has a large image of Guru Rinpoche, with 12 other interesting metal statues to the side. A small, dark-skinned image of Thangtong Gyalpo stands to the left. The goemba has a basic four-roomed guesthouse.

Thangbi Goemba

The yellow-roofed Thangbi (or Thankabi) Goemba was founded in 1470 by Shamar Rinpoche and, after a dispute, was taken over by Pema Lingpa. The main chapel of the Dusum Sangay (past, present and future Buddhas) is entered under another of Pema Lingpa's famous chainmails. Around 20 *gomchen* (lay or married monks) live here, celebrating a *drup* (festival) in October.

The goemba is a 3.5km drive north of Kurjey Lhakhang on an unpaved road, branching across the river at Toktu Zampa. It's worth a visit if you are headed to Ngang Lhakhang. This is also the starting point for the Bumthang Cultural trek (see p166).

Ngang Lhakhang

Several hours' walk up the Chokhor Chhu from Thangbi Goemba is the small region known as Ngang-yul (Swan Land). The site was visited by Guru Rinpoche, but the present Ngang Lhakhang (Swan Temple) temple was built in the 15th century by Lama Namkha Samdrup, a contemporary of Pema Lingpa.

Despite the rustic exterior, the interior contains some lovely statues and paintings. Look also for the saddles by the entrance. The primary statue is of Guru Rinpoche, flanked by his two consorts. There is a mural of the Zhabdrung on the wall opposite the altar and an image of Guru Rinpoche on a lotus surrounded by swans.

The upper chapel is a *goenkhang,* with statues of Tsepame, Chenresig, Vijaya and Drolma. The statue of Guru Rinpoche to the bottom right was fashioned by Pema Lingpa. Protector deities lurk in the shadows. Hanging from the rafters are masks used in the three-day **Ngang Shey**, a festival held here in the 10th month in honour of the temple's founder.

It's possible to drive here with a 4WD but it's a much nicer walk along the true left bank of the river. You could walk one way and arrange to be picked up at nearby Damphey.

For a map of the region see p166.

EASTERN SIDE OF THE VALLEY

The best way to visit the eastern side of the Chokhor valley is to walk a couple of hundred metres north from Kurjey Lhakhang, then follow a path east to cross a footbridge, then uphill to a trail on the opposite side. Downstream of the bridge you can see a natural formation named **Do Zam**, said to be the remains of a stone bridge that was built by a goddess trying to meet Guru Rinpoche, and destroyed by a demon.

From here you can follow the east-bank trail south for 30 minutes to **Tamshing Goemba**. A more interesting 45-minute detour is to take a left after the bridge for 10 minutes to an impressive **rock painting** of Guru Rinpoche in the form of Dorje Drolo, astride a tiger. From here, head uphill to the **Dorji Bi Lhakhang**, with its large white chorten, and then descend past a former country mansion, across a stream, to the turn-off to **Pema Sambhava Lhakhang** and then Tamshing Goemba. You can send your vehicle back through Jakar to meet you here.

The major influence in the temples on this side of the valley was Pema Lingpa, the great *terton* of the 16th century.

Tamshing Goemba

This goemba, formally the Tamshing Lhendup Chholing (Temple of the Good Message), is at the northern end of the eastern road, 5km from Jakar. It was established in 1501 by Pema Lingpa and is the most important Nyingma goemba in the kingdom. Pema Lingpa built the unusual structure himself, with the help of *khandromas*, who made many of the statues. On the inner walls are what are believed to be original unrestored images that were painted by Pema Lingpa, though recent research has uncovered even older paintings underneath.

The entrance to the lhakhang is via an inner courtyard lined with monks' quarters. To the left is the small **Mani Dungkhor Lhakhang**, built in 1914 to hold a huge prayer wheel.

The main lhakhang has an unusual design, with the key chapel screened off in the centre of the assembly hall, almost like a separate building. In the chapel are three thrones for the three incarnations (body, mind and speech) of Pema Lingpa. During important ceremonies the reincarnations sit here, although a photograph is substituted if one of the incarnations is not present.

The primary statue in the inner sanctuary is of Guru Rinpoche flanked by Jampa (Maitreya, the Buddha of the Future) and Sakyamuni. This statue is particularly important because it was sculpted by the *khandroma*s. The statue's eyes are looking slightly upward, following the angels in their flight; another unique aspect of the statue is that the Guru is not wearing shoes. Above the altar are two *maksara*s (mythological crocodiles) and a *garuda*. On the walls are the eight manifestations of Guru Rinpoche, four on each side. A small statue of Pema Lingpa occupies a glass case in front of the chapel.

The upper floor forms a **balcony** around the assembly hall. Pema Lingpa was a short man and it is said that he built the low ceiling of the balcony to his exact height. Around the outside are 100,000 old paintings of Sakyamuni. In the **upper chapel** is a statue of Tsepame, the Buddha of Long Life, and a large collection of masks that are used for lama dances. Also here, but closed to visitors, is a statue of Pema Lingpa fashioned by the man himself.

There are good views from Tamshing back across the river to Kurjey Lhakhang.

Konchogsum Lhakhang

Just 400m below Tamshing is a small rural-looking temple – the source of many interesting stories. It was renovated in 1995 and almost destroyed by a butter-lamp fire in 2010. It was still awaiting restoration at the time of writing.

The original building probably dates back to the 6th or 7th century. The current structure, however, dates from the 15th century, when Pema Lingpa restored it. There is a pedestal in the courtyard upon which a large and ancient bell used to sit.

PEMA LINGPA'S CHAINMAIL

At the far end of the dimly lit inner *kora* path within Tamshing Goemba is a cloak of chainmail made by Pema Lingpa. It weighs about 25kg, and if you can hoist it on to your shoulders it is an auspicious act to carry it around the *kora* three times.

It is said that when this bell was rung, it could be heard all the way to Lhasa in Tibet. A 17th-century Tibetan army tried to steal the bell, but the weight was too great and they dropped it, which cracked the bell. It is said to comprise 10% gold, 20% silver, 50% bronze and 20% tin. After a period on display in the National Museum in Paro, a fragment of the lost bell is back inside the lhakhang.

Pema Sambhava Lhakhang

At the end of the road a short steep climb above the valley floor leads to the small Pema Sambhava Lhakhang. The original lhakhang was built in 1490 by Pema Lingpa around the cave where Guru Rinpoche meditated and assumed his manifestation of Padmasambhava. It was expanded by Jigme Namgyal, the father of the first king, and restored in the early 1970s.

There are several rock paintings here, as well as a representation of the local protector Terda Norbu Zangpo, and the cave itself is painted in rainbow colours. The interesting bamboo weaving that looks like a shield is an unusual representation of Chenresig.

Tang Valley

Tang is the most remote of Bumthang's valleys. As it is higher than Chokhor and the soil is not as fertile, there's not as much agriculture here, although the valley turns bright pink with buckwheat flowers in October. The people of this valley raise sheep and at higher elevations, yaks. For a map of the region, see p166.

From Jakar it's 10.5km to the unpaved road that branches north up the Tang valley. This road climbs past the trail to **Membartsho** (1.3km from the turn-off) and the **Pema Shedrup Choeki Gatsheling Shedra**, a large nunnery with about 120 *anim*, to reach the jumping-off point for the hike

THE BURNING LAKE

Two of Pema Lingpa's most celebrated discoveries took place at Membartsho.

The first took place when a dream told him to go to a point where the river forms a large pool that looks like a lake. After a while, standing on a large rock, he saw a temple with many doors, only one of which was open. He plunged naked into the lake and entered a large cave where there was a throne, upon which sat a life-size statue of Lord Buddha and many large boxes. An old woman with one eye handed him one of the chests and he suddenly found himself standing on the rock at the side of the lake holding the treasure.

Pema Lingpa's second treasure find was the most famous. His previous *terma* had instructed him to return to the lake, but when he did, many people gathered to watch the event and the sceptical *penlop* of the district accused him of trickery. Under great pressure to prove himself, Pema Lingpa took a lighted lamp and proclaimed: 'If I am a genuine revealer of your treasures, then may I return with it now, with my lamp still burning; if I am some devil, then may I perish in the water'. He jumped into the lake, was gone long enough that the sceptics thought they were proven right, and then suddenly he emerged back on the rock with the lamp still burning and holding a statue and a treasure chest. The lake became known as Membartsho, or Burning Lake.

to Kunzangdrak, 7km from the turn-off. The road then climbs high above the river, crossing the bridge at Pangshing and then passing **Gemtshong**, a particularly picturesque village and lhakhang perched on a ridge. After a short descent to the river it's 3km to a school at Mesithang (Tang) and 1km further to the Tang Rimochen Lhakhang. The owner of River Lodge in Jakar runs a rural retreat called the **Mesithang River Lodge** (☑631287; pemadawa@druknet.bt; s/d Nu 1500/1600) for those wishing to experience authentic rural Bhutan.

The road becomes rougher as it approaches the bridge at **Kizum** (Ki Zam), 22km from the road junction. This is generally the end point of the Bumthang Cultural trek, though the increasingly rough road does continue a few kilometres further to Gamling and Wobtang.

You can take in all the sites in this section in a good day trip from Jakar, or on the drive back to Jakar at the end of the Bumthang Cultural trek. Better still, overnight at the secluded Ogyen Chholing Guest House (see opposite).

MEMBARTSHO

A five-minute walk from a parking spot at a bend in the road leads to a picturesque pool in the Tang Chhu that is known as Membartsho (Burning Lake). Pema Lingpa found several of Guru Rinpoche's *terma* here. It's a lovely spot, where nature, religion and mythology blur into one.

A wooden bridge crosses the prayer-flag-strewn gorge and offers a good vantage point over the 'lake'. Only the enlightened will spot the temple that lurks in the inky depths. The sanctity of the site is made obvious by the numerous small clay offerings called *tsha-tsha* piled up in various rock niches.

Under a rock shrine with a carving of Guru Rinpoche flanked by Sakyamuni and Pema Lingpa is a cave that virtuous people can crawl through, no matter how big they are. Beware: it's quite small, and very dusty.

KUNZANGDRAK GOEMBA

A stiff hour-long, Stairmaster-style climb up the hillside above Drangchel leads to one of the most important sites related to Pema Lingpa. He began construction of the goemba in 1488, and many of his most important sacred relics are kept here.

The first chapel has a *kora* path around it, with Chenresig, Guru Nazey (Guru Rinpoche) and Namkhai Ningpo inside. Walk around the back of the building to the gravity-defying **Khandroma Lhakhang**, spectacularly situated against a vertical rock face that seeps holy water. Ask to see the stone anvil bearing the footprint of Pema Lingpa. Finally, cross over the small bridge, past a fire-blackened cleft in the cliff, to the *goenkhang*.

Figure on three to four hours for the return trip.

TANG RIMOCHEN LHAKHANG

Tang Rimochen Lhakhang was built by Pema Lingpa in the 14th century to mark a sacred place where Guru Rinpoche meditated. The original name 'Tag (or Tak) Rimochen' (an impression of tiger's stripes) is derived from the yellow stripes that appear on the rock cliff behind the building.

There are handprints and footprints of the Guru and his consort Yeshe Tsogyal on the cliff face and at the top of the steps leading to the temple. The two huge rocks below the lhakhang represent male and female *jachung,* as well as the bathing spot of the Guru.

OGYEN CHHOLING PALACE

From either Gamling or Kizum it's a 45-minute uphill walk to this hilltop 16th-century *naktshang,* or country manor, originally built by Deb Tsokye Dorje, the one-time *penlop* of Trongsa and a descendant of the *terton* Dorji Lingpa. The present structures, including the *tshugl-hakhang* (main temple), *utse* (central tower), *chamkhang* (dance house), *shag-kor* (servants' quarters) and *nubgothang* (guesthouse) are more recent, having been rebuilt after their collapse in the 1897 earthquake.

The family that owns Ogyen (or Ugyen) Chholing has turned the complex into a **museum** (admission Nu 150) to preserve its legacy and provide a place for religious studies, research and solitude. The fascinating and well-captioned exhibits offer real insights into the lifestyle of a Bhutanese noble family. Highlights include a book of divination, a *dakini* dance costume made of bone and the revelation that petrified yak dung was one of the ingredients for Bhutanese gunpowder. Bring a torch. The complex is supported through the Ogyen Chholing Trust, which produces an excellent museum booklet (Nu 350).

The superbly rustic **Ogyen Chholing Guest House** (☏03-680704; r Nu 700-1300) in the palace grounds has two excellent suites and six smaller basic rooms and offers a tranquil overnight retreat. Proceeds go to the trust.

If you walk to the palace from Kizum it's well worth returning via the lovely village of Gamling. Road access to the palace will improve with a road bridge over the river: it's being constructed a few hundred metres beyond Kizum.

THOWADRAK HERMITAGE

The remote hermitage of Thowadrak (or Thowa Drak) clings to the highest rocks above the north end of the Tang valley. It is said to have been founded by Mandarava, the Indian consort of Guru Rinpoche, and the Guru himself is believed to have meditated here. The goemba was built by Dorji Lingpa. There are numerous small meditation retreats on the hillside above (don't disturb the hermits) and dramatic views over the valley. Texts relate that the upper valley conceals a sealed gateway to one of Bhutan's *bey-yul.* The only sounds here are of rushing water and the rustle of bamboo.

The six-hour return hike could be done as a day trip from the Ogyen Chholing Guest House or can be tagged on to the end of the Bumthang Cultural trek (see p166).

Ura Valley

Southeast of Jakar, Ura is the highest of Bumthang's valleys and is believed by some to have been the home of the earliest inhabitants of Bhutan.

JAKAR TO URA
48KM / 1½ HOURS

The road crosses the bridge to the east of Jakar, then travels south along the east bank of the Chamkhar Chhu, winding around a ridge past the turn-off to the Tang valley. Just past the turn-off is an impressive new chorten. As the road climbs, look back at excellent views up the Chokhor and Chhume valleys.

The few houses and potato fields that make up Tangsibi are 24km from Jakar. The road climbs to a false summit, then finally crosses the Shertang La (3590m), also known as the Ura La. Just before the pass you'll get a view of Gangkhar Puensum (7541m) to the northwest and the yellow-roofed lhakhang of Somrang village to the south.

It's then a long descent into the Ura valley. The descent on foot from the pass makes for a nice hour-long walk into Ura village. A couple of kilometres before the turn-off to the village of Ura, which lies below the road, is the turn-off to Shingkhar.

SHINGKHAR
POP 250 / ELEV 3400M

The traditional village of Shingkhar, made up of only 35 households, is 9km up a good gravel side road from Ura. The small

Rinchen Jugney Lhakhang, on a hill 50m from the Shinkhar Guest House, was founded by the Dzogchen master Longchen Rabjampa (1308–63).

The village's central **Dechen Chholing Goemba** is headed by Shingkhar Lama, whose predecessor featured prominently in the Bhutanese novel *Hero with the Thousand Eyes,* by Karma Ura. The central lhakhang has its floorboards exposed to show the stone teaching throne of Longchen. The protector deities are appropriately fierce, except for Rahulla who looks embarrassed wearing a gorilla mask. The **Shingkhar Romney** (festival) held here in the ninth month (October) features an unusual yak dance, without the tour groups that often crowd out Ura.

There are several good hiking options in the valley. Day hikes lead up to the Singmu La, along the former trade route to Lhuentse and bordering the Thrumshing La National Park, or try the four- to five-hour return hike to the cliff-hanging Shamsul Lhakhang.

Shingkhar Retreat (☑03-323206; masagang@druknet.bt; s/d Nu 1800/2300) is a great base from where to explore the village. The rooms are basic but cosy, with mud walls and solar electricity. Meals are available.

URA
☑03 / ELEV 3100M

Ura is one of the more interesting villages in Bhutan. There are about 40 closely packed houses along cobblestone streets, and the main **lhakhang** dominates the town, giving it a medieval atmosphere. In colder weather Ura women wear a sheepskin shawl that serves as both a blanket and a cushion.

Ura gets a rush of visitors during the **Ura yakchoe**, a notoriously unreliable festival that regularly changes dates at the last minute, leaving behind lots of disappointed tour groups on tight schedules. If you do decide to visit the festival, normally in May, it would be wise to budget a couple of days' leeway in your itinerary. The three days of masked dances starts on the 12th day of the third month with a procession carrying an image of Chana Dorje (Vajrapani) from the nearby Geyden Lhakhang down to the main lhakhang. The eve of the festival sees the frantic brewing of *sinchhang* (a spirit distilled from millet, wheat or rice) and late-night exorcisms.

Hotel Arya Zambala (☑680025; azherbal05@yahoo.com; s/d Nu 1750/2000), beside the main road before the turn-off to Ura, has basic rooms, some with attached bathrooms, and can provide simple meals. Their main business is in herbal medicines and dried mushrooms.

During the Ura festival even camping spots are scarce and some groups commute from Jakar, 90 minutes' drive away.

A few hundred metres beyond the hotel (towards Mongar) is the start of the **Ura-Geyzamchu Walking Trail**, a 9km-long, 4½–hour trail crossing two passes and rejoining the road at Geyzamchu, a rushing mountain stream. It's an easy walk through rhododendron and pine forests and alpine meadows along an old trade route. Visit the **Park Visitor Centre** (tnp@moa.gov.bt) in Ura for more information.

SOUTHERN DZONGKHAGS

Two dzongkhags lie on the southern border of central Bhutan. For a few years now, tourists have not been permitted to travel far into these regions because of the threat posed by Assamese separatist groups, but moves are afoot to reopen the region to nature-based tourism. When that happens, the Royal Manas National Park in particular will offer an amazing experience in an area of extreme biodiversity.

Zhemgang Dzongkhag

Zhemgang, along with neighbouring Mongar, was once a collection of tiny principalities, collectively known as Khyeng, absorbed into Bhutan in the 17th century. Panbang, near the Indian border, is known for its round baskets called *bangchung*.

As you approach the town of Zhemgang from Trongsa, keep an eye out for golden langurs swinging in the trees. At the time of writing, a community-based tourism project was under construction below the town in the village of **Dankala**. When finished, the cabins and camping ground will provide a unique village experience as well as a base for birdwatching and other ecotourism pursuits. A two-day walk from near Zhemgang town leads to Nabji (see p176), where a stone pillar commemorates the settlement of the dispute between the Sindhu Raja and Naochhe that was mediated by Guru Rinpoche (see p185).

Sarpang Dzongkhag

Sarpang is on the southern border and a large part of the district is protected within the Royal Manas National Park. Kalikhola in the far west is a border town that has no road connection with the rest of Bhutan; all travel here involves passing through India.

GELEPHU
♪06

The large border town of Gelephu is the gateway to the south and to the Manas area. There's a *tsachhu* (hot spring) in nearby Shershong, 15km from town, and you could also check out the town's whisky distillery. At the time of writing, foreigners were allowed to exit Bhutan at Gelephu in an emergency, but entry was not allowed. This situation is expected to change in 2012 when the new airport is completed.

There are several local hotels, including the **Dragon Guest House** (☎251019), **Hotel Chorten** (☎251252), and **Hotel Dechen** (☎251293).

ROYAL MANAS NATIONAL PARK

This remote national park continues to suffer from security issues involving poachers and militants and is closed to visitors. There are simple lodges at Kanamakra, Rabang and Panbang, and, if the area is reopened, a tented camp may be established at Pantang. A 25km road leads from Gelephu to Kanamakra at the southwestern corner of the park. There is also a road from Tingtibi on the Trongsa–Gelephu road. This 40km road passes along the northern boundary of the park from Gomphu to Panbang village.

The park and surrounds are home to a wide variety of animals including elephants, water buffalos, leopards, tigers, rhinoceros and many species of bird.

Eastern Bhutan

Best Places to Stay

» Wangchuck Hotel (p133)

» Druk Deothjung Resort (p138)

» Rangjung Woesel Chholing Monastery (p139)

» Bomdeling Wildlife Sanctuary Guesthouse (p143)

Best Buddhist Architecture

» Lhuentse Dzong (p134)

» Gom Kora (p141)

» Trashigang Dzong (p138)

» Old Trashi Yangtse Dzong (p141)

Why Go?

The east of Bhutan sees far fewer tourists than the western regions – reason enough to go! Intrepid visitors will be rewarded with exquisite dzongs and temples, beautiful handicrafts, and lush, bird-filled monsoon forests. Even though this is the most densely populated region, the rugged east remains the kingdom's hinterland. Roads reach the major towns, but most of the population live in remote settlements; secreted high above the road or in isolated valleys, some are home to minority ethnic groups comprising less than 1000 people.

Eastern Bhutan is separated from the rest of the country by a chain of extremely rugged and steep hills that runs from the Tibetan border almost all the way down to the Indian border. The road from Bumthang crosses these hills over Thrumshing La (3750m), Bhutan's highest road pass. Other than trails, this one spectacular drive is the region's only road link to the rest of the country. New airports being built at Gelephu and Yongfula will provide easier access to eastern Bhutan and facilitate increased tourism in region.

When to Go

The lower altitudes mean that spring and summer here are hot, humid and sweaty, with insects aplenty. This is also the best time for bird-watching in the lush broadleaf forests. Monsoon rains, however, regularly cause havoc on the fragile roads carved into the steep mountains, so expect delays after heavy downpours.

Snowfalls in winter can also result in temporary road blockages on the high passes.

Eastern Bhutan Highlights

① Wander the bustling narrow streets of **Trashigang** (p137), one of Bhutan's most attractive and lively towns

② Fasten your seatbelt for a trip on the dramatic cliff-hugging road over the 3750m **Thrumshing La** (p130)

③ Take the picturesque drive up to **Lhuentse Dzong** (p134)

④ Watch some of Bhutan's finest cloth being woven at the remote weaving village of **Khoma** (p135)

⑤ Check your sin levels at the serene pilgrimage spot of **Gom Kora** (p141)

⑥ Walk around the serene Chorten Kora, and witness traditional crafts in far-flung **Trashi Yangtse** (p142)

⑦ Explore the remote **Bomdeling Wildlife Sanctuary** (p143), one of the best places to see the black-necked crane

It's a *looong* drive out to the far east, though the good news for tourists is that the border crossing at Samdrup Jongkhar is open to foreigners, so you can avoid a long and winding return drive by exiting into India. Guwahati, the capital of Assam, with regular flights to Kolkata and Mumbai, is just a two-hour drive from the border.

The dominant language of the east is Sharchop (language of the east), although there are many local languages and dialects. Sharchop is different enough from Dzongkha that people from eastern and western Bhutan usually have to use English or Nepali to communicate. Eastern Bhutanese love their home-brewed *arra* (rice wine) and locally grown green chillies. Because of the slash-and-burn system of shifting cultivation called *tseri*, the forest cover at lower elevations is less extensive than in other parts of Bhutan.

History

In ancient times, eastern Bhutan was ruled by a collection of separate petty kingdoms and was an important trade route between India and Tibet. Goods flowed via Bhutan through what is now Singye Dzong in the Lhuentse district to the Tibetan town of Lhodrak.

The most important figure in this region's history was Chhogyel Mingyur Tenpa. When he was *penlop* (governor) of Trongsa, he led his armies to eastern Bhutan to quell revolts in Bumthang, Lhuentse, Trashigang, Mongar and Zhemgang. His efforts were responsible for bringing eastern Bhutan under the rule of the *desi* (secular ruler of Bhutan) and went a long way towards the ultimate unification of the country. Mingyur Tenpa built the dzong at Trongsa and was responsible for the construction of most of the dzongs in eastern, as well as central, Bhutan. In 1668 he was enthroned as the third *desi* and ruled until 1680.

MONGAR DZONGKHAG

The Mongar district is the northern portion of the ancient region of Khyeng. Shongar Dzong, Mongar's original dzong, is in ruins, and the new dzong in Mongar town is not as architecturally spectacular or historically significant as others in the region. Drametse Goemba, in the eastern part of the district, is an important Nyingma monastery, perched high above the valley.

Jakar to Mongar

193KM

It takes about seven hours to travel between Jakar and Mongar. The trip crosses two passes and takes in numerous sheer drops on what is one of the most spectacular drives in the country, descending 3200m in a distance of 84km. During winter Thrumshing La is occasionally closed for a day or two during heavy snowfall.

URA TO THRUMSHING LA
36KM / 1¼ HOURS

Beyond the office of the Thrumshing La National Park and the Japanese-funded hydroelectric plant, the road crosses the small Lirgang Chhu on a bridge called Liri Zam to enter the territory of the national park. It climbs past overhanging cliffs and cedar trees, more often than not framed in mist, and crosses a ridge that is labelled Wangthang La on some maps. It then drops into the Gayzam Chhu valley and starts climbing again past a road workers' camp. Because the soil is very sandy, the road is unstable and has left a large scar on the hillside.

Three kilometres before the pass there is a small park that features over 40 species of rhododendron. It's possible to follow the trail inside the **Rhododendron Garden** and hike up through the forest for 40 minutes to the pass. If you have a keen interest in rhododendrons, it's often possible to get the park ranger to accompany you and point out the different species; mention this to your guide in advance and ask at the national park office in Ura.

If you are lucky enough to travel on a clear day, watch for a view of Gangkhar Puensum (at 7541m it is often cited as the world's highest unclimbed mountain) as you approach the pass. A *mani* wall (Buddhist dry-stone wall with sacred inscriptions) and prayer flags adorn the pass and a fallen sign proclaims: 'You are at highest point'. This is Thrumshing La (3750m), 85km from Jakar, and the border of Mongar Dzongkhag; you are now officially in eastern Bhutan.

THRUMSHING LA TO SENGOR
22KM / 1 HOUR

Once you've crossed into eastern Bhutan, you'll find this side of the pass much rockier. The road switchbacks down through a fir forest past a road sign that says 'Life is a journey, complete it'. At about 3000m, 20km from the pass, the route emerges from the trees and enters the pastures of the Sengor valley. The settlement at Sengor has a few houses near the road, although the main part of the village, about 20 houses, is in the centre of the valley. If you're carrying a picnic lunch and have not already eaten it, this is an excellent place to do so – there is no good place to stop for the next two hours. Another option is the rustic **Kuenphen Hotel**; adorned by a sign in Dzongkha, you can get a simple local-style meal here. A large road-construction contingent here toils to keep the pass open.

SENGOR TO KURI ZAMPA
62KM / 1¾ HOURS

The next stretch of road is the wildest in Bhutan. Five kilometres beyond the Sengor valley the road begins a steep descent into the Kuri Chhu valley, clinging to the side of a rock cliff, with numerous streams and waterfalls leaping out onto the road. The frequent fog and cloud on this side of the pass makes it difficult to see what's below – for which you should be profoundly grateful, since more often than not, there's nothing.

There are several chortens here – erected as memorials to the almost 300 Indian and Nepali contract labourers who were killed during the construction of this portion of the road. As you drive along the narrow track that was hacked into the side of a vertical cliff, it's hard not to be concerned that you might well join them soon. Prayer plaques and Shiva tridents offer some limited spiritual protection. There are no settlements here except for a camp at **Namling**, 22km from Sengor, where a crew works frantically to protect the road from tumbling down the mountainside. About 2km before the camp the **Namling Waterfall** plunges from beneath the road and is spectacular after monsoonal rainfalls.

About 17km from Namling, after a long descent that traverses the side of a cliff, the road reaches safer ground and leaves the territory of the Thrumshing La National Park. At Yong Khola it emerges into the upper part of a large side valley of the Kuri Chhu, a lush land of bamboo, ferns and leeches (and good bird-watching). You pass cornfields and descend to the valley floor on a road that winds around like a pretzel. Rice terraces appear and tropical fruits such as mango and pineapple flourish.

Atop a hill on the opposite side of the river, near the kilometre marker 123, is a view of the ruined **Shongar Dzong**. There's not much to see – just some stone walls almost hidden by trees on the top of a hillock – but this is believed to have been one of the earliest and largest dzongs, perhaps built as early as 1100. Like Trongsa, Shongar was powerful because the dzong was ideally situated to control movements between eastern and western Bhutan. The new dzong was built in Mongar town when the old one was destroyed by fire in 1899. You can hike to the dzong on a sweaty overgrown trail rich with birdlife.

A few kilometres further, **Lingmethang** (650m), 57km from Sengor, boasts four adjacent roadside hotels, including the **Dorje Hotel Cum Bar**, all offering good local food, hot drinks and cold beer.

The road turns north at a chorten that marks the junction of the main Kuri Chhu valley. At Kuri Zampa (570m) you finally hit the valley floor with a bump – an amazing descent of 3200m from the pass. Step out of your vehicle and breathe in the thick syrupy air before frantically stripping off three layers of clothing. On the east side of a prayer flag-strewn bridge is a large concrete **chorten** that is patterned after Bodhnath in Nepal; it is said to contain relics from the original Shongar Dzong. Beside the bridge is a deserted factory that used to extract oil from the wild lemongrass that is so abundant here.

A secondary road leads downstream to the new town of Gyalpozhing and the Kuri Chhu power project, beyond which a new road leads further downstream to Nanglam on the Indian border.

KURI ZAMPA TO MONGAR
25KM / 45 MINS

The road to Mongar climbs through chirpine forests up the eastern side of the Kuri Chhu valley. To the north you can see the road to Lhuentse traversing the side of the valley. This road leaves the Mongar road at Gangola, 12km before Mongar, and travels 65km to Lhuentse (see p134).

The Mongar road climbs up and up through cornfields towards a cluster of houses on top of the hill. A final switchback leads into Mongar.

Mongar

♪04 / ELEV 1600M

Most towns in the west of Bhutan are in valleys. In eastern Bhutan most towns, including Mongar, are on the tops of hills or ridges.

There is little of real interest to see in Mongar, but many people spend a night here before continuing to Trashigang. It takes about 11 hours to drive from Jakar to Trashigang, which often means driving at night, which is a waste in such interesting countryside.

The pleasant main street is lined with traditionally painted stone Bhutanese buildings decorated with wooden facades with colourful potted plants and prayer wheels on their verandas. Archers sharpen their aim on the football ground on most afternoons.

A large **prayer wheel** near the clock tower attracts reverential travellers and those just wishing to catch up on local news.

◉ Sights

Mongar Dzong   DZONG

The Mongar Dzong, unusual because it has two entrances and because the monk and administrative bodies share the same courtyard, was rebuilt in 1953. The dzong was established here in 1930 to replace the original Shongar Dzong, although the original *utse* (central tower) dates from an earlier age. There are 80 monks in the dzong, about 70 of them young boys aged eight to 10 years old plus their teachers. The week-long **Mongar tse-**

Mongar

chu is held here in November. There are four lhakhangs in the *utse*; the Sangay Lhakhang is probably the only one in Bhutan equipped with comfy sofas!

🛏 Sleeping

Wangchuk Hotel   HOTEL **$$**
(☎641522; www.wangchukhotel.com; s/d Nu 2000/2500; @) The impressive and modern Wangchuk dominates the accommodation scene in Mongar with spacious rooms, good food and a delightful setting. The large carpeted rooms equipped with comfy beds, bathtubs, TVs, phones, room safes and fans, have views over town or forested hills. The multi-cuisine restaurant and adjacent bar has balcony seating with great valley views. It's the perfect place to reminisce over the drive from Bumthang with a stiff drink.

Hotel Druk Zom   HOTEL **$$**
(☎641206; fax 641207; r Nu 2000-2500; @) A bright and welcoming boutique hotel with a range of rooms whose sizes and configurations vary according to what appears to be rather haphazard building plans. All rooms have a ceiling fan, a TV and phone. Mattresses, though, are on the firm side and bathrooms vary in size. The multi-cuisine restaurant is light and bright with views over town.

Druk Zhongar Hotel   HOTEL **$$**
(☎641121; drukzhongar@druknet.bt; s/d from Nu 1800/2000, ste Nu 2500; @) This well-run, friendly hotel has average rooms equipped with TVs and fans and some have a balcony. The smaller rooms are rather cramped. The Phuntso Delek Restaurant here is also decent, if a little gloomy.

Zhongar Guest House   GUESTHOUSE **$**
(☎641107; s Nu 500-1200, d Nu 800-1400) This government-owned guesthouse is in a charming traditional-style wooden building, complete with royal quarters, great views over the dzong and a fabulous sense of history. Unfortunately, staying here is a bit of a gamble; if at any time government employees turn up, you'll be turfed out, even with a reservation, so agents are naturally reluctant to book you here. Some of the rooms have shared bathrooms.

There are many small local-style hotels in Mongar that usually don't accommodate foreign tourists, but cater primarily to passengers travelling on the Trashigang–Thimphu bus, which stops here on the first night of its three-day journey. Three of these are:

Dolma Hotel   HOTEL **$**
(☎641508; r Nu 500) An acceptable place with rooms with attached bathrooms and a balcony.

Hotel Tashiling   HOTEL **$**
(☎641207; r Nu 250-350)

Samling Hotel   HOTEL **$**
(☎641111; r Nu 200-300)

✗ Eating

Almost everyone eats in their hotel, but if you want a light lunch of *momos* (dumplings) or samosas try the local hotels lining the main street. The **Wangchuk Hotel** (☎641522) has a great balcony attached to its restaurant and bar for a meal or drink with a view. The **Phuensom Bakery** (☉9am-6pm) is the place to load up for the following day's picnic lunch, whereas the **Doeyen Jamtsho Pizza Hut** (☉9am-8pm) is a rather dim downstairs joint with cheese pizza at Nu 35 per slice.

ℹ Information

Bank of Bhutan (☎641123; ☉9am-1pm Mon-Fri, to 11am Sat)

Bhutan National Bank (☎641495 ☉9am-4pm Mon-Fri, to 11am Sat)

Post Office (☉8.30am-5pm Mon-Fri, to 1pm Sat)

ℹ Getting There & Away

Buses run daily to Trashigang (Nu 85, departing at 6am) and Lhuentse (1pm), and on Tuesday, Thursday and Saturday to Thimphu (Nu 370; two days, 6am) and to the border at Samdrup Jongkhar (6.30am).

LHUENTSE DZONGKHAG

Formerly known as Kurtoe, the isolated district of Lhuentse is the ancestral home of Bhutan's royal family. Although geographically in the east, it was culturally identified with central Bhutan, and the high route over Rodang La was a major trade route until the road to Mongar was completed. Many Lhuentse women have looms at home and the village of Khoma is especially famous for its *kushuthara* (brocade) weaving.

Mongar to Lhuentse

76KM

Lhuentse is 63km from the junction at Gangola and a three-hour drive from Mongar. It's a dramatic trip, frequently taking you alongside cliffs high above the river valley, but it's a comfortable ride if there have not been any recent landslides. A new road avoiding a notorious slippage zone was under construction at the time of writing.

MONGAR TO AUTSHO

38KM / 1¼ HOURS

It is 12km down the hill from Mongar to the junction of the Lhuentse road at Gangola (1110m). The Lhuentse road winds around the hill to Chali and passes the few houses of Palangphu and then passes the new suspension bridge to Banjor village the previous bridge further upstream was washed away when a glacial lake burst, sending floodwaters surging down the valley). The road descends through an unstable slide area to the banks of the Kuri Chhu and the two shops that make up the village of Rewan. Passing a large Tibetan-style brick chorten surrounded by 108 smaller chortens, the road reaches the extensive cornfields and impressive riverside location of **Autsho** (920m). Near the river you may be able to spot rhesus monkeys playing on stones, and black cormorants diving for fish.

AUTSHO TO TANGMACHU

26KM / 1 HOUR

The road passes towering cliffs, often half hidden in the mist, en route to Fawan. It then switchbacks 100m above the river to the scruffy roadside settlement of Gorgan opposite the large valley of the Noyurgang Chhu, which enters from the west. Near this part of the road, in Umling, are said to be the remains of an ancient underground stone castle built by Bangtsho Gyalpo in about 1500 BC.

After a while the Kuri Chhu valley begins to widen. Beyond a large white chorten, the road crosses to the west bank of the river on a suspension bridge. On the hillside high above the bridge locals are building a 41m-high statue of Guru Rinpoche, above the improbably located settlement of **Tangmachu** (known locally as Darkila). The statue will be one of the world's tallest and will cost at least 100 million ngultrum. A rough unpaved road leads 10km up to the village and high school, 600m above the road, but it is often impassable if it's been raining.

TANGMACHU TO LHUENTSE

13KM / 30 MINS

The road traverses the foot of the Tangmachu valley for about 6km, passing a road construction camp and a hydrology station at Sumpa. Rounding a corner there's a view of **Lhuentse Dzong**, which dominates the head of the valley. A small suspension bridge leads across the river here, providing access to the trail to Khoma and Singye Dzong (see p135).

A short distance on, the valley narrows and the road begins climbing towards the town. As the road passes the hospital there is an excellent view of the dzong perched dramatically atop a bluff. The road to Dungkhar branches off by the hospital.

Lhuentse

📞 04 / ELEV 1440M

There is little to see in Lhuentse and there's no actual village here, but the dzong is one of the most picturesque in Bhutan. As you enter Lhuentse, just above the current collection of wooden shops and bars, is the construction site for another of Bhutan's new towns. The pillared pavilion nearby is a cremation ground.

The road terminates in front of the dzong. Adjoining the parking lot are quarters for government officials who have been posted to this remote area where housing is scarce.

It's worth driving up to the Royal Guest House for views of the dzong and the snow peaks at the head of the Kuri Chhu valley. The peak at the head of the valley to the northwest of the guesthouse is Sheri Nyung.

As you leave Lhuentse for Mongar, look out for the ancient ruined bridge down in the valley below, just before the bend in the river.

⊙ Sights

Lhuentse Dzong   DZONG

Lhuentse Rinchentse Phodrang Dzong, as it is correctly known, sits high on a rocky outcrop overlooking the Kuri Chhu valley, with near-vertical drops on all sides.

Although Pema Lingpa's son Kuenga Wangpo established a small goemba on this site early in the 16th century, the dzong itself was built by the Trongsa *penlop* Mingyur Tenpa in 1654. It has been renovated several times and numerous lhakhangs have been added. A three-day **tsechu** fills the dzong to capacity in December/January.

Visitors can visit seven lhakhangs, assuming you can find someone with the keys. The 100 or so resident monks see few tourists and are very friendly, which perhaps explains why visitors here have more freedom to explore than they do in any other dzong in Bhutan.

🛏 Sleeping & Eating

Royal Guest House GUESTHOUSE **$**
(☑545102; bed Nu 120-200) Lhuentse's only hotel is this government guesthouse, on a hill 100m above the town. It's possible to get a booking here but it's a hassle (the local *dzongkhag* administration prefers you have permission from the Home Ministry in Thimphu) and you could get bumped by visiting officials.

It's best to arrive in Lhuentse with a packed lunch, otherwise you can get *ema datse* (chillies with cheese) and perhaps *momos* at the basic **Shangrila Hotel** (☑545123) or nearby **Karma Hotel**.

ℹ Getting There & Away
Buses run three times a week to Thimphu, overnighting in Bumthang.

Around Lhuentse

A highly recommended excursion from Lhuentse is the hike to the weaving village of Khoma (see the boxed text). Several Bhutanese travel companies offer three-day tours of surrounding weaving villages, including Gonpokarpo, Chenling, Minje and Nyilamdun (Ngangladung).

DUNGKHAR
An unpaved road runs from Lhuentse for 39km to the small village of Dungkhar, named because the ridge upon which it sits is shaped like a conch *(dungkhar)*. Pema Lingpa's son Kuenga Wangpo settled here, and it is through him that Bhutan's royal family, the Wangchucks, trace their ancestry to the Kurtoe region. Jigme Namgyal, father of the first king, was born here in 1825 and left home when he was 15 to eventually become Trongsa *penlop* and the 51st *desi*.

Special permission is required to visit Dungkhar, although check with your travel agency as this situation may change. The Jigme Namgyal Naktshang and the renovated 16th-century Dungkhar Naktshang are above the village. (A *naktshang* is a

If you are interested in weaving (and even if you're not), it's worth making the hike up to this traditional weaving village. The village produces some of Bhutan's most soughtafter and expensive *kushutara* weavings and almost all of the 30 or so houses in the village have traditional back-strap looms set up in their porches. The weavings are so elaborate that they resemble embroidery and are generally used as *kiras* (women's traditional dress), though bags and other pieces are produced. The village's comparative wealth has translated into TVs and carbon-fibre bows, and mule caravans frequently shuttle consumer goodies up to the well-stocked shops. The Zangto Pelri Lhakhang sits on a spur overlooking the river junction.

It's an easy 90-minute hike up to the village, passing the Drak Kharpo and White Hermitage Cave of Guru Rinpoche, visible high on the far cliffs.

temple dedicated to a warlord or protective deity.) Also here is the renovated Dungkhar Choeje, the birthplace of the first king. Guru Rinpoche meditated in a cave overlooking Dungkhar, and Pema Lingpa visited the area many times and built Goeshog Pang Lhakhang near the river below the village.

SINGYE DZONG
Singye Dzong is on the old trade route from Bhutan to Lhobrak in Tibet. Guru Rinpoche meditated here and it's an important pilgrimage place for Bhutanese. The trek takes three days in each direction, but is off-limits to tourists. Yeshe Tsogyal, the consort of Guru Rinpoche who concealed many *terma* (sacred texts and artefacts) here, founded the goemba.

TRASHIGANG DZONGKHAG

Trashigang is the heart of eastern Bhutan and was once the centre of important trade with Tibet. There are several goembas and villages that make a visit worthwhile, but a lot of driving is required to reach this remote region.

Mongar to Trashigang

92KM

The Mongar to Trashigang stretch is easier and shorter than the journey from Jakar to Mongar, but you still need about 3½ hours to cover the 92km between the two towns, plus an extra two hours if you detour to Drametse Goemba. The road crosses one low pass, then follows a river valley before making a final climb to Trashigang.

MONGAR TO KORI LA

17KM / 30 MINS

Leaving Mongar, the road climbs past fields of corn to the power substation and *shedra* (Buddhist college) at Kilikhar, then through rhododendron and blue-pine forests to the few houses in the scattered settlement of **Naling**. Soon the road is clinging to the side of a cliff, passing through a deep forest of rhododendrons and orchids.

About 3km past a forest nursery is **Kori La** (2400m), where there is an array of prayer flags, a small *mani* wall, and the **Coffee Café** (⊙7am-8pm), where you can get a hot coffee or tea with biscuits. The forest surrounding the pass is under a management plan regulating the harvest of trees and bamboo and is a good place for bird-watching. Keep an eye out for great Indian hornbills. Nearby is the start of the **Kori La to Golishing Phurtuma Nature Trail**, which traverses 2.75km of jungle trail before returning to the road where your driver can pick you up.

KORI LA TO YADI

21KM / 1 HOUR

The road drops from the pass into the upper reaches of the extensive Manas Chhu drainage, switchbacking down through broadleaf forests to the small private Guru Lhakhang, near the village of **Naktshang**. Above the road are several small buildings used by monks as retreat and meditation centres.

The road continues its descent past fencelike prayer flags (the Bhutanese equivalent of road safety barriers) and through fields of corn and mustard, past the road-crew camp at Ningala, finally reaching the substantial village of **Yadi** (1480m). The **Choden Hotel General Shop Cum Bar & Lodge** (☎04-539113) here is a good place to break for a cup of masala tea. Passengers pile out of buses from Trashigang to Mongar to breakfast here.

Below Yadi, a dirt road branches off 17km to **Shershong** (or Serzhong) and, for Bhutanese pilgrims only, a two-day walk to Aja Ney. The 'A' of Aja is a sacred letter and 'ja' means 'one hundred'. Guru Rinpoche placed one hundred letter As on rocks here, and for devotees it's like a spiritual treasure hunt: the more you see the more merit you gain. Those without sin usually find the most.

YADI TO THUNGDARI

33KM / 1 HOUR

Beyond Yadi a long stretch of prayer flags lines the road; below are numerous switchbacks, nicknamed the **Yadi Loops**, that lead down through a forest of sparse chir pine with an understorey of fragrant lemongrass, dropping 350m in 10km. There is a good viewpoint where you can see the road weaving down the hill; pictures taken from here often appear in books and brochures to illustrate just how circuitous Bhutan's roads are. The unpaved road that heads west before the loops begin leads to the village and hydro plant of Chaskhar. Three kilometres beyond Yadi, the **Zalaphangma Cafeteria** (☎04-539113; ⊙6.30am-8.30pm) has pleasant indoor and outdoor seating and serves set meals by arrangement as well as tea, coffee and snacks.

After more switchbacks, the road crosses a bridge painted with the eight Tashi Tagye symbols and continues for 10km to the nondescript bazaar of **Sherichhu** (600m). Climb out of the Sherichhu valley to a chorten and cross a ridge to meet the large Drangme Chhu, which flows from the eastern border of Bhutan and is a major tributary of the Manas Chhu. The road winds in and out of side valleys for 12km to Thungdari, 71km from Mongar, where a side road leads to Drametse Goemba.

DRAMETSE GOEMBA

Drametse is the biggest and most important monastery in eastern Bhutan. It's an 18km, hour-long detour on a dirt track off the main road, gaining 1350m, and you'll need a 4WD vehicle if it's been raining.

There are about 60 *gomchen* (lay or married Nyingma monks) at Drametse. The monastery was founded in 1511 by the great-granddaughter of Pema Lingpa, Ani Chhoeten Zangmo, and her husband, Yeshe Gyalpo, in a place she named Drametse, which means 'the peak where there is no enemy'.

The monastery is famous as the home of the Nga Cham drum dance that features in many tsechus and which was proclaimed a masterpiece of oral and intangible heritage by Unesco in 2005.

The murals of the guardian kings in the entryway were painted in the 1950s and repainted in 1982. In the main chapel, to the right of a central Guru Rinpoche, is the gold chorten of Chhoeten Zangmo, next to a statue of her great-grandfather.

The middle floor has chapels dedicated to the protectors Palden Lhamo (Sri Devi) and the 'horse-necked' Tamdrin (Hayagriva). The upstairs **Goenkhang Chenmo** (Great Protector Chapel) is jam-packed with weapons, a stuffed lynx, a dead flying fox (that looks like it's been blown up with a foot pump), lots of arrows and the three local protector deities of Gyelpo, Drametse and Tsong Tsoma. Make an offering and you'll be blessed with a sacred thread. The next-door **Tseringma Lhakhang** houses the black hats used in the annual tsechu in September/October, as well as five versions of Tseringma, all riding different mythological beasts. Finally, the **Kanjur Lhakhang** houses a box of sacred relics, including bowls and *drilbu* (Tantric bells).

This is potato-growing country, and in the autumn there are huge piles of potatoes waiting for trucks to carry them down to eventual sale in India and Bangladesh. In the distance to the southeast you can see the college at Kanglung (see p144).

THUNGDARI TO CHAZAM
11KM / 30 MINS

Back down on the main road you'll catch glimpses of Trashigang Dzong high above the south bank of the Drangme Chhu. Much of the hillside beside the road is made up of loose alluvial deposits. Boulders embedded in the sand often break loose during rainstorms and fall onto the road, causing delays while road crews scramble to remove them.

After passing a PWD (Public Works Department) camp at Rolong, the road reaches a 90m-long bridge at Chazam (710m). This place was named after the original chain-link bridge here, said to have been built by the Tibetan bridge builder Thangtong Gyalpo (see the boxed text, p86) in the 15th century (*cha* means 'iron', *zam* means 'bridge'). The large building that formed the abutment of the old bridge has been partially restored and can be seen a short distance upstream of the new bridge. Look for the ruins of watchtowers on the ridge above the old bridge.

CHAZAM TO TRASHIGANG
9KM / 15 MINS

On the south side of the bridge is an immigration checkpoint where police inspect your travel permit. The road north from here follows the Kulong Chhu valley and then climbs to Trashi Yangtse (p142).

The road switchbacks up through cornfields towards Trashigang, passing a turnoff that leads down to the small settlement of Chenary. The Druk Seed Corporation here produces seeds for subtropical fruit.

At the top of the hill is a collection of motor workshops and a road junction. The road to southern Bhutan leads to the right. The left fork leads to Trashigang, 3km away. Go round a bend where there's a good view of Trashigang Dzong, then follow the road into Trashigang, which is well hidden in a wooded valley.

Trashigang
04 / ELEV 1070M

Trashigang is one of Bhutan's more interesting towns and a good base for excursions to Trashi Yangtse, Khaling, Radi, Phongme and elsewhere in eastern Bhutan. The picturesque town is at the foot of a steep wooded valley with the tiny Mithidang Chhu channelled through it. Trashigang's focal point is a tiny plaza that becomes crammed with parked cars. A large prayer wheel sits in the centre of the plaza. The covered pedestal holding the prayer wheel is a favourite sleeping place for villagers waiting for buses and becomes an ad hoc vegetable market most days. Surrounding the plaza are several hotels, restaurants, bars, and a bakery and handicraft shop.

A side road leads downhill from the chorten past a handsome collection of shops, bars and small restaurants, then past a chorten to the dzong.

Accommodation here is fairly limited, but there is a variety of restaurants and you're bound to find at least one amusing place to drink among the town's numerous bars. Not many tourists make it to Trashigang, but there used to be many Canadian teachers working here and the people of Trashigang are used to Westerners.

Villagers come to town on holy days, which occur on the first, 10th and 15th of

Trashigang

To Phongme (35km)
To Trashigang Dzong (100m)
Mithidang Chhu
Royal Guest House
Town Gate
To Mongar (92km); Samdrup Jongkhar (180km)
To Druk Deothjung Resort (500m)
Chorten
Telecom Tower
Shops
Prayer Wheel

Trashigang

◎ Top Sights
Prayer Wheel..B3

⊜ Sleeping
1 Druk Deothjung Hotel............................B3
2 Hotel Ugyen...B3

⊗ Eating
Druk Deothjung Bakery & Confectionary...............................(see 1)
3 Karmapa Restaurant and Bar.............B3
4 Pema Bakery & General Store...........A3
5 TT Restaurant B3

⊙ Shopping
Druk Deothjung Eastern Rural Handicraft....................................(see 1)
6 Rural Handicrafts Sales Centre.......... B1

the Bhutanese month, to trade and sample the local *arra* (spirit distilled from rice).

◉ Sights

Trashigang Dzong
DZONG

The dzong is on a high promontory that overlooks the confluence of the Drangme Chhu and the Gamri Chhu. It was built in 1667 by Mingyur Tenpa, Bhutan's third *desi*.

The entire eastern region was governed from this dzong from the late 17th century until the beginning of the 20th century.

This dzong is unusual in that both the administrative and monastic bodies face onto a single *dochey* (courtyard). As always, the *gorikha* (porch) has paintings of the Four Guardian Kings. Inside are several lhakhangs. One lhakhang holds the statue of the deity of Gasin-re or Yama, the wrathful aspect of Chenrisig. He is a protector of the faith, the god of death and the king of law, and the one that weighs up the good and evil at the end of a person's life. You can see him in the vestibule of most lhakhangs holding the Wheel of Life in his mouth. Many lama dances are performed in Trashigang to appease Yama, especially during the four-day **tsechu** in November/December.

🛏 Sleeping & Eating

An alternative to staying in Trashigang is to continue 16km east of town and overnight at the pleasant guesthouse of the Rangjung Wodsel Chholing Monastery (see p139).

Druk Deothjung Resort
HOTEL $$

(☎521145; s/d Nu 1800/2000, deluxe r Nu 2500; @) Under management of the Druk Deothjung Hotel, this erstwhile government guesthouse makes for a comfortable though hardly luxurious stay. The resort is 1km uphill from the town centre and has a view over the dzong. Standard rooms have hotwater showers and the two top-floor deluxe rooms are marginally better than the standard rooms and have TVs.

Druk Deothjung Hotel
HOTEL $$

(☎521214; fax 521269; s/d Nu 1800/2000; @) This family-run hotel near the central prayer wheel is still the best place in the centre of town. It's comfortable, with satellite TV and hot-water showers, but it's far from luxurious, with concrete grills in the walls that let in bugs and street noise. Balconies overlook the town plaza and the pleasant al-fresco dining area serves up the best food and coldest beer in town. The owner is also building a tourist hotel 1.5km west of town.

Hotel Ugyen
HOTEL $

(☎521140; s/d Nu 100/200) This basic place is very much a third choice and will only be used by your agent in the unlikely event that all tourist-friendly rooms are booked out. It has rooms that are similar in standard to a trekking lodge in Nepal, with very basic bathrooms down the corridor.

Pema Bakery & General Store
GENERAL STORE **$**

(☑521196) On the road to the dzong, this bakery and general store serves bread and pastries, and stocks a huge range of imported goodies from Pringles to Coffee Mate. The odd smell comes from the sacks of dried fish.

Druk Deothjung Bakery & Confectionary
BAKERY **$**

(☉6am-9pm) In the Druk Deothjung, this bakery has fresh bread and colourful cakes.

If you prefer something more local in flavour, try the **Karmapa Restaurant & Bar**, or the **TT Restaurant**, for a quick meal of rice, *ema datse* and meat.

🛍 Shopping

The small **Druk Deothjung Eastern Rural Handicraft** (☉9am-7pm) shop at the Druk Deothjung Hotel is your last place to load up on hand-crafted souvenirs.

ℹ Information

Bank of Bhutan (☑521294; ☉9am-1pm Mon-Fri, to 11am Sat)

Bhutan National Bank (☑521129; ☉9am-4pm Mon-Fri, to 11am Sat)

Jigme Wangmo Photo Studio Sells *Kuensel* and prints digital photos.

Kuenphen Medical Shop (☑521175) For medical supplies.

Post Office (☉9am-5pm Mon-Fri, to 1pm Sat) Above the town centre, near the high school.

ℹ Getting There & Away

From Trashigang it's 281km to Bumthang, 349km to Trongsa and 551km to Thimphu.

The local jeep drivers that wait at the bus stand say that if you leave Trashigang at 3.30am, you can reach Thimphu at 8.30pm, a total of 17 hours' gruelling driving.

There are daily local buses to Thimphu, Samdrup Jongkhar and Radhi, as well as less-frequent services to Mongar (Monday to Saturday), Trashi Yangtse (Wednesday and Saturday) and Phongme (Wednesday, Friday and Sunday).

Far Eastern Bhutan

The paved road east from Trashigang travels up the valley of the Gamri Chhu to Rang-

jung, and then continues as a gravel road and dirt track to Radi and Phongme. This is the end of the line, as far east as you can go in a vehicle in Bhutan. If you're short on time, you won't miss much by skipping this route.

TRASHIGANG TO RANGJUNG
16KM / 45 MINS

The road descends from Trashigang, weaving in and out of side valleys to the banks of the Gamri Chhu at 820m. A side road crosses the river here and leads uphill for 19km in great zigzagging gashes to the town and goemba at **Bartsam**. The Rangjung road stays on the south side of the river, passing through a flat area affected by flooding (the chorten in the middle of the flood plain provides divine protection against floods). Shortly afterwards is the village of **Lungtenzampa**.

After traversing fields for 6km, past the large Vocational Training Institute at Buna, the road crosses the small Kharti Chhu and makes a short climb to **Rangjung** at 1120m. Beyond the high school, an elaborate chorten dominates the pleasant centre of town, while a new road layout is catering to the town's gradual expansion just to the north of the old village.

Above the town is the **Rangjung Woesel Chholing Monastery**, a large Nyingma goemba founded in 1990 by Garub Rinpoche. The brightly painted main chapel has some impressive *torma* (sculptures of barley and butter), including one depicting the five senses, with eyeballs, earlobes, nostrils, a tongue and skin. The lower courtyard hosts *cham* dancing at the end of a 10-day **drup** (festival) in the 12th month.

The monastery has two good guesthouses (☑04-561145; s Nu 800-1100, d Nu 1200-1500) up the hill that are occasionally booked by tourists, particularly Buddhist groups. The main guesthouse has rooms that smell like a hospital but they have private bathrooms and offer great views over the goemba. More rooms, with shared bathrooms, exist in a small building higher up the hill. Meals can be arranged at either guesthouse.

RANGJUNG TO PHONGME
17KM / 1 HOUR

The road continues east, climbing through large rice terraces and fields of corn to **Radi** (1570m).

For an unusual outing, hike downhill for about 30 minutes from the Yeshi Lhundup shop, at a hairpin loop just before Radi

EASTERN BHUTAN FAR EASTERN BHUTAN

Naturally, Bhutanese yetis have different characteristics from yetis found (or not found) in Tibet and other Himalayan regions. The Bhutanese name for a yeti is *migoi* (strong man) and they are believed to exist throughout northern and northeastern Bhutan, particularly in the **Sakten Wildlife Sanctuary** (see below).

The *migoi* is covered in hair that may be anything from reddish-brown to black, but its face is hairless, almost human. It is similar to the yetis of Nepal and Tibet in that the breasts of the female are large and sagging, and both sexes have an extremely unpleasant smell. But Bhutanese *migoi* are special because they have the power to become invisible, which accounts for the fact that so few people have seen them. Another feature that helps them escape detection is that their feet may face backwards, confusing people who try to follow them.

The book *Bhutanese Tales of the Yeti* by Kunzang Choden is a wonderful collection of tales told by village people in Bhutan who have seen, or have met people who have seen, a *migoi*.

(kilometre marker 23), to the small village of Tzangkhar. Most of the women here are weavers who specialise in fabrics made from *bura* (raw silk), and it is fun to walk from house to house to see the results. Enough cloth to make a *gho* or *kira* costs about Nu 35,000 for a flower design and about Nu 10,000 for a plainer pattern. It's a stiff uphill climb back to the road, gaining 130m.

Beyond Radi the road climbs past terraced hillsides and above the large modern **Thakcho Kunzang Choeden Anim Goemba**. A few kilometres later, past Khardung village, is the collection of shops that is Phongme (1840m).

On the hill above the village is the 150-plus-year-old **Phongme Lhakhang**. The central statue is of Chenresig with 1000 arms and 11 heads. A rolled-up *thondrol* (a building-sized *thangka*) hangs from the rafters and *cham* masks are stored in boxes at the foot of the statues.

SAKTEN WILDLIFE SANCTUARY

From Phongme, a trail leads east to the remote minority villages of Merak and Sakten, which are inhabited by seminomadic tribesmen called Brokpa. Tourists are again permitted to make this trek (p177), but it was closed to foreigners in 1995 out of concern for the unique culture of the people living there. Rugged Brokpa men often come into Phongme, Khaling and Trashigang to trade. You can recognise them by their sheepskin and yak-hair clothing and unusual yak-felt hats called *shamo*, which have hanging spider-like legs that act as rainspouts.

Katie Hickman gives a good description of her visit to the region on horseback in her travelogue *Dreams of the Peaceful Dragon*.

Apart from the Brokpas, the sanctuary's most famous resident is the *migoi*, or yeti, for whom the park was allegedly established in 2002. The sanctuary office is 1km east of Phongme, at the end of the motorable road.

TRASHI YANGTSE DZONGKHAG

Previously a *drungkhag* (subdistrict) of Trashigang, Trashi Yangtse became a fully fledged *dzongkhag* (district) in 1993. It borders the Indian state of Arunachal Pradesh, and there is some cross-border trade. The old trade route between east and west Bhutan used to go through Trashi Yangtse, over the mountains to Lhuentse and then over Rodang La (4200m) to Bumthang. This difficult route fell into disuse when the road from Trashigang to Bumthang via Mongar was completed. The district lies at the headwaters of the Kulong Chhu, and was earlier known as Kulong.

Trashigang to Trashi Yangtse

53KM

The drive from Trashigang to Trashi Yangtse takes about 1¾ hours' driving time, but you should budget extra time to visit Gom Kora on the way. There's lots to see en route and it's a great day trip from Trashigang.

Even if you don't have time to drive all the way to Chorten Kora, do make the effort to make the short trip to Gom Kora.

To get from Trashigang to **Chazam** (9km, 15 minutes), follow the switchbacks down to the bridge at Chazam. Just past Chazam, an unpaved side road leads steeply uphill to Gangthung and **Yangnyer**. The complex that is visible a short distance up this road is a jail.

From Chazam, the road is level as it winds its way through sparse clumps of chir pine above the west bank of the Drangme Chhu to Gom Kora (13km, 30 minutes). A couple of kilometres before Gom Kora, by the side of the road, is a *ney* (holy spot), where a rock shrine is covered in *tsha-tshas* (small offerings moulded in clay) and brass images of the Rigsum Goempo – the Buddhist trinity of Chenresig, Jampelyang/ Manjushri and Chana Dorje.

Gom Kora

Gom Kora is an extraordinarily picturesque temple 13km north of Chazam. The lush green fields, the red robes of the monks and the yellow roof of the temple combine with colourful Buddhist carvings and the rushing river to create an idyllic scene.

The correct name for the site is Gomphu Kora. Gomphu denotes a sacred meditation site of Guru Rinpoche and *kora* means 'circumambulation'. The Guru meditated here and left a body impression on a rock, similar to that in Kurjey Lhakhang in Bumthang.

The central figure in the temple is Guru Rinpoche. To the right is Chenresig, in his 1000-armed aspect. To the far right is an image of the snake demon Gangan Yonga Choephel, who holds a golden mirror in his right hand. The murals on the walls are believed to date from the 15th century.

There are numerous sacred objects locked in a glass cabinet that either miraculously appeared here or were brought by the Guru. The largest item is a *garuda* egg, which is a very heavy, perfectly shaped, egg-like stone. Other relics include the traditional boot print of the Guru, the footprint of his consort Yeshe Tsogyal (aged eight), the hoof print of Guru Rinpoche's horse and a phallus-shaped rock belonging to Pema Lingpa.

Gom Kora's celebrated old *thondrol,* unique because it is painted, not appliquéd, is now kept in Chorten Kora. Gom Kora has a new *thondrol,* which is displayed at the **tsechu** in the second lunar month (March/ April). This festival is different from most other tsechus and pilgrims circumambulate the goemba and sacred rock throughout the night. The evening's activities are said to result in many marriages!

Behind the goemba is a fantastical large **black rock**. It is said that Guru Rinpoche was meditating in a small cave near the bottom of the rock when a demon in the shape of a cobra suddenly appeared. The Guru, alarmed, stood up quickly (as you would), most likely swore and left the impression of his pointed hat at the top of the cave. The Guru then made an agreement with the demon to stay away until the end of his meditation. The contract was sealed with thumb prints, which are still visible on the rock. The serpent also left a print, with his hood at the top of the rock.

A small **sin-testing passageway** leads from the cave to an exit below the rock – one successful participant reported that you must indeed move like a snake to get through the cave. Visitors also test their sin levels and rock climbing skills by trying to climb up the side of the rock (the 'stairway of the *dakinis*'); only the virtuous can make it. On certain auspicious days, holy water, believed to be the Guru's nectar of immortality, flows down from a crevice in the rock and pilgrims line up to spoon it into bottles. You may also see childless women carrying a hefty holy stone around the *kora* path to boost their chances of conceiving.

The monastery is home to about 25 student monks.

Gom Kora to Trashi Yangtse

28KM / 1¼ HOURS

Two kilometres from Gom Kora is the sleepy village of **Duksum** (860m), the roadhead for many large villages higher in the valley. A couple of shops (try the Dondup Tsongkhag) sell colourful patterned cloth and belts woven by the local women using back-strap looms. Duksum's iron chain-link bridge, believed to be the last surviving example of those built by Thangtong Gyalpo (see the boxed text, p86) was tragically washed away by flooding in 2004, but some links were recovered and used in the reconstructed bridge at Tamchhog Lhakhang (see p85). Duksum has had a difficult time of late; a rockfall caused the villagers to abandon the upper section of the bazaar.

The road turns northwest and follows the Kulong Chhu valley towards Trashi Yangtse. The eastern fork of the river flows from Arunachal Pradesh in India and is known as the Dawung Chhu. There are proposals to build a dam along this section of the Kulong Chhu.

Climbing high above the Kulong Chhu the road passes the junction of a paved road at Zangpozor that leads 9km to the village of **Tshenkarla**. Above the village school are the ruins of **Tshenkarla dzong**, which was built in the first half of the 9th century by Prince Tsangma, the eldest son of Tibetan king Trisong Detsen. The prince established himself in eastern Bhutan after he was banished from Tibet. The old name of this town is Rangthang Woong.

Beyond the small settlement of Shali the habitation gets more sparse as the valley becomes steeper and less suitable for cultivation. Snowy peaks at the head of the valley come in and out of focus. After traversing along a rocky cliff, a house-like building appears on a promontory where a side stream, the Dongdi Chhu, joins the valley. This is the original Trashi Yangtse Dzong, built by Pema Lingpa alongside the former trade route; it now houses the town's community of 100 monks. The *dratshang* (monastic college) has a dramatic main assembly hall and an *utse*, which holds the dzong's most precious relic, a statue of Chenresig that flew here from Ralung in Tibet. The dzong is 1.5km up a side road, past a wonderful traditional cantilevered bridge.

Trashi Yangtse

♪04 / ELEV 1700M

The new settlement of Trashi Yangtse is near the Chorten Kora, 3km from the old dzong. The new dzong and rapidly growing town occupies a large bowl in one of the furthest corners of the kingdom, 550km from Thimphu. The road enters from the south passing the large Chorten Kora before it enters a subdued bazaar area with a few shops and a tall, elaborately decorated Bhutanese-style chorten. From here, one road leads to the headquarters and visitor centre of the Bomdeling Wildlife Sanctuary and another climbs to the new dzong and administrative offices, on a ridge 130m above the town. The dzong was inaugurated in 1997 and, being new, has little historical or architectural significance.

The town is known for the excellent wooden cups and bowls made here from avocado wood and maple wood using water-driven and treadle lathes. Trashi Yangtse is also a centre of paper making. They use the *tsasho* technique with a bamboo frame, which produces a distinctive pattern on the paper.

◉ Sights

Chorten Kora   CHORTEN

Chorten Kora is large, but not nearly as large as the stupa of Bodhnath, after which it was patterned. It was constructed in 1740 by Lama Ngawang Loday in memory of his late uncle, Jungshu Phesan, and to subdue local spirits. The lama went to Nepal himself and brought back a model of Bodhnath carved in a radish. He had it copied here so that people could visit this place instead of making the arduous trip to Nepal. The reason that Chorten Kora is not an exact copy of Bodhnath is because the radish shrank during the trip and distorted the carving.

During the second month of the lunar calendar there is a **kora** here, whereby people gain merit by walking around the chorten. It is celebrated on two separate dates, 15 days apart. The first day is for the people from the Dakpa community in Arunachal Pradesh, India, who make the three-day pilgrimage here to celebrate the sacrifice of an eight-year-old girl from Arunachal Pradesh who was enshrined in the chorten during its construction to appease a troublesome demon. The second *kora* is for the Bhutanese, who come from all over eastern Bhutan. A month before the festival the chorten is whitewashed anew, with funds earned from rice grown in the fields immediately surrounding the chorten.

In front of the chorten is a natural stone stupa, the *sertho,* which is referred to as the 'mother' of the chorten. There's also a small goemba here. The hugely popular Bhutanese film *Chorten Kora* was shot here.

National Institute for Zorig Chusum
ART SCHOOL

(☎781141; fax 781149; ⊙9am-noon & 1-3.30pm Mon-Fri, to 12.30pm Sat) This art and craft institute was opened in 1997 to provide opportunities in vocational training for those who do not continue in the system of higher education. The school strives to produce technically proficient craftspeople, while providing them with a basic educational foundation. Six of the Zorig Chusum (13 arts and crafts) are studied here, including *thangka* painting, embroidery, sculpture, metalwork and woodturning. You can visit the school, watch the students at work and take photographs, though the selection of crafts for sale is rather disappointing. The students are on holiday from December to March and for two weeks in July.

🛏 Sleeping & Eating

Karmaling Hotel and Bakery   HOTEL **$$**
(☎781113; s/d Nu 1200/1500) This is the main tourist hotel in town, with attached Western bathrooms with hot-water geysers but no showers or tubs – just a bucket. The main building boasts a veranda, bakery and restaurant. This place could be nice if it weren't for the hard beds, bare walls and lack of showers.

Bomdeling Wildlife Sanctuary Guest House   GUESTHOUSE **$**
(☎781155; s/d Nu 400/500) The sanctuary visitor centre (see the boxed text below) has several basic rooms with attached bathrooms in its guesthouse, which you could use as a base to visit the sanctuary. Upper-floor rooms are the best.

Thinley Dendup Hotel   HOTEL **$**
(☎781192; r with/without bathroom Nu 500/350) This local hotel has basic rooms with hard beds and hot water, and you can get a simple meal here.

Dzongkhag Guest House   GUESTHOUSE **$**
(☎781148; r Nu 500-600) If you have connections, you might be able to stay at this tin-roofed government guesthouse, just below the dzong and the Royal Guest House (off-limits to visitors). All rooms have a bathroom but only half have hot water.

🛍 Shopping
The **Thinley Dendup General Shop & Handicraft** (☺7am-7pm) store near the Bomdeling turn-off, stocks textiles, wooden bowls, brass butter lamps and other religious paraphernalia.

ℹ Getting There & Away
Public buses run to Thimphu on Monday and Friday and to Trashigang on Wednesday and Saturday.

Around Trashi Yangtse

BOMDELING WILDLIFE SANCTUARY
Bomdeling is a two- to three-hour walk or a 13km 4WD drive north of Chorten Kora. It is the winter (November to early March) roosting place of a flock of black-necked cranes (see p250). The flock of 120 to 150 cranes, smaller than the flock in Phobjikha, returns here year after year. The sanctuary is also home to black-capped langurs, red pandas, tigers and snow leopards.

Apart from crane-watching, there are possible hikes up to the Buddhist sites of Rigsum Goempo, Dechen Phodrang and Minkhar Goemba. Under development is a community information centre and cafeteria at Bomdeling village and a day-trip hiking trail from the village to Trashi Yangtse. Visit the helpful visitor centre (opposite) in Trashi Yangste to get the latest information on these developments.

SAMDRUP JONGKHAR DZONGKHAG

The only reason to make the tortuous drive into southeastern Bhutan is to leave it, at the border crossing with India at Samdrup Jongkhar. Although it is rarely done, you can also enter the country at this border crossing and wind your way north and west into Bhutan. For further information, head to shop.lonelyplanet.com to purchase a downloadable PDF of the Northeast States chapter of Lonely Planet's *India* guidebook.

DON'T MISS

BOMDELING WILDLIFE SANCTUARY VISITOR CENTRE

This **visitor centre** (☎781155; bws@druknet.bt; ☺9am-5pm Mon-Fri) in Trashi Yangtse town has some interesting displays (dioramas, stuffed animals etc) on the geology and natural history of the 1445-sq-km sanctuary. The helpful manager can advise on hiking and camping options (in the central part of the sanctuary only) and how community-based tourism is being developed in the sanctuary buffer zones.

Trashigang to Samdrup Jongkhar

180KM

The winding drive from Trashigang to Samdrup Jongkhar takes at least six hours.

TRASHIGANG TO KANGLUNG
22KM / 45 MINS

Three kilometres from Trashigang bazaar, the southern road turns off the Mongar road and climbs past the petrol station.

Climbing around a ridge and heading south the road passes the settlement of **Pam**. There are a few houses near the road, but there is an extensive settlement and a lhakhang on the hillside above. The narrow unpaved road that leads uphill from here goes to Rangshikhar Goemba.

Descend into a side valley, cross a stream and climb through rice terraces to the prosperous farming community of **Rongthung**, 17km from Trashigang. The road then climbs to a ridge and enters **Kanglung** (1870m), where you can see the clock tower and extensive campus of **Sherubtse College**.

The late Father William Mackey, a Jesuit priest, was instrumental in setting up Sherubtse (Peak of Knowledge), Bhutan's only college, in the late 1970s. India aided in the construction of the original school in 1964 as part of the construction of the road from Trashigang to the Indian border. Most foreigners know of the college through reading Jamie Zeppa's *Beyond the Sky and the Earth,* which chronicles her time teaching here as a Canadian volunteer. The clock tower and green lawns give the town the feel of a Himalayan hill station.

KANGLUNG TO KHALING
32KM / 1 HOUR

The road climbs through fields of corn and potatoes, then switchbacks around a line of eight chortens. There are fine views down over the college and as far as Drametse Goemba (p136), far across the valley. Above the road is the Yongphula army camp and further on is Yongphu Goemba. Hidden on a ridge above the road is Bhutan's second airstrip. Work had commenced in 2010 to convert the small military airstrip into one able to handle domestic commercial flights, making eastern Bhutan much more accessible (plans were to have it operational by late 2010).

The road crosses the **Yongphu La** (2190m), offering you a last glimpse of the Himalaya, and swoops along the top of the Barshong valley, cutting across a ridge into another valley, before winding down again. A short climb leads over yet another ridge marked by chortens. It then descends to **Gumchu**, below which is a lush valley dotted with traditional houses.

Rounding a corner, the road enters **Khaling**, spread out in a large valley high above the Drangme Chhu. Above the valley is a small lhakhang. In the centre of the valley below Khaling is the **National Institute for the Disabled**. This very well-organised institution tries to assimilate students from all over Bhutan who are blind or otherwise disabled into the local educational system by providing special resources and training. One of their accomplishments is the development of a Dzongkha version of Braille. The school was originally set up by missionaries but has been run by the government since 1987.

Three kilometres beyond Khaling is the **National Handloom Development Project** (☎04-581122; nhdp@druknet.com; ⊗8am-1pm & 2-5pm Mon-Fri, 8am-noon Sat), operated by the National Women's Association of Bhutan (NWAB). It contracts out weaving and provides cotton yarn on credit to about 400 villagers, who then return the finished product to be sold here or at Handicraft Emporiums in Thimphu, Paro and Bumthang. It has samples of about 300 designs and, although it doesn't have fabric from every design in stock, it will take orders.

Particularly interesting are samples of the plants that are used to produce the natural dyes, including rhododendrons (pale yellow), an insect secretion called *lac* (purple) and the stem of the madder creeping plant (pale pink). Photography of the workshops and of the design samples is strictly prohibited. Prices for a length of woven cloth vary from Nu 1000 up to Nu 20,000, and there are also shawls for sale. Most of the basic cotton is imported from Kolkata.

KHALING TO WAMRONG
27KM / 45 MINS

Beyond Khaling, the road traverses above scattered houses and cornfields before climbing to the head of a rhododendron-filled valley and crossing the **Kharung La** at 2350m. There's a short descent through crumbling hills, then another climb to another pass at 2430m.

Curling around the valley, the route descends past a side road to Thrimshing, then curves round the **Zangto Pelri Lhakhang**. This may well be the last Bhutanese goemba you see, so consider stopping to check out the wonderfully detailed murals and ceiling mandalas. Two kilometres below the lhakhang is the pleasant town of **Wamrong** (2130m), where you can get a good lunch at one of the local-style restaurants. More than half of Wamrong's bazaar was razed in a fire suffered in late 2009 and rebuilding was continuing at the time we visited. **Dechen Wangdi Restaurant** has Bhutanese staples, and try **Jerme Fast Food** for fresh *momos*. Wamrong is a *drungkhag* and so has a small dzong.

WAMRONG TO PEMAGATSHEL JUNCTION
20KM / 45 MINS

The road here descends for 6km to Riserboo and its Norwegian-funded hospital. There is a good view down the huge valley as the road traverses in and out of side valleys past the hamlet of **Moshi**, halfway between Trashigang and Samdrup Jongkhar. At a bend in the road at kilometre marker 77 you get your first glimpse of the Assam plain below.

Before long you meet the junction to **Pemagatshel**, from where you can see Yongla Goemba on a hill across the valley.

The name Pemagatshel means 'blissful land of the lotus'. This rural dzongkhag in the southeastern part of the country is Bhutan's smallest district. Its headquarters, Pemagatshel, is reached via a side road that leads off the Samdrup Jongkhar to Trashigang road.

Yongla Goemba is one of the holiest shrines in eastern Bhutan. It was founded in the 18th century by Kheydup Jigme Kuenduel, who was advised by the great *terton* Rigzin Jigme Lingpa to establish a monastery on a mountain that looked like a *phurba* (ritual dagger) and overlooked the vast plains of India. Later the goemba was used as a base for religious ceremonies by Trongsa *penlop* Jigme Namgyal during the great Duar War with the British in 1865.

PEMAGATSHEL JUNCTION TO DEOTHANG
55KM / 1¾ HOURS

Below the junction comes the day's most dangerous section of road, the **Menlong Brak** (*brak,* or *brag,* means cliff in Sharchop), high above the upper Bada valley. The fragile road passes prayer flags, prayer

plaques and chortens to reach the Dantak-sponsored Hindu shrine at **Krishnagiri**, where your car (and occupants) will get a *tikka* from the resident sadhu. It's an amazing descent, with sheer drops putting the fear of Shiva into you.

From the two-road village of **Narphung** (with its one-way system!), the road passes a checkpoint to the Narphung La at 1698m. It crosses a ridge and climbs to 1920m before beginning the final descent to the plains.

The road weaves down, reaching the PWD camp at Morong at 1600m, whose workers are responsible for the Indian-style homilies that line the roads here: 'speed thrills but kills', 'After whisky driving is risky', and our favourite: 'it is not a rally, enjoy the valley'.

The Choekey Gyantso Institute for Advanced Buddhist Philosophy marks the outskirts of **Deothang** at 850m. The town's old name town was Dewangiri, and it was the site of a major battle between the Bhutanese and the British in 1865. The town is dominated by a large Royal Bhutan Army (RBA) camp and to the south is a chorten with the names of all those who died building Bhutan's roads. A side road branches off here to Bhangtar, a border town not open to foreigners.

DEOTHANG TO SAMDRUP JONGKHAR
18KM / 30 MINS

The road eventually hits the valley floor with a thud, as a rock painting of Guru Rinpoche marks the end of the Himalayan foothills. The road curves through the final ripples of the continental collision zone passing the Dickensian Bhutan Chemical Industries to the fairly cursory checkpoint at **Pinchinang**, 4km or so before Samdrup Jongkhar.

Samdrup Jongkhar
🕿 07 / ELEV 170M

The highway enters the town from the north, passing the small modern dzong, post office, Dzongkhag (former Hifi) Guest House and Bank of Bhutan. The main road crosses a bridge then turns left into the compact bazaar area, where you'll find hotels, shops and restaurants. If you go straight instead of turning left, you will hit the border.

There's little reason to linger in this sweltering border town. The streets are jammed with Tata trucks and every morning and afternoon a tide of Indian workers crosses the border to work in the town. A Bhutanese-style gate decorated with a dragon and *garuda* bids you farewell as you collect your exit stamp in your passport and cross into the heat and chaos of India.

🛏 Sleeping & Eating

TLT Guesthouse   HOTEL **$$**
(☎251470; fax 251502; s/d Nu 1000/1200, with air-con Nu 1500/1800) This well-run hotel next to the market area is the best option in town with soft mattresses, clean attached bathrooms, satellite TVs in every room and a good multi-cuisine restaurant with mouth-watering Indian food.

Hotel Mountain   HOTEL **$$**
(☎251178; fax 251130; r with/without air-con Nu 1800/1400) Take the stairs up one floor to this modern hotel with functional and spacious rooms with satellite TVs, attached bathrooms and a bright, airy, multi-cuisine restaurant and bar.

Hotel Menjong   HOTEL **$**
(☎251094; s/d Nu 650/850) The Menjong has spacious rooms but check the mattresses as these vary. There's a decent though dimly lit lobby restaurant and bar.

Other options include the basic Indian-style **Hotel Shambhala** (☎251222; s/d Nu 275/375) and **Hotel Friends** (☎251544; r with/without air-con Nu 750/400), where simple rooms with TVs and attached bathrooms can be found on the 1st floor.

ⓘ Information

Bank of Bhutan (☎251149; ◷9am-1pm Mon-Fri, to 11am Sat) Will change ngultrum into Indian rupees but not US dollars.

Rita Internet (◷8am-9pm; per min Nu 1)

ⓘ Getting There & Away

The easiest way to get to Guwahati is to arrange an Indian taxi through your hotel. A non-air-con 4WD costs Nu 2500 for the 100km drive. Buses from the Indian town of Darranga, a 10-minute walk or rickshaw ride over the border, depart for Guwahati (Rs55 to Rs70) at 6.30am and 2pm.

Due to security concerns, all Bhutanese vehicles have to travel in a convoy as far as Rangiya (convoys do not run on Thursday or Sunday), 49km from the border. Indian vehicles face no such restrictions. For more on immigration and onward travel into India, see p269

Treks

Treks in This Book

All told, there are more than 25 treks in Bhutan that are officially approved by the government. However, not all are open at the same time, so double-check with your operator before zeroing in on an itinerary. Apart from approved treks, alternate routes are constantly explored by the Tourism Council of Bhutan (TCB), and may be walked with prior permission obtained by tour operators. Variations within prescribed itineraries are also possible, and many routes can be trekked in the reverse direction, logistics permitting. This chapter details 14 major treks across the country, including two brand-new trails, the itineraries for which are still in the process of being finalised. Between them, these trails offer everything that a trekker could want, including what is claimed to be the world's most difficult trek. All were open at the time of research.

Route Descriptions

The route details in this chapter provide a comprehensive overview of the terrain and cultural background, but are not self-guiding trail descriptions by themselves. Once on the trail, it's your guide who knows best. Some treks that follow old trade routes are seldom used by people today. Since there is usually no one around to ask for directions, you need to stay reasonably close to your guide or horsemen to ensure you are on the correct path.

Daily Stages

Route descriptions are divided into daily stages, and give an estimate of the number of days required for each trek. The stages are marked by campsites designated by TCB, and the rules state that you must camp at these places, although new campsites are sometimes identified.

Before you start out, make sure you have a detailed itinerary, including rest days, worked out in advance. While discussing the trek with your staff, be careful to ensure that everyone agrees on the places where you will camp. In the past, horsemen have sometimes set off for a campsite beyond the expected stage, leaving trekkers stranded in the wilderness. Besides, some Bhutanese trekking staff have a rather relaxed approach to schedules, and late morning starts are common – often resulting in arrivals to camp after dark.

Times & Distances

The route descriptions list approximate daily walking times, based on personal experience and information produced by TCB. The estimates are 'tourist times', factoring in a leisurely pace with plenty of breaks and sightseeing. Bhutanese horsemen and over-enthusiastic trekkers can reduce walking times considerably. The distances shown are those published by TCB. They are estimates and have not been determined by any more empirical method of measurement.

Rest Days

The route descriptions are based on a reasonable number of days needed to complete the trek. You will enjoy the trek more if you add the occasional day for rest, acclimatisation or exploration – even at the cost of an extra US$200 (US$250 from 2012).

Maps in this Chapter

The maps in this chapter are based on the best available maps of each region. To make them legible, only those villages and landmarks mentioned in the text are marked. The maps show elevations for peaks and passes only – other elevations, including camps, are given in the descriptions. Trails and roads follow the general direction indicated on the maps; small switchbacks and sharp twists are not marked.

Instead of contour lines, the maps depict ridge lines, or the line of the highest point on a ridge. If the trail crosses one of these lines, you walk uphill. If the trail leads from a ridge line to a river, you're going downhill.

Altitude Measurements

The elevations given in this chapter are composites, based on measurements with an altimeter or GPS and checked against maps. There is no definitive list of elevations or names of peaks and passes in Bhutan, and various maps and publications differ significantly. In most cases, peak elevations are those defined in the mountain database produced by the Alpine Club in Britain. All other elevations are rounded to the nearest 10m.

Directions & Place Names

Bhutan is a complex maze of valleys and rivers that wind around in unexpected twists and turns. It is, therefore, difficult to define the exact compass direction of a river at a particular spot. So instead of referring to north or south banks, the slightly technical 'river right' or 'river left' have been used. This refers to the right or left side of the river as you face downstream, which is not necessarily the direction you are walking. In the route descriptions, right and left in reference to a river always refers to river right or river left.

Several mountains and places in the descriptions do not match names in other descriptions or maps of the same route. The variance occurs because most maps were made before the Dzongkha Development Commission produced its guidelines for Romanised Dzongkha. This book uses the Romanised Dzongkha standards for all place names in Bhutan.

Many streams and landmarks remain nameless in some trail descriptions. Most routes go through sparsely populated country, where there is less formality about place names. Although some places have official, historically accurate names, many camping places are in meadows or yak pastures, the names of which were made up by local herders or trekking guides and now appear on maps. Numerous small streams, valleys and other landmarks do not have names at all. Even if they do, there is usually nobody nearby to ask.

Druk Path Trek

The Druk Path is currently the most popular trek in Bhutan. The main draws are a nice mixture of monasteries and fine alpine scenery, a convenient length and the compelling sense of journey that comes from walking between Paro and Thimphu, Bhutan's two most popular destinations.

The trek is possible from late February to May and from September to December, although snow sometimes closes the route in late autumn and early spring. Afternoon showers are common in April and May. Days are normally warm, but nights can be very cold and you should always be prepared for snow. Avoid the monsoon season of July and August.

It is quite possible to shorten the trek to four days, but then you must walk six to eight hours for two of the days. With the shorter schedule you could camp at Jili La, Jimilang Tsho and Phajoding, arriving in Motithang at lunchtime of the fourth day. For a five-day trek, simply combine days four and five. Some agents modify the trek into a four-day trek in the reverse direction, starting at Motithang and finishing by hiking down from Jimilang Tsho to the road head at Tsaluna in the Bemang Rong Chhu valley. If you're a masochist you can even race through the trek in a single day: an old punishment for Bhutanese soldiers was a forced one-day march along this route.

DAY 1: NATIONAL MUSEUM TO JILI DZONG

10KM / 3½-5 HOURS / 1115M ASCENT, 40M DESCENT

The first day is fairly short but it's all uphill, gaining more than 1000m. Most groups start from a trailhead outside Paro's National Museum at 2470m. The route follows a dirt road for 30 minutes before making the

THE TREK AT A GLANCE

Duration 6 days

Max Elevation 4235m

Difficulty Medium

Season February to May, September to December

Start Paro Ta Dzong

Finish Motithang

Access Towns Paro, Thimphu

Summary One of the most scenic and popular treks in Bhutan, following a wilderness trail past several remote lakes and a famous meditation retreat. Trekking days are short but the trail goes to a relatively high altitude, making it moderately strenuous.

JILI DZONG

The 15th-century Jili Dzong has long occupied an important site. It was the residence of Ngawang Chhogyel (1465–1540), the cousin of Lama Drukpa Kunley, and the Zhabdrung is said to have meditated here before heading down to Paro to defeat an invading Tibetan army. The impressive main lhakhang contains a large statue of Sakyamuni almost 4m high. One can only wonder what kinds of mischief the 13 resident monks must have perpetrated to warrant banishment to such a high and isolated monastery!

first of many short cuts that avoid the looping road. After 40 minutes, pass Kuenga Choeling Lhakhang (unusually a Gelugpa-school chapel; thus the photos of the Dalai Lama) at 2650m. A further hour's climb takes you to the stone houses and apple orchards of **Damchena** (2880m), 10 minutes before a *mani* (carved stone) wall and campsite in a clearing known as **Damche Gom** (2985m).

It's then a long, but not steep, climb through forests of golden moss to a herders' camp just before Jili La (3540m). Cross the pass (marked by a cairn and broken chorten) and drop to an excellent camping place in a meadow surrounded by rhododendron forests just below **Jili Dzong**.

DAY 2: JILI DZONG TO RABANA
10KM / 3-4 HOURS / 425M ASCENT, 50M DESCENT

Today's walk is a short and enjoyable ridge walk, full of short ascents and descents, so there's plenty of time for a morning visit to Jili Dzong. You might see or hear monal pheasants during the day.

From the dzong the route first follows prayer flags and then descends through rhododendrons to a saddle at 3550m, before climbing for 40 minutes to great views of Paro and the Bemang Rong valley. If the weather is clear, look for Jhomolhari and other snow-capped peaks in the distance.

The trail crosses to the east side of the ridge offering views down to Gimena village (look for its large goemba). Climb again and traverse around the west side of a cone-shaped hill to a saddle (3750m) and two clearings, the latter below some prayer flags. Five minutes' further is **Jangchhu**

Lakha, a yak pasture at 3760m. From here a lower trail continues 10 minutes to an often-boggy camping spot at **Tshokam** (3770m). A better option is to take the higher trail for 25 minutes to the yak herders' camp of **Rabana** (3890m), surrounded by mauve rhododendron forests.

DAY 3: RABANA TO JIMILANG TSHO
11KM / 4 HOURS / 375M DESCENT, 370M ASCENT

There are two trails to Jimilang Tsho. Most groups take the high trail (described here) because it offers better views, including (in good weather) Jhomolhari and 6989m Jichu Drakye, the peak representing the protective deity of Paro. The lower trail descends from Tshokham into the upper Bemang Rong valley and then climbs via the yak pasture of Langrithang.

From Rabana a horse trail ascends the ridge diagonally to a viewpoint marked by a lone prayer flag at 3960m. Traverse for 30 minutes to a meadow, then descend through rhododendrons, heading just left of a miniature peak topped with prayer flags. An hour from camp you crest the minor **Langye Ja La** (Ox Hump Pass) at 4070m. You can climb 50m to the top of the mini-peak for impressive 360-degree views.

The rocky descent is hard on the feet, passing a small herders' shelter by an overhanging rock, and then climbing 80m to a pass for fine views of Jhomolhari. Far below in the Do Chhu valley you can see the yellow roof of Chumpu Ney, a pilgrimage spot famous for its statue of Dorje Phagmo. Five minutes later you see isolated Jimilang Tsho far below you. Descend to a saddle for lunch and then climb and angle around the ridge to a chorten at 4180m for a final view of Jhomolhari. A steep 30-minute descent leads to the shore of **Jimilang Tsho**, with pleasant camping five minutes' further at the far end of the lake (3885m).

Jimilang Tsho means 'Sand Ox Lake', and was named for a bull that emerged from the lake and joined the cattle of a family that uses the area as a summer grazing ground. The lake is also known for its giant trout, which were introduced in the 1970s.

DAY 4: JIMILANG TSHO TO SIMKOTRA TSHO
11KM / 4 HOURS / 820M ASCENT, 400M DESCENT

The trail climbs from the lower end of the lake through yellow rhododendrons to a ridge at 4010m, traverses the ridge, then descends to a single stone shelter. Following the ridge, you crest at some prayer flags at 4050m overlooking **Janye Tsho**. Descend to a yak herders' camp near the lake at 3880m before climbing again, veering eventually to the right, to a ridge at 4150m and views of overlooking **Simkotra Tsho**. Descend to some stone ruins and a camp at 4100m.

Be sure everyone is clear on where to camp on this day. Horse drivers often push to continue over the next ridge to a better camp and grazing land at **Labana**.

DAY 5: SIMKOTRA TSHO TO PHAJODING
10KM / 3-4 HOURS / 130M ASCENT, 680M DESCENT

It's a long climb past three false summits, before the trail descends to Labana camping place at 4110m, near a stone hut beside an almost-dry lake. There's a final longish climb to a group of cairns atop **Labana La** at 4235m. The hill above the trail marks a seldom-used sky burial site. The trail descends gently to crest a minor pass at 4210m. There are views of Dochu La and Jhomolhari along this stretch.

From here the trail descends to a final 4090m pass marked by a chorten. Below sprawls the entire Thimphu valley. Weather permitting, there are views of Gangkhar Puensum and other Himalayan peaks. The main trail descends northeast towards Phajoding below but after 10 minutes it's worth taking the side trail for 20 minutes southeast down to Thuji Drak, a remote meditation centre that clings to the side of a precipitous rock face at 3950m.

Meditation centres and lhakhangs are scattered across the hillside. A descent on a maze of eroded trails through juniper and rhododendrons leads to a campsite beside the main Jampa Lhakhang at 3640m. See p66 for details of Phajoding Goemba. Darkness brings the bright city lights far below you and the feeling that you have arrived back at the edge of the world.

DAY 6: PHAJODING TO MOTITHANG
4-5KM / 2½ HOURS / 1130M DESCENT

This day's trek is all downhill through forest so tie your laces tight and keep your trekking poles handy. A wide trail passes a chorten at 3440m, 40 minutes after which there is a trail junction. The left branch descends via Chhokhortse Goemba to the BTC telecom tower at Sangaygang, offering an interesting alternative end to the trek.

The normal route branches right and descends more steeply towards Motithang.

There are numerous short cuts, but they all eventually lead to the same place. Pass another chorten at 3070m and descend steeply to a stream, crossing it at 2820m. Climb to a rough road and follow it down to your waiting vehicle.

Dagala Thousand Lakes Trek

This trek is off the beaten track; you will probably encounter no other trekkers along the way. It's not particularly demanding (despite a few steep climbs), and most trekking days are short. The route is best walked in April and late September through October. However, snow in the high country can often block out the route, compelling you to return.

It's a 29km drive from Thimphu to the junction of an unpaved road, which crawls up 8km to a Basic Health Unit (BHU) at Khoma, high above the Geynitsang Chhu at 2850m. The trail head lies another 3km ahead at the suspension bridge in Geynizampa.

DAY 1: GEYNIZAMPA TO GUR
5KM / 4 HOURS / 550M ASCENT, 60M DESCENT

Crossing the suspension bridge, the trail turns south along the east side of the Geynitsang Chhu (river left) to a side stream, the Dolungu Chhu. Cross the stream on a log bridge and start uphill on an eroded trail through an oak forest. Currently used only by yak herders, woodcutters and a handful of trekkers, this trail was once a major trading route between Thimphu and **Dagana**, headquarters of Dagana Dzongkhag. This accounts for the walls, well-crafted stone

THE TREK AT A GLANCE

Duration 5 days

Max Elevation 4520/4720m

Difficulty Medium

Season April, September to October

Start Geynizampa

Finish Chamgang

Access Town Thimphu

Summary A short trek near Thimphu, to a number of lovely, high-altitude lakes (far fewer, however, than the name suggests).

YAK! YAK!

Westerners tend to oversimplify its many manifestations into a single name, yet it is only the full-blooded, long-haired bull of the species *Bos grunniens* that truly bears the name yak. In Bhutan, the name is pronounced 'yuck'. Females of the species are called *jim*, and are prized for their butterfat-rich milk, used to make butter and cheese.

Large, ponderous and clumsy looking, yaks can move very quickly when startled. If you are trekking with yaks, give them a wide berth, and don't put anything fragile in your luggage. If an animal becomes alarmed, it charges up a hill, and your baggage could fall off and get trampled while the yak bucks and snorts, even as its keeper tries to regain control.

Though some yaks are crossbred with local cows, there are many purebred yaks in Bhutan – massive animals with thick furry coats and impressive sharp horns.

staircases and other developments along portions of the route.

A long climb leads to an outstanding lookout point at 3220m. The ascent is now gentler, and the trail climbs to the top of the ridge where it makes a hairpin turn at 3350m. The way to the campsite is an inconspicuous path that leads off the trail here, going southward through the forest to **Gur**, amid yak pastures at 3290m.

DAY 2: GUR TO LABATAMBA
12KM / 5 HOURS / 1040M ASCENT, 110M DESCENT

Climb back from camp to the main trail and continue gently up the ridge on a wide track. A long, stiff climb through blue pines leads to a rocky outcrop where the vegetation changes to spruces, dead firs and larches. The trail traverses into a side valley, crosses a stream at 3870m and begins a long, gentle climb through scattered birches and rhododendrons, weaving in and out of side valleys and crossing several tiny streams. At **Pangalabtsa**, a pass marked by cairns at 4250m, there is a spectacular view of the whole Dagala range. This is prime yak country, with numerous herders' camps scattered across the broad Labatamba valley. Descend from

the pass to the first herders' hut at 4170m and traverse around the head of a small valley to the main valley floor. Climb beside a stream to **Labatamba**, a camp at 4300m near Utsho Lake, a beautiful high-altitude *tsho* (lake) with a thriving population of golden trout. The area near the lakes bursts with alpine wildflowers in September. There are numerous other pretty lakes in the vicinity, and you could schedule an extra day here to explore them.

DAY 3: LABATAMBA TO PANKA
8KM / 6-7 HOURS / 260M ASCENT, 520M DESCENT

There are two possible routes ahead, and pack animals will take the lower one. The trail here is undefined (more of a cross-country traverse), and climbs along the western side of the Dajatsho lake to a saddle at 4520m, with good mountain views. If you want a better view, you could scramble to the top of a 4720m peak to the east. From the pass, the trail descends past several herders' camps before dropping to the Dochha Chhu, rejoining the lower trail at about 4200m. Subsequently, it climbs over three ridges and descends to **Panka** at 4000m. Water is scarce here during spring, and it may thus be necessary to descend to an alternative camp 20 minutes below.

DAY 4: PANKA TO TALAKHA
8KM / 6-7 HOURS / 180M ASCENT, 1100M DESCENT

The route leads north to a crest at 4100m, where several trails lead off in different directions. The trail to Talakha climbs steeply up a slate slope to the ruins of a house. From here, it is a long traverse to **Tale La** at 4180m, which offers a view of the Dagala range and Thimphu, far away to the north. Finally, it's a long descent – first through a mixed forest of spruce, birch, juniper and rhododendron, and then through bamboo – to the goemba at **Talakha** (3080m).

DAY 5: TALAKHA TO CHAMGANG
6KM / 3 HOURS / 440M DESCENT

There is a road passing just below the goemba, and you can choose to end your trek here by requesting a 4WD pick-up. However, it's a rough and bumpy ride to Simtokha, so it's better to walk three hours down the road, taking a few short cuts to avoid switchbacks, and reach **Chamgang** at 2640m, where you can meet your vehicle. There is an alternate trail that leads to Simtokha, but it is steep and eroded, with numerous apple orchard fences standing in the way, and is best avoided.

Jhomolhari Trek

The Jhomolhari Trek is to Bhutan what the Everest Base Camp route is to Nepal: a trekking pilgrimage. With two different versions (The TCB counts them as two separate treks), it's one of the most trodden routes in the country, and almost 40% of all trekkers who come to Bhutan end up following one of the Jhomolhari routes. The first three days of the trek follow the Paro Chhu valley to Jangothang, climbing gently, but continually, with a few short, steep climbs over side ridges. It crosses a high pass and visits the remote village of Lingzhi, then crosses another pass before making its way towards Thimphu. The last four days of the trek cover a lot of distance and require many hours of walking. The trek also affords an excellent opportunity to see yaks.

The trek is possible from April to early June and September to November; April and October are most favourable. The day-light hours are normally warm, but nights can be very cold, especially above Jangothang. There is a lot of mud on this trail and it can be miserable in the rain. Snow usually closes the high passes mid-November onward, and they don't reopen until April.

DAY 1: DRUKGYEL DZONG TO SHARNA ZAMPA

17KM / 4-6 HOURS / 360M ASCENT, 80M DESCENT

The trek traditionally starts from the ruins of Drukgyel Dzong at 2580m (although a 4WD vehicle can drop you further up the trail at Mitshi Zampa on a feeder road). From Drukgyel Dzong, the trek starts with a short, 80m descent to the Paro Chhu river. Upstream is the small settlement of Chang Zampa, with an outreach clinic and a shop. A *zam* (bridge) crosses to river left here – don't cross it. The trek stays on the south bank (river right), among fields of potatoes and wheat. On the opposite side, it's all red rice.

Jhomolhari Treks

THE TREK AT A GLANCE

Duration 9 days

Max Elevation 4930m

Difficulty Medium–hard

Season April to June, September to November

Start Drukgyel Dzong

Finish Dodina

Access Towns Paro, Thimphu

Summary Bhutan's popular showcase trek offers a spectacular view of the 7314m Jhomolhari from a high camp at Jangothang.

Half an hour later, you arrive at the settlement of Mitshi Zampa. Here, the route leaves the road and crosses to the left bank of the Paro Chhu via a Swiss-built suspension bridge at 2540m. The well-worn trail climbs gently, through well-maintained rice terraces and millet fields. A short walk leads to a small stream and a white chorten. Beyond is Sangatung, a pleasant farmhouse surrounded by fields.

The route now enters an area of apple orchards and blue-pine and fir forests, and the trail is littered with rocks sticking out of the mud. In some places, logs have been placed to form bridge-like structures to provide a smoother walking surface. You can divert to a less-muddy alternate route here, cutting across fields and following a telephone line. Don't cross the cantilever bridge leading south; stay on river left, climbing gently to Chobiso, a single house at 2800m.

Soon the valley widens and you reach the army post of Gunitsawa (2810m), close to the border with Tibet, with a primary school and a shop. All army personnel and civilians are required to report to the checkpoint; your trek permit will be checked and endorsed here. The large dormitory-style buildings across the river are quarters for enlisted men and their families.

Below the shop at Gunitsawa, the trail crosses the Paro Chhu to river right on a wooden cantilever bridge at 2790m. It then climbs to Sharna Zampa, a camping place amid meadows surrounded by trees at 2850m. On the opposite side of the river is a helipad and archery field.

DAY 2: SHARNA ZAMPA TO THANGTHANGKA

22KM / 7-8 HOURS / 770M ASCENT, 10M DESCENT

Brace yourself for a long, hard day with lots of ups and downs, made worse by all the rock-hopping required to avoid mud holes.

Begin the day by climbing through conifers and rhododendrons flanking the Paro Chhu. If the water is high, you might have to scramble over a few small hills to get around the river in places. About 15 minutes beyond Sharna Zampa are the remnants of an old bridge with a house and a chorten on the other side. Welcome to Jigme Dorji National Park.

After about two hours of trekking through oaks, rhododendrons and ferns, and crossing several streams, you will reach Shing Karap, a stone house and a clearing at 3110m. Consider stopping here for lunch. Further ahead is the stone-paved trail leading left to Tremo La. This is the old invasion and trade route from Phari Dzong in Tibet, and still looks well-beaten since it's used by army caravans to ferry rations to the border post. Beware; many trekkers have casually ambled down this trail in the past and made a long, exhausting side trip to nowhere.

Immediately after the trail junction is a wooden bridge over a side stream. Climb a short set of switchbacks over a little ridge, then descend and cross the Paro Chhu to river left on a wooden cantilever bridge at 3230m. The route now goes up and down a rocky trail through forests of birch and fir, followed by blue pine, maple and larch woods, crossing an old landslide along the way.

About three hours ahead, there's a bridge back to river right at 3560m. The trail climbs to a place where you can see a white chorten on the opposite side of the river. There is a bridge here that leads back across the river. Don't cross it, or it'll take you up the Ronse Ghon Chhu towards Soi Yaksa, the campsite on Day 5 of the Jhomolhari trek 2.

Follow the trail on river right, and climb over a small ridge as the Paro Chhu makes a noticeable bend. Fifteen minutes from the bridge is a lovely meadow with Jhomolhari looming majestically at the head of the valley. This is Thangthangka (3610m), with a small stone shelter and a Bhutanese-style house in a cedar grove at the edge of the meadow.

DAY 3: THANGTHANGKA TO JANGOTHANG

19KM / 5-6 HOURS / 480M ASCENT

This is not a long day, but you'll be left breathless due to the significant elevation gain at high altitude.

Wake up early for good views of Jhomolhari, which will disappear behind a ridge as you climb beyond camp. Less than an hour ahead, at 3730m, there's an army post with rough stone barracks housing personnel from both the Bhutan army and the Indian Military Training Team (IMTRAT).

The trail crosses a wooden bridge over a fast-flowing stream a short distance beyond the army post. The hillside on the opposite side of the Paro Chhu is a near-vertical rock face with a few trees clinging to it. Along this stretch the trail can be extremely muddy; there are lots of big stones you can use to rock-hop around mud holes. At 3770m, about one hour from camp, the trail turns sharply right at a whitewashed *mani* wall.

A short climb leads to a small chorten on a ridge. You are now entering yak country and will see these huge beasts lumbering across hillsides and lazing in meadows. There are two trails from here, both contouring up the valley and ending near the river bank, hugging the valley floor as the river bends sharply to the right. Parts of the hillside are covered with larches, which turn a light yellow in autumn. Above the trail is the village of **Soe**. You cannot see it until you are beyond and above it, but you may meet people herding yaks near the river.

One hour beyond Soe is **Takethang**, a cluster of stone houses on a plateau at 3940m. The villagers grow barley and a large succulent plant called *kashaykoni* that is fed to yaks during winter.

The trail follows straight across the plateau, high above the river, crossing a little stream on a bridge made of big stones laid on logs. On the opposite side are a white chorten, an outreach clinic and the few houses of **Dangochang**. The people of this village raise yaks and a few sheep, and some households grow potatoes, turnips and radishes. This area is snowbound from mid-November until the end of March. From here, it's slow going, uphill beside a side stream to the camp at **Jangothang** (4080m), offering a spectacular view of Jhomolhari.

The guidelines for pack animals require that you now exchange your horses for yaks from Soe or horses from Dangochang. Don't be alarmed when your loads get dumped at the camp and the animals disappear down the valley, leaving you alone with a mountain of baggage. If all goes well, the replacement pack animals will show up on schedule when you are ready to leave.

DAY 4: ACCLIMATISATION DAY & EXPLORATION OF JANGOTHANG

If you're pressing on to Lingzhi, you should spend a day lazing in Jangothang for acclimatisation. If you are returning to Drukgyel Dzong via Jhomolhari trek 2, a day in Jangothang is the highlight of the trek; the views don't get any better than here. The horsemen also take the day off, and can be seen lazing around and playing *dego*, a traditional discus game.

There are four major possibilities for day hikes from Jangothang. The first, and best, is a four-hour excursion up the ridge to the north of the camp. There's no trail, but it's a broad open slope and you can just scramble up. The ridge seems endless, but after an hour or so, you get an excellent view of **Jichu Drakye**. Jhomolhari is hidden behind

CAMPING AT JANGOTHANG

Jangothang is clearly among the most popular campsites in the entire Himalayas. It's packed to its gills with trekkers in October, and the joke among guides is that if you're yearning to catch up with a long-lost mountain-loving pal, simply land up in Jangothang in autumn! You are unlikely to have the camp to yourself even in the lean season.

The campsite derives its name (meaning 'land of ruins') from the remains of a small fortress that sits atop a rock in a side valley leading northwest to Jhomolhari. There's a community hall with a kitchen here for the benefit of trekkers, and several large flat spots for camping. A chain of snow peaks line the eastern side of the Paro Chhu valley, and it's possible to spot blue sheep on the lower slopes. Despite being located at the foot of Jhomolhari, Jangothang has interestingly never been used as base camp by any expedition scaling the summit.

the ridge here, but becomes visible if you continue to the highest point at 4750m. You are likely to encounter grazing yaks, and, occasionally, blue sheep, on the upper slopes.

An alternative, which can be combined with the walk up the ridge, is to trek up the main valley towards the last house, then continue up the valley towards Jichu Drakye. This is the same country you'll be walking through if, later, you decide to continue trekking over the Nyile La to **Lingzhi**.

A third hike goes up towards the head of the valley in the direction of **Jhomolhari**. There is a very rough overgrown trail that cuts across moraines and brush, leading to the foot of the mountain. You can't get very far, but there are good views in the upper part of the valley.

The last alternative is an expedition to **Tshophu**, a pair of lakes that sit high on the opposite side of the river to the east, with a good supply of brown trout. To get to the lakes, follow the trail north to the last settlement in the valley (as described, p158). It takes about one hour to get to the top of the ridge and then another 30 minutes following a stream to the lake.

DAY 5: JANGOTHANG TO LINGZHI
18KM / 6-7 HOURS / 840M ASCENT, 870M DESCENT

If you are having problems with the altitude at Jangothang, consider returning. Otherwise, push ahead past three stone houses inhabited by park rangers and a few elderly people. This is the last settlement in the valley and it's extremely isolated. Around a corner, there's a spectacular view of Jichu Drakye.

Descend and cross a log bridge at 4160m to the left bank of the Paro Chhu, then start up a steep traverse heading back downstream. The trail crests at the foot of a side valley and goes eastwards. Jichu Drakye towers above the Paro Chhu valley and soon the top of Jhomolhari appears over the ridge above the camp at Jangothang. The snow peak in the middle is a secondary summit of Jhomolhari.

At 4470m, the trail traverses under the big rocks that were visible from the camp, leads left and enters a large east–west glacial valley with numerous moraines. Apart from a few small gentians, it's just grass, tundra and small juniper bushes that grow here. You may spot blue sheep on the hillside above and see marmots darting into their burrows.

Past a false summit with a cairn at 4680m, the trail approaches the ridge and you can see Jichu Drakye to the northwest. The trail dips and then climbs back up a moraine, offering spectacular views of the sharp ridge jutting out from Jichu Drakye. The final pull is up a scree slope to **Nyile La** (4870m), about four hours from camp. You can climb higher to the northwest, where you'll see Jhomolhari 2 and Jichu Drakye on one side, and Tserim Kang (6789m) on the other. Nyile La is frequently very windy, so descend quickly through scree along the hillside, down to a stream on the valley floor at 4450m. There is some vegetation here, mostly grass, juniper and cotoneaster. It's an excellent lunch spot.

The trail now goes north, contouring along the hillside high above the valley. It's a good trail with a few small ups, but mostly down and level. Eventually you can see an army camp near the river below; the white tower of Lingzhi Dzong is visible in the distance. Following a long walk to a lookout at 4360m, the trail now descends into the large Jaje Chhu valley, making many switchbacks through rhododendrons and birches to a yak pasture on the valley floor. Jichu Drakye and Tserim Kang tower over the head of the valley and you can see some remarkable examples of moraines on their lower slopes. The camp is at **Chha Shi Thang** near a large stone community hall (4010m) used by both Bhutanese travellers and trekking groups. **Lingzhi** is up the obvious trail on the opposite side of the Jaje Chhu.

If you take a spare day here, you can make an excursion to Chhokam Tsho at 4340m near the base camp of Jichu Drakye. During the hike you may encounter blue sheep and musk deer. If you are continuing to Thimphu, schedule a rest day here. The village and dzong at Lingzhi are worth visiting, and it's useful to rest up for the following strenuous trek day.

DAY 6: LINGZHI TO SHODU
22KM / 8-9 HOURS / 940M ASCENT, 920M DESCENT

Start early today; you have a long and tiring trek ahead of you. Climb towards a white chorten on a ridge above the camp, then turn south up the deep Mo Chhu valley. The trail stays on the west side of the valley, crossing numerous side streams, most without bridges. About three hours from camp, it crosses the Mo Chhu. There is no bridge and the river has broken into many small channels, presenting a tedious route-finding exercise through hummocks of grass and slippery rocks.

The trail climbs steeply up the side of the main valley and crosses into a large side valley, climbing above a stream. It then makes an impressive climb up the headwall, zigzagging through rocks to a large cairn atop Yeli La at 4930m. Avoid walking with the pack animals because the trail here is carved into a rock cliff and is quite narrow. From the pass, on a clear day, you can see Jhomolhari, Gangchhenta and Tserim Kang.

Descending to a hanging valley after passing a small lake at 4830m, the trail tracks the outflow from the lake, and goes down to another huge valley with a larger lake, Khedo Tsho, at 4720m. Watch for grazing blue sheep. The trail then crosses the upper reaches of the Jaradinthang Chhu and descends along the valley, following the river southwards, crossing several side streams. After crossing back to the east bank on a log bridge at 4340m, the trail reaches a chorten at 4150m where it turns eastwards into the upper Wang Chhu valley. Descending and crossing to the south bank (river right) on a log bridge, the trail traverses a narrow, sandy slope to a camping place at **Shodu** (4080m), just at the tree line.

DAY 7: SHODU TO BARSHONG
16KM / 5-6 HOURS / 250M ASCENT, 670M DESCENT

Upon leaving Shodu, you cross to river left and pass an abandoned army camp and a small alternative campsite. The trail traverses under steep yellow cliffs with a few meditation caves carved into them, where the Zhabdrung supposedly spent some time. Down a steep stone staircase, the trail reaches the river, crossing it on a log bridge at 3870m. For the next three hours, the trail crosses the river five more times, slopping through muddy cypress forests on the south slope and hugging the steep canyon walls and crossing large side streams on the north slope, eventually ending up on the north bank (river left) at 3580m.

The route climbs gradually for one hour to **Barshong**, where there is a dilapidated community hall and the ruins of a small dzong. The designated camp is below the ruins at 3710m, but it is in a swampy meadow and most groups elect to continue to a better camp by the river, about 1½ hours beyond.

DAY 8: BARSHONG TO DOLAM KENCHO
15KM / 4-6 HOURS / 290M ASCENT, 640M DESCENT

The trail descends gently through a dense forest of rhododendrons, birches and conifers, and then drops steeply on a rocky trail to meet the Wang Chhu. Thirty minutes of walking through a larch forest leads to a clearing known as **Ta Gume Thang** (Waiting for Horses) at 3370m. Most groups camp here or 15 minutes further on at **Dom Shisa** (Where the Bear Died) instead of Barshong.

Stay on river left, climbing over ridges and descending to side streams. From here, the route then makes a steep climb to 3340m. After traversing for about 30 minutes through rhododendron forests, a trail leads off to the right. This descends to **Dolam Kencho**, a pleasant camp in a large meadow at 3320m. If your group has elected to shorten the trek and continue on to Dodina, stay on the left-hand trail, bypassing Dolam Kencho, and climb to a crest at 3430m.

DAY 9: DOLAM KENCHO TO DODINA
8KM / 3-4 HOURS / 500M ASCENT, 930M DESCENT

From the camp, a track climbs back to the main trail, reaching a crest with a cairn at 3430m. The trail descends to a stream at 3060m, then climbs again to a pass at 3120m. Another short descent and climb through bamboo forest leads to a rocky stream bed, which the trail follows down to the remains of a logging road along the Wang Chhu at 2720m. It is then a 15-minute walk south along a rocky route to the road head at **Dodina** (2640m), opposite the bridge that leads to Cheri Goemba.

Jhomolhari Trek 2

If you fancy sighting Jhomolhari and Jichu Drakye from up close, but nonetheless want to avoid the tiring slog all the way to Lingzhi, this trek is just right for you. While it's possible to return from Jangothang to Drukgyel Dzong by the same route taken on the way up, most trekkers choose to take an alternate route described here, which is less strenuous than the classic Jhomolhari trek and can be completed in less time. Despite its relative ease, however, be warned that this route still goes up to an elevation that could cause altitude problems.

THE TREK AT A GLANCE

Duration 8 days

Max Elevation 4890m

Difficulty Medium

Season April to June, September to November

Start/Finish Drukgyel Dzong

Access Town Paro

Summary The shorter and easier version of the main Jhomolhari trek goes to the Jhomolhari base camp at Jangothang, returning either via the same route or by an alternate trail.

DAYS 1-4: DRUKGYEL DZONG TO JANGOTHANG

Follow days 1 to 4 of the main Jhomolhari trek.

DAY 5: JANGOTHANG TO SOI YAKSA

16KM / 6-7 HOURS / 810M ASCENT, 1090M DESCENT

From Jangothang, the return trail initially leads north to the last settlement in the valley, before dropping to the Paro Chhu, crossing it on a wooden bridge. After crossing the river, you begin a gradual climb, following a set of sharp switchbacks for about 300m up the side of the hill. Along the way, you can get fabulous views of Jhomolhari, Jhomolhari 2, Jichu Drakye and Tserim Kang if the weather is good. From here, it's a relatively even and smooth hike all the way to a large cirque nestling the lakes of **Tshophu** (4380m), a pair of splendid high-altitude water bodies, inhabited by a flock of ruddy shelducks and known to foster a healthy population of brown trout deep in their placid waters. While it's possible to set up camp in between the two lakes, you could always carry on along the trail, which now climbs high above the eastern side of the first lake, passes the second lake along the way and finally climbs across a scree slope to the crest of a ridge. From here, it descends into a hidden valley, before climbing steeply to **Bhonte La** at 4890m, the highest point on this route.

Descending from Bhonte La, the route now runs past a scree slope, and then winds down a ridge with a lot of crisscrossing yak trails. Finally, it switchbacks down to the **Soi Yaksa** valley (also known as the Dhumzo Chhu valley), a beautiful setting for a camp at 3800m with rocky cliffs, wildflower meadows, a few nomadic settlements and a waterfall at the end of the valley. All through this day, keep your eyes trained on the wilderness for a host of regional wildlife, such as blue sheep, golden marmots, and the elusive snow leopard.

DAY 6: SOI YAKSA TO THOMBU SHONG

11KM / 4-5 HOURS / 720M ASCENT, 340M DESCENT

Starting out from camp, today's walk initially takes you past hillsides lush with a crop of azalea and rhododendron, before gradually climbing above the tree line. You will also cross forests of birch and oak on the way. The trail ascends about 100m over a ridge, before dropping to a meadow with a chorten and a *mani* wall, and another stream flowing nearby. If you have enough time on your hands, you can make a quick detour from this place to the ruins of the **Sey Dzong**, located in one of the side valleys nearby. Otherwise, you can simply continue ahead from the *mani* wall, cross the stream on a wooden bridge, and follow the trail heading up the hillside. Not long after, it drops into a small side valley, before emerging onto a ridge. Here the trail bifurcates, and it can be quite confusing since both the tracks look very similar. Don't go left – this route will eventually take you to Lalung La, a pass that leads on to an extremely roundabout way back to Drukgyel Dzong. Go right instead. The track will first take you through a wooded area, and then climb steeply for about an hour, ascending past a few huts and chortens to **Takhung La** (4520m). Spectacular views of Jhomolhari, Jichu Drakye and Tserim Kang can be seen from the pass, and on a clear day, the formidable Kanchenjunga (8586m) can be sighted far away on the western horizon.

From Takhung La, the trail holds out for a while, before gradually meandering down to **Thombu Shong** (4180m). It's a grassy pasture dotted with three yak herders' huts, and has traditionally been used by animal herders as a campsite through various times of the year.

DAY 7: THOMBU SHONG TO SHARNA ZAMPA

13KM / 4-5 HOURS / 200M ASCENT, 1650M DESCENT

After breaking camp, follow the trail leading out of the valley through a marshy patch. From here, the well-defined track suddenly begins to gain elevation, and climbs steeply for a good 200m. This hike can prove tiring, especially since you now have an entire week's vigorous trekking behind you, although you will have adjusted well to the altitude by now, if that's any consolation. All along, you will be traversing through a gloriously beautiful garden of wildflowers, also rich with a crop of rhododendron, which is especially breathtaking through late spring and summer. At the end of the climb, you will finally cross over **Thombu La** at 4380m, where the trail eventually exits the valley. Stop here for a last good look at Kanchenjunga and Drakye Gang (5200m), among other peaks.

On the other side of Thombu La, the trail begins to amble down steeply through upland forest, and the long descent ahead can prove to be rather brutal on your knees. Leading down from the pass, the total loss in elevation all the way to the final campsite of the trek is a whopping 1800m, all within a span of about three hours. The first part of the descent is gradual, winding down to about 4000m, after which the trail makes a steep descent, zigzagging down the ridge through wildflower bushes, mostly edelweiss, before finally reaching the helipad at **Gunitsawa** (2730m). You can either camp here or – if you are looking for a quieter experience – cross the river and go upstream to camp at **Sharna Zampa** (2580m), the same place where you pitched tent on Day 1.

DAY 8: SHARNA ZAMPA TO DRUKGYEL DZONG
17KM / 4-6 HOURS / 80M ASCENT, 360M DESCENT

Follow the itinerary of Day 1 of the Jhomolhari trek in the reverse direction to **Drukgyel Dzong**.

Laya-Gasa Trek

This trek takes you into remote and isolated high country, introducing you to the unusual culture of the Layap community and allowing you to cross paths with takins. If you're lucky, you might also spot the exotic blue poppy, Bhutan's national flower. The natural hot springs in Gasa, a further attraction on this trek, were washed away by heavy rains in mid-2009. However, don't let that dampen your spirits; the rest of the trek remains eminently enjoyable.

The trek begins in the Paro valley and follows the same route as the Jhomolhari trek

as far as Lingzhi, before heading north into the highlands. Snow can sometimes close the high passes, but they are generally open from April to June and mid-September to mid-November. The best trekking month in the Laya region is April.

DAYS 1-5: DRUKGYEL DZONG TO LINGZHI

Follow Days 1 to 5 of the Jhomolhari trek (p153).

DAY 6: LINGZHI TO CHEBISA
10KM / 5-6 HOURS / 280M ASCENT, 410M DESCENT

Cross the stream below the Chha Shi Thang camp on a wooden bridge and climb up the opposite side to a chorten below Lingzhi Dzong, sitting at 4220m atop a ridge and accessible via a diversion from the trail. Also known as **Yugyel Dzong**, it was built to control travel over the Lingzhi La, a trade route between Punakha and the Tibetan town of Gyantse.

Walk down from the dzong and rejoin the lower trail leading into Lingzhi village, hidden in a valley formed by the ridge. Wheat and barley fields carpet the upper part of the side valley. The trail crosses the lower part, dotted by a few houses, a school

---

THE SHY PREDATOR

Locally referred to as *chen*, the critically endangered snow leopard is a solitary and elusive creature that lives in rocky mountain folds above the tree line, descending to lower altitudes during winter. While its white fur works as a wonderful camouflage in its icy habitat, the snow leopard is also extremely agile in high terrain, and can effortlessly walk through nearly three feet of snow. Preying on blue sheep and the occasional yak calf, it can sometimes stray into human territory in search of food. However, direct confrontations with humans are rare.

The holy grail of an entire generation of wildlife photographers and filmmakers, the snow leopard remains one of the most pursued creatures in the wild, although there's very little data on hand to portray the animal accurately. If you manage to spot one of these cats on your trek, consider yourself blessed.

THE TREK AT A GLANCE

Duration 13 days

Max Elevation 5005m

Difficulty Medium–hard

Season April to June, September to November

Start Drukgyel Dzong

Finish Damji

Access Towns Paro, Punakha

Summary This trek is an extension of the Jhomolhari trek. It offers diverse flora and fauna, with a pit stop at the far-flung village of Laya and offers a good opportunity to spot blue sheep.

and post office (with a telephone) at 4080m. The Lingzhi region has a wide variety of herbs, many of medicinal value. The National Institute of Traditional Medicine in Thimphu has a herb-collecting and -drying project here.

About one hour from Lingzhi, the trail turns into a side valley past a cairn and prayer flags on a ridge at 4140m. It then makes a long gradual descent to **Goyul** (3870m), a cluster of unusual stone houses by a stream, with dramatic rock walls towering above. Leaving Goyul, the trail climbs for an hour to a chorten. A short descent leads into the spectacular Chebisa valley, with a frozen waterfall at its head. The campsite is on a meadow opposite **Chebisa** (3880m). Upstream of the camp is the village of **Chobiso**.

DAY 7: CHEBISA TO SHOMUTHANG
17KM / 6-7 HOURS / 890M ASCENT, 540M DESCENT

Start out by climbing the ridge behind Chebisa, and then tackling a long, steep ascent up a featureless slope. There are large herds of blue sheep living in the rocks above. Watch for bearded vultures and Himalayan griffons flying overhead. At about 4410m the trail levels out and traverses to **Gogu La** (4440m), before crossing a ridge and descending into a side valley through rhododendrons.

Descend to a stream at 4170m, and then climb over a small ridge through a cedar forest. The trail crests the ridge at 4210m and descends on a muddy path into the main Jholethang Chhu valley, in a deep forest of fir and birch. There's a little climb over the side of the valley and down to **Shakshepasa** (3980m), the site of a helipad, marked by a big H. Below, there's a marsh and a messy stream crossing, with a good lunch spot on the other side.

The trail now goes steeply up the northern side of the valley, levelling out at about 4200m, passing a couple of herders' huts and traversing high above the valley floor on river right to Chachim, a yak pasture at 4260m. The camp is in a cluster of brush beside a stream at the base of the valley, at **Shomuthang** (4220m).

DAY 8: SHOMUTHANG TO ROBLUTHANG
18KM / 6-7 HOURS / 700M ASCENT, 760M DESCENT

The trail climbs up the valley, starting on river right, crossing to river left and then crossing back again at 4360m. Edelweiss abounds along the trail; the snow peak visible to the southeast is Kang Bum (6526m).

Climb out of the valley through desolate country to Jhari La (4750m), about two hours from camp. North of the pass, the trail switchbacks down to a little stream at 4490m, then becomes a rough, rocky route through rhododendrons on the stream's left. Follow the stream gently downhill through bushes on river left as it makes its way to the main valley. It's a gradual descent to a meadow by the Jholethang Chhu at 3990m, which you cross on a log bridge about 1km upstream.

There is a camp called **Tsheri Jathang** by the river. Herds of takin migrate to this valley in summer and remain here for about four months. Takins are easily disturbed by the presence of other animals, including humans. Sometimes, it might be neces-

Built by the third *druk desi*, Mingyur Tenpa, who ruled from 1667 to 1680, Yugyel Dzong is perched on a hill about 200m above Lingzhi village and is quite close to the Tibetan border. The dzong was destroyed in the 1897 earthquake, but was rebuilt in the 1950s to serve as an administrative headquarters.

The dzong is quite small, with a few offices along the outside wall and a two-storey *utse* (central tower) in the centre. Until some years ago, the basement was used as a jail to house murderers and temple robbers. However, the facilities were quite primitive and the dzong is no longer used for this purpose. The dzong is also home to a few monks.

sary to take a one-hour diversion, in order to leave the beasts undisturbed. The valley has been declared a special takin sanctuary and yak herders have agreed not to graze their animals in the valley while the takins are here.

The trail climbs steeply on the northern side to a crest at about 4150m. It then traverses into a side valley past a tiny lake. There are good camping places in a rocky meadow named **Robluthang** at 4160m.

DAY 9: ROBLUTHANG TO LIMITHANG
19KM / 6-7 HOURS / 850M ASCENT, 870M DESCENT

Climb past the remnants of a burned forest and up the hillside through some boggy patches. Switchback to a shelf at 4390m, before turning into another large glacial side valley. Follow a stream for a while, crossing to river right on an icy log bridge at 4470m, then climb onto a moraine and traverse past lots of marmot holes. You may be able to spot blue sheep high on the slopes to the north before the trail crosses back to stream left.

It's a tough climb from here to the pass at **Sinche La** (5005m), passing a false summit with a cairn. The trail levels out a little before reaching the cairns and prayer flags on the pass, with the snow-covered peak of Gangchhenta filling the northern horizon.

The descent is on a rough, rocky trail that follows a moraine into another glacial valley. Eventually you arrive at the Kango Chhu, a

LORE OF LAYA

Spread out over a hillside near the Tibetan border, Laya is one of the highest and remotest villages in Bhutan, at 3700m. The terrain forms the country's primary yak-breeding area. Villagers raise turnips and mustard and produce a crop of wheat or barley each year before winter. During summer, people move to high pastures and live in black tents woven from yak hair.

The Layaps have their own language, customs and distinct dress. The women keep their hair long and wear conical bamboo hats with a bamboo spike at the top, held on by a beaded band. They dress in black woollen jackets with silver trims and long woollen skirts with a few stripes in orange or brown. They wear lots of silver jewellery on their backs; on many women, this display includes an array of silver teaspoons.

The village women are easily encouraged to stage an evening 'cultural show', which consists of Bhutanese circle dancing accompanied by traditional Bhutanese and Layap songs. The womenfolk often offer to sell their bamboo hats for about Nu 150. Be wary of the ones offering to sell beads, as they are often family heirlooms. Laya women also frequent trekking camps selling jewellery; most of this is made in Nepal.

Zhabdrung Ngawang Namgyal passed through Laya, and in a small meadow below the village is a chorten with the footprints of the Zhabdrung and his horse. The region is believed to be a bey-yul (hidden land) protected by an ancient gate that leads to Laya village. The Layaps perform an annual ceremony in honour of the protective forces that turned all the stones and trees around the gate into soldiers to repel Tibetan invaders.

stream below a terminal moraine that forms the end of another valley to the west.

Cross the Kango Chhu to river left on a small log bridge at 4470m. A short distance beyond is a yak pasture and camping spot next to a huge rock. However, it's best to continue to Limithang to camp. Follow the valley northwards, staying high as the stream falls away below you. Beyond an uninhabited stone house, the trail descends steeply to the valley floor. It switchbacks down with the terminal moraine looming above, crossing the Kango Chhu on a bridge at 4260m. After a short climb through rhododendrons, the trail levels out on a plateau above the Zamdo Nangi Chhu. It's then a short walk through a cedar forest interspersed with small meadows to **Limithang** (4140m), a lovely campsite in a big meadow by the river. Gangchhenta towers over the campsite in the distance.

DAY 10: LIMITHANG TO LAYA
10KM / 4-5 HOURS / 60M ASCENT, 340M DESCENT

After 20 minutes of walking, the trail crosses to river left and enters a deep cedar forest, crossing several muddy side streams. Ahead, there's a herders' hut of stone where

the vegetation changes to fir trees draped with lichen.

Cross a large stream that flows in from the north and make a steep rocky descent down the side of the valley to the river at 3800m, then cross to river right on a wooden cantilever bridge. A short distance later, cross back and make a stiff climb.

It's a long walk through the heavily wooded, uninhabited valley. Descend to cross a waterfall flowing across the trail, then traverse several small ups and downs. Near a point where you can see a single house on a ridge to the east, there is an inconspicuous trail junction. The lower trail leads to the lower part of the village. If you take the upper trail, you will cross a ridge and see the stone houses and wheat fields of **Laya** laid out below you with some abandoned houses and a goemba above.

Gangchhenta dominates the skyline to the west of the village, and from some places you can get a glimpse of Masang Gang (7165m). In the village centre is a community school, hospital, archery field and the first shop since the Paro valley. You can camp in the fields below the school at 3840m.

DAY 11: LAYA TO KOINA
19KM / 6-7 HOURS / 260M ASCENT, 1070M DESCENT

Layaps are not noted for their reliability and punctuality, so horses may arrive late. Below the village, the trail drops back to the river. The trail exits the village through a *khonying* (arch chorten), then passes another chorten at Taje-kha as it descends on a muddy trail to a stream.

There is an alternative camping place on a plateau at 3590m, next to the large Togtsherkhagi Chhu. Cross the river on a wooden bridge and climb to the stone buildings of the army camp. There's a radio station here, and a checkpoint where your names will be registered.

The route now follows the Mo Chhu downstream to Tashithang. About 30 minutes from the army post is an inconspicuous trail junction at 3340m, where the route for the Snowman trek leads uphill on a tiny path. The route to Gasa keeps going downstream on a muddy trail. Soon, it turns a corner into a side valley before crossing the Bahitung Chhu at 3290m, the lunch spot for the day.

Post meal, the trail trudges along the Mo Chhu to an overhanging rock forming a cave, then crosses to river right at 3240m on a cantilever bridge. The canyon closes in, and the trail makes several climbs over side ridges while making its way downstream. Beyond, another cave formed by a large overhanging rock is a long steep climb, cresting on a ridge at 3390m. It's a 150m descent to a clear side stream, and the trail then wanders up and down near the river, before climbing once again to Kohi La at 3300m.

The muddy trail stays high for about 30 minutes until it reaches a stone staircase, where it turns into a side valley, before dropping to the Koina Chhu. Welcome to **Koina** (3050m), a muddy bog in the forest filled with ankle-deep sludge. This is the worst camp on the whole trek and perhaps the most unpleasant camp in all of the Himalayas. A new – and considerably drier – camp has recently been identified about two hours ahead at **Chempsa** (3700m). Feel free to use it instead.

DAY 12: KOINA TO GASA
14KM / 6-7 HOURS / 900M ASCENT, 1710M DESCENT

Today's walk sees you tackling one last obstacle on this trek – the Bari La.

Cross the bridge at Koina and start up the hill. Parts of the trail are so muddy that logs have been placed to form little bridges. The muddy trail keeps going through a deep forest of fir for almost three hours, until you reach a small rock cairn and a few prayer flags atop **Bari La** (3900m). Then it's a reasonably level walk to another chorten.

The route then begins to descend, sometimes steeply, through a bamboo forest to a stream. At 3080m it rounds a corner where you can finally see Gasa Dzong on the opposite side of a large wooded side valley. The trail descends past an old chorten, then crosses a ridge into a big side valley. It drops and crosses a large stream at 2780m, then traverses along the side of the valley to four chortens on the ridge at 2810m.

The chortens mark the southern boundary of **Gasa town** (2770m). The trail traverses above the football and archery ground, past several small teashops, then intersects Gasa's main street. Trek downhill to the bazaar, with about nine shops and a police checkpoint. The police post checks permits, providing a perfect excuse to stop for a soft drink or beer at one of the shops.

You must camp in a field near the town – the alternative campsite 1½ hours downhill at the *tsachhu* (hot spring) has become unusable since heavy rains washed away the springs in 2009. See Day 1 of the Gasa Hot Spring trek (p164) for details of the site. If it is raining, the remainder of this trek is perfect country in which to closely study how leeches become attached to humans.

DAY 13: GASA TO DAMJI
18KM / 5-6 HOURS / 470M ASCENT, 280M DESCENT

Follow the trail generally south, passing a few houses and *mani* walls, as it descends to the primary branch of the Mo Chhu, flowing in through the mountains from Lingzhi to join the other branch of the Mo Chhu that flows from Gasa. Look back for a good view of the dzong that sits on top of the hill. Be careful as you follow this trail; near a chorten there is a fork where a second trail leads steeply downhill to the hot spring. The trail towards Damji goes straight on.

After a long descent, cross the river at 2360m on a cable suspension bridge high above the water. This is where you meet the road head, and your operator can arrange to have you picked up from here and driven down to Tashithang.

Gasa Hot Spring Trek

Much of this trek is now drivable, thanks to a new road that crawls up from Tashithang to Damji. Since 2009, after a deluge caused by heavy rains washed away the hot spring and laid the site to waste, people have found little reason to come on this trek. However, there has been talk of restoring the site (owing to its therapeutic qualities and religious significance), and it's possible that the hot spring may soon be revived through collective effort. Being at a lower elevation, this trek is possible from February to March and October to December. There are leeches in the lower part of the trek, making it particularly unpleasant during the rainy season.

DAY 1: DAMJI TO GASA TSACHHU
16KM / 4-5 HOURS / 470M DESCENT

Follow Day 13 of the Laya–Gasa trek in reverse direction along the side of the valley, then drop to the large stream below Gasa. A trail leads north from here, following the stream directly to the hot spring at 2240m. The Jigme Dorji National Park administers the hot-spring complex and offers various kinds of accommodation in a grove of large birch trees. There are some houses that can be rented, a few buildings that can be used as kitchens, a dormitory and numerous good camping places. It is a pleasant place to spend a day. Women often sell souvenirs around the site; it's mostly Tibetan-style jewellery made in Nepal.

DAY 2: A DAY AT GASA TSACHHU
You can laze around the site of the hot springs or take a packed lunch and climb about two hours to Gasa village and the dzong.

DAY 3: GASA TSACHHU TO DAMJI
Follow Day 13 of the Laya-Gasa trek.

THE TREK AT A GLANCE

Duration 3 days

Max Elevation 2430m

Difficulty Easy

Season February to March, October to December

Start Damji

Finish Damji

Access Town Punakha

Summary This trek is the last part of the Laya-Gasa trek in reverse.

Gangte Trek

Much of this trek's charm has been compromised in recent times due to the construction of a feeder road running parallel to (and, at times, criss-crossing) the route, connecting Phobjikha to neighbouring valleys. Nonetheless, it's recommended as a spring trek, especially around April, when blooming rhododendrons make it a particularly enjoyable excursion.

DAY 1: PHOBJIKHA TO ZASA
15KM / 6-7 HOURS / 610M ASCENT, 410M DESCENT

The trek starts near the village of Tabiting, just before the Black Mountain National Park warden's office at 2890m. Go uphill beside a stream, and climb through blue pines to **Kelwag**, a scrub bamboo meadow at 3120m. The trail then gently ascends through pines and rhododendrons to **Tsele La** at 3430m.

From the pass, descend into the Kangkha Chhu valley and traverse to **Tsele Pang** (3280m). Descend further into a forest of cypress, juniper, rhododendron and daphne (the plant used for handmade paper) to the small village of **Tserina** at 3120m. It's then a long traverse through forests to a few houses at Gogona (3090m).

Gogona Lhakhang is dominated by statues of Chenresig, Atisha and several manifestations of Guru Rinpoche. The walls are covered with elaborate paintings and on the *gorikha* (porch) is a painting of Lama Drukpa Kunley. Camping is not allowed at the monastery, so trek around the ridge to the pretty village of **Dangchu** (3040m). The women here weave blankets and speak a different dialect called Bjop-kha (language of the nomads). A small campsite sits near the head of the grassy valley beside a small stream in a yak pasture called **Zasa** (3130m). Larger groups usually camp at Dzomdu Gyakha or near the cheese factory at Sha Gagona.

DAY 2: ZASA TO CHORTEN KARPO
16KM / 5-7 HOURS / 450M ASCENT, 860M DESCENT

The trail leads up the meadow above Zasa, entering a forest of fir, oak, spruce, dwarf rhododendron, miniature azalea, cypress and juniper. Climb for about two hours to a crest at 3360m, then again for another 30 minutes to **Shobe La**, a forested ridge marked by a rock cairn at 3480m.

Descend to join a rough forest road at 2970m. The trek to the Tashila ropeway strays on and off this road, used by tractors to transport timber. Cross a stream and take a few short cuts through an oak forest to arrive at **Dolando**, with an isolated sawmill and wooden houses at 2790m. The road makes a small detour around a rock that is said to be the remains of a demon. If you look closely you may be able to see the marks left when Guru Rinpoche beat the demon with his stick. Follow the road alongside a stream, crossing to river right at 2730m, and continue to another sawmill near Gangri Chi village at 2670m. Below is the village of Kokotkha, with about 60 houses.

Atop a ridge to the southwest is the large Rinchenling monastery. High above to the south is Dolay Goemba. The route turns north here and follows the small Paza Chhu, then climbs over a ridge on a narrow trail, recrosses the road and climbs gently to **Chorten Karpo**, four chortens in a forest of blue pines at 2680m. The Nepali chorten is in honour of a Je Khenpo. The second one commemorates a rich merchant from Kokotkha; next is a *kani* (archlike chorten) with its middle filled in; the southernmost chorten was built by a flour merchant from Kokotkha.

DAY 3: CHORTEN KARPO TO TIKKE ZAMPA

12KM / 4-5 HOURS / 120M ASCENT, 1340M DESCENT

Climb from camp to join the forest road at 2720m, and gently hike to the ridge top at 2800m. If possible, continue a few minutes to the top of the **Tashila ropeway** (p97) and watch rice and building supplies coming up and logs going down. It's not officially allowed, but you may be able to get a

THE TREK AT A GLANCE

Duration 3 days

Max Elevation 3480m

Difficulty Easy

Season March to May, September to November

Start Phobjikha

Finish Tikke Zampa

Access Towns Phobjikha, Wangdue Phodrang

Summary A short trek at relatively low elevations, visiting several remote villages and monasteries, and offering birding opportunities.

ride down the 6km-long cableway and save yourself a knee-cracking descent.

The walk down is through a beautiful forest, where the vegetation gradually changes from rhododendrons and magnolias to ferns and dwarf bamboo. Experts claim that this stretch of trail is one of the finest bird-watching areas in Bhutan. Among the birds found here are laughing thrushes, shrikes, magpies and woodpeckers.

There's a trail junction at 2250m. Take the right-hand fork and go down until you reach the houses and fields of Wachay at about 1880m. Traversing through fields and farmyards, the trail finally plunges past steep terraced wheat fields to two shops at 1460m on the road about 300m east of the bridge at **Tikke Zampa**.

TREKS GANGTE TREK

Bumthang Cultural Trek

This is another trek that is fast losing popularity due to the construction of roads in the region. Although it is a short itinerary, the Bumthang trek is strenuous in sections, and packs in a tiring 500m climb to Phephe La at 3360m. This trek is usually possible from March to May and again from September to November. The start of the trek is a 3km drive up the unpaved road from Kurjey Lhakhang to Toktu Zampa at 2540m, then a short drive to Thangbi Goemba. With luck, packhorses will be waiting and you can start walking with minimal delay.

DAY 1: THANGBI GOEMBA TO SAMBITANG
10KM / 2-3 HOURS / 170M ASCENT

Although it's possible to drive further up the valley, most groups choose to start this trek at Thangbi Goemba (see p122 for a brief description), with its distinctive yellow roof, near the small village of Thangbi.

The trail now courses a broad ledge above the river past a 70m-long painted *mani* wall and a *khonying* with a mandala painted on the roof inside. Just beyond the arched chorten is a trail junction. Take the trail leading to a suspension bridge across the Bumthang Chhu (known locally as the Choskhor Chhu). Follow the left bank of the river through pleasant meadows and forests of blue pine and scrub.

After about an hour, you pass the Zangling Lhakhang on the hill to the right. From here it's 15 minutes to a trail junction next to a chorten and prayer wheels. Fifteen minutes down the right branch is the campsite at **Sambitang**. The left branch leads to Ngang Lhakhang (Swan Temple). It's located about 30 minutes above, near a settlement of old-looking houses at 2800m. There are two water-driven prayer wheels; the water comes down an interesting sluiceway of carved wooden pipes. For more information on this interesting temple, see p122.

Bumthang Cultural & Duer Hot Springs Treks

THE TREK AT A GLANCE

Duration 3 days

Max Elevation 3360m

Difficulty Medium

Season March to May, September to November

Start Thangbi Goemba

Finish Kizum

Access Town Jakar

Summary This trek is so named because it offers ample opportunities to visit villages and lhakhangs.

DAY 2: SAMBITANG TO OGYEN CHHOLING
18KM / 6-7 HOURS / 750M ASCENT, 670M DESCENT

The day's walk starts out across meadows, with a lot of dwarf bamboo and several little streams to cross. The trail cuts across the top of some fields, goes over a small hill and down to a stream. Soon, the trail starts climbing, cutting back and forth across a stream on slippery logs and stones. Birches, sycamores, dwarf bamboo and lots of tall bamboo form a cold, sunless forest. Spanish moss drapes the ancient trees, giving an eerie feel to the steep climb.

Finally, the stream disappears and the climb continues through a rhododendron forest in a dry gully to a rock cairn and a little stone shrine. Tattered prayer flags stretch across the path atop **Phephe La** (3360m), on a forested ridge with big birch and fir trees.

The trail leads down to a stream at 3200m, then into a side valley covered in dwarf bamboo, passing a small *mani* wall and a *khonying* chorten. Breaking out into broad meadows full of grazing yaks and cows, it continues through ploughed fields into a broad valley, surrounded by rounded, treeless hills.

Going downhill, the route then approaches the base of the valley, with several side trails leading to pastures and buckwheat fields. Take the most prominent trail downhill to a large stream and a wooden bridge at 2790m near the village of **Tahung**. From Tahung, time permitting, you can take a detour left, and embark on a four-hour return trek to the remote Thowadrak Hermitage. Perched high on the rocks, it's believed to date back to Guru Rinpoche's

time. Behind Tahung is the Australian-assisted Wobtang sheep development project. A rough tractor road follows the right bank of the Tang Chhu, from the project to Tang village down the valley. The route leads downstream in meadows next to the river. Crossing the stream on a road bridge, it turns a corner into the main valley of the Tang Chhu at 2640m.

Cross the Tang Chhu near Gamling, a large, wealthy village noted for its *yathra* weaving, about 45 minutes downstream. The trail crosses a stream, goes around a farmyard, and then climbs onto a ridge, reaching four chortens and several large houses at 2760m. **Ogyen Chholing** is atop the hill to the right. You can camp near the palace or splurge on a room in the guesthouse. For more information about Ogyen Chholing Palace and its fascinating museum, see p125.

DAY 3: OGYEN CHHOLING TO KIZUM
1.6KM / 1 HOUR / 130M DESCENT

It's a short walk downhill to **Kizum** where your vehicle should be waiting to pick you up. From here, it's a 25km drive to the junction of the road near Membartsho.

Duer Hot Springs Trek

This is a less-walked route, owing to its high difficulty rating. With special permission, it might be possible to extend this trek to the base camp of Gangkhar Puensum itself, although the trail is rough and often remains closed. It's also possible to vary either the upward or return route, and travel via the Mangde Chhu valley to meet a gravel road leading west from Trongsa.

THE TREK AT A GLANCE

Duration 8 days

Max Elevation 4700m

Difficulty Medium–hard

Season March to April, September to November

Start/Finish Duer

Access Town Jakar

Summary This trek takes you on the old expedition route to Gangkhar Puensum, the world's highest unclimbed peak and offers a full day at the hot springs.

Snow covers the route during winter so the trek is usually open from March to April and from September to early November. Its starting point, Duer village, is an hour (5km) of rough driving from Toktu Zampa. The trek includes a day at a *tsachhu* (hot spring).

DAY 1: DUER TO GORSUM
18KM / 6 HOURS / 380M ASCENT

Starting out of Duer, the route goes north, following the valley of the Yoleng Chhu (also known as Gorzam Chhu), which is famous for its trout population. En route, you will cross the Lurawa Goemba. The campsite for the day is at **Gorsum** at 3120m; for those who want to push ahead, there's an alternate site about two hours ahead.

DAY 2: GORSUM TO LUNGSUM
12KM / 5 HOURS / 40M ASCENT

The route travels through a forest of cypress, juniper, spruce, hemlock and maple. The trail is muddy and climbs gradually to the camp at **Lungsum** (3160m). On the way, you might cross paths with Bhutanese wild dogs. Keep your cameras ready.

DAY 3: LUNGSUM TO TSOCHENCHEN
15KM / 6-7 HOURS / 620M ASCENT

Today's trek remains more or less the same as yesterday's, passing through similar ter-

rain and flora. Along the way, you'll come across a bifurcation; from here, the trail to the right leads to Gangkhar Puensum via Thole La. The left trail leads to the springs. Towards the end of today's hike, the vegetation begins to thin out, before camp is reached at **Tsochenchen**, above the tree line at 3780m.

DAY 4: TSOCHENCHEN TO DUER HOT SPRINGS
18KM / 8-9 HOURS / 1340M ASCENT, 1530M DESCENT

The day starts with a long climb to a small lake and on to Juli La (4700m), a rocky saddle with a few prayer flags and a good view of the surrounding mountains. After crossing the pass, the trail goes all the way down to a lake at 4220m, before climbing again to Gokthong La (4640m). Finally, it switchbacks steeply down through jungle to a camp near the **Duer hot springs** at 3590m. It may be possible to see musk deer, Himalayan bears and blue sheep through the day's trek.

DAY 5: A DAY AT DUER HOT SPRINGS

Take a rest day to relax in the *tsachhu*. There are several wooden tubs set into the ground inside a rough wooden shelter for you to soak in.

DAY 6-8: DUER HOT SPRINGS TO DUER

Return via the same route from the hot springs to Duer.

OWL TREK

Keen to sample some 'nightlife' out in the mountains? Well, you could always consider walking the Owl trek, a new route in the Bumthang region that owes its name to the constant hooting of owls, which can be heard at campsites through the night. A three-day itinerary, the Owl trek starts at Menchugang village and ends at Jakar Dzong.

After an early pit-stop at Duer village, the trek passes through ageless forests of birch, fir and spruce, climbing to the 3870m Kitiphu ridge with magnificent views of the mountains. Then, after passing the remote monasteries of Tharpaling and Choedrak (where Guru Rinpoche is said to have meditated), the trek courses the ridge of the 3915m Kiki La, before heading towards Jakar. Chalked out in 2008, the Owl trek is now rapidly gaining in popularity, possibly at the expense of the classic Bumthang Cultural trek.

Rodang La Trek

Ever since a highway was rolled out to connect its end points, this trek – once an important trade route – has remained largely untrodden by foreigners. However, its high difficulty level can come as a draw for the more adventurous types. Few locals travel this path, and most trekkers tend to combine it with the Bumthang Cultural trek, starting at Thangbi Goemba. Alternatively, you can start the trek by driving up the Tang valley to Kizum, saving two days of walking.

Rodang La is subject to closure because of snow, and is best trodden in October, early November or late spring. The trek crosses the road near Lhuentse, which breaks up the continuity of the trekking experience, but offers a chance to visit the remote dzong.

THE TREK AT A GLANCE

Duration 10 days

Max Elevation 4160m

Difficulty Medium–hard

Season October to November

Start Thangbi Goemba

Finish Trashi Yangtse

Access Town Jakar

Summary This trek across eastern Bhutan is tough and involves a tremendously long, steep descent. The logistics are complicated and horses are often difficult to obtain for the final four days of the trek.

DAYS 1-2: TOKTU ZAMPA TO OGYEN CHHOLING

Follow Days 1 and 2 of the Bumthang Cultural Trek to **Ogyen Chholing**, at an elevation of 2760m (p125).

DAY 3: OGYEN CHHOLING TO PHOKPEY
17KM / 5-6 HOURS / 920M ASCENT

The long climb to Rodang La takes two days. Above Ogyen Chholing, the trail is rutted with cattle hoof prints, and can be slippery when wet. The trail levels out around 2900m, meeting a stream. At about 3000m the cow trails turn into a small footpath through muddy fields and dwarf bamboo.

At 3400m the trail crosses a meadow with more dwarf bamboo. High on the opposite hill is the Phokpey Goemba. Climb through the meadow and traverse through forest to another steep, high meadow, finally turning a corner into a side valley, and heading to **Phokpey**, a camp at 3680m.

DAY 4: PHOKPEY TO PEMI
20KM / 6-7 HOURS / 480M ASCENT, 1160M DESCENT

The trail goes through a small notch onto a ridge at 3700m. After a long crossing at 3770m is the final climb to the pass, up big stone slabs and a steep stone staircase. **Rodang La** (4160m) is about two hours from camp.

Across the pass, it's a steep descent of nearly 2500m to the valley floor, down an unbelievably long and steep stone staircase. This is a tough route for horses, and it is said that even the king had to walk downhill here. Part of the route is along a vertical face, and the trail is on wooden galleries fastened into the side of the cliff. Past a few meadows, the trail winds through a region where sightings of ghosts and yetis have been reported. Leaving the rhododendrons and conifers, the trail descends to a big meadow called **Pemi** at about 3000m. Up ahead are the ruins of a royal granary and a campsite at 2950m. Water is 15 minutes down the side of a hill; go easy on the washing here.

DAY 5: PEMI TO KHAINE LHAKHANG
21KM / 7-8 HOURS / 350M ASCENT, 1340M DESCENT

The trail tumbles into the Noyurgang Chhu valley, leading through dwarf bamboo and a damp, mossy, rock-filled gully. Around 2600m, the vegetation changes to ferns and tropical species, and the trail goes down towards a meadow called Sang Sangbe (2300m), apparently haunted by a ghost. The trail drops to a bridge over a stream at 1700m. It's then a short walk across rice fields to a suspension bridge over the Noyurgang Chhu at 1660m.

Cross to river left and start climbing through ferns and tropical jungle to Bulay village (1800m). Next is Kulaypang (1930m) – with a few simple houses and cornfields – where there's a false trail going down towards the next ridge; the correct trail goes up.

The trail passes below Gomda village (2040m). Passing a chorten, it crosses a stream at 2000m, then climbs to a *mani* wall at 2020m. Then it's a level walk to Gongdra. Beyond Chanteme, you cross a stream and climb to **Khaine Lhakhang**. Follow the cement irrigation canal and climb onto the ridge where the temple sits at 2010m. There are two tall cedars by the monastery and fields of soya beans surrounding it. Pephu Goemba is high above and the town below is Songme.

DAY 6: KHAINE LHAKHANG TO TANGMACHU
18KM / 6-7 HOURS / 520M ASCENT, 810M DESCENT

The trail goes down to a stream and up to a Basic Health Unit (BHU) and community school in **Gorsam**. It then climbs to 2130m, levelling out for 15 minutes, before climbing gently through trees. You can see a glimpse of the road at the bottom of the Kuri Chhu valley.

The Tibetan-style Umling Mani at 2180m is at the corner between the Noyurgang Chhu and the Kuri Chhu valleys. It was

TREKS

KHAINE LHAKHANG

Some people believe that the remote Khaine Lhakhang is one of the 108 temples built by King Songtsen Gampo in AD 659. Three small statues from here are said to have flown of their own accord to Konchogsum Lhakhang in Bumthang, believed to have been built at the same time. The primary statue is a 2.5m Sakyamuni figure. A statue of the Karmapa is on his right and Zhabdrung Rinpoche is above him on the left. There are also smaller statues of Milarepa and Guru Rinpoche. The main protective deity is a ferocious god named Taxan, who is depicted riding a horse.

A two-day festival is celebrated here in mid-November.

built by a lama from Tibet and marks the boundary between the two *gewogs* (administrative blocks). Here the route turns north up the Kuri Chhu.

Traversing through four large side valleys, you then descend to a stream and climb to the next ridge. The trail emerges from the first valley at Gumbar Gang (2120m). After going up to a chorten on Zerim La (1940m), it winds down to the head of a valley at 1840m, with a chorten and a prayer wheel, then starts climbing back through chir pines to 1890m, traversing grassy slopes to another ridge and several herders' huts.

Descend to a *mani* wall, pass Menjabi village, cross the stream at 1540m, then start a long climb on a grassy slope with chir pines to some chortens and a *mani* wall on Tage La (1760m). Southeast of the pass is the Tangmachu High School, where 400 students study atop a windswept ridge. The campsite is near the school. If you have time, you could request a vehicle to drive you 21km north to Lhuentse to visit the dzong, and then drop you back at **Tangmachu** for the night. The vehicle can then drive on to Trashi Yangtse to pick you up four days later.

DAY 7: TANGMACHU TO MENJI
16KM / 4-5 HOURS / 690M ASCENT, 620M DESCENT

From the bridge (1140m) below Tangmachu, the trek goes gradually up through rice terraces and cornfields to Chusa. It then becomes a steep haul up a treeless slope, although the path is beautifully scented with wild mint, lemon grass and artemisia. Camp is at 1830m, above **Menji**, beside the Darchu Pang Lhakhang. The temple's well-kept garden is full of flowers – marigolds, geraniums, dahlias and nasturtiums – and has a vegetable patch that often has tomatoes and huge cucumbers. There are banana trees, too, and dozens of long-tailed birds in the trees.

DAY 8: MENJI TO PEMI
10KM / 3-4 HOURS / 620M ASCENT

Continue uphill through the thick, humid forest packed with a dense foliage of ferns and creepers and a constant whistle of cicadas. The trail is narrow, steep and rutted. Climb steadily for two hours to a ridge-top meadow, then plunge back into the forest to reach some herders' huts at **Pemi** (2450m) on a narrow ridge-top clearing with a view to a forested gorge. There's not a village or house in view, although Menji villagers use this area as a summer pasture. Much of the trail for the next two days has fallen into disuse and is narrow and slippery.

DAY 9: PEMI TO TAUPANG
21KM / 7-8 HOURS / 1450M ASCENT, 1450M DESCENT

The trail stays largely in damp, cold forest, with occasional pastures. The area is a botanist's delight, with shrubs of every kind, pungent with a sweet fermented smell, thick with humus. The trail then traverses nine passes, nicknamed the **Nine Sisters**, the highest of which is **Dong La** (3900m), with good mountain views and some prayer flags on a pile of rocks.

Cross the remaining ridges, each adorned with prayer flags, and descend steeply through thick evergreen forests on a trail strewn with rocks, logs and slippery leaves to a ridge-top meadow called Lisipang. The last part of the trek is easy at first, turning right and down through a pasture at Yesupang, but then becomes rocky and muddy near the Dongdi Chhu. There's no bridge, and once you rock-hop across, it's even muddier and rockier on the other side, and parts of the trail are layered with logs placed in a bridge-like manner to provide a smoother walking surface over the uneven terrain. The camp is at **Taupang** (2450m), a clearing with a wooden cowherds' shelter.

DAY 10: TAUPANG TO TRASHI YANGTSE
24KM / 8-9 HOURS / 720M DESCENT

The path through the forest beside the river is damp and muddy with huge ferns, red-berried palms and occasional leeches. The forest is alive with birds and monkeys. Two hours of sloshing through mud or stone-hopping brings you to **Shakshing**, a cluster of houses surrounded by corn, millet, banana and grazing cows.

The trail stays on the ridge to the north of the valley, passing above Tongshing village. It then descends past swampy areas, crossing to the southern bank of the Dongdi Chhu on a large bridge. The small, old **Trashi Yangtse** dzong suddenly appears on a hilltop above the river. The trail crosses back to the north bank of the river below the dzong on an old cantilever bridge. Finally, it crosses the Kulong Chhu at 1730m. Your vehicle will either be waiting here, or 3km ahead at Chorten Kora.

Snowman Trek

The combination of distance, altitude, remoteness and weather makes this a tough journey, and when trekking fees were set at US$200 a night, it suffered a sharp decline in the number of trekkers attempting it. Even though there are reduced rates for long treks, many baulk at a 25-day trek costing US$4280.

If you plan to trek this route, double-check your emergency evacuation insurance (p259). If you get into Lunana and snow blocks the passes, the only way out is by

THE TREK AT A GLANCE

Duration 25 days

Max Elevation 5320m

Difficulty Hard

Season September to October

Start Drukgyel Dzong

Finish Sephu

Access Town Paro

Summary The Snowman trek travels to the remote Lunana district and is said to be one of the most difficult treks in the world. Fewer than half the people who attempt this trek eventually finish it, either because of problems with altitude or heavy snowfall on the high passes.

helicopter, an expensive way to finish an already expensive trek. Another obstacle that often hampers this trek is bridges in remote regions that get washed away by deluges.

The Snowman trek is frequently closed because of snow, and is impossible to undertake during winter. The season for this trek is generally considered to be from late September to mid-October. Don't plan a summer trek; this is a miserable place to be during the monsoon.

This classic trek follows the Jhomolhari and Laya-Gasa treks to Laya. Many walking days can be saved by starting in Tashithang and trekking north up the Mo Chhu, following the Laya-Gasa trek in reverse.

DAYS 1 TO 5: DRUKGYEL DZONG TO LINGZHI

Follow Days 1 to 5 of the Jhomolhari trek (p153).

DAYS 6 TO 10: LINGZHI TO LAYA

Follow Days 6 to 10 of the Laya-Gasa trek (p159).

DAY 11: REST & ACCLIMATISATION DAY IN LAYA

If you have trekked from Drukgyel Dzong you should spend a day recuperating in Laya and preparing for the rigours ahead. If you've trekked from Tashithang, you should also walk up to Laya to acclimatise. The army post below Laya has a radio; you will need to send a runner here with a message in an emergency.

DAY 12: LAYA TO RODOPHU

19KM / 6-8 HOURS / 1030M ASCENT, 70M DESCENT

The trek leads down to the Lunana trail junction, then climbs for 40 minutes to a hilltop with good views over the Mo Chhu and the Rhodo Chhu. It continues up the Rhodo Chhu valley, first through mixed conifers, then through rhododendron, above the tree line. Atop a large rock slide, there is a view of the glacial valley and a massive glacier on Tsenda Kang (7100m). The **Rodophu** camp is just beyond a wooden bridge across the Rhodo Chhu at 4160m.

If you're acclimatising here for a day, consider a short 2km hike up the valley to a knoll with excellent views of the valley and mountains, continuing to the base of the glacier. Another option is to follow a small trail starting about 500m upstream from camp and up the hill to the north, ending in a small yak pasture with a hut at 4500m.

DAY 13: RODOPHU TO NARETHANG

17KM / 5-6 HOURS / 720M ASCENT

The path crosses the wooden bridge and follows the river for 20 minutes through rhododendron shrubs before turning right up the hill. Climb to a high open valley at 4600m and then through meadows to **Tsomo La** (4900m), which offers good views towards the Tibet border and Jhomolhari. Next up is a flat, barren plateau at around 5000m with yak trails crisscrossing everywhere – your guide should know the way. The camp is at **Narethang** (4900m), below the 6395m peak of Gangla Karchung.

DAY 14: NARETHANG TO TARINA

18KM / 7-8 HOURS / 270M ASCENT, 1200M DESCENT

It's a one-hour climb to the 5120m **Gangla Karchung La**, with Kang Bum (6526m) to the west and Tsenda Kang, Teri Gang (7300m) and Jejekangphu Gang (7100m) due north. The path descends along a large moraine to the edge of a near-vertical wall with breathtaking views. A massive glacier descends from Teri Gang to two deep turquoise lakes at its foot, 1km below you. The glacial lake to the left burst through its dam in the early 1960s, causing widespread damage downstream, and partially destroying Punakha Dzong.

The path now becomes very steep as it descends into the valley. When wet, this stretch can be rather nasty, with lots of roots and slippery mud. At the base of the U-shaped valley, the trail turns right, following the Tang Chhu downstream. There are several good campsites along the river, both before and after the trail crosses the river at **Tarina**.

DAY 15: TARINA TO WOCHE

17KM / 6-7 HOURS / 275M ASCENT, 330M DESCENT

The walk leads through conifers down the Tang Chhu on river left, passing some impressive waterfalls. The trail climbs gently out of the valley past several huge landslides, and eventually climbs steeply to the northeast into the high side valley of **Woche**. The first village in the Lunana region, Woche is a small settlement of five houses at 3940m.

Looking up the valley you can see the following day's route to Lhedi. There have been reports of theft here; keep all your gear safely inside your tent.

DAY 16: WOCHE TO LHEDI

17KM / 6-7 HOURS / 980M ASCENT, 950M DESCENT

The trail climbs the Woche valley, crossing a stream and going over a moraine before descending to a wooden bridge across the Woche Chhu. It then climbs on a wide trail past a clear lake to **Keche La** (4650m), with excellent views of the surrounding mountains, including Jejekangphu Gang's triple peak, the source of the Woche Chhu.

The route now descends into the Pho Chhu valley and reaches Thaga village (4050m). Dropping towards the Pho Chhu, the path then turns northeast towards Lhedi. Passing a few scattered settlements and crossing below a waterfall on a wooden bridge, the trail descends to the banks of the Pho Chhu, continuing along the river bed to **Lhedi** at 3700m.

Lhedi is a district headquarters with a school, BHU and wireless station, but there is no shop here (or anywhere else in the Lunana district). Everything is carried in by yak trains across 5000m passes. Strong winds blow up the valley in the late afternoon, making it bitterly cold in autumn and winter.

'DON'T TAKE MY THREE DAYS AWAY!'

Ask experienced mountain guides in Bhutan, and they'll all agree in unison that it's impossible to sum up the magical experience of the Snowman trek in mere words. However, 38-year-old Robin Pradhan Joshi cites an incident that might give an idea of the overwhelming charm the trek possesses. As a climber, instructor and trek leader who has been roving the Bhutan Himalayas for nearly a decade, Joshi was leading a party on the Snowman trek in 2008, when a female guest took a fall somewhere between Jichu Dramo and Chukarpo, and severely injured her knee. 'I was concerned that she may not be able to walk the remaining three days of the trek, so I offered to put her on a horse,' recalls Joshi.

However, the guest flatly refused the offer. '"Don't take my three days away from me, Robin!", she scolded me,' laughs Joshi, sipping mango juice at a Thimphu cafe. Despite the injury, the guest was determined to walk every step on the trail, and no amount of persuasion made her swap her once-in-a-lifetime experience for a 'boring' horse ride. 'She actually hobbled all the way down,' smiles Joshi. Nuff said.

DAY 17: LHEDI TO THANZA
17KM / 4-5 HOURS / 400M ASCENT

The trail follows the north bank of the Pho Chhu past several small farms. Floods have destroyed parts of the trail so a temporary path winds its way among boulders in the river bed. Around lunchtime the trail passes **Chozo** village at 4090m, with a functional dzong.

If you are pressed for time, you can take a direct trail to Tshochena from here, but most trekkers continue to Thanza (4100m), a couple of hours up the valley. The first part of the trail leads through yak pastures on river flats, giving way to a large expanse of fine glacial sand. Eventually, the trail leaves the river bed and climbs a bluff overlooking the villages of **Thanza**, straight ahead, and **Toencha**, on the other bank of the river. The 7100m Zongophu Gang (Table Mountain) forms an immense, 3000m-high wall of snow and ice behind Thanza. Most groups camp in Toencha (4150m), but there are places to camp in Thanza as well.

DAY 18: REST DAY IN THANZA

Schedule a rest day here. This is as far as yak drivers from Laya go, and it takes time to round up yaks for the rest of the trek. Capitalise on the day by exploring the villages and glacial lakes up the valley. The closest lake, Raphstreng Tsho, is 100m deep and caused a flood in 1994 when a moraine holding back its waters burst. A large crew of Indian workers dug a channel through the moraine to prevent a recurrence, but there are other lakes in the area posing a similar risk.

DAY 19: THANZA TO DANJI
8KM / 3-4 HOURS / 80M ASCENT

If you're feeling fit, you can hike to Tshochena in one day, but it's a long, hard walk at high altitude and is best split in two parts.

Climbing to a large boulder on the hill south of the village, the trail turns east up a side valley. After a couple of hours of easy walking, the trail enters **Danji**, a yak meadow with some herders' huts. It's an excellent camp, with blue sheep often grazing above and occasionally walking into camp.

A few hundred metres up the valley, a small trail climbs the ridge to the left, leading to a higher valley. The top of the ridge offers excellent views of surrounding mountains.

DAY 20: DANJI TO TSHOCHENA
12KM / 5-6 HOURS / 490M ASCENT, 240M DESCENT

From the junction near camp, the trail up the valley leads to Gangkhar Puensum base camp and Bumthang. The path to the end of the trek crosses the creek and leads up a rocky side valley – a long climb across several false summits to **Jaze La** at 5150m, with views of mountains in all directions. From the pass, the path descends between snow-covered peaks past a string of small lakes. The camp is near the shore of **Tshochena** at 4970m. This is the first of two nights' camping above 4900m.

DAY 21: TSHOCHENA TO JICHU DRAMO
14KM / 4-5 HOURS / 230M ASCENT, 140M DESCENT

The trail follows the shore of the blue-green lake before climbing to a ridge at 5100m, with a 360-degree panorama of snowy peaks. Far below, the Pho Chhu descends towards Punakha. The road and microwave tower at Dochu La are visible in the distance.

The path makes several ups and downs over small rounded hills, but the altitude can slow you down. Past a glacial lake before Loju La at 5140m, many trails wander around high-altitude yak pastures, and it's easy to wander astray. The correct path is across a small saddle at 5100m into a wide glacial valley, and then down to the camp at **Jichu Dramo** (5050m), a small pasture on the east of the valley.

DAY 22: JICHU DRAMO TO CHUKARPO

18KM / 5-6 HOURS / 320M ASCENT, 730M DESCENT

The trail climbs through a moraine to the picturesque Rinchen Zoe La (5320m), dividing the Pho Chhu and Mangde Chhu drainages. Rinchen Zoe peak (5650m) towers above, Gangkhar Puensum is visible in the east, while the Thampe Chhu valley stretches below to the south.

Descending into a broad, marshy valley with a string of lakes, the trail follows the left (east) side of the valley. Eventually, it descends steeply down the face of a moraine to a yak pasture in the upper reaches of the Thampe Chhu. Cross to the west bank (river right) here, as there is no bridge further down. The vegetation begins to thicken, and consists of rhododendron and juniper. The camp is a couple of hours away at **Chukarpo** (4600m); a better site sits an hour ahead at **Thongsa Thang** (4400m).

DAY 23: CHUKARPO TO THAMPE TSHO

18KM / 5-6 HOURS / 400M ASCENT, 640M DESCENT

Descend along the right bank of the river until you reach a yak pasture at Gala Pang Chhu (4010m). From here, the path begins to climb steeply through junipers and silver firs towards **Thampe Tsho**. The path generally follows a stream to the beautiful, clear, turquoise lake, set in a bowl and surrounded by steep mountain walls. The camp is at the far end of the lake at 4300m.

DAY 24: THAMPE TSHO TO MAUROTHANG

14KM / 5 HOURS / 280M ASCENT, 1020M DESCENT

The trail climbs steeply to **Thampe La** at 4600m. You may see blue sheep high on the slopes above the trail.

The path descends to Om Tsho, a sacred site where Pema Lingpa found a number of *terma* (sacred texts and artefacts). The path

skirts the northwestern shore of the lake before crossing its outlet, marked by prayer flags, and then drops steeply past a waterfall to a smaller lake, about 100m lower.

From the second lake to the headwaters of the Nikka Chhu is a descent so steep that even yaks are reluctant to come down this stretch. The path eventually levels out, following the left bank of the Nikka Chhu. After about 2km, it reaches a large open glade near the confluence of a major tributary coming from the east. A wooden bridge crosses the Nikka Chhu to river right, where a broad path leads through mixed forest to **Maurothang** (3610m), a large clearing by the river beside a few herders' huts.

DAY 25: MAUROTHANG TO SEPHU

18KM / 5-6 HOURS / 990M DESCENT

If horses are not available at Maurothang, your guide will probably send someone ahead to arrange for them further down. Yaks cannot walk all the way to the road because of the low altitude and the many cows in the area.

A well-used trail continues down the west side of the Nikka Chhu for about 30 minutes before crossing to the east bank into a mixed deciduous and bamboo forest. It descends gradually through forests and pastures, emerging onto a large grassy area overlooking the road and Sephu village. There are many confusing trails here; look for a large track about 25m above the river and you'll soon pass a large suspension bridge over the Nikka Chhu, which you shouldn't cross. Soon the trail turns into a narrow tractor road leading to the main road at **Sephu**, next to the Nikka Chhu bridge at 2600m, marked by shops and a small restaurant.

Samtengang Winter Trek

This is a low-altitude trek southeast of Punakha. The low elevation makes it possible to walk this trek throughout the off-season in winter, but it's miserable during summer, when other treks are in commission. This route sees few trekkers.

DAY 1: PUNAKHA TO LIMUKHA

12KM / 4 HOURS / 880M ASCENT

Go past the Paro Dzong, and proceed to cross the Pho Chhu on the footbridge, continuing up to Shengana. This is the longest footbridge in Bhutan. After Shengana, the trek begins to climb gradually through a

THE TREK AT A GLANCE

Duration 4 days

Max Elevation 1830m

Difficulty Easy

Season April, September to October

Start Punakha

Finish Chhuzomsa

Access Town Punakha

Summary A short trek passing through villages in the Punakha valley, offering a glimpse into the culture of the region.

forest of chir pine; if the weather is good, you might be able to catch glimpses of Jhomolhari and Kang Bum in the distance. Finally, the trail reaches the quaint village of **Limukha** at 1980m. A lovely campsite is located at the far end of the village, under an oak forest.

DAY 2: LIMUKHA TO CHHUNGSAKHA
14KM / 5 HOURS / 430M DESCENT

Start the day by climbing through a stretch of rhododendron and oak forests. The vegetation is dense, and the branches hang low, thus ruling out the possibility of riding on horses. The trail finally rises to a pass, and then winds down to **Chhungsakha** (1550m), a tiny hamlet with about a dozen houses. A holy stone and a cypress tree in the village supposedly date back to the days of Drukpa Kunley, the Divine Madman.

DAY 3: CHHUNGSAKHA TO SAMTENGANG
13KM / 5 HOURS / 650M ASCENT, 270M DESCENT

Trek down from Chhungsakha to the Pe Chhu, crossing it at 1420m. Hereafter, it's a brisk ascent through daphne bushes, past the settlement of Sha to **Samtengang** village at 1830m. The campsite is located next to a small lake near the village school. About two hours above the village is a lhakhang you can visit in the afternoon.

DAY 4: SAMTENGANG TO CHHUZOMSA
15KM / 5-6 HOURS / 730M DESCENT

The trail leads steeply downhill along a treeless slope carpeted with agricultural areas. From here, it's basically an amble along farm tracks until you reach the road at **Chhuzomsa**.

Nabji Trek

The Nabji trek was first drafted in 2006, but it's only recently that the route has begun to grab attention. To minimise the impact on the fragile ecosystem of the region, only one group – not exceeding 11 trekkers – is allowed to walk the trail at a time. Nabji is an early stab at community-based tourism in Bhutan, where local villagers are employed to offer services and amenities such as porterage, village tours, cultural shows and food at semi-developed campsites along the route.

The trailheads of this winter trek are on the road between Trongsa and Zhemgang, and the trek itself offers a chance to spot some exotic local creatures such as the golden langur, the rufous-necked hornbill and the serpent eagle, among others.

DAY 1: RIOTALA TO NIMSHONG
6.5KM / 3-4 HOURS / 625M ASCENT, 365M DESCENT

From Riotala, the trek begins with a steep descent to the Mangde Chhu valley, before climbing for about two hours to a lunch spot called Matling (800m). Another 30 minutes ahead, at the end of a steep climb, stands a chorten, which marks the entry into **Nimshong**, a village of about 60 households at 1320m. You will be welcomed into Nimshong with much song and dance, before being served dinner cooked by villagers.

DAY 2: NIMSHONG TO NABJI
13KM / 5-6 HOURS / 20M DESCENT

After a village tour of Nimshong, hike through a lush broadleaf forest teeming with regional fauna such as golden langurs and rufous-necked hornbills, to the village of **Nabji** (1300m). There's a temple here, with a stone pillar commemorating a peace

THE TREK AT A GLANCE

Duration 6 days

Max Elevation 1635m

Difficulty Easy

Season October to March

Start Riotala

Finish Tongtongphey

Access Town Trongsa

Summary A low-altitude trek passing through the land of the isolated Monpa people.

easy hike to **Jangbi** village (1370m), where you'll pitch tent in a scenic spot overlooking the Mangde Chhu valley.

DAY 6: JANGBI TO TONGTONGPHEY
8.5-9.5KM / 3-4 HOURS / 640M ASCENT, 950M DESCENT

After breaking camp, descend steeply to the bridge crossing the Mangde Chhu, before one last push to **Tongtongphey** (1060m), where you will be met by your vehicle and driven back to Trongsa.

Merak-Sakten Trek

This is the newest trek to be commissioned in Bhutan, and promises an unparalleled cultural and natural experience in the eastern outreaches of the country. To maintain its exclusivity, only one team (not exceeding 12 people) is allowed to walk the trek at a time, and tours start every third day through two open seasons adding up to five-and-a-half-months. To further regulate the exposure of the trek, a special fee is also being discussed.

The trek passes through the Sakten Wildlife Sanctuary, an unspoilt and extremely delicate ecosystem that's home to several exotic species such as the endangered snow leopard and red panda, the Himalayan black bear, the Himalayan red fox and perhaps even the legendary *migoi* or yeti. The region is also home to the isolated Brokpa tribe; you'll probably be among the first outsiders to cross paths with them.

Being a brand-new route, this trek itinerary still misses a few details compared to other treks, such as daily walking distances,

treaty once signed between the kings of Bumthang and Assam. In the village, you'll also see the rocky remains of a blacksmith, believed to be one of the reincarnations of Pema Lingpa. The camp is located amid rice fields near the village.

DAY 3: REST DAY IN NABJI
Use this day to do a pleasant two-hour hike (gaining about 200m) to **Korphu**, a village of about 600 people perched at 1500m. After gorging on a locally cooked lunch, visit the village temple, housing the sacred relics of Pema Lingpa. Trudge back to Nabji down the same trail by late afternoon.

DAY 4: NABJI TO KUDRA
13-14KM / 6-7 HOURS / 335M ASCENT

Today's trek leaves Nabji at a spot marked by a holy tree, before passing through a dense forest of clippers, orchids and bamboo. The forest is supposedly a habitat for tigers and leopards, although sightings are rare. The campsite at **Kudra** (1635m) is smack in the middle of the forest, with three Monpa households nearby.

DAY 5: KUDRA TO JANGBI
13-14KM / 6-7 HOURS / 265M DESCENT

Today's trail is littered with fabulous evidence of Guru Rinpoche's visit to the region – footprint, dagger, hat, you name it. Lunch is at Phrumzur village (1400m), which has a temple from where one can take in good views of the valley. From Phrumzur, it's an

THE TREK AT A GLANCE

Duration 6 days

Max Elevation 3480m

Difficulty Moderate

Season Mid-March to May, September to November

Start Chaling

Finish Phongmay

Access Town Trashigang

Summary A star attraction offering a sneak peek into one of the most secluded regions in Bhutan, previously unknown to the outside world.

MEET THE BROKPAS

The Brokpas are a semi-nomadic tribe who migrate through eastern Bhutan with their yaks, moving between the highlands in summer and lower pastures in winter. Their population exceeds 5000. They are culturally different from neighbouring tribes and dress differently; most notable is their scalp-hugging headgear made of yak hair, with tail-like extensions descending from its edges.

The Brokpas still engage in the barter system, and travel down to Phongmay, Radhi and Trashigang in winter to trade their stocks of cheese, butter and dried meat in exchange for salt, tea and grains. Most families own livestock, barring a few who stay back in their village dwellings through the cold season.

altitude gain/loss and a well-marked map. Hopefully, they will be made available soon.

1: CHALING TO DAMNONGCHU
7 HOURS

Starting out of Trashigang, drive along a feeder road to the village of Rangjung. The trailhead is at Chaling, a further hour's drive ahead. From Chaling, it's a brisk walk past Mindrula to the camp at **Damnongchu** (3070m).

DAY 2: DAMNONGCHU TO MERAK
5 HOURS

The trail leading out of Damnongchu involves a series of gentle ups and downs along a stream. The final stretch is an easy and gradual ascent that takes you into the village of **Merak** (3480m). Camp will be made just before the village, in a spot offering fantastic views of the mountains and the village. Alternately, you can choose to stay at the village guesthouse.

DAY 3: MERAK TO MIKSA TENG
7-8 HOURS

Today's trek scales the Nagchung La pass, after which the route descends steadily to a river. After following the river for an hour, it's another steep one-hour climb to **Miksa Teng** (2850m). The campsite is in a clearing by the village, surrounded by rhododendrons. To catch them in a riotous bloom, plan your trek in April.

DAY 4: MIKSA TENG TO SAKTEN
3-4 HOURS

From Miksa Teng, it's an easy day walk through beautiful woods to **Sakten** (2985m). If you're lucky, you might see a red panda amid the greens along the way. There's a campsite on the outskirts of the village, but you can also sleep at the village guesthouse if you want.

DAY 5: SAKTEN TO JYONGKHAR
6-7 HOURS

Today's walk is mostly downhill, along a plain path, to the village of **Jyongkhar** (1850m), which has a community school. The campsite is located near a river.

DAY 6: JYONGKHAR TO PHONGMAY
5 HOURS

The last stretch of the trek passes through the village of **Radhi**, a beautiful agrarian settlement also known as the 'rice bowl of the east', for obvious reasons. Radhi is also extremely popular for its woollen textiles, generically called Bura weaving. From Radhi, it's a direct drive to Phongmay, and on to Trashigang.

Understand
Bhutan

population per sq km

BHUTAN   USA   INDIA

† ≈ 20 people

Bhutan Today

Bhutan remains a unique and special country. For better or worse, the country has opened its doors and hearts to the outside world and joined the global community. There is now at least one mobile phone for every three Bhutanese and there are more than 45,000 registered vehicles (though there are still no traffic lights). The challenge ahead for the government is to bring the benefits of globalisation and capitalism to Bhutan without undermining the very things that Bhutanese cherish about their unique culture.

Democracy & Parliament

In 2005 Bhutan's much-loved king announced that he would abdicate in favour of the crown prince and he set about drawing up the country's first ever constitution to prepare for democratic elections in 2008. This peaceful ceding of power in favour of a parliamentary democracy stood in stark contrast to that other Himalayan former monarchy, Nepal.

In March 2008 the world's eyes were focussed on this small mountain kingdom as its populace went to the polls. With royal encouragement this sparse population spread over a rugged country managed a remarkable 80% turnout. And the result was extraordinary and unpredicted – a landslide victory to one of the two contesting parties. The Druk Phuensum Tshogpa (DPT) party grabbed 45 of the 47 seats in the parliament's lower house, the National Assembly. The People's Democratic Party (PDP) won the other two seats; however, it lost its leader in the landslide.

Bhutan's shiny new parliament consists of the king or Druk Gyalpo, the upper house or National Council, and the aforementioned National Assembly. The **National Council** consists of 25 members, 20 of who each represent one of the *dzongkhags* (political districts) and there are five additional members nominated by the king. Interest-

» Population: 699,847 (2009)

» Life expectancy: 66 years

» GDP: US$2155 per capita (2009)

» Human Development Index ranking: 132 out of 182 countries

» Chilli production: 10,500 tonnes per year

Dos & Don'ts

» Do use the word *la* at the end of a sentence in either Dzongkha or English as a sign of respect, eg *kuzo zangpo la* (hello).

» Do bring a small gift if you are invited to a Bhutanese home, perhaps a bottle of wine or box of sweets.

» Do remove your shoes and hat upon entering the important rooms of a temple.

» Do leave a small offering of money on the altar of temples.

» Don't use your finger to point, especially at deities or religious objects; use an open hand with the palm up.

» Don't touch the crown of the head, for example of a young child; this is considered a special part of the body.

» Don't take photos inside any temples and don't embarrass your guide by asking to be the exception.

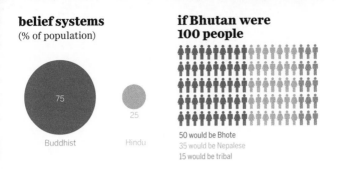

belief systems
(% of population)

75 Buddhist

25 Hindu

if Bhutan were 100 people

50 would be Bhote
35 would be Nepalese
15 would be tribal

---

ingly, candidates for the National Council must not be members of a political party.

For the first election, the **National Assembly** had 47 seats across the 20 *dzongkhags*. The constitution allows for adjustments to be made to the National Assembly as the population increases (to a maximum of 55 seats), and as the distribution of voters across *dzongkhags* changes.

Modernisation & Gross National Happiness

Despite the rapid and recent uptake of technology, democracy and global trends, Bhutan is very aware of the dangers of modernisation and the government continues to assume a protective role in Bhutanese society. Bhutan was the world's first country to ban not only smoking in public places but also the very sale of tobacco. Also banned are Western-style advertising billboards and plastic bags.

Issues of sustainable development, education and health care, and environmental and cultural preservation are therefore at the forefront of policy making; as are the tenets of Buddhism, which forms the base of Bhutan's legal code. Every development project is scrutinised for its impact on the local population, religious faith and the environment. Bhutan's strict adherence to high-value, low-impact tourism is a perfect example of this. Bhutan is one of the few places on earth where compassion is favoured over capitalism and wellbeing is measured alongside productivity. This unique approach is summed up in the much-celebrated concept of Gross National Happiness.

Challenges

Bhutan is a tiny nation with abundant natural riches and a small, sustainable population surrounded by much larger countries experiencing

Although Buddhism plays a central role in Bhutan it has not been made the official state religion. The constitution stresses that all Bhutanese have freedom of religion and foreign religious personnel are permitted to work in Bhutan, but are not allowed to proselytise.

Top Books

» **The Raven Crown** by Michael Aris

» **Treasures of the Thunder Dragon** by Ashi Dorji Wangmo Wangchuck

» **The Hero with a Thousand Eyes** by Karma Ura

» **The Circle of Karma** by Kunzang Choden

» **Bhutan, Kingdom of the Dragon** by Robert Dompnier

Top Films

» **Travellers & Magicians** (Khyentse Norbu) A whimsical tale within a tale tackling the conflict of new and old

» **The Other Final** (Johan Kramer) The world's bottom football team, Monserratt, meets second from bottom, Bhutan resource-hungry population growth. This situation has presented opportunities (the export of hydroelectricity to India provides 49% of government revenue), but also threats in recent decades.

Along the southern border of Bhutan, immigrants from Nepal, seeking to break free from the rigid caste system of their home country, began settling in the late 19th and early 20th centuries. They are called **Lhotshampa** (literally, 'the people of the southern border') and are mainly Hindu and form approximately 25% of Bhutan's population.

Major problems between the **Drukpa**, or northern Bhutanese, and the Lhotshampa emerged in the late 1980s. At that time, the government began to focus on preserving what it saw as Bhutan's threatened national identity. Mindful of Bhutan's porous border and attractiveness because of its fertile land, low population and free health and education facilities, the government conducted a nationwide census to identify illegal immigrants. Thousands of ethnic Nepalis lacked proper documentation and a sense of fear and insecurity led to an exodus of Nepali-speakers from Bhutan. How much of the migration was voluntary remains a matter of debate, but tens of thousands of Nepali-speakers left Bhutan for camps in neighbouring Nepal between 1988 and 1993. In 2010 there were about 90,000 people left in the UNHCR protected camps. Despite thousands of refugees being resettled in the West, the issue of the refugees still languishing in camps in eastern Nepal is far from resolved.

In 2004, on another porous border, Bhutanese troops flushed out Assamese separatist militants from Bhutanese territory, destroying their jungle refuges. While the struggle for independence from Delhi in these regions of India continues, the security of the bordering Bhutanese lands, including the spectacular Royal Manas National Park, remains compromised (see also p204).

The Centre of Bhutan Studies (www.bhutanstudies.org.bt) has an excellent website explaining the celebrated Bhutanese concept of Gross National Happiness (GNH; www.grossnationalhappiness.com) including how and why the index is measured.

News Sources

Bhutan Broadcasting Service (BBS) Government-run, it provides TV and radio services
Bhutan Times (www.bhutantimes.bt) Sunday newspaper
Bhutan Today (www.bhutantoday.bt) Daily newspaper

Bhutan Observer (www.bhutanobserver.bt) Friday newspaper
Drukpa (www.drukpa.bt) Monthly news magazine
Kuensel (www.kuenselonline.com) Wednesday and Saturday newspaper

The Journalist (www.thejournalist.bt) Sunday newspaper

History

Bhutan's early history is steeped in Buddhist folklore and mythology; it features tremendous deeds and beings with supernatural powers. It's said that a saint who had the ability to appear in eight different forms, one of them being Guru Rinpoche, visited Bhutan on a flying tiger and left the imprint of his body and his hat on rocks. School texts describe demons that threatened villages and destroyed temples until captured through magic and converted to Buddhism. Tales abound of ghosts who destroyed temples, and angels who rebuilt them.

Researchers have attached dates to many events, though these often do not seem to fit together into a credible and accurate chronology. When reading Bhutanese history, it's easier to let your imagination flow. Try visualising the spirit of the happenings rather than rationalising events as historical truth. This will, in part, help prepare you for a visit to Bhutan, where spirits, ghosts, yetis, medicine men, and lamas reincarnated in three different bodies are accepted as a part of daily life.

Bhutan's medieval and modern history is better documented than its ancient history, but is no less exotic. This is a time of warlords, feuds, giant fortresses and castles, with intrigue, treachery, fierce battles and extraordinary pageantry all playing feature roles. The country's recent history begins with a hereditary monarchy that was founded in the 20th century and continued the country's policy of isolationism. It was not until the leadership of the third king that Bhutan emerged from its medieval heritage of serfdom and seclusion.

Until the 1960s the country had no national currency, no telephones, no schools, no hospitals, no postal service and no tourists. Development efforts have now produced all these – plus airports, roads and a national system of health care. Despite the speed of modernisation, Bhutan has been famously cautious in opening its doors to tourism, TV and the internet in an effort to preserve its national

The most authoritative and complete history of Bhutan in English is Michael Aris' *Bhutan, the Early History of a Himalayan Kingdom*.

TIMELINE	1500–2000 BC	6th Century AD	7th Century
	Present-day Bhutan is inhabited by nomadic herders who seasonally migrated between low-lying valleys and alpine pastures.	The animist Bon religion is established across the Himalayan region including several valleys of what is now Bhutan.	Buddhism becomes established in Bhutan with the first Buddhist temples built in AD 659, including Kyichu Lhakhang near Paro, and Jampey Lhakhang in Bumthang.

ORIGIN OF THE NAME BHUTAN

Few agree on the origin of the name Bhutan. It may have evolved from the Sanskrit 'Bhotant', meaning the end of Tibet, or from 'Bhu-uttan' meaning high land'. Early British explorers called it Bootan or Bhotan, and they believed the name derived from 'Bhotsthan', meaning 'Land of the Bhotias' (Bhotia is Sanskrit for people from Tibet).

Although now known as Bhutan to the outside world, the country has been known as Druk Yul, 'land of the thunder dragon', to its inhabitants since the 13th century. The people call themselves the Drukpa.

identity and the environment. More recently the exceedingly popular fourth king ensured his special place in history and the beginning of a new era for Bhutan by forsaking absolute power, introducing democracy and abdicating in favour of his son.

Early History & the Arrival of Buddhism

Archaeological evidence suggests the low-lying valleys of present-day Bhutan were inhabited as early as 1500 to 2000 BC by nomadic herders who moved their grazing animals to high pastures in summer. Many Bhutanese still live this way today. The valleys of Bhutan provided relatively easy access across the Himalaya, and it is believed that the Manas River valley, in particular, was used as a migration and trade route from India to Tibet.

Some of the early inhabitants of Bhutan were followers of Bon, the animistic tradition that was the main religion throughout the Himalayan region before the advent of Buddhism. It is believed that the Bon religion was introduced in Bhutan in the 6th century AD.

Buddhism was possibly first introduced to parts of Bhutan as early as the 2nd century AD, although most historians agree that the first Buddhist temples were built in the 7th century under the instruction of the Tibetan king Songtsen Gampo. See the boxed text, p83, for the remarkable story behind the construction of these temples.

Many of the important events in the emerging country's early history involved saints and religious leaders and were therefore chronicled only in scriptures. Unfortunately, most of these original documents were destroyed in fires in the printing works of Sonagatsel in 1828 and in Punakha Dzong in 1832. Much of what was left in the old capital of Punakha was lost in an earthquake in 1897 and more records were lost when Paro Dzong burned in 1907. Therefore much of the early history of Bhutan relies either on reports from British explorers, on legend and folklore, and the few manuscripts that escaped these disasters.

The Centre for Bhutan Studies (www.bhutan studies.org.bt) is dedicated to promoting research and scholarship on Bhutan; it publishes many detailed historical research articles, among other subjects.

746
Guru Rinpoche (Padmasambhava) is invited by the king of Bumthang to visit his land and subdue evil spirits. He is credited with converting the king and others to Buddhism.

841
The Tibetan king Langdharma bans Buddhism in Tibet and banishes his brother prince Tsangma to eastern Bhutan.

» Bumthang, where Guru Rinpoche first visited Bhutan

Guru Rinpoche

Guru Rinpoche, or Precious Master, is one of the most important of Bhutan's historical and religious figures and his visit to Bumthang in AD 746 (see following) is recognised as the true introduction of Buddhism to Bhutan. He is a notable historical figure of the 8th century and his statue appears in almost all Bhutanese temples built after this first visit.

He is also regarded as the second Buddha possessing miraculous powers, including the ability to subdue demons and evil spirits, and his birth was predicted by Sakyamuni, the historical Buddha. His birthplace was Uddiyana in the Swat valley of what is now Pakistan. Uddiyana is known in Dzongkha as Ugyen, and some texts refer to him as Ugyen Rinpoche. He is also known as Padmasambhava. *Padma* is Sanskrit for 'lotus flower' and is the origin of the Tibetan and Bhutanese name Pema; *sambhava* means 'born from'.

He travelled in various manifestations throughout Tibet, Nepal and Bhutan, meditating in numerous caves, which are now regarded as important 'power places'. He preserved his teachings and wisdom by concealing them in the form of *terma* (hidden treasures) to be found by enlightened treasure discoverers called *tertons*. His consort and biographer, Yeshe Chhogyel, urges us not to regard Guru Rinpoche as a normal human being, because by doing so we will fail to perceive even a fraction of his enlightened qualities.

Bhutanese and Tibetans differ over a few aspects of his life; the text following, reflects the Bhutanese tradition.

> Artistic styles and traditional practices are greatly similar between Buddhists and Bonpo, followers of Bon. Noteworthy differences: Bonpo circumambulate their temples anticlockwise and vote in their lamas, whereas Buddhist lamas are reincarnated.

The Story of Kurjey Lhakhang

In 746 Guru Rinpoche made his first visit to Bhutan. At this time, the Indian Sendha Gyab had established himself as the king of Bumthang, with the title Sindhu Raja. He was feuding with Naochhe (Big Nose), a rival Indian king in the south of Bhutan, when Naochhe killed the Sindhu Raja's son and 16 of his attendants. The raja was so distraught that he desecrated the abode of the chief Bumthang deity, Shelging Kharpo, who then angrily took revenge by turning the skies black and stealing the king's life force, bringing him near to death.

One of the king's secretaries thus invited Guru Rinpoche to Bumthang to use his supernatural powers to save the Sindhu Raja. The Guru came to Bumthang and meditated, leaving a *jey* (imprint) of his *kur* (body) in the rock, now surrounded by Kurjey Lhakhang (see p121).

Guru Rinpoche was to be married to the king's daughter, Tashi Khuedon. He sent her to fetch water in a golden ewer. While she was away the Guru transformed into all eight of his manifestations and, together, they started to dance in the field by the temple. Every local

9th Century	10th Century	12th Century	1180
Many Tibetan Buddhists take up refuge in Bhutan as the Bonpo gain power and Buddhists are persecuted	Further turmoil and the decline of Buddhism in Tibet sees various schools of Tibetan Buddhism established in Bhutan.	Gyalwa Lhanangpa, founder of the Lhapa Kagyu lineage, establishes Tango Goemba in the Thimphu valley and a system of forts based on Tibetan dzongs.	The founding of Druk Monastery in Ralung (Tibet) by Lama Tsangpa Gyarey Yeshe Dorji signals the beginning of Drukpa Kagyu lineage.

deity appeared to watch this spectacle, except the stony-faced Shelging Kharpo who stayed hidden away in his rocky hideout.

Guru Rinpoche was not to be set back by this rejection, and when the princess returned he changed her into five separate princesses, each clutching a golden ewer. The sunlight flashing off these ewers finally attracted Shelging Kharpo, but before he ventured out to see what was going on, he first transformed himself into a white snow lion. On seeing the creature appear the Guru changed into a *garuda*, flew up and grabbed the lion and told Shelging Kharpo in no uncertain terms to behave himself. He therefore recovered Sendha Gyab's life force, and for good measure converted both the rival kings to Buddhism, restoring the country to peace.

Shelging Kharpo agreed to become a protective deity of Buddhism; to seal the agreement the Guru planted his staff in the ground at the temple where its cypress tree descendants continue to grow and tower over the Kurjey Lhakhang.

Guru Rinpoche is credited with the founding of the Nyingma lineage – also known as the old 'red hat' sect – of Mahayana Buddhism, which became for a time the dominant religion of Bhutan. Its followers are known as Nyingmapa.

Further Visits by Guru Rinpoche

The Guru returned to Bhutan via Singye Dzong in Lhuentse and visited the districts of Bumthang and Mongar as well as Lhuentse. He was returning from Tibet where, at the invitation of the Tibetan king Trisong Detsen, he had introduced Nyingma Buddhism and overcome the demons that were obstructing the construction of Samye Monastery.

At Gom Kora, in eastern Bhutan, he left a body print and an impression of his head with a hat. He flew in the form of Dorji Drakpo (one of his eight manifestations) to Taktshang in Paro on a flaming tigress, giving the famous Taktshang monastery the name 'Tiger's Nest'.

It is believed that Guru Rinpoche also made a third visit to present-day Bhutan during the reign of Muthri Tsenpo (764–817), the son of Trisong Detsen and the 39th king of Tibet.

The Eight Manifestations of Guru Rinpoche

The Guru is depicted in eight forms (Guru Tshengay). These are not really different incarnations, but representations of his eight main initiations, in which he assumed a new personality that was symbolised by a new name and appearance. Because initiation is equivalent to entering a new life, it is a form of rebirth. Therefore the eight forms follow the chronology of Guru Rinpoche's life.

He emerged as an eight-year-old from a blue lotus on Lake Danakosha in Uddiyana, and was adopted by King Indrabodhi. Then he was called Tshokye Dorji (diamond thunderbolt born from a lake). He later renounced his kingdom and went to receive teachings and ordination from the master Prabhahasti in the cave of Maratrika (near the village of Har-

12th Century	1184–1251	1433	1450–1521
Many Drukpa lamas leave Tibet for Bhutan because of persecution at the hands of the rival Gelugpa. Most settle in western Bhutan and establish Drukpa monastic orders.	Lifespan of Lama Phajo Drukgom Shigpo, who establishes Drukpa Kagyu as the dominant school of Buddhism in Bhutan giving the region its distinctive form of Buddhism.	Thangtong Gyalpo, the Iron Bridge Lama, visits Bhutan from Tibet in search of iron ore and builds eight bridges.	The much-heralded life of Pema Lingpa, the most important *terton* (discoverer of sacred texts and artefacts) in Bhutan.

PAINTINGS & STATUES OF GURU RINPOCHE

Most representations of Guru Rinpoche are in his manifestation as Padmasambhava, wearing royal robes and holding the insignia of spiritual realisation (see p223).

Often, a statue of Padmasambhava will be flanked by two statues of female devotees. These are the Indian princess Mandarava, the lady of wisdom, and the Tibetan *khandroma* Yeshe Chhogyel, who is regarded as an incarnation of Saraswati, the goddess of knowledge. She was gifted with such a perfect memory that she was able to remember the Guru's every word and became his sole biographer. She is depicted as a white, heavenly being with traditional ornaments and flying scarves; Mandarava is usually depicted as an Indian hill princess.

Guru Rinpoche's celestial abode or paradise is a copper-coloured mountain named Zangto Pelri. The Guardians of the Four Directions guard the four gates, and in the centre is a three-roofed pagoda, with Guru Rinpoche enthroned on the ground level, flanked by his two consorts.

ishe in eastern Nepal), becoming Sakya Senge (lion of the Sakya clan). In this form he is identified with Sakyamuni, the historical Buddha.

After studying the teachings of the Vajrayana and mastering the sciences of all Indian *pandits,* he obtained full realisation and was able to see all the gods and deities. Then he was called Loden Chogsey (possessor of supreme knowledge). He took as his consort Mandarava, the daughter of the king of Zahor (in the Mandi district of Himachal Pradesh, India). This enraged the king, who condemned them both to be burned, but through his powers the Guru turned the pyre into a lake and converted the kingdom to Buddhism. Then he was called Padmasambhava.

He returned to Uddiyana to convert it to Buddhism, but was recognised as the prince who had renounced his kingdom and was condemned to be burned along with his consort. Again he was not consumed by the fire and appeared sitting upon a lotus in a lake. This lake is Rewalsar – also called Tsho Pema (the lotus lake) – in Himachal Pradesh, and is an important pilgrimage spot. His father, King Indrabodhi, offered him the kingdom and he became Pema Gyalpo (the lotus king), remaining for 13 years and establishing Buddhism.

When he was preaching in the eight cremation grounds to the *khandromas* (female celestial beings), he caught the life force of the evil deities and he turned them into protectors of Buddhism. Then he was called Nyima Yeozer (sunbeam of enlightenment). Later, 500 heretic masters tried to destroy the doctrine of Buddha, but he vanquished them through the power of his words and brought down a thunderbolt

Sampa Lhundrup Lhakhang, part of the Kurjey Lhakhang complex in Bumthang's Chokhor Valley, houses an impressive 10m statue of Guru Rinpoche flanked by his eight manifestations.

1455–1529

Lifespan of Lama Drukpa Kunley, the Divine Madman, who travelled throughout Bhutan preaching an unconventional approach to Buddhism and life.

1616

The first Zhabdrung, Ngawang Namgyal, arrives in Bhutan from Ralung, Tibet, marking the ascendancy of the Druk Kagyu lineage.

JOHNNY HAGLUND

» The phallus symbol is a legacy of the Divine Madman

destroying the non-Buddhists in a flash of hail and lightning. He was then called Sengye Dradrok (roaring lion).

When he came to Bhutan the second time and visited Singye Dzong in Kurtoe and Taktshang in Paro, he was in the form of Dorji Drakpo (fierce thunderbolt). He subdued all the evil spirits hindering Buddhism and blessed them as guardians of the doctrine. In this form, Guru Rinpoche rides a tigress.

Medieval Period

The grandson of Trisong Detsen, Langdharma, ruled Tibet from AD 836 to 842. As a follower of Bon, he banned Buddhism, destroyed religious institutions and banished his brother, Prince Tsangma, to Bhutan. It is believed that many monks fled from Tibet and took refuge in Bhutan during this period. Despite the assassination of Langdharma and the reintroduction of Buddhism, Tibet remained in political turmoil and many Tibetans migrated to western Bhutan.

Between the 9th and 17th centuries numerous ruling clans and noble families emerged in different valleys throughout Bhutan. The various local chieftains spent their energy quarrelling among themselves and with Tibet, and no important nationally recognised political figure emerged during this period.

The three main lineages spreading Buddhist teachings in Bhutan were the Nyingmapa, the Kagyupa and the Sakyapa. A fourth school, the Gelugpa, emerged in Tibet in the 15th century. This lineage was viewed by the Bhutanese from the 17th century onwards as hostile to Bhutan.

Establishing the Bhutanese Form of Buddhism

Back in Tibet, Lama Tsangpa Gyarey Yeshe Dorji (1161–1211) founded a monastery in the town of Ralung, just east of Gyantse, in 1180. He named the monastery Druk (Dragon), after the thunder dragons that he heard in the sky as he searched for an appropriate site upon which to build a monastery. The lineage followed here was named after the monastery and became known as Drukpa Kagyu.

In the 11th and 12th centuries there was a further large influx of Tibetans into Bhutan. Many Drukpa lamas left Tibet because of persecution at the hands of the followers of the rival Gelugpa lineage. Most of these lamas settled in western Bhutan and established branches of Drukpa monastic orders. Western Bhutan became loosely united through the weight of their teachings. Charismatic lamas emerged as de facto leaders of large portions of the west, while the isolated valleys of eastern and central Bhutan remained separate feudal states.

One of the most important of these lamas was Gyalwa Lhanangpa, who founded the Lhapa Kagyu lineage. He established the Tango Goemba (monastery) on a hill above the northern end of the Thimphu valley and established a system of forts in Bhutan similar to the dzongs found in Tibet.

1621	1627	1629	1637
First monk body established at Cheri Goemba, which was built by Zhabdrung Ngawang Namgyal a year earlier.	Portuguese Jesuits, Fathers Cacella and Cabral are the first European visitors to Bhutan.	A coalition of five Bhutanese lamas representing opposing lineages attacks Simtokha Dzong, the first dzong in the country, and challenges the Zhabdrung.	Punakha Dzong constructed as second dzong in country. The town remains capital of Bhutan until the mid 1950s.

Lama Phajo Drukgom Shigpo (1184–1251), a disciple of Lama Tsangpa Gyarey, came to Bhutan from Ralung and defeated Lama Lhanangpa. He and his companions established the small Dho-Ngen Dzong on the west bank of the Wang Chhu and took control of the Tango Goemba. Lama Phajo is credited with establishing the Bhutanese form of Buddhism by converting many people to the Drukpa Kagyu lineage. Other lamas resented his presence and success, and they tried to kill him through the casting of magic spells. Phajo, though, turned the spells back on these lamas, destroying several of their monasteries.

Between the 13th and 16th centuries, the Drukpa Kagyu lineage flourished and Bhutan adopted a separate religious identity. Several important Druk Kagyu teachers from Ralung were invited to preach and establish monasteries in western Bhutan. Among the visitors to Bhutan during this period was Lama Ngawang Chhogyel (1465–1540). He made several trips and was often accompanied by his sons, who established several monasteries. They are credited with building the temple of Druk Choeding in Paro and Pangri Zampa and Hongtsho goemba near Thimphu.

Perhaps the most famous Druk Kagyu teacher was the colourful and unconventional Drukpa Kunley (1455–1529; see p92). He is remembered today with immense affection and faith by the Bhutanese and is closely associated with the beautiful temple of Chimi Lhakhang between Lobesa and Punakha.

Hidden Treasures & Pema Lingpa

Between the 11th and 16th centuries numerous *terma* (sacred texts) hidden by Guru Rinpoche in caves, rocks and lakes were discovered, as he had prophesied, by tantric lamas called *tertons* (treasure-finders).

Pema Lingpa (1450–1521) was one of the five great *tertons* of Nyingma Buddhism, and the most important *terton* in Bhutan. The texts and artefacts he found, the dances he composed and the art he produced have significantly shaped Bhutan's cultural heritage. He is also considered to be a reincarnation of Guru Rinpoche.

He was born in the hamlet of Drangchel in Bumthang's Tang valley, near Kunzangdrak Goemba. As a boy he learned the craft of blacksmithing from his grandfather; indeed, two of the chainmails he forged are still on display at Tamshing and Thangbi goembas.

At age 25 he discovered his first *terma* after he dreamed a monk handed him a scroll in *dakini* script that gave instructions on how to find a treasure chest deep in a pool in the Tang valley (see p124). Pema eventually managed to translate the scroll but this was a huge project, because in *dakini* script each word stands for 1000 human words.

The Divine Madman by Keith Dowman is a wonderful translation of the poems and works of the extraordinary Lama Drukpa Kunley.

In his visions, Pema Lingpa often visited Zangto Pelri, Guru Rinpoche's celestial paradise, where he observed the dances *(pa-cham)* of the *khandromas* and *yidam* (tutelary deities). He taught three of these dances to his disciples, and several are still performed as part of Bhutan's tsechus.

HISTORY HIDDEN TREASURES & PEMA LINGPA

1639	1668	1705
Tibet finally recognises Zhabdrung Ngawang Namgyal as the supreme authority in Bhutan.	Mingyur Tenpa is enthroned as the third *desi*. He rules for 12 years, during which time he extends the boundaries of Bhutan westwards to Kalimpong, now part of India.	The much-delayed announcement of the demise of the Zhabdrung Ngawang Namgyal.

ANTONY GIBLIN

Later, assisted by the *khandromas (dakinis),* he used the text as a basis for teachings. His residence at the time was in Kunzangling, which is on a cliff above the Tang valley and is now the site of the Kunzangdrak Goemba.

During Pema Lingpa's life he found a total of 34 statues, scrolls and sacred relics in Bhutan and as far away as Samye in Tibet. Many of the statues and relics he discovered are preserved in lhakhangs (inner temples) throughout Bhutan, including Bumthang's Tamshing and Kunzangdrak goembas, which he founded.

After his death he was reincarnated in three forms, consisting of *ku* (body), *sung* (speech) and *thug* (mind) and these lineages continue to this day.

Through his six sons, one daughter and numerous reincarnations, Pema Lingpa's legacy still influences much of Bhutan. One of his grandsons, Gyalse Pema Thinley, who was also a reincarnation of Pema Lingpa, founded Gangte Goemba in the Phobjikha valley, and the Gangte Trulku lineage continues there, with Kuenzang Pema Namgyal, born in 1955, as the ninth 'mind' reincarnation. The royal family of Bhutan, the Wangchuck dynasty, is also descended from this line.

The Rise of the Zhabdrung

The arrival in 1616 of the Zhabdrung Ngawang Namgyal marks the transformation of Bhutan and the ascendancy of the Druk Kagyu lineage.

By the 16th century the political arena was still fragmented between many local chiefs, each controlling their own territory and engaging in petty feuds with the others. There were numerous monasteries competing for superiority and the lamas of western Bhutan were working to extend their influence to the east of the country.

Everything changed in 1616 when Ngawang Namgyal (1594–1651) came to Bhutan from Ralung, the original home of the Drukpa Kagyu in Tibet. He was a descendent of Tsangpa Gyarey, the founder of Ralung Monastery. At age 12 he was recognised as the reincarnation of Pema Karpo, the prince-abbot of Ralung. This recognition was challenged by the ruler of another principality in Tibet, and Ngawang Namgyal found his position at Ralung very difficult. When he was 23, the protective deity Yeshe Goenpo (Mahakala) appeared to him in the form of a raven and directed him south to Bhutan. He travelled through Laya and Gasa and spent time at Pangri Zampa (Thimphu), which was established by his great-great-grandfather, Ngawang Chhogyel.

As Ngawang Namgyal travelled throughout western Bhutan teaching, his political strength increased. Soon he established himself as the religious ruler of Bhutan with the title Zhabdrung Rinpoche (precious jewel at whose feet one prostrates), and so becoming the first in the line of *zhabdrungs.* He built the first of the present system of dzongs at

1730	**1768**	**1772**	**1774**
Druk Desi Mipham Wangpo assists Gya Chila, the ruler of Cooch Behar, to defeat invaders and to settle a family feud; Bhutan is then allowed to station a force in that southern kingdom.	The *desi* tries to suppress the influence of the religious establishment in Bhutan. To do so he establishes alliances with the Panchen Lama in Tibet and with King Prithvi Narayan Shah of Nepal.	Bhutan invades Cooch Behar and kidnaps its king. The British East India Company agrees to assist Cooch Behar in return for payment.	George Bogle leads a trade mission to Bhutan and Tibet, and plants potatoes in Bhutanese soil.

Simtokha, just south of present-day Thimphu. While the primary function of earlier Bhutanese dzongs was to serve as invincible fortresses, the Simtokha Dzong also housed a monastic body and administrative facilities, as well as fulfilling its defensive function. This combination of civil, religious and defensive functions became the model for all of Bhutan's subsequent dzongs.

The Zhabdrung's rule was opposed by the leaders of rival Buddhist lineages within Bhutan. They formed a coalition of five lamas under the leadership of Lama Palden and attacked Simtokha Dzong in 1629. This attack was repelled, but the coalition then aligned itself with a group of Tibetans and continued its opposition. The Zhabdrung's militia thwarted the Tibetans in battle on several occasions, and the influence of the rival lineages diminished. Finally, after forging an alliance with the brother of King Singye Namgyal of Ladakh, the Zhabdrung's forces defeated the Tibetans and their coalition ally. In 1639 an agreement was reached with the Tsang Desi in Tibet recognising Zhabdrung Ngawang Namgyal as the supreme authority throughout Bhutan.

The Zhabdrung further enhanced his power by establishing relations with neighbouring kings, including Rama Shah, the king of Nepal, and Raja Padmanarayan of Cooch Behar (India). It was at this time that the king of Ladakh granted the Zhabdrung a number of sites in western Tibet for the purpose of meditation and worship. These included Diraphuk, Nyanri and Zuthulphuk on the slopes of the holy Mt Kailash.

The Bhutanese administration of these monasteries continued until the Chinese takeover of Tibet in 1959. Other Tibetan monasteries that came under Bhutanese administration were Rimpung, Doba, Khochag, and De Dzong, all near Gartok. A Bhutanese lama was sent as representative to Nepal, and Bhutanese monasteries were established at Bodhnath (Chorten Jaro Khasho) and Swayambhunath in Kathmandu. Bhutan administered Swayambhunath until after the Nepal-Tibet war of 1854–56, when it was retaken by Nepal on the suspicion that Bhutan had helped the Tibetans.

The Zhabdrung established the first *sangha* (community of monks) at Cheri Goemba near Thimphu. When Punakha Dzong was completed in 1635, the *sangha* was moved there and became the *dratshang* (central monk body), headed by a supreme abbot called the Je Khenpo.

Invasions from Tibet

In the meantime, strife continued in Tibet, between the Nyingmapa (known as 'red hat') group of Buddhists and the Gelugpa ('yellow hat'); the latter are headed by the Dalai Lama. The Mongol chief Gushri

During his reign, Zhabdrung Ngawang Namgyal ordered the construction of many monasteries and dzongs throughout Bhutan. Of these, the dzongs at Simtokha, Paro, Wangdue Phodrang, Punakha and Trongsa are still standing.

1776 & 1777
Dr Alexander Hamilton travels to Punakha and Thimphu to negotiate land disputes between Britain and Bhutan.

1783
Captain Samuel Turner leads a grand British Raj expedition to Bhutan and Tibet.

ANTONY GIBLIN

» The Punakha countryside was a source of land disputes

FATHERS CACELLA & CABRAL MEET THE ZHABDRUNG

The first Western visitors to Bhutan were two Portuguese Jesuit priests. In early 1627 Fathers Cacella and Cabral travelled from Calcutta to Bhutan en route to Shigatse in Tibet. They stayed for a few months in Cheri Goemba, north of Thimphu, with the Zhabdrung.

There is no complete account of their journey, but one of their letters provides an insight into Ngawang Namgyal's character: 'He received us with a demonstration of great benevolence, signifying this in the joy which he showed on seeing us and on knowing where we had come from, where we were from, that is from what country or nation, and he asked the other questions normal at a first meeting.'

Khan, a patron of the Dalai Lama, led his army in an attack on Tibet's Tsang province, where he overthrew the Rinpong dynasty and established the supremacy of the Gelug lineage in the region.

In 1644 the Mongols and Tibetans, who were used to the extremely high plains of Tibet, launched an assault from Lhobrak into Bumthang, but found themselves overpowered by the forests and heat of Bhutan. Zhabdrung Ngawang Namgyal personally led the successful resistance and several Tibetan officers and a large number of horses were captured. Drukgyel Dzong was built at the head of Paro valley in 1647 to commemorate the victory and to prevent any further Tibetan infiltration.

One of the strongest of Tibet's Dalai Lamas was the 'Great Fifth'. During his administration, he became jealous of the growing influence of the rival Drukpa on his southern border and mounted further invasions into Bhutan in 1648 and 1649. Each attempt was launched via Phari in Tibet, from where the Great Fifth's forces crossed the 5000m-high Tremo La into Paro valley. They were repelled, and again the Bhutanese captured large amounts of armour, weapons and other spoils. Some of this booty may still be seen in the National Museum in Paro.

Much of the armour and many weapons that were taken during the 1644 battle with the Mongols and Tibetans are on display in Punakha Dzong.

Ngawang Namgyal's success in repelling the Tibetan attacks further consolidated his position as ruler. The large militia that he raised for the purpose also gave him effective control of the country. Mingyur Tenpa, who was appointed by the Zhabdrung as *penlop* (governor) of Trongsa, undertook a campaign to unite all the valleys of the central and eastern parts of the country under the Zhabdrung's rule, which he accomplished by about 1655. At this time the great dzongs of Jakar, Lhuentse, Trashi Yangtse, Shongar (now Mongar), Trashigang and Zhemgang were constructed.

1826	1828	1832	1862
Bhutan and Britain start bickering over the sovereignty of the *duars* (the southern Bhutanese hills).	Many original historical documents are destroyed in fires in the printing works of Sonagatsel.	Further losses of historical documents occur in the devastating fire in the library of Punakha Dzong.	Birth of Ugyen Wangchuck, the son of 'the Black Regent' Jigme Namgyal, the battle-hardened Trongsa *penlop*.

A Bhutanese Identity Emerges

The Zhabdrung realised that Bhutan needed to differentiate itself from Tibet in order to preserve its religion and cultural identity. He devised many of Bhutan's customs, traditions and ceremonies in a deliberate effort to develop a unique cultural identity for the country.

As a revered Buddhist scholar, he had both the astuteness and authority to codify the Kagyu religious teachings into a system that was distinctively Bhutanese. He also defined the national dress and instituted the tsechu (series of dances) celebrations.

The Zhabdrung created a code of laws that defined the relationship between the lay people and the monastic community. A system of taxes was developed; these were paid in kind in the form of wheat, buckwheat, rice, yak meat, butter, paper, timber and clothing. The people were subject to a system of compulsory labour for the construction of trails, dzongs, temples and bridges. These practices lasted almost unchanged until the third king eliminated them in 1956.

In the 1640s the Zhabdrung created the system of Choesi, the separation of the administration of the country into two offices. The religious and spiritual aspects of the country were handled by the Zhabdrung. The political, administrative and foreign-affairs aspects of the government were to be handled by the *desi* (secular ruler), who was elected to the post. The office of the Zhabdrung theoretically had the greater power. Under the system at that time, the Zhabdrung was the spiritual ruler and the Je Khenpo was the Chief Abbot and official head of the monastic establishment. The Je Khenpo had a status equal to the *desi* and sometimes held that office.

The first *desi* was Tenzin Drugyey (1591–1656), one of the monks who came with Ngawang Namgyal from Ralung Monastery. He established a system of administration throughout the country, formalising the position of *penlop* as that of provincial governor. There were initially three districts: Trongsa in the centre, Paro in the west and Dagana in the south. The *penlops* became the representatives of the central government, which was then in Punakha. There were three officers called *dzongpens* (lords of the dzong) who looked after the affairs of the sub-districts of Punakha, Thimphu and Wangdue Phodrang.

Zhabdrung Ngawang Namgyal went into retreat in Punakha Dzong in 1651. He didn't emerge again, and although it is likely that he passed away very early in the period of retreat, his death remained concealed until 1705. It is believed that the four successive *desis* who ruled during this period felt that the continued presence of the Zhabdrung was necessary to keep the country unified and Tibet at bay. Nonetheless, Tibet mounted seven attacks on Bhutan between 1656 and 1730.

A Political and Religious History of Bhutan by CT Dorji chronicles the major personalities in the religious and political spheres of Bhutan's history.

HISTORY A BHUTANESE IDENTITY EMERGES

1864	1865	1865	1870
The ill-fated Ashley Eden expedition gets a humiliating reception in Punakha and sours relations between Bhutan and Britain.	Bhutan and Britain go to war over the *duars*; it is finally resolved with the Treaty of Sinchula, which sees Bhutan's territory greatly reduced.	After the *duar* war, the saying goes that Bhutan's border is where a rock rolled down the hill finally stops.	The Penlop of Trongsa, Jigme Namgyal, is enthroned as the 51st Desi, consolidating his growing power and influence.

Civil Wars

When the Je Khenpo finally announced the death of the Zhabdrung in 1705, he said that three rays of light emanated from the Zhabdrung's body, representing the *ku sung thug* (body, speech and mind) of Ngawang Namgyal. This indicated that the Zhabdrung would be reincarnated in these three forms, though only the reincarnation of the Zhabdrung's mind was considered to be the head of state. Because the position of *zhabdrung* was a continuing one, it was necessary for the mind incarnation to be reborn after the death of the previous incarnation.

This structure resulted in long periods when the *zhabdrung* was too young to rule and the *desi* often became the de facto ruler. Because the *desi* was an elected position, there was considerable rivalry among various factions for the office. These factions also took advantage of uncertainty over which of the three incarnations of the Zhabdrung was the 'true' incarnation. None of the successive incarnations had the personal charisma or political astuteness of Ngawang Namgyal.

The next 200 years were a time of civil war, internal conflicts and political infighting. While there were only six mind incarnations of the Zhabdrung during this period, there were 55 *desis*. The longest-serving *desi* was the 13th incumbent, Sherab Wangchuck, who ruled for 20 years; and the most important was the fourth, Gyalse Tenzin Rabgye, who ruled from 1680 to 1694. Few of the rulers finished their term; 22 *desis* were assassinated or deposed by rivals.

The political situation became so unstable that some of the rival factions appealed to the Tibetans for assistance. In 1729 and 1730 Tibet took advantage of Bhutan's instability and invaded the country three times. The lamas in Tibet initiated a truce that eventually ended the hostilities. The rival Bhutanese factions submitted their case to the Chinese emperor in Beijing for mediation. But the issue was only finally resolved when several of the Bhutanese protagonists died, leaving the currently recognised mind incarnation of the Zhabdrung as the ruler. At the same time, formal diplomatic relations were established between Bhutan and Tibet, which the late historian Michael Aris said 'helped to guarantee the fact of Bhutanese independence'.

Bhutan and the British by Peter Collister is a comprehensive account of the interaction between Britain and Bhutan from 1771 to 1987.

BRITAIN

Involvement of the British

In his book, *Lands of the Thunderbolt,* the Earl of Ronaldshay wrote: '... it was not until 1772 that the East India Company became conscious of the existence, across its northern frontier, of a meddlesome neighbour.' The first contact the British had with Bhutan was when the claimants to the throne of neighbouring Cooch Behar (in present-day West Ben-

1878

At just 16 years of age Ugyen Wangchuck, the son of Jigme Namgyal, is briefly taken hostage in Paro's Ta Dzong while accompanying his father's campaign to recapture Paro Dzong.

1885

After decades of civil unrest and the Battle of Changlimithang, Ugyen Wangchuck emerges as the most powerful figure in the country.

ANTONY GIBLIN

» Ugyen Wangchuck was held hostage in Paro's Ta Dzong

gal) appealed to the East India Company to help drive the Bhutanese out of their kingdom.

Because the East India Company was a strictly commercial enterprise, its officers agreed to help when the deposed ruler of Cooch Behar offered to pay half of the revenues of the state in return for assistance. In December 1772 the British governor of Bengal, Warren Hastings, sent Indian troops and guns to Cooch Behar and, despite suffering heavy losses, routed the Bhutanese and restored the king to the throne. However, Cooch Behar paid a very high price for this assistance. Not only did its rulers pay Rs50,000, but in 1773 they also signed a treaty ceding substantial powers and future revenue to the East India Company.

The British pushed the Bhutanese back into the hills and followed them into Bhutan. The British won another major battle in January 1773 at the garrison of Chichacotta (now Khithokha) in the hills east of what is now Phuentsholing. A second battle was fought near Kalimpong in April 1773. The Bhutanese troops were led by the 16th *desi* but, after the second defeat, he was deposed by a coup d'état.

First Treaty with the British

The new *desi* wanted to make an agreement with the British and appealed to the Panchen Lama in Tibet for assistance. The Panchen Lama then wrote what the British described as 'a very friendly and intelligent letter' that was carried to Calcutta (now called Kolkata) by an Indian pilgrim. The British, although more eager to establish relations with Tibet than to solve the issue of Bhutan, agreed to comply with the Tibetan request. The result was a peace treaty between Bhutan and the British signed in Calcutta on 25 April 1774. In this treaty the *desi* agreed to respect the territory of the East India Company and to allow the company to cut timber in the forests of Bhutan. The British returned all the territory they had captured.

Several records of the early European exploration and missions to Bhutan have been reprinted by Indian publishers and are readily available in bookshops in Thimphu, Delhi and Kathmandu.

Exploration by Western Travellers

Some of the most interesting stories of Bhutan, and much of Bhutan's recorded history, came from the descriptions provided by early European explorers. These records provide an insight into what they observed and also reveal the extraordinary attitudes of some of the envoys Britain sent to negotiate with Bhutan.

George Bogle

The first British expedition arrived in Bhutan in 1774, just after the first British treaties with Bhutan and Tibet were signed. The Court of Directors of the East India Company sent a mission to Tibet via Bhutan

1897	1904	1906	1907
On 12 June the great Assam earthquake destroys the dzongs and many original documents in Punakha and Lingzhi, and severely damages many other buildings.	Ugyen Wangchuck assists Francis Younghusband in his invasion of Tibet and assists with the negotiations for a treaty between Britain and Tibet.	Sir Ugyen Wangchuck is invited to Calcutta to attend the reception for the Prince of Wales.	Ugyen Wangchuck is unanimously elected as the hereditary ruler of Bhutan, the Druk Gyalpo, in Punakha.

to find out about goods, 'especially such as are of great value and easy transportation'. The expedition team, led by George Bogle, planted potatoes wherever they went, providing a new food crop for Bhutan and a lasting legacy of this mission. They spent five months in Thimphu and then travelled on to Tibet. The written account of this mission provides the first Western view into the isolated kingdom of Bhutan. Bogle found the Bhutanese 'good-humoured, downright, and so far as I can judge, thoroughly trustworthy'. He did, however, note that the practice of celibacy by many monks led to 'many irregularities' and the cold resulted in 'an excessive use of spirituous liquors'.

Alexander Hamilton & Samuel Turner

In the next few years two small expeditions travelled to Bhutan. Dr Alexander Hamilton led a group to Punakha and Thimphu in 1776, and another in 1777, to discuss Bhutanese claims to Ambari Falakati (a town northwest of Cooch Behar) and to consolidate transit rights through Bhutan to Tibet that had been negotiated by Bogle's mission.

The next major venture into Bhutan was in 1783, when Samuel Turner led a grand expedition with all the accoutrements of the British Raj. They travelled through the *duars* (lowest Bhutanese hills) in palanquins (sedan chairs) and followed Bogle's route to Thimphu. They also visited Punakha and Wangdue Phodrang before crossing to Tibet. Among the members of the 1783 expedition was Samuel Davis, who was a draftsman and surveyor. His journal and outstanding paintings provide one of the earliest views of Bhutan. Much of Davis' material is presented in *Views of Mediaeval Bhutan* by Michael Aris.

The Humiliation of Ashley Eden

Lands of the Thunderbolt, Sikhim, Chumbi & Bhutan by the Earl of Ronaldshay is a very readable, very British account of regional history and an expedition to Bhutan in the early 20th century.

Minor British expeditions to Bhutan were made in 1810, 1812, 1815 and 1837, for the most part in order to settle border disputes and conflict over the *duars* (see p242). The Ashley Eden expedition attempted to settle these issues.

The British had managed to extend their influence into Sikkim, making it a British protectorate, and subsequently decided to send a mission to Bhutan to establish a resident British representative and encourage better communication. Among the members of Eden's expedition was Captain HH Godwin-Austin of the Indian topographical Survey. Godwin-Austin had explored (present-day) Pakistan's Baltoro Glacier in 1861 and on some maps K2, the second-highest peak in the world, is named after him.

Despite reports of political chaos in Bhutan, Ashley Eden, the secretary of the government of Bengal, set out from Darjeeling in November 1864 to meet the *desi,* or *deb raja*. Ignoring numerous messages from

1907	1910	1926	1927
Numerous collections of historical documents and treasures are lost when Paro valley's Rinpung Dzong is engulfed in a devastating fire.	The Treaty of Punakha is signed, guaranteeing Bhutan's sovereignty and giving Britain a hand in its external relations.	His Majesty Ugyen Wangchuck dies and is succeeded by his son Jigme Wangchuck, the second Druk Gyalpo.	British officer Lt Col FM Bailey attends the official coronation of the second king of Bhutan, Jigme Wangchuk.

the Bhutanese that the British mission was not welcome, Eden pushed on past Kalimpong, through Daling, Haa and Paro, reaching Punakha on 15 March.

It's not clear whether it was more by accident or by design, but Eden's party was jeered, pelted with rocks, made to wait long hours in the sun and subjected to other humiliations. Both Bhutanese and British pride suffered badly. As Eden describes it in *Political Missions to Bootan:* 'The Penlow [*penlop*] took up a large piece of wet dough and began rubbing my face with it; he pulled my hair, and slapped me on the back, and generally conducted himself with great insolence.'

Eden exacerbated the situation by sending the Lhengyal Shungtshog a copy of a draft treaty with terms that he had been instructed to negotiate. His actions implied that this was the final version of the treaty that the Bhutanese were to sign without any discussion. The Bhutanese took immediate exception to Eden's high-handedness and soon presented him with an alternative treaty that returned all the *duars* to Bhutan. One clause in the treaty stated: 'We have written about that the settlement is permanent; but who knows, perhaps this settlement is made with one word in the mouth and two in the heart. If, therefore, this settlement is false, the Dharma Raja's demons will, after deciding who is true or false, take his life, and take out his liver and scatter it to the winds like ashes.'

Reading this, it's little wonder that Eden feared for the safety of his party. He signed the treaty, but under his signature added the English words 'under compulsion', which, naturally, the Bhutanese could not read.

Eden's party crossed the Cheli La from Haa into the Paro valley in February and had an extremely difficult time in the deep snow. Some years later, John Claude White suggested that Eden might have been given incorrect directions, perhaps on purpose. It is astounding that, even having admitted failure, Eden still viewed his as a 'friendly mission'. His report certainly was a major factor in British annexation of the *duars*. He advocated a punitive policy to teach the Bhutanese that they would not be allowed to 'treat our power with contempt'. He later went on to build the toy train in Darjeeling.

John Claude White

There were no formal expeditions to Bhutan for more than 40 years after Eden's, but the Survey of India sent several agents disguised as lamas and pilgrims to explore Bhutan and Tibet in 1883 and 1886.

By 1905 the Bhutanese and British were friends due to the assistance that the *penlop* of Trongsa, Ugyen Wangchuck, had provided the 1904 Younghusband expedition to Lhasa. John Claude White, a

Political Missions to Bootan by Ashley Eden is a pompous Victorian account of the history of Bhutan. After reading a few pages, you'll have some idea as to why Eden was treated so badly when he arrived in Punakha.

HISTORY EXPLORATION BY WESTERN TRAVELLERS

1928	1931	1949	1952
The future third king, Jigme Dorji Wangchuck, is born at Thruepang Palace in Trongsa on 2 May.	Lt Col JLR Weir travels to Bumthang to present King Jigme Wangchuk with the insignia of Knight Commander of the Indian Empire.	Bhutan signs a treaty with newly independent India in Darjeeling and gains a small concession of land bordering the region known as the *duars.*	King Jigme Wangchuck, the second king, dies and is succeeded to the throne by his 24-year-old son Jigme Dorje Wangchuck.

British political officer, came to present the insignia of Knight Commander of the Indian Empire to the *penlop*. White had been a member of the 1904 expedition and was an old friend of Ugyen Wangchuck.

White and his large party travelled into from Gangtok, in Sikkim, into Haa and Paro, en route to the investiture ceremony in Punakha. Later, White and his party were guests of Ugyen Wangchuck at his new palace of Wangdichholing in Bumthang. The expedition later returned with the first photographs of dzongs and the court of Bhutan.

In 1906 White made a reconnaissance through eastern Bhutan to southern Tibet. He made a third trip in 1907 when he was invited as the British representative to the coronation of Ugyen Wangchuck as the first king of Bhutan. A summary of White's account appeared in the April 1914 issue of the *National Geographic,* and made Bhutan known to the world for the first time.

Sikhim and Bhutan, Twenty-one Years on the North-east Frontier by J Claude White describes the 1905 expedition to present the first king, Ugyen Wangchuck, with the insignia of Knight Commander of the Indian Empire.

Other British Political Officers

Between 1909 and 1947 the British government dealt with Bhutan in the same way as it did with other Indian princely states, but it never specifically defined its relationship with Bhutan. Starting with CA Bell in 1909, several British political officers visited Bhutan and presented the king with decorations. In 1921 the Earl of Ronaldshay, who was described as a 'closet Buddhist', travelled to Bhutan as a guest of the first king. He travelled from Gangtok to Paro, where he was met with great fanfare. The party visited Taktshang Goemba and witnessed the Paro tsechu, but never met the king, who was in Punakha, ill with influenza.

The Duar Wars & the Rise of Ugyen Wangchuck

In 1931 Lt Col JLR Weir travelled to Bumthang to denominate the king Knight Commander of the Indian Empire – the basis for the book and TV documentary *Joanna Lumley in the Kingdom of the Thunder Dragon.*

The area of plains between the Brahmaputra River up to and including the lowest of the hills of Bhutan was known as the *duars,* which means doors or gates (see p242). The western part of this area, known as the Bengal Duars, had been annexed by the third *desi,* Mingyur Tenpa, in the late 17th century and the Bhutanese considered it their territory. The eastern part, the Assam Duars, had long been administered in a complex rental agreement between Bhutan and Assam.

After the Burmese war (1825–26), the British took over the peculiar land rental arrangement for the Assam Duars, along with what were described as 'very unsatisfactory relations of the Assamese with the Bhutanese'. Disagreements over payments and administration between Britain and Bhutan escalated into military skirmishes. Other than the area's strategic importance, the British were attracted to the *duars* because they were excellent tea-growing country.

1953	1956	1958	1959
The 130-member National Assembly (Tshogdu), the country's first legislature, is established by the king to promote democratic governance.	The age-old system of serfdom is abolished by King Jigme Dorji Wangchuck, who also decrees that all derogatory terms associated with serfs be abolished.	The Indian Prime Minister, Jawaharlal Nehru, and his daughter, Indira Gandhi, visit Bhutan to symbolise improving communications with India.	Bhutan loses administrative control of several monasteries on the slopes of Mt Kailash and near Gatok after the Chinese annexation of Tibet.

The British annexed the two easternmost *duars* in 1840 and the rest of the Assam Duars in September 1841, agreeing to pay Bhutan an annual compensation of Rs10,000. Lord Auckland wrote to the *deb* and *dharma rajas* that the British were '...compelled by an imperative sense of duty to occupy the whole of the duars without any reference to your Highnesses' wishes, as I feel assured that it is the only course which is likely to hold out a prospect of restoring peace and prosperity to that tract of country.'

Perhaps more revealing is a letter from Colonel Jenkins, the agent of the governor-general, outlining the need for taking over the Assam Duars. He wrote: 'Had we possession of the Dooars, the Bhootan Government would necessarily in a short time become entirely dependent upon us, as holding in our hands the source of all their subsistence.'

The Trongsa Penlop Gains Control

During this period the Trongsa *penlop,* Jigme Namgyal (1825–82), established effective control of the country through a series of shrewd alliances. This was the first time peace had prevailed since the time of the first Zhabdrung. Jigme Namgyal was working to strengthen his power and that of the central government when he had an inconvenient visit from the British government representative Ashley Eden (see p196).

Although the British considered Eden's mission a failure, and reprimanded him for his conduct, they continued the dispute with Bhutan over payment for the Bengal Duars. The Bhutanese, in turn, were furious the British had renounced the treaty Eden had signed. In November 1864 the British summarily annexed the Bengal Duars, gaining effective control of the entire south of Bhutan. The Trongsa *penlop* mounted a carefully planned counterattack. His troops, protected by shields of rhinoceros hide, captured two British guns and drove the British forces out of Bhutan in January 1865.

The British regrouped and recaptured various towns, including Samtse (then called Chamurchi). A fierce battle at Dewangiri on 2 April essentially ended the war, with the British destroying all the buildings and slaughtering their captives. Negotiations continued through the summer. Eventually the Bhutanese returned the captured guns and accepted a treaty. The treaty of Sinchula was signed, under duress, by the Bhutanese on 11 November 1865. In it the Bhutanese ceded the *duars* to Britain forever and agreed to allow free trade between the two countries.

Through this treaty, Bhutan lost a major tract of valuable farmland and a large portion of its wealth. Its borders became the foot of the hills bordering the plain of India. It is often said that Bhutan's border

Although the *duars* were excellent for growing tea, they were also a malarial jungle, and the British had a very difficult time keeping their troops healthy.

DUARS

1961	1964	1968	1971
Bhutan warily emerges from self-imposed isolation and begins a process of controlled development, undertaking modernisation.	Prime Minister Jigme Palden Dorji, a leading proponent of change, is assassinated on 5 April in Phuentsholing.	King Jigme Dorji Wangchuck continues to reform the government by surrendering his veto power on the decisions of the National Assembly.	Bhutan finally joins the UN as a full member after spending three years holding observer status.

is where a rock rolled down the hill finally stops. Among the important landmarks the Bhutanese lost were the town of Ambari Falakati, northwest of Cooch Behar, the town of Dewangiri (now called Deothang) in the east and the territory on the east bank of the Teesta River, including what is now the town of Kalimpong.

Back in Bhutan's heartland there were continuing civil wars, but the *penlop* of Trongsa, Jigme Namgyal, retained his power and in 1870 was enthroned as the 51st *desi*. The next 10 years were again a time of intrigue, treachery, power broking and continual strife. The *penlop* of Paro and the *dzongpens* of Punakha and Wangdue Phodrang conspired to challenge the position of Desi Jigme Namgyal and his successor, who was his half-brother. After he retired as *desi,* Jigme Namgyal remained in firm control of the country and in 1879 appointed his 17-year-old son, Ugyen Wangchuck, as Paro *penlop*. Michael Aris' book *The Raven Crown* gives a detailed description of this extraordinary period.

After Jigme Namgyal died, his son consolidated his own position following a feud over the post of *penlop* of Trongsa. At the age of 20, Ugyen Wangchuck marched on Bumthang and Trongsa and in 1882 was appointed *penlop* of Trongsa, while still retaining the post of *penlop* of Paro. Because his father had enhanced the powers of the office of the Trongsa *penlop*, this gave him much more influence than the *desi*. When a battle broke out between the *dzongpens* of Punakha and Thimphu, Ugyen Wangchuck tried to mediate the dispute.

He sent in his troops after unsuccessful negotiations and his forces defeated the troops loyal to both *dzongpens* and seized control of Simtokha Dzong. The monk body and the *penlop* of Paro tried to settle the conflict and in 1885 arranged a meeting at the Changlimithang parade ground in Thimphu. During the meeting a fight broke out, the representative of the Thimphu *dzongpen* was killed and the *dzongpen* fled to Tibet. Following the battle, Ugyen Wangchuck emerged as the most powerful person in the country, assumed full authority, installed his own nominee as *desi,* and reduced the post to a ceremonial one.

THE 1897 EARTHQUAKE

One of the most devastating natural disasters in Bhutan was the great Assam earthquake that occurred at 5.06pm on 12 June 1897. The epicentre was about 80km south of Bhutan in Assam and had an estimated magnitude of 8.7 on the Richter scale, which seismologists categorise as 'catastrophic'. The earthquake destroyed the dzongs in Punakha and Lingzhi and severely damaged the dzongs of Wangdue Phodrang, Trongsa, Jakar and the *utse* (central tower) of Trashi Chhoe Dzong. Paro Dzong escaped largely unharmed.

1972	1974	1974	1980s
King Jigme Dorje Wangchuck is succeeded to the throne by his son, 16-year-old Jigme Singye Wangchuck.	The official coronation of King Jigme Singye Wangchuck, the fourth Druk Gyalpo.	The first 'tourist group' explores the country's sights, paving the way for international visitors.	Government policies aimed at preserving national identity begin to polarise the Nepali-speaking southerners.

The First Dragon King

In order to re-establish Bhutan's sovereignty and help consolidate his position, Ugyen Wangchuck developed closer relations with the British. He accompanied Francis Younghusband during his invasion of Tibet in 1904 and assisted with the negotiations that resulted in a treaty between Tibet and Britain. The British rewarded the *penlop* by granting him the title of Knight Commander of the Indian Empire. In 1906 the then Sir Ugyen Wangchuck was invited to Calcutta to attend the reception for the Prince of Wales and returned to Bhutan with a better appreciation of the world that lay beyond the country's borders.

In 1907 the secular ruler, the *desi,* died and Ugyen Wangchuck was elected as the hereditary ruler of Bhutan by a unanimous vote of Bhutan's chiefs and principal lamas. He was crowned on 17 December 1907 and installed as head of state with the title Druk Gyalpo (Dragon King). This coronation signalled the end of the *desi* system and the beginning of a hereditary monarchy – among the youngest in existence today. King Ugyen Wangchuck continued to maintain excellent relations with the British, partly in an effort to gain some security from the increasing Chinese influence in Tibet.

Michael Aris' book *The Raven Crown* gives a detailed description of Bhutan in the early 20th century; it is lavishly illustrated with rare photographs and provides a perspective based on Bhutanese accounts.

The Treaty of Punakha

British-Bhutanese relations were enhanced in the treaty of Punakha, which was signed in 1910. This treaty stated that the British government would 'exercise no interference in the internal administration of Bhutan'. It was agreed, though, that Bhutan would 'be guided by the advice of the British Government in regard to its external relations'. The compensation for the *duars* was doubled to Rs100,000 per year and Bhutan agreed to refer disputes with Cooch Behar and Sikkim to the British for settlement.

Bhutan still refused to allow the appointment of a British resident, and continued to maintain a policy of isolation aimed at preserving its own sovereignty in an era of colonisation. In 1911 King Ugyen Wangchuck attended the great durbar (royal court) held by King George V at Delhi and was given the additional decoration of Knight Commander of the Order of the Star of India.

The Second King

Ugyen Wangchuck died in 1926 and was succeeded by his 24-year-old son, Jigme Wangchuck. He ruled during the time of the Great Depression and WWII, but these catastrophic world events did not affect Bhutan because of its barter economy and isolation.

Jigme Wangchuck refined the administrative and taxation systems and brought the entire country under his direct control. He made

HISTORY THE FIRST DRAGON KING

1988	1991	1992	1993
The government conducts a nationwide census aimed at identifying illegal immigrants, defined as those who could not prove family residence before 1958.	The start of an eventual mass movement of Nepali-speakers from Bhutan to refugee camps just over the border in Nepal.	Up to 80,000 Nepali speakers who claimed they were from Bhutan are housed in seven camps in the Jhapa district of southeastern Nepal.	The exodus of Nepali speakers stops and the UN High Commissioner for Refugees establishes a screening centre at Kakarbhitta on the Nepal–India border.

Wangdichholing Palace in Bumthang his summer palace, and moved the entire court to Kuenga Rabten, south of Trongsa, in the winter.

After India gained independence from Britain on 15 August 1947, the new Indian government recognised Bhutan as an independent country. In 1949 Bhutan signed a treaty with independent India that was very similar to its earlier treaty with the British. The treaty reinforced Bhutan's position as a sovereign state. India agreed not to interfere in the internal affairs of Bhutan, while Bhutan agreed to be guided by the government of India in its external relations. The treaty also returned to Bhutan about 82 sq km of the *duars* in the southeast of the country, including Dewangiri, that had been annexed by the British.

The Third King & the Modernisation of Bhutan

King Jigme Wangchuck died in 1952. He was succeeded by his son, Jigme Dorji Wangchuck, who had been educated in India and England and spoke fluent Tibetan, English and Hindi. To improve relations with India he invited the Indian prime minister, Jawaharlal Nehru, and his daughter, Indira Gandhi, to visit Bhutan in 1958.

When the Chinese took control of Tibet in 1959, it became obvious that a policy of isolationism was not appropriate in the modern world. The king knew that in order to preserve Bhutan's independence, the country had to become a member of the larger world community. In 1961 Bhutan emerged from centuries of self-imposed isolation and embarked on a process of planned development.

Bhutan joined the Colombo Plan in 1962. This gave it access to technical assistance and training from member countries in Southeast Asia. The first 'five-year plan' for development was implemented in 1961 and India agreed to help finance and construct the large Chhukha hydroelectric project in western Bhutan. Not all Bhutanese approved of the pace of change. There were clashes between rival power groups and the prime minister, Jigme Palden Dorji, who was a leading proponent of change, was assassinated on 5 April 1964.

Bhutan joined the Universal Postal Union in 1969 and became a member of the UN in 1971. In the same year, Bhutan and India established formal diplomatic relations and exchanged ambassadors.

The king's domestic accomplishments were also impressive. In 1953 he established the Tshogdu (National Assembly) and drew up a 12-volume code of law. He abolished serfdom, reorganised land holdings, created the Royal Bhutan Army (RBA) and police force, and established the High Court. However, as he led Bhutan into the modern world, he emphasised the need to preserve Bhutanese culture and tradition.

Karma Ura's book *The Hero with a Thousand Eyes* gives a wonderful insight into the protocol and workings of the Bhutanese court in the days of the second king, Jigme Wangchuck, and is available in Thimphu.

King Jigme Dorje Wangchuck, the third king, became known as the father of modern Bhutan owing to his reforms to society and economics.

1998	**1998**	**1999**	**2001**
King Jigme Singye Wangchuck transfers full executive authority to an elected Council of Ministers.	Taktshang Goemba, the most famous monastery in Bhutan, is all but destroyed in a fire.	TV and the internet are officially introduced to Bhutan in a managed continuation of the modernisation process.	Drafting of the first Constitution of the Kingdom of Bhutan begins.

Until the beginning of King Jigme Dorji Wangchuck's modernisation efforts in 1960, most of the non-Indian foreigners who entered Bhutan were British explorers. A few foreigners were permitted into the country during the 1960s, but only the royal family had the authority to issue invitations, so almost all visitors were royal guests.

Early trekkers included Desmond Doig, a friend of the royal family who trekked in 1961 on assignment for *National Geographic*. In 1963 Professor Augusto Gansser travelled throughout the country studying geology, and in 1964 a group of British physicians, Michael Ward, Frederic Jackson and R Turner, mounted an expedition to the remote Lunana region.

The coronation of the fourth king in 1974 was the first time that a large number of foreign visitors had entered the kingdom. After the coronation, small groups of tourists were allowed into the country and given permission to visit the dzongs and goembas in Thimphu and Paro. From these beginnings, the pattern for Bhutan's tourism industry evolved.

The first group of paying tourists arrived in 1974, organised and led by Lars Eric Lindblad, founder of Lindblad Travel in Connecticut, USA, a pioneer of modern-day group tours. Lindblad encouraged the government to limit tourism and to charge high fees.

Paro airport was opened in 1983 and the newly formed national airline, Druk Air, started operating flights from Kolkata. The airport runway was extended in 1990 and Druk Air began operating jet aircraft, with direct international connections. Until 1991 tourists were handled by the Bhutan Tourism Corporation, a government agency. Tourism was privatised that year and soon numerous agencies were established, most run by ex-employees of the now-disbanded government agency.

The Fourth King & the Introduction of Democracy

King Jigme Dorji Wangchuck died in 1972 at age 44. He was succeeded by his 16-year-old son, Jigme Singye Wangchuck. Like his father, he was educated in India and England, but he also received a Bhutanese education at the Ugyen Wangchuck Academy in Paro. He pledged to continue his father's program of modernisation and announced a plan for the country to achieve economic self-reliance. This plan took advantage of Bhutan's special circumstances – a small population, abundant land and rich natural resources. Among the development goals set by the king was the ideal of economic self-reliance and what he nicknamed 'Gross National Happiness' (GNH). GNH is not a simple appraisal of the smiles on the faces of the populace; rather it encompasses explicit

2001	2003	2003	2005
A verification process of refugees in the Nepal camps is initiated under a bilateral process between Nepal and Bhutan.	Disagreements over appeals from the first round of verification escalate and Bhutanese officials are attacked in one camp.	The Royal Bhutan Army, led by the fourth king, removes Bodo militant camps from Bhutanese territory.	The fourth king announces intended abdication and plans for succession of the throne by the crown prince.

BODO GROUPS & THE UNITED LIBERATION FRONT OF ASSAM

The northeastern region of India has suffered years of separatist violence carried out by militants, some of whom have established bases in the jungles of southern Bhutan from which they mount assaults. The actions of these groups have claimed the lives of more than 20,000 people in the Indian state of Assam.

The Bodos are Mechey tribal people that have two militant groups, the Bodo Liberation Tiger Force and the Bodo Security Force, both of which are fighting for a Bodo homeland. The United Liberation Front of Assam, more commonly known as ULFA, is a separatist group formed in 1979 with the goal of an independent Assamese nation. It has staged numerous attacks on trains, buses and vehicles carrying both Bhutanese and Indian citizens.

In December 2003, after the government felt it had exhausted all peaceful means, the Royal Bhutan Army, led from the front by the king, flushed out the militants from Bhutanese territory. The continued presence of these militants across the border has made travel in the southeastern part of the country risky for both Bhutanese and tourists and is the reason for restrictions on visiting such places as Royal Manas National Park and Pemagatshel.

Of Rainbows and Clouds: The Life of Yab Ugyen Dorji As Told to His Daughter by Yab Ugyen Dorji and Ashi Dorje Wangmo Wangchuck is a fascinating and intimate account of life in changing Bhutan.

criteria to measure development projects and progress in terms of society's greater good. A more sustainable happiness for the individual is believed to derive from such an approach.

The coronation of King Jigme Singye Wangchuck as the fourth Druk Gyalpo on 2 June 1974 was a major turning point in the opening of Bhutan, and was the first time that the international press was allowed to enter the country. A total of 287 invited guests travelled to Thimphu for the event, and several new hotels were built to accommodate them. These hotels later provided the basis for the development of tourism in Bhutan, see the boxed text, p203.

The fourth king emphasised modernisation of education, health services, rural development and communications. He continued the reforms begun by his father in the areas of administration, labour and justice, including the introduction of a secret ballot and the abolishment of compulsory labour. He was the architect of Bhutan's policy of environmental conservation, which gives precedence to ecological considerations over commercial interests. He promoted national identity, traditional values and the concept of 'One Nation, One People'.

In 1988 the royal wedding solemnised the king's marriage to the sisters Ashi Dorji Wangmo, Ashi Tshering Pem, Ashi Tshering Yangdon and Ashi Sangay Choedon. In 1998 he gave up absolute power, sharing authority with the National Assembly and Council of Ministers.

2005 & 2006	2007	2007	2008
The draft Constitution for the Kingdom of Bhutan is finally released and circulated, and a referendum planned to vote on its acceptance.	The major political parties, Druk Phuensum Tshogpa (DPT, Bhutan Peace & Prosperity) and Peoples Democratic Party (PDP) are formed for the upcoming democratic elections.	First-ever election to vote for the 20 members each representing a *dzongkhag* (district) of the 25-member National Council (upper house).	Unprecedented numbers of Bhutanese turn out to vote for the 47-member National Assembly (lower house).

In December 2005 the 50-year-old king announced a plan to abdicate the throne in favour of his eldest son, Crown Prince Jigme Khesar Namgyal Wangchuck, and help move the country from an absolute monarchy to a democratic constitutional monarchy in 2008. He is quoted as saying 'Monarchy is not the best form of government because a king is chosen by birth and not by merit'.

The Fifth King & the First Elected Parliament

King Jigme Singye Wangchuck did not wait until 2008. He formally abdicated in December 2006 bestowing all his authority to his son, Jigme Khesar Namgyel Wangchuck, who was already travelling to every corner of the country to explain the new constitution, the up-coming election, and their beloved fourth king's dramatic decision.

In December 2007 the first elections for the new parliament were held for the 25-member upper house, called the National Council. This was followed in March 2008 with the first election for the 47-member National Assembly (lower house). This election became a landslide victory for Druk Phuensum Tshogpa (DPT) party, which won 45 of the 47 seats. The Peoples Democratic Party (PDP) won the other two seats. For more on Bhutan's system of government and political parties, see p180.

The unprecedented sight of the former king crowning the new king with the raven crown was witnessed on 6 November 2008 at the official coronation of 27-year-old Jigme Khesar Namgyel Wangchuck. The momentous occasion took place in the Golden Throne room of Thimphu's Tashichhodzong in front of national and international dignitaries. The following day, the fifth king gave his coronation speech to a packed Changlimithang Stadium, in which he pledged: 'As the king of a Buddhist nation, my duty is not only to ensure your happiness today but to create the fertile ground from which you may gain the fruits of spiritual pursuit and attain good Karma.'

The UN refugee agency (www
.unhcr.org) provides the latest facts and figures on the refugee camps in Jhapa, Nepal.

2008	2008	2009	2010
Formal coronation of the fifth Druk Gyalpo (Dragon King) Jigme Khesr Namgyel Wangchuck on 6 November 2008.	The Constitution of the Kingdom of Bhutan is officially adopted.	Bhutan and India agree on the construction of 10 new hydropower projects in Bhutan to be completed by 2012 and provide 10,000MW of electricity.	Bhutan hosts the 16th summit of the South Asian Association for Regional Cooperation (SAARC) in Thimphu.

The Bhutanese Way of Life

Bhutan decided long ago that we will never be a military power, we will never be an economic force, so to survive we must have a distinct identity. This is the identity you see; our clothes, language, the architecture. You look around and you feel that you are in a different world. This is not an accident.

Dasho Kinley Dorji, Secretary,
Ministry of Information and Communication

Bhutan was relatively isolated until the early 1950s and traditional Bhutan has changed more in the last 50 years than in the previous 400 years. The country has retained its traditional social structures so far and has actively sought to preserve its cultural identity in the face of modernisation and increasing external influences.

The smiles of the children walking to school in the morning light, the laughter overheard in a family house, the shy greetings from women weaving outside their homes – these will quickly entrance the traveller. The Bhutanese are a warm and open people – quick to smile and laugh. As with the other peoples of the Himalayas, the Bhutanese have an infectious sense of humour and quickly overcome barriers to communication. You should not be surprised to be offered a seat and a cup of tea even if you do not speak Dzongkha or one of the other 18 languages of Bhutan. These simple acts are spontaneous and provide the traveller with both fond memories and a brief insight into the generous nature of the Bhutanese.

An excellent introduction to the people and culture is *Bhutan: Mountain Fortress of the Gods* (eds C Schicklgruber and F Pommaret, Serindia).

Everyday Buddhism

Buddhism permeates everyday life in Bhutan, and a basic knowledge of Buddhism is essential to understanding the Bhutanese. Prayer flags flutter throughout the land, prayer wheels often powered by mountain streams clunk gently by the roadside, images of the Buddha and other religious figures are carved into cliffs, reminding the visitor that every aspect of daily life is shaped by Buddhist beliefs and aspirations. This can be daunting, even alien, for many Western visitors. The idea of accumulating merit, having a deep respect of the natural and often sacred environment, respect for religious practitioners: all are central elements of the unique fusion of Buddhism and older non-Buddhist beliefs.

Buddhism is practised throughout the country though, in the south, most Bhutanese people of Nepali and Indian descent are Hindu. Relations between Buddhists and Hindus are very good, with major Hindu festivals marked by national holidays. Minority groups practise various forms of ancient animistic religions, including Bon, which predates Himalayan Buddhism. Bhutanese Buddhism is discussed in more depth on p215.

Urban Bhutan

Until the 1960s there were no major urban settlements. Since then Thimphu and Phuentsholing have both grown significantly, leading to pressure on land availability in these areas. Elsewhere there has been an increase in land acquisition, most notably in Gelephu.

As a result of the opportunities created by education and the creation of alternative employment (as civil servants, teachers, army personnel or police), Bhutan has experienced increased social mobility. The rate of rural–urban migration is increasing, particularly as young educated Bhutanese seek employment in offices and other businesses in the capital. There has been growing concern over the increasing unemployment rate among educated school leavers, as well as rapidly rising property values and rents in Thimphu.

The Living Standard Survey 2007 revealed that 37% of Bhutanese rely on wages and salaries as their main source of income, and 41% on agriculture. For many living in urban areas average household expenditure can represent all or most of their salary, which is why many Bhutanese women now work in offices or seek to supplement their husband's income through some form of small business enterprise.

Until the mid-20th century there were no large urban settlements in Bhutan. By 2005, the population of Thimphu was over 50,000.

THE BHUTANESE WAY OF LIFE

Rural Life

Despite rapid urbanisation, the majority of people still live in rural Bhutan, dependent on the cultivation of crops and livestock breeding. Accordingly, daily life revolves around the care of crops and livestock. In Bumthang, the woman is the head of the household, and it will be she who decides on the division of farm labour. Bhutanese women are viewed as equal to Bhutanese men and accordingly there are only a few forms of labour traditionally viewed as exclusively male or female. Weaving and spinning have been reserved for women, while harrowing and ploughing were reserved for men. However, it is not uncommon to see a husband and wife working together ploughing their land. Other tasks such as collecting the harvest, threshing and so forth are done by both men and women. Usually women brew the homemade alcohol such as *arra, bang chhang* or *sinchhang*, and are responsible for household chores.

Life for most rural households starts around dawn and ends with sunset. Each morning the family will make offerings, typically of water, before the household shrine and a simple breakfast of rice will be prepared. Men and women share equally in the day-to-day care of the

The main crops grown in central Bhutan are rice, buckwheat, barley, potatoes and winter barley. Chillies are also grown, then dried on the roofs of houses before being stored.

BHUTAN BEAT

The music scene in Bhutan is small and the most popular music, *rigsar*, is still evolving. *Rigsar* is typically performed on modern instruments, notably electric piano and synthesiser. *Rigsar* blends elements of traditional Bhutanese and Tibetan tunes, and is influenced by Hindi film music.

Popular male and female performers, including Lhamo, Dechen Pem and Rinchen Namgay, often appear in locally produced films. There is a range of contemporary and classical music now available from little booths throughout Bhutan.

In addition to *rigsar* performers, there are a few rock and rollers seeking fame if not a taste of fortune. Groups such as Thimphu's *Who's Your Daddy* struggle in a small market where massively popular karaoke has all but plundered every centimetre of available stage space.

children, and although women are usually in charge of the household, men are equally able, and expected, to assist with the cooking. Meals are eaten sitting on the floor, often with personal bowls for rice and a selection of simple shared dishes set out in front – *ema datse,* perhaps a meat dish or some buckwheat noodles. Children are expected to help with the household and farm chores, like cleaning, collecting water or firewood, or herding the livestock.

In the evening, the water from the offering bowls will be poured away and a butter lamp may be lit and left to burn before the household shrine.

Traditionally Bhutanese were very self-sufficient, often making their own clothing, bedding, floor and seat covers, tablecloths, and decorative items for daily and religious use. There remains a degree of self-sufficiency among the rural Bhutanese, though many day-to-day items are increasingly imported from Bangladesh, China, India and Thailand.

Bhutan has 542 schools and male literacy is at 69% and female literacy at 51% (2005 Census). For more information on education in the Himalayas, and on supporting young students, see www.loden.org.

Learning

Until the introduction of Western-style education by the third king in the 1960s, the only education available in Bhutan was from the monasteries. Prior to this a few students travelled to Darjeeling or Kalimpong to receive a secular education. Western-style education has expanded to cover the whole country.

The school system aims to provide basic literacy skills, and knowledge of Bhutan's history, geography and traditions. Most villages have a primary school, though it is not uncommon for children to board at a junior high school or high school. Free education and textbooks are provided to all students until tertiary level. Morning prayers and the national anthem start the day for all students throughout Bhutan. The government provides adult education classes, especially aimed at improving literacy.

A key aspect of Bhutan's development plan involves training doctors, engineers and other professionals. Important trade skills in plumbing, construction and electrics are now being taught to young men and women. In 2003 the Royal University of Bhutan was established to provide tertiary education in Bhutan. All the existing tertiary institutions were incorporated in the new university.

Women in Bhutan

Compared to other areas of South Asia, Bhutanese women enjoy greater equality and freedom with men. The right to inherit often passes property to women rather than men.

The women of Laya are particularly noted for their distinctive conical bamboo hats and long black wool dresses.

Traditionally, women look after the household, preparing food and weaving textiles for family use and for sale. However, they also work in the fields, notably at harvest times when all available labour is required. Decisions affecting the household are jointly made. Travelling in Bhutan you will notice that Bhutanese women are independently minded and possess a strong entrepreneurial spirit. In Thimphu and the emerg-

DZOE – SPIRIT CATCHER

Sometimes you will come across a strange construction of twigs, straw and rainbow-coloured thread woven into a spider-web shape. You may see one near a building or by a roadside, with flower and food offerings. This is a *dzoe* (also known as a *tendo*), a sort of spirit catcher used to exorcise something evil that has been pestering a household. The malevolent spirits are drawn to the *dzoe.* After prayers the *dzoe* is cast away, often on a trail or road, to send away the evil spirits it has trapped.

DOMA

Doma is an integral part of Bhutanese culture. A popular gift throughout Bhutanese society, it is made up of three main ingredients: *doma* or areca nut (Areca catechu), *pani* or betel leaf (Piper betel) and *tsune* or lime (calcium carbonate).

According to Bhutanese tradition, in 1637 a huge gathering of people had come with a variety of food products to offer to the Zhabdrung in Punakha. Deeply touched by their gesture, the Zhabdrung instructed that those present should be served with various gifts of food and *doma pani*. JC White, the British political officer who attended Gongsar Ugyen Wangchuck's enthronement in 1907, reports that *doma* was served to those attending the enthronement.

Eating *doma* was an aristocratic practice, with the various ingredients kept in ornate rectangular silver boxes called *chaka,* while lime had a separate circular box with conical lid called *trimi*. Today, people may keep their *doma* in bamboo *bangchung* or a cloth pouch called a *kaychung*. Young people appear to be turning away from eating *doma*, particularly as it may cause a variety of cancers.

ing urban centres such as Trongsa, Gelephu and Phuentsholing, women may seek to boost family income by engaging in trade, selling goods from home or renting a small shop.

Rural women are often presented as the custodians of traditional values. Urbanisation and increasing rural–urban migration have brought new challenges for women separated from their families and social networks.

The introduction of education in the 1960s enabled Bhutanese women to become literate and to seek employment outside of both their homes and their local villages. Teaching, the civil service and other office positions provided important opportunities for young, educated Bhutanese women.

However, there are areas in which Bhutanese women are still not equal with their male counterparts. Levels of literacy remain higher among men than women, though this is being tackled by the government through adult learning classes. Although some women have been appointed to higher positions in the government and NGOs, including the first female district court judge appointed in 2003, there remains a gender imbalance at all levels of government. In the first elections for the new parliament's National Council in 2007, four of the successful 20 candidates were women. For the 47-member National Assembly elections in March 2008, four women were elected from the winning DPT party. In all, 10 women stood for election between the two parties and the female voter turnout outnumbered the male turnout.

The major women's organisation in the country is the National Women's Association of Bhutan. It was established in 1981 and headed by Dasho Dawa Dem, one of the few women to have received the honorific title of Dasho from the king. In 2004 Respect, Educate, Nurture & Empower Women (Renew; www.renew.org.bt), an NGO for women, was established by HM Ashi Sangay Choeden Wangchuck. RENEW is highly respected and tackles major issues facing contemporary Bhutanese women.

MONKS

Of approximately 5500 formal monks in Bhutan, half are under the patronage of the Je Khenpo, the other half subsidised by private support. About 15,000 lay or married monks are called *ngakpa*s or *gomchen*s.

Marriage

In the past, marriages were arranged. However, since the 1970s the majority of marriages are love matches. The minimum age is 16 for women and 21 for men. In rural areas, it is quite common for the husband to move into his wife's household and if they divorce he will return to live with his own family.

Polyandry, the practice of taking more than one husband, still exists in certain parts of Bhutan and polygamy is restricted. There remain a large number of Bhutanese couples who, although living together as a couple, are not formally married. The divorce rate is increasing and there is legal provision for alimony to be paid to take care of children.

Personal Names

The system for personal names in Bhutan differs between the north and south of the country. In the north, with the exception of the royal family, there are no family names. Two names are given to children by monks a few weeks after birth. These are traditional names of Tibetan origin and are chosen because of their auspicious influence or religious meaning. Two names are always given, although a few people have three names.

It is often impossible to tell the sex of a Bhutanese person based on their name. A few names are given only to boys, and others apply only to girls, for example Choekyi, Drolma and Wangmo, but most names may apply to either.

In the south, with an evident Hindu influence, a system resembling family names exists. Brahmans and Newars retain their caste name, such as Sharma or Pradhan, and others retain the name of their ethnic group, such as Rai or Gurung.

At night, do not shout a person's name, as it's believed this may attract a ghost.

Health & the Wheel of Life

Bhutan has made significant progress in its provision of health facilities and provides free health care to all its citizens. The main hospital is the National Referral Hospital in Thimphu, and two further regional referral hospitals. There are smaller hospitals in each district. Rural health care is provided through Basic Health Units staffed with a health assistant, nurse midwife and a basic health worker.

Child immunisation is at almost 100%, and iodine deficiency has been eliminated. Infant and maternal mortality rates have decreased. According to the 2005 census, over 80% of Bhutanese have access to clean drinking water.

Although Bhutan has tackled endemic health problems, it is also facing the emergence of HIV and AIDS. The Bhutanese authorities have taken a proactive stance, emphasising the importance of safe sex and awareness of HIV. Monks and nuns have been trained (in addition to teaching rural communities about basic hygiene) to provide advice on HIV and to act as HIV counsellors for those infected. In August 2004 the former king issued a *kasho* (royal command or statement) stressing the threat of HIV and the need to show compassion towards those infected.

Bhutan's press freedom has steadily improved in the last decade and was ranked 70th out of 175 countries in the 2009 Reporters Sans Frontiers index.

The frescoes of the Wheel of Life show that, to Bhutanese, death is part of the cycle of samsara separating loved ones and leading to rebirth. Accordingly, death is treated as a major life event. Family and friends are informed and monks, *gomchen* (lay or married monks) or nuns begin to recite from the *Bardo Thodrel* to guide the deceased through the intermediate phase.

Until the cremation, the deceased is placed in a wooden box and covered in a white cloth and kept separate from the family. At the cremation, the corpse is placed on the pyre facing the officiating lama. The first funeral service is held on the seventh day after death, with other rituals performed on the 14th, 21st and 49th days. The lama reminds the deceased that they are dead and during the ritual seeks to help them move on to their next and (it is hoped) fortunate rebirth, either as a human being or preferably in a Buddha realm.

At the end of the 49 days the ashes of the deceased may be scattered; some are placed in a sacred image and donated to a monastery or temple. The anniversary of the death will be marked for the following three years. Manidhar prayer flags (see p224) are also erected in memory of the deceased.

Titles & Forms of Address

Titles are extremely important in Bhutan. All persons of rank should be addressed by the appropriate title followed by their first or full name. Members of the royal family are addressed as 'Dasho' if they are male, and 'Ashi' if female. A minister has the title 'Lyonpo' (pronounced 'lonpo').

The title Dasho is given to those who have been honoured by the king, receiving also the accompanying red scarf. In common practice, many senior government officials are addressed as Dasho even if they have not received the title, but officially this is incorrect.

You would address a senior monk or teacher with the title 'Lopon' (pronounced 'loeboen') or, if he has been given the title, as Lam. A *trulku* (reincarnate lama) is addressed as 'Rinpoche' and a nun as 'Anim'.

A man is addressed as 'Aap' and a boy as 'Busu'; a woman is addressed as 'Am' and a girl as 'Bum'. If you are calling someone whose name you do not know, you may use 'Ama' for women and 'Aapa' for men. In the same situation, girls are 'Bumo' and boys 'Alou'. When Bhutanese talk about a foreigner whose name they don't know, they use the word 'Chilip' or, in eastern Bhutan 'Pilingpa'.

Bhutanese basic schooling takes 11 years: one year of pre-primary schooling, six years of primary and two years each of junior high and high school. Examinations mark the move from primary to junior high, and from there to high school.

THE BHUTANESE WAY OF LIFE

TRADITIONAL MEDICINE

Historically, Bhutan was referred to as the 'Land of Medicinal Herbs' and exported herbs to Tibet. Bhutanese were trained in medicine, known as So-ba Rig pa. It represents a blending of Ayurveda from India with Chinese medicine, in the reading of pulses. The earliest medical works date from the 7th and 8th centuries and the main medical teachings are believed to have been transmitted from the Medicine Buddha, Sangye Menlha. They are contained in four volumes, called the *Gyuzhi*.

When the Zhabdrung Ngawang Namgyal came to Bhutan, he brought with him a highly esteemed physician, Tenzin Drukey, who spread the teachings on So-ba Rig pa in Bhutan. Although the basic texts are the same, the Bhutanese tradition of So-ba Rig pa developed independently from its Tibetan origins. Since 1967 the Bhutanese tradition has been formally incorporated into the national health system.

The decision about the kind of treatment necessary for a particular condition is made mainly through reading of the pulses. Unlike Western medicine, which only uses reading of pulses to detect anomalies of the heart or the circulatory system, using the So-ba Rig pa method it is possible to detect diseases of organs through the pulses. The eyes, tongue and urine are also examined for signs that will help with the diagnosis, and sometimes the physician will record the patient's medical history.

Several forms of treatment are applied in Bhutanese traditional medicine. Hundreds of medicinal plants, minerals and animal parts from the basic medicines used by the practitioner. These basic ingredients are processed and mixed in different combinations to make 300 medicines in the form of pills, tablets, syrups, powders and lotions. The practitioner may also offer advice on, or treatment for, diet and lifestyle.

There are also procedures that include *gtar* (bloodletting), *bsregs* (cauterisation by herbal compounds), *gser bcos* (acupuncture with a golden needle), *tshug* (cauterisation with instruments of different materials), *dugs* (applying heat or cold to parts of the body), *byugs pa* (medicated oil massage), *sman chu* (stone heated bath), *tshachhu* (bath at a hot spring, such as the springs in Gasa) and *lum* (vapour treatment).

DRIGLAM NAMZHA

The Zhabdrung Ngawang Namgyal established a code of etiquette for monastic and government officials. Over the centuries this system of etiquette spread to lay people. Called *driglam namzha*, the code of conduct specifies how to dress when visiting a dzong, the polite way to greet one's boss and officials, the correct way to sit, eat and so forth. Many of the ceremonies performed at the start of an official event *(chipdrel, marchang)*, or an archery match are part of *driglam namzha*.

The government has actively promoted *driglam namzha* since 1989 in an attempt to preserve Bhutanese traditions, notably enforcing the requirement to wear *gho* and *kira* when visiting government offices, dzongs and temples.

Closely linked to *driglam namzha, thadamthsi* refers to the Bhutanese belief in respect towards ones' parents, elders, and other members of the community. Based on the Buddhist teachings on devotion, *thadamtshi* is an important concept in Bhutanese society. It is often illustrated by the story of the Four Friends (see the boxed text, p228).

Linked to *thadamtshi* and less formal than *driglam namzha* is the concept of *bey cha. Bey cha* emphasises the aesthetics of performing everyday tasks gracefully and with care and consideration for others.

White silk scarves called *kata* are exchanged as customary greetings among ranking officials and are offered to high lamas as a sign of respect, but they are not exchanged as frequently as they are in Tibet and Nepal.

Dress: Gho & Kira

Bhutan's traditional dress is one of the most distinctive and visible aspects of the country. It is compulsory for all Bhutanese to wear national dress in schools, government offices and formal occasions. Men, women and children wear traditional clothing made from Bhutanese textiles in a variety of colourful patterns.

The Bhutanese version of shot put is called *pungdo*, and is played with large heavy stones.

Men wear a *gho,* a long robe similar to the Tibetan *chuba.* The Bhutanese hoist the *gho* to knee length and hold it in place with a woven cloth belt called a *kera.* The *kera* is wound tightly around the waist, and the large pouch formed above it is traditionally used to carry a bowl, money and the makings of *doma.* One man suggested that the best part of the day was when he was able to loosen his uncomfortably tight belt.

According to tradition, men should carry a small knife called a *dozum* at the waist. Traditional footwear is knee-high, embroidered leather boots, but these are now worn only at festivals. Most Bhutanese men wear leather shoes, trainers or trekking boots.

Ghos come in a wide variety of patterns, though often they have plaid or striped designs. Flowered patterns are taboo, and solid reds and yellows are avoided because these are colours worn by monks; otherwise patterns have no special significance. Historically, Bhutanese men wore the same thing under their *gho* that a true Scotsman wears under his kilt, but today it's usually a pair of shorts. In winter it's correct to wear thermal underwear, but it's more often a pair of jeans or a track suit, which gives the costume a peculiar look that some people liken to a dressing gown. Formality in Thimphu dictates that legs may not be covered until winter has arrived, which is defined as the time that the monks move to Punakha.

Formal occasions, including a visit to the dzong, require a scarf called a *kabney* that identifies a person's rank. The *kabney* has to be put on correctly so it hangs in exactly the right way. In dzongs, and on formal occasions, a *dasho* or someone in authority carries a long sword called a *patang*.

Ordinary citizens wear a *kabney* of unbleached white silk and each level of official wears a different coloured scarf: saffron for the king and Je Khenpo; orange for *lyonpos*; blue for National Council and National Assembly members; red for those with the title Dasho and for senior officials whom the king has recognised; green for judges; white with a central red stripe for *dzongdags* (district governors); white with red stripes on the outside for *gups*.

Women wear a long floor-length dress called a *kira*. This is a rectangular piece of brightly coloured cloth that wraps around the body over a Tibetan-style silk blouse called a *wonju*. The *kira* is fastened at the shoulders with elaborate silver hooks called *koma* and at the waist with a belt that may be of either silver or cloth. Over the top is worn a short, open, jacketlike garment called a *toego*. Women often wear large amounts of jewellery. The whole ensemble is beautiful and Bhutanese women are very elegant in their finery.

The *kira* may be made from cotton or silk and may have a pattern on one or both sides. For everyday wear, women wear a *kira* made from striped cloth with a double-sided design, and on more formal occasions they wear a *kira* with an embellished pattern woven into it. The most expensive *kira*s are *kushutara*s (brocade dresses), which are made of hand-spun, hand-woven Bhutanese cotton, embroidered with various colours and designs in raw silk or cotton thread. Lhuentse is celebrated for its *kushutara* designs.

When visiting dzongs, women wear a cloth sash called a *rachu* over their shoulders or simply over their left shoulder in the same manner as men wear a *kabney*.

Bhutan's first foray into the Olympic Games happened when an archery team of three men and three women participated in the 1984 games. Since then Bhutan has participated in all the Olympics.

Bhutanese at Play

Bhutan's national sport is archery *(datse)*. It is played wherever there is enough space and remains the favourite sport for all ages. There are archery tournaments held throughout the country.

Archery contests act as an affirmation of Bhutanese cultural identity as well as popular entertainment. The tournaments begin with a short ceremony and breakfast. The targets are placed 140m apart. Players often stand close to the targets and call how good or bad the

BHUTAN'S SILVERSCREEN

The first feature film produced by a Bhutanese film-maker for a non-Bhutanese audience was *The Cup* by Khyentse Norbu, which was nominated as best foreign-language film for the 2000 Academy Awards. *Travellers and Magicians* (2003), also produced by Khyentse Norbu, is the first Dzongkha-language film to be made for an international audience. The film contains two parallel tales and its main theme is very pertinent to contemporary Bhutan. The main story focuses on a young frustrated civil servant, Dhundup, who dreams of leaving Bhutan for the United States. He likes rock and roll and Western clothes. Yet on the road to the capital, he encounters a series of people who suggest that contentment can be found among his own people.

Bhutanese of all ages enjoy these films, and part of the enjoyment for many is identifying friends and relatives, as well as the locations. Bhutanese films such as *Khorwa*, made for a Bhutanese audience, often tackle contemporary social problems such as domestic violence, the issues facing stepchildren, alcoholism and more recently, unemployment. Presently, the production values and acting are of varying quality, yet a stronger sense of Bhutanese film-making is gradually appearing, with annual awards recognising local film-makers. One recent film, *Sha Dha Semo*, bagged 11 awards, including 2009's best film at the Ninth National Film awards in Thimphu 2010.

aim of their opponent is – if the contestant hits the target, his team mates will perform a slow dance and sing his praises, while he slips a coloured scarf into his belt. If he misses, the opposition mock his ability.

Women, usually wearing their finest clothes and jewellery, often stand to one side of the archery field and act as cheerleaders. They dance and sing during breaks from the shooting. Their songs and shouts can be quite ribald!

Monks are forbidden to participate in archery, so they often play a stone-throwing game called *daygo*. A round, flat stone rather like a discus is tossed at a target and the winner is the one who gets the closest.

Khuru is a darts game played on a field about 20m long with small targets similar to those used by archers. The darts are usually home-made from a block of wood and a nail, with some chicken feathers for flights. If a chicken can't be found, bits of plastic make a good substitute. Teams compete with a lot of shouting and arm waving, designed to put the thrower off his aim. The game is a favourite of monks and young boys; beware of dangerous flying objects if you are near a *khuru* target or archery field.

Modern sports, notably basketball, football (soccer), cycling, golf, tae kwon do, shooting and tennis, continue to grow in popularity. Basketball is a favourite, especially since the fourth king used to regularly play basketball in public. Football teams such as DrukStar in Thimphu have emerged, and you may see matches taking place on the playing fields at Changlimithang. Cricket has recently gained popularity despite the current lack of suitable cricket pitches and there are several cricket clubs in Thimphu alone.

Bhutanese footballers came to the world's attention in 2002 when Bhutan played against the small island of Montserrat. *The Other Final* documentary narrates the lead-up to the football match between the world's two lowest ranked teams and the crowd's enthusiastic participation.

Buddhism in Bhutan

Buddhism is inscribed into the landscape of Bhutan – prayer flags, white-and-red chortens and images of Buddhist saints carved into the rock dot the countryside. To understand Bhutan it is essential to have a basic understanding of Buddhism. The experience of entering a dzong or monastery, or even a private household shrine room, will be enriched by understanding Buddhist concepts, and how these are encapsulated in some of the common religious images and practices encountered in Bhutan.

The Buddhism of Bhutan has a complex and rich visual tradition that can seem overwhelming. The bright and intricate mandalas decorating temple entrances, wrathful protective deities and the Wheel of Life all serve the same purpose: to encapsulate basic Buddhist teachings.

Buddhism is perhaps the most accommodating of the world's religions. As Buddhism has spread, it has adapted to local conditions, creating new schools of thought. However, its basic tenets have remained the same and all schools of Buddhism are united by their faith in the value of the original teachings of Sakyamuni (Sakya Thukpa), the historical Buddha.

To learn more about Tibetan Buddhism try the book *What Makes You Not a Buddhist* by Dzongsar Jamyang Khyentse, the celebrated Bhutanese rinpoche and director.

The Buddha

Buddhism originated in northern central India around the 6th or 5th century BC, from the teachings of Sakyamuni Buddha (at present, some historians consider that he lived in the 6th century and others in the 5th century). When he was born the local religion was based on Brahmanism. Some Brahmins (in order to purify themselves before performing rituals to their gods) would wander in remote areas and engage in ascetic practices – fasting, practising yogic techniques and meditation. The young Siddhartha Gautama, who would become known as the Buddha, was one of many such wandering ascetics. His teachings became the basis for a new religion, Buddhism.

The Buddha is known in Bhutan as Sakyamuni Buddha or Sakya Thukpa.

Little is known for certain about the young Siddhartha Gautama. According to legend his parents, King Suddhodana and Queen Maya, lived in a small kingdom, Sakya, which lay on the border between the present-day states of Nepal and India. Shortly after his birth a wandering ascetic prophesied to King Suddhodana that the young prince would either be a world-conquering king or a liberator of living beings from suffering. The king took various precautions to ensure that his son would never have cause to follow a spiritual path. However, the young prince grew restless and during various excursions from his palace Siddhartha Gautama saw a number of examples of suffering that inspired him to escape from his palace life.

After fleeing the palace, Siddhartha became a wandering ascetic, fasting and meditating. Finally at Bodhgaya in Bihar, India, Siddhartha

SAKYAMUNI

BUDDHISM IN BHUTAN BUDDHIST CONCEPTS

began meditating beneath a bo *(pipal)* tree, declaring that he would not stop until he had achieved enlightenment. He had realised there must be a middle path between the extremes of his former life in the palace and the ascetic practices he had been taught. As dawn broke on the morning of his third night of meditation Siddhartha became a Buddha (an awakened one).

Buddhist Concepts

Shortly after gaining enlightenment, the Buddha gave his first public teaching in the Deer Park at Sarnath. For the remainder of his life, the Buddha continued to give teachings and established the early Buddhist monastic community. These early teachings by the Buddha are collected in the Sutras and form the basis for all later Buddhist thought. The Mahayana school, which developed later, diverged from these earlier teachings in some respects, but not fundamentally.

The Buddha started his teachings by explaining that there was a middle way that steered a course between sensual indulgence and ascetic self-torment. The Middle Way can be followed by taking the Eight Fold Noble Path, underpinned by the Four Noble Truths. The Four Noble Truths set out the laws of cause and effect. These basic concepts are the core of early Buddhist thought. In Bhutan, these are contained in a series of meditations that lamas and religious teachers view as the foundation for spiritual growth leading to enlightenment: the Four Mind Turnings.

Seeds of Faith: A Comprehensive Guide to the Sacred Places of Bhutan (Volume 1, West Bhutan) by the KMT Research Group is an expensive but excellent locally produced guide to Bhutan's spiritual places.

Four Noble Truths

The Four Noble Truths underpin Buddhist philosophy and are the basic tenets about ignorance and enlightenment, suffering and freedom set forth by the Buddha in his first formal discourse in Sarnath.

The first Noble Truth is that life is suffering, the Truth of Suffering. This suffering is the misery of an unenlightened life and the constant process of rebirth in the different realms of existence. At its root is the inherent imperfection of life – the inability to find true satisfaction in samsara (the cycle of birth, death and reincarnation). The suffering of life is inherent in the pain of birth, ageing, sickness and death, in having to associate with the unpleasant things of life and to lose that which brings us pleasure.

The reason for this dissatisfaction and suffering is contained in the second Noble Truth, True Origins. This refers to our desire for things to be other than they actually are. The Buddha taught that in order to gain

OTHER RELIGIONS

Not all Bhutanese are Buddhist. Many of the Lhotshampas, the descendants of Nepalese migrants, are Hindu – as are the majority of the casual labourers from Assam and Bengal. There are still traces of the earlier pre-Buddhist beliefs in the countryside and there's a small number of Christian converts. Bhutan is tolerant of all religions but does not permit proselytisation. The constitution upholds freedom of belief and does not make any religion the official religion of Bhutan. It does, however, recognise the importance of Bhutan's Buddhist heritage to Bhutan's cultural identity.

Vestiges of Bon, the pre-Buddhist beliefs of Tibet, can still be found in Bhutan. Moreover, Bhutan has a rich folk religion *(luso)* and Bhutanese folk beliefs are primarily concerned with a range of spirits, like *nep* or local deities who act as the custodian of particular valleys such as Chungdu in Haa, or Radak in Wangdue Phodrang. Other spirits reside in rocks or groves of trees; there are *tshomens*, goddesses who inhabit the lakes; *lus* or *nagas* – snake-bodied spirits who dwell in the lakes, rivers and wells. *Sadaks* are lords of the earth and *tsens* are air spirits who can bring illness and death. All these have subsequently merged into mainstream Buddhism.

EIGHT-FOLD PATH

The Fourth Noble Truth, True Paths, set out by the Buddha refers to the correct means through which an individual is able to overcome attachment and desires in the pursuit of liberation from samsara. These are often described as the Eight-Fold Path: with dedication and practice it may lead to accumulation of merit, then enlightenment and liberation. The eight components of the path to enlightenment: right understanding, right thought, right speech, right action, right livelihood, right effort, right mindfulness and right concentration.

liberation from suffering we need to abandon our delusions and selfish actions, which are the cause for our rebirth in samsara. Due to our ignorance, we create the causes for our rebirth and maintain the cycle.

The third Noble Truth was described by the Buddha as True Cessation – the stopping of all delusions, our desires and attachment to samsara. With the cessation of desire and attachment, we are able to break the cycle of rebirth and suffering and reach the state of nirvana, the ultimate goal of Buddhism. The final Noble Truth, True Paths, is the truth of the path leading to cessation.

The doctrine of the Four Noble Truths is the foundation on which the whole path to liberation and enlightenment is built. Therefore a deep understanding of these truths, cultivated through reflection and meditation, is an indispensable basis for following the Buddhist path.

Karma

As beings are reborn in samsara their rebirths in the different realms of existence are determined by their karma. In Buddhist doctrine, karma refers to three important components: actions, their effects and their consequences. Actions are divided into those of the body, speech and mind and the main concern is with the imprint of each action on the mind or mental continuum that follows each being from rebirth to rebirth. Buddhist teachings liken karma to a seed (action) that ripens into a fruit (effect).

Mahayana teachings say it is important to dedicate the merit of one's wholesome actions to the benefit of all living beings, ensuring that others also experience the results of one's positive actions. Therefore, in Bhutan and elsewhere in the Himalayan region, the accumulation of merit is not a selfish act. Rather, it is dedicated to all living beings with the aspiration that they gain liberation from samsara, demonstrating the belief that through action all beings, as one, affect each other.

Rebirth

In Buddhism, life is a cycle of rebirth, and these rebirths are countless as living beings 'wander' in samsara. There is not just one world but a myriad of worlds in which beings may be reborn – according to Buddhist doctrine there are six different realms of existence. Rebirth, or cyclic existence, emerges from fundamental ignorance through a process known as the 12 links of dependent origination. When this fundamental ignorance is reversed, cyclic existence itself can be reversed and nirvana attained, free from suffering and the processes of rebirth. The six realms of existence and the 12 links of dependent origination are commonly depicted in the Wheel of Life and according to Buddhist teachings it is important during one's lifetime to accumulate enough merit to avoid being reborn in one of the three lower realms. This emphasises the preciousness of a human life and the importance of engaging in virtuous actions.

BUDDHISM IN BHUTAN BUDDHIST CONCEPTS

MONKS

Some monks may be trained as painters or sculptors, or as tailors and embroiderers for the various items required for the monastery.

Buddhism in Modern Bhutan

The modern state of Bhutan reflects an age-old system constructed by the first Zhabdrung (see p190). At the pinnacle of the new structure was the Zhabdrung. Below him he created the Je Khenpo, or Chief Abbot, who was responsible for all religious matters. His secular counterpart was the *desi,* who was responsible for all political matters. For a background to the origins of Buddhism in Bhutan and the important historical figures that influenced the spread and organisation of Buddhism in Bhutan, see History (p183).

Organisation of the Religious Community

The *dratshang* (central monk body) refers to the government-supported monks who are under the authority of the Je Khenpo. He is assisted by five *lonpons* (masters), each in charge of religious tradition, liturgy, lexicography or logic. The Je Khenpo moves between Punakha dzong in winter and Thimphu dzong in summer. On these occasions the roads are lined with Bhutanese seeking his blessings and the journey by road takes two days.

Each dzong has a *lam neten,* who is responsible for the monk body in the each *dzongkhag.* Each dzong will have a master of grammar, master of liturgy, master of philosophy, an *umdze* (choirmaster) and a *kundun* (disciple master), who carries a rosary of large beads and a whip.

SCHOOLS OF BUDDHISM

Shortly after the death of Sakyamuni, disputes began to arise among his disciples over the interpretation of his teachings. The Sutras were composed after his death and subsequently different schools of thought appeared, leading to a schism and the emergence of the two principal schools of Buddhism, Theravada and Mahayana.

Theravada, sometimes referred to as Hinayana, focused on pursuing liberation for the individual. Mahayana took Buddhism in a different direction, emphasising compassion and the liberation of all living beings. The Theravada teachings retreated to southern India before becoming established in Sri Lanka, Thailand, Burma and Cambodia. The Mahayana teachings were developed in the new Buddhist universities in northern India before being transmitted northwards through the Himalayas, to China, Japan and Korea. The Mahayana teachings on compassion permeate the religious beliefs and practices of the Bhutanese.

Tantrism (Vajrayana)

A new school emerged from the Mahayana in about AD 600. Both the Theravada and Mahayana schools studied the Sutras that recorded the teachings of Sakyamuni; however, the followers of Tantrism believed that he had left a collection of esoteric teachings to a select few of his early disciples. These were known as Tantra *(gyu).*

Tantra (Sanskrit meaning 'continuum') has two meanings in Buddhism. It refers to the literature dealing with tantric teachings and secondly to the continuum of development from ignorance to enlightenment. Tantra involves identifying with a tutelary deity through deep meditation and the recitation of mantra. The two most well-known mantras are *om mani padme hum* of Chenresig (Avalokiteshvara) and *om vajra guru padme siddhi hum* of Guru Rinpoche (Padmasambhava).

In Bhutan many of the ritual objects and the imagery in the monasteries and temples are derived from tantric teachings. They display the many different aspects of enlightenment – at times gentle as in the image of Chenresig or the Medicine Buddha, at times wrathful as in the image of Dorje Drolo. The meditational deities sit at the centre of an elaborate mandala, a representation of the pure land where the deity resides. Through years of careful meditation the tantric practitioner identifies with the deity by visualising in detail the three-dimensional mandala.

DOS & DON'TS WHEN VISITING TEMPLES

Himalayan Buddhism has a generally relaxed approach to religious sites, but you should observe a few important rules if you are invited to enter a lhakhang or go-emba. It is customary to remove one's shoes and hat upon entering the important rooms of a temple. You will most likely be escorted by a caretaker monk, and you can follow his example in removing your shoes at the appropriate doorway. Leave cameras, umbrellas and hats outside. Always move in a clockwise direction and do not speak loudly. If there is a ceremony being performed inside, always check that it's OK before entering. It is customary to leave a small offering of money (Nu 10) on the altar. When you make this offering, the monk accompanying you will pour a small amount of holy water, from a sacred vessel called a *bumpa*, into your hand. You should make the gesture of drinking a sip of this water and then spread the rest on your head. While male visitors may be permitted (please ask before entering) to enter the *goenkhang* (shrine dedicated to protector deities), this is off-limits to all women. Do not walk behind an altar set before the *goenkhang*.

Traditionally, Bhutanese families would, if they were able, send one son to join a monastery. This was viewed as creating merit for the family and household and a blessing for the child. The fourth *desi,* Tenzin Rabgye, introduced a monk tax in the late 16th century. The reason for this tax, which required one child to be sent to become a monk, was to promote the Drukpa Kagyu sect.

There is no longer a monk tax, and young boys continue to enter the monasteries. Any visitor to Bhutan will see long snaking lines of maroon-robed boy monks walking near the dzongs in Paro and Punakha. Often they come from poor rural families and may or may not have expressed an interest to become a monk. Once in the monastery, their daily lives revolve around learning to read and write.

Typically, the young monks will sit in class with a monk-teacher in the mornings and in the afternoon sit with friends in small groups, reciting their texts. Monastic schools for younger monks are known as *lobdra*s, as opposed to more advanced *shedra*s. Throughout a monk's education there is an emphasis on memorisation. So each day the monk will memorise a set amount of text and prayers, and will be tested by his teacher. When they are still young the monks do not understand the meaning of the texts. Once they are in the midteens they will be examined individually and they will either proceed to the *shedra* (philosophy school) or perhaps join the ritual school. The *shedra* develops the young monk's knowledge and understanding of a range of Buddhist texts and teachings, while the ritual college trains the monk in the correct procedures for a wide range of rituals.

While the government currently provides basic needs (accommodation, food and clothing), the monks are permitted to keep money received from lay people for performing rituals. They may be requested to attend the blessing of a new house, the consecration of a new chorten or to conduct prayers for the wellbeing of the household. These events take a great deal of preparation for the sponsor, who will need to ensure that all the necessary ritual items are available. The sponsor will provide food to the monks and often the household will be filled with neighbours attending the ceremony. These events renew and strengthen the bonds between the lay and religious community.

Monks continually take vows, as they progress from novice to fully ordained monk. A few monks join monastic orders after adolescence, but they are not the norm. Monks may renounce or return their vows at any time in order to return to lay life, often to start a family, and have

Monks are celibate and must abstain from smoking and drinking alcohol, but they are not required to be vegetarian and may eat in the evening, unlike their counter-parts in Southeast Asia.

to pay a token fine. These former monks are called *getre*s or 'retired' monks and there is no social stigma attached to this choice. Some may even act as lay religious figures, called *gomchen*s, and perform prayers and ceremonies for a range of daily activities, especially if there is no monastery nearby.

Domestic Rituals

Every house has a *choesum* (altar or shrine room). Each altar usually features statues of Sakyamuni, Guru Rinpoche and the Zhabdrung. In most homes and temples, devotees place seven bowls filled with water on altars. This simple offering is important because it can be given without greed or attachment. If offerings are made to the protective deities, such as Mahakala, then there are only five offering bowls. As all Himalayan Buddhists do, Bhutanese devotees prostrate themselves in front of altars and lamas, first clasping hands above the head, again at throat level and then at the chest. This represents the ultimate desire to attain the body *(ku)*, speech *(sung)* and mind *(thug)* of a Buddha.

Rites are performed for events and crises in life such as birth, marriage, promotion, illness and death. The rituals take place in front of the household shrine, or outside with an altar erected with an image of Buddha (representing the Buddha's body), a religious text (representing the Buddha's speech) and a small stupa or chorten (representing the Buddha's mind). The basic rituals of initiation, purification, consecration and the offering of a *torma* are included. For example, a water or incense purification ceremony is performed after a birth, while more elaborate rituals involving the offering of the eight lucky signs (ie Tashi Tagye) may be offered at a promotion or marriage. Astrology may be used to decide the timing of the rituals. Bhutanese often consult *tsip*s (astrologers) before embarking on a journey or a new undertaking. Astrology plays an important role in overcoming misfortune and deciding the most appropriate time to perform rituals to avert misfortune.

Ordinary men and women do not typically engage in meditation or Buddhist philosophical studies, though many will attempt to complete the preliminary practices and will seek the blessings of lamas before embarking on new ventures, for their children and prosperity.

On special occasions monks prepare *torma* (ritual cake), multicoloured sculptures made from *tsampa* (barley flour) and butter, as symbolic offerings to deities. Each deity is associated with a particular form of *torma*.

TORMA

LUSO (FOLK RELIGION)

The invocation of local and protective deities, and the offering of incense to the mountain deities, are everyday rituals in Bhutan. Every locality, mountain, lake, river or grove of trees has its deities and they are worshipped by the local communities. In the morning, leaves or aromatic herbs (juniper) are burned as an offering to the mountain deities. On certain days, a single flag is raised on every house and particular deities are invoked. Many of the local deities are believed to have originally been Bon deities converted to Buddhism by Guru Rinpoche. Bon traditions and rituals are still practised in parts of Bhutan during the celebration of local festivals. Bon may have spread to Bhutan from Tibet prior to the arrival of Guru Rinpoche.

Each locality has its own local practices and often women play a major role in these local ceremonies and celebrations. An interesting, if rare, category of female religious figures is the *delog. Delog*s are women, occasionally men, who have died and travelled to the other side, where they have watched the judgment of the dead and encountered various Buddhas (eg Chenresig or Guru Rinpoche), before returning to life. The *delog*s stress the importance of leading virtuous lives and refraining from causing harm to living beings. The anthropologist Françoise Pommaret encountered several *delog*s in eastern Bhutan during the 1980s and the biographies of historical *delog*s remain popular in Bhutan.

Buddhism has numerous important deities and protectors of the faith, but there are also many other deities that have special significance only within a certain region. These local protector or guardian deities, as well as *yidam* (tutelary deities), may be wrathful manifestations of enlightened beings, spirits or malevolent beings that were subdued and converted by Tantric forces. They are an important element of Bhutan's spiritual beliefs and they occupy a special place in lhakhangs. A locally crafted statue, which is often terrifying or wrathful, of a protective deity is found in a corner or in the *goenkhang* of most of Bhutan's lhakhangs.

The deity Mahakala (Great Black One) assisted Zhabdrung Ngawang Namgyal all his life and is recognised as the guardian deity of Bhutan. He is also known as Yeshe Goenpo, often described as the overlord of all the mountain gods, and is a Tantric Buddhist form of the Hindu god Shiva. Mahakali (Wisdom Defender) is the female form, also known as Palden Lhamo, the dark-blue protector.

Most of Bhutan's valleys have a local protective deity. Statues of Thimphu's protector, Gyenyen Jagpa Melen, appear in Dechenphug Lhakhang near Dechencholeing and in Ney Khang Lhakhang next to the dzong. He is also seen as a national protective deity, with Bhutanese visiting his temple to seek his blessings before a new venture or if leaving the country for any length of time. Among the other regional protective deities are Jichu Drakye in Paro, Chhundu in Haa, Talo Gyalpo Pehar in Punakha, Kaytshugpa in Wangdue Phodrang and, in Bumthang, Keybu Lungtsan and Jowo Ludud Drakpa Gyeltshen. These deities are gods who have not left the world and therefore have not gained enlightenment. For more on protective deities, see p223.

Important Figures of Buddhism in Bhutan

This is a brief guide to the iconography of some of the main figures of Buddhism in Bhutan. The images are divided into Buddhas, Bodhisattvas, Protective Deities, and Historical Figures. This guide is neither exhaustive nor scholarly; rather it seeks to enable you to identify the main figures on altars and in the temple murals encountered during your trip. The Bhutanese names are given first with the Sanskrit (where applicable) in parenthesis.

Buddhas

Sakyamuni

Sakyamuni is the historical Buddha (of the present age), whose teachings are the foundation of Bhutanese Buddhism. Typically in Bhutan, as in Tibet, Sakyamuni is represented as seated with his legs crossed in the adamantine (diamond/*vajra*) position on a lotus-flower throne. His hair is bluish-black and there is a halo of light around his head. His right hand touches the ground in the 'witness' *mudra* (hand gesture) and his left rests on his lap, usually with an alms bowl in the left palm. His body is marked with 32 signs of enlightenment. Often seen is the trinity of Three Buddhas, the Dusum Sangye/Sangey: past, present and future Buddhas.

Opagme (Amitabha)

The Buddha of Infinite Light is one of the five *dhyana* (meditational or cosmic) Buddhas and resides in the Blissful Pure Land of the West (Sukhavati or Dewachen in Dzongkha, also the name of several hotels in Bhutan.). He is closely associated with Tsepame and Chenresig and represents the transformation of lust into wisdom. He is depicted seated cross-legged on a lotus throne, with his hands resting on his lap in meditative pose and holding an alms bowl. His body is red in colour.

Sakyamuni

Jampa (Maitreya)

The future Buddha is said to be residing as a Bodhisattva in Tushita heaven, a heaven realm where bodhisattvas reside awaiting full enlightenment and rebirth, until his time to incarnate on earth as a Buddha. Statues of Jampa are the focal point in most older lhakhangs built before the visit of Guru Rinpoche. He is shown seated with his feet on the ground and hands in front of his chest, in the 'turning the wheel' *mudra*.

Sangye Menlha

According to Mahayana tradition, Sakyamuni transformed himself into a deep-blue Buddha who emanates healing rays of light and teaches the science of medicine. Buddhism values medicine as a means to alleviate suffering and prolong human life, thereby improving the opportunity to attain enlightenment. Sangye Menlha (medicine Buddha) is seated cross-legged on a lotus throne, with a bowl containing three medicinal fruits. He may be surrounded by a group of eight other medicine Buddhas.

Jampa

Bodhisattvas

A bodhisattva ('hero of enlightenment') seeks enlightenment for the sake of all living beings, out of heartfelt compassion and self-sacrifice, rather than seeking liberation from samsara for her or himself. This altruistic attitude is referred to as bodhicitta, or mind of enlightenment, and involves cultivating love and great compassion towards others through the practice of the six perfections: generosity, moral discipline, patience, effort, concentrations and wisdom.

Keep a look out in goembas and lhakhangs for the Rigsum Goempo – a trinity of Chenresig, Jampelyang and Chana Dorje.

Chenresig

Chenresig (Avalokiteshvara)

The Bodhisattva of compassion is probably the best-known deity in Bhutanese Buddhism, outside Bhutan. Chenresig appears in a variety of forms. He is the 'glorious gentle one' – one of the four great bodhisattvas and the special guardian of Bhutanese religion – pictured sitting in a lotus position, with the lower two (of four) arms in a gesture of prayer. He also appears with 11 heads and 1000 arms arranged in a circle, also known as Chuchizey in Bhutan.

Jampelyang (Manjushri)

The 'princely lord of wisdom' – the embodiment of wisdom and knowledge – carries a sword in his right hand to destroy the darkness of ignorance. He is the patron of learning and the arts, and is generally yellow.

Jampelyang

Chana Dorje (Vajrapani)

'Thunderbolt in hand' – this is the god of power and victory. His thunderbolt, representing power, is a fundamental symbol of Tantric faith; it is called a *dorji* in Tibetan and *vajra* in Sanskrit. He is pictured in a wrathful blue form with an angry face and one leg outstretched.

Drolma (Tara)

There are many different emanations of Drolma, and a popular prayer recited daily mentions 21 different activities that she performs to protect people and to enable them to gain enlightenment. The two most common representations are as Drolma, a green, female Bodhisattva

Chana Dorje

seated on a lotus flower with her right leg extended, ready to leap down to assist. Green Tara is said to have been born from Chenresig's tears of compassion and from her determination to achieve enlightenment in the body of a woman. The other form, known as Drolkar (White Tara), is seated in the full lotus posture and with seven eyes, including one in her forehead and two on her palms and the soles of her feet.

Green Tara

Protective Deities
Nagpo Chenpo (Mahakala)

Mahakala (The Great Black One) appears in a variety of forms in Bhutan and is one of the fiercest protective deities. Most Bhutanese monasteries and temples have a shrine dedicated to him (*goenkhang;* not open to women). Mahakala may be invoked to help remove obstacles to a new undertaking, or in times of danger. His worship in Bhutan was popularised by the Zhabdrung Ngawang Namgyal, whose personal protective deity he was. According to legend, Mahakala appeared to the Zhabdrung in his raven form (Gompo Jarodanden) and advised him to go to Bhutan. The Raven Headed Mahakala is the basis for the Raven Crown worn by the Bhutanese monarchs.

Mahakala is black with reddish hair that rises upwards. He has three eyes and is surrounded by fire and smoke. He wears various bone ornaments and a skull garland. He carries a curved *vajra* knife in his right hand and a skull cup in his left. Depending on the form depicted he may have two, four, six or more arms.

Drolkar

Palden Lhamo (Mahakali)

The Glorious Goddess is a fierce protective deity and is closely associated with Yeshe Gompo (Wisdom Mahakala). She is an important protector of the Kagyu order and is equally important to the other lineages of Nyingma, Sakya and Gelug (in Tibet). Palden Lhamo is invoked in times of difficulty and special pujas are performed to avert misfortune, like natural disasters and wars. She has a ferocious appearance and is quite distinctive. Her body is dark blue, while the palms of her hands and the soles of her feet are red. She wears a crown of five skulls and her long hair rises upwards. She carries a skull cup in her left hand and brandishes a club in her right. She rides on a wild ass and her saddlecloth is a flayed human skin.

Guru Rinpoche

Historical Figures
Guru Rinpoche (Padmasambhava)

'The Lotus Born' is an Indian Buddhist Great Adept who, according to Bhutanese tradition, arrived in Bhutan before he went to Tibet in the 8th century. Popularly known as Guru Rinpoche, he is viewed as the Second Buddha by the Nyingma lineage. He is depicted seated in a half-lotus position on a lotus throne. He wears a blue inner robe with a golden robe and an outer red cloak. His hat is known as the 'lotus cap' and is adorned with a crescent moon, the sun and a small flamelike protuberance that signifies the union of lunar and solar forces. The hat is surmounted by a *dorji* (thunderbolt) and also an eagle's feather, which represents the Guru's soaring mind, penetrating the highest realms of reality. He has long flowing hair and a curly moustache. In his extended right hand he holds a *vajra* and in his left hand, resting on his lap, is a skull cup filled with nectar. A staff topped with a freshly severed head, a decaying head and a skull rests in the crook of his left arm. A ritual dagger, for subduing demons, is tucked into his belt. Guru Rinpoche also appears in eight manifestations (see p185).

Milarepa

Zhabdrung Ngawang Namgyal

Milarepa

A great Tibetan magician (1040–1123) and poet of the Kagyu lineage, he is believed to have attained the supreme enlightenment of Buddhahood in the course of one life. He travelled extensively throughout the Himalayan border lands and is said to have meditated at Taktshang in Bhutan, where he composed a song. Most images of Milarepa picture him smiling and holding his hand to his ear as he sings. He is normally depicted in green due to his extended diet of nettle soup.

Drukpa Kunley

The wandering ascetic, Drukpa Kunley (1455–1529), is one of the main figures of the Druk Kagyu. His ribald songs and poems were unconventional and have earned him the affection of the Bhutanese. In Bhutan he is often depicted with a bow-and-arrow case and accompanied by a small hunting dog. In Chimi Lhakhang, Drukpa Kunley is depicted dressed similarly to the great Mahasiddhis, with a bare torso and a loin cloth. Elsewhere he is shown wearing normal lay dress with boots. For more on Drukpa Kunley, see p92.

PRAYER FLAGS

Prayer flags are ubiquitous in Bhutan, found fluttering on mountain passes, rooftops, and dzong and temple courtyards.

Prayer flags come in five colours – blue, green, red, yellow and white – symbolising the elements of water, wood, fire, earth and iron, respectively. They also stand for the five *dhyani* or meditation Buddhas; the five wisdoms; the five directions; and the five mental attributes or emotions. The prayer for the flag is carved into wooden blocks and then printed on the cloth in repeating patterns.

Goendhar

The smallest prayer flags, *goendhar*s, are those mounted on the rooftops of homes. These white banners have small blue, green, red and yellow ribbons attached to their edges. They invoke the blessings and patronage of Mahakala, the main protective deity of Bhutan. The flags are replaced annually during a ceremony that honours the family's personal local deities.

Lungdhar

The *lungdhar* (wind flag) is erected on hillsides or ridges and can be for good luck, protection from an illness, the achievement of a personal goal, or the acquisition of wisdom. These flags are printed with the Wind Horse, or Lungta, which carries a wish-fulfilling jewel on its back.

Manidhar

The *manidhar* is erected on behalf of a deceased person, and features prayers to the Bodhisattva of Compassion, Chenresig. These prayer flags are generally erected in batches of 108 and are placed at strategic high points from which a river can be seen. In this way, the belief is that the prayers will waft with the wind to the river, and be carried by the river on its long and winding journey.

Lhadhar

The largest flag in the country is the *lhadhar* (god flag). These huge flags can be seen outside dzongs and other important places and represent victory over the forces of evil. There is normally no text on these flags; they are like a giant version of the *goendhar*. The only difference, apart from size, is at the top, where the *lhadhar* is capped by a colourful silk parasol. You must be formally dressed in traditional Bhutanese attire for Bhutanese and in appropriate dress for foreigners to enter any place where a *lhadhar* stands.

Spinning prayer wheels are a ubiquitous sight in Bhutan. The revolving cylinders are filled with printed prayers which are 'said' each time the wheel is turned. Prayer wheels can be intricately decorated hand-held affairs or building-sized and every size in between. Some are effortlessly turned by diverted streams of water, whereas monks and devotees turn man-powered wheels to gain merit and to concentrate the mind on the mantras and prayers they are reciting.

Pema Lingpa

The *terton* (treasure finder) Pema Lingpa (1450–1521) was born in Tang valley, Bumthang. The best-known statue of Pema Lingpa was made by Pema Lingpa himself and is kept at Kunzangdrak Goemba, Bumthang. Usually depicted in the *vajra* position, Pema Lingpa holds a *bumpa* (vase symbolising long life) in his hands and wearing a hat similar to that worn by Guru Rinpoche, with the notable addition of two *vajras* crossed at the front of it. For more on Pema Lingpa, see p189.

Zhabdrung Ngawang Namgyal

The Zhabdrung Ngawang Namgyal (1594–1651) is regarded as the founder of Bhutan, where he arrived from Tibet in 1616. The Zhabdrung has a distinctive white, pointed beard and wears monastic robes, and is seated in the lotus posture. In his left hands he holds a *bumpa* and his right hand is in the 'witness' *mudra*. Over his right shoulder is a meditation belt. The Zhabdrung wears a distinctive ceremonial hat of the Druk Kagyu order. For more details on him, see p190.

Traditional Arts

Practically all Bhutanese art, dance, drama, music and even architecture has its roots in Buddhism. The highly distinctive architecture of Bhutan is discussed on p233. Almost all representation in art, music and dance is a dramatisation of the Buddha's teachings about the path to liberation and the constant struggle to overcome the delusions that lead to the cycle of rebirth in samsara.

The Artistic Tradition in Bhutan

The development of Buddhist arts and crafts in Bhutan can be traced to the 15th-century *terton* (discoverer of sacred texts) Pema Lingpa, who was an accomplished painter, metalworker, sculptor and architect. The country's artistic tradition received a further boost when, in 1680, the fourth *desi* (secular ruler), Gyalse Tenzin Rabgye (r 1680–94), opened the School of Bhutanese Arts & Crafts, which has evolved into the National Institute for Zorig Chusum.

Traditional Bhutanese artistry is maintained through the support of all levels of society. The royal family, nobility and clergy continue to provide important patronage. Meanwhile, the common people support the arts because they depend on artisans to provide the wide variety of wooden and metal objects indispensable to typical Bhutanese households and painting, both inside and outside homes.

Traditional art has two important characteristics: it is religious and anonymous. The Bhutanese consider commissioning paintings and statues as pious acts, which gain merit for the *jinda* (patron). The name of the *jinda* is sometimes written on the work so that their pious act may be remembered. However, the artist's name is rarely ever mentioned, although there are some artists whose names do become well known due to the exceptional quality of their work.

There are strict iconographical conventions in Bhutanese art and the Bhutanese artists observe them scrupulously. However, artists do express their own personality in minor details (for example, the shading of clouds or background scenes).

Bhutan's Department of Trade has introduced the Bhutan SEAL (www.bhutanseal .gov.bt) to establish a quality and authenticity benchmark for handicraft products.

The Thirteen Arts

The Thirteen Arts are the 13 traditional arts and crafts (Zorig Chusum) believed to have been categorised during the reign of the fourth *desi,* Tenzin Rabgye. Zorig Chusum refers to those physical activities that assist, teach or uplift others.

If you are interested in actually creating your own Bhutanese art, look out for *Tibetan Thangka Painting: Methods and Materials* by David P Jackson and Janice A Jackson.

Shingzo (Carpentry)

Skilled carpenters are involved in a range of activities ranging from building dzongs and temples, houses and palaces, to making tools and other practical instruments used in the everyday life of the Bhutanese people.

Dozo (Masonry)

This covers the building of stupas, dzongs and temples as well as making the heavy millstones and stone pestles.

Parzo (Carving)

The Bhutanese are highly skilled at wood, stone and slate carving. Examples of their work are evident throughout Bhutan, from the slate carvings depicting the Buddha and other religious figures inserted in stupas, to the wooden printing blocks used for printing sacred texts.

Lhazo (Painting)

Lhazo encompasses drawing and painting in Bhutan. It includes the painting of *thangkas* (religious pictures), murals and frescoes in temples and dzongs as well as the colourful images on the exterior walls of Bhutanese homes. Drawing and painting are governed by strict geometric rules of proportion and iconography. For more on *lhazo* see p228.

Jinzo (Sculpture)

One of the arts in which the Bhutanese excel is the creation of delicate clay sculptures, occasionally set in amazing landscapes. These sculptures, ranging from small- to large-scale statues, are generally created around a hollow frame with the mud or clay built up to form the image.

As well as statues, *jinzo* includes the production of a range of ritual items, notably the moulded offerings *(torma)* and masks worn during tsechu, and the more prosaic activity of preparing mud walls on new buildings.

Lugzo (Casting)

Casting, usually in bronze, refers to the production of musical instruments, statues, tools and kitchen utensils, as well as slip casting for pottery and jewellery.

Garzo (Blacksmithing)

Generally, these craftsmen produce axes, plough blades, chains, knives and swords and other practical items.

Troko (Gold- & Silver-smithing)

This includes all ornaments made from gold, silver or copper. They are often cut out, beaten, drawn or engraved.

Tshazo (Bamboo work)

There is a wide variety of these products, as seen in the markets across the country. They include *bangchung* (covered bowls with intricate designs), long *palang* (used to store beer or other liquor), the *tshesip* (box), *belo* (small hat worn for sun protection), *redi* (mat), *luchu* (used for storing grain), *balep* (bamboo thatch) and of course, the bow and arrow.

Thagzo (Weaving)

Thagzo covers the whole process: from the preparation of the yarn, dyeing and the numerous designs. This is the largest craft industry in terms of the variety and number of craftspeople involved throughout Bhutan. See p229 for more on *thagzo*.

BURLS

Bhutan's wonderful wooden bowls are turned from lumpy 'burls' that usually grow around an infection or insect attack on a tree. Only the most intricately patterned burlwood goes into making the magnificent and highly valued *Woogzo* bowls, so named for their owl-feather patterns.

Although some men do practise weaving, the majority of weavers are women and it is the only one of Bhutan's 13 traditional arts and crafts that is dominated by women.

One of Bhutan's favourite paintings is based on the popular fable of the Four Friends. In Dzongkha the name of the story is *Thuenpa Puen Shi* (Cooperation, Relation, Four) and it illustrates the concept of teamwork. You will see paintings illustrating this story on temples, homes and shops throughout the country.

The story tells how the elephant, monkey, peacock and rabbit combined forces to obtain a continual supply of fruit. The peacock found a seed and planted it, the rabbit watered it, the monkey fertilised it and the elephant guarded it. When the fruit was ripe the tree was so high that they could not reach the top. The four animals made a tower by climbing on one another's back, and plucked the fruit from the high branches.

Tshemzo (Embroidery)

There are two special categories within this craft. The first are those items which are sewn and embroidered (ranging from clothing to intricate and rare embroidered *thangkas*). The second refers to appliqué and patchwork items made from stitching cloth together. This includes the large *thondrols* displayed in the dzongs during tsechu, as well as hats and the elaborate boots worn with the *gho* on official occasions.

Shagzo (Woodturning)

Skilled woodturners produce a range of delicate wooden bowls, turned with expertise from special parts of a tree or roots. The large wooden *dapa* (serving dishes), wooden plates, buckets, ladles and *phop* (small cups), as well as the various small hand drums beaten during religious ceremonies, are among the products of this craft.

Dezo (Papermaking)

The art of making paper from the daphne plant, and more recently bamboo and rice stalks, is under threat from the loss of skilled craftsmen. The word *de* refers to the daphne plant, from which traditional insect-repellent paper is made.

Painting

Aside from spectacular architecture, the most visible manifestation of Bhutanese art is painting. There are three forms of traditional painting: *thangkas,* wall paintings and statues. A painting is invariably religious in nature depicting a deity, a religious story, a meditational object or an array of auspicious symbols (such as the Tashi Tagye – Eight Auspicious Symbols – or Four Friends). Paintings were traditionally done not for sale, but for specific purposes – though this is slowly changing.

Paintings, in particular the portrayal of human figures, are subject to strict rules of iconography. The proportions and features must be precise, and there is no latitude for artistic licence in these works. The initial layout is constructed with a series of geometrical patterns, using straight lines to lay out the proportions of the figure, which are defined in religious documents called *zuri pata*. In other cases the initial sketch is made with a stencil of the basic outline, which is transferred to the canvas by patting the stencil with a bag filled with chalk dust. Traditionally, paints were made from earth, minerals and vegetables, though now chemical colours are also used. The material is first reduced into powder and then mixed with water, glue and chalk. The brushes are handmade from twigs and animal hair.

LHUENTSE

The royal Wangchuck dynasty's ancestral home is in the pre-eminent weaving district of Lhuentse, and perhaps this is why royal patronage has been so influential in the development of textile art, with dozens of weavers employed by all the royal households.

Thangkas are painted on canvas that is stretched and lashed to a wooden frame. When the work is completed it is removed from the frame and surrounded by a border of colourful brocade, with wooden sticks at the top and bottom used for hanging. Although some *thangkas* are hung permanently, most are rolled up and stored until they are exhibited at special occasions. This applies particularly to the huge appliqué *thondrols* that are displayed briefly in the early morning during the annual tsechus. The same iconographical rules apply to the massive *thondrol,* which demonstrates the skills of the Bhutanese tailors.

The inner walls of dzongs and lhakhangs are usually covered with paintings. In Bhutan most wall murals are painted on a thin layer of cloth applied to the wall using a special paste. Nowadays, old paintings are treasured because of their historic and artistic value; however, until quite recently old wall paintings were often repainted or even painted over during restoration work.

Most statues are finely painted to sharply define the facial features, which are individualised for each figure. Many religious statues in lhakhangs, especially the larger statues, are made from unfired clay. In addition to the face, the entire surface of these large figures is painted, often in a gold colour, giving them a bronze aspect. Examples of these statues can be seen in Punakha dzong. On bronze statues, some of which are quite small, only the face is painted.

Statues only gain their sanctity when they are stuffed with texts and juniper incense, blessed and their eyes painted open. You'll sometimes see unfinished statues with bandages around their unpainted eyes.

Textiles

Weaving, more than the other Zorig Chusum, is the most distinctive and sophisticated of the arts and crafts. The richness of this art form can be seen at the permanent exhibition in the National Textile Museum in Thimphu. Everyday articles such as clothing, wrappers for goods, and cushion covers are stitched from cloth woven at home. Until the mid-20th century, certain taxes were paid in cloth and collected at the regional dzong. The authorities distributed the cloth as 'payment' to monastic and civil officials and to monasteries. Until quite recently, it was common to present cloth as a gift to mark special occasions or promotions. Bhutanese women still have trunks filled with fine fabrics that may be sold when money is required.

Paintings and sculptures are usually executed by monks or laymen working in specialist workshops. The disciples of a master, as part of their training, will do all the preliminary work, while the fine work is executed by the master himself.

The non-state-funded Choki Traditional Art School (www .chokischool. com) in Kabesa offers free training to young students from poor families in painting, sculpting and carving. See p66.

TRADITIONAL ARTS

TEXTILE TRAVELS

Watching the mesmerising weaving while appreciating the fine skills and sheer hard work is just part of the fun of chasing traditional textiles. With your guide you can start conversing with the weavers, perhaps picking up a few century-old tricks of the trade. Some friendly bartering is sure to follow. Hand-woven fabric is the most traditional and useful item you can buy in Bhutan. The quality is almost always good, but the price will vary depending on the intricacy of the design and whether any expensive imported silk was used in the weaving. Hand-woven fabric is sold in 'loom lengths' that are 30cm to 45cm wide and 2.5m to 3m long. Bhutanese sew three of these lengths together to make the traditional dress of *gho* and *kira*.

The traditional centres of sophisticated weaving are in eastern Bhutan, especially Dungkhar and Khoma in Lhuentse, Khaling and Radi in Trashigang and Duksum in Trashi Yangtse. Zungney village in Bumthang is the centre for the weaving of wool into strips called *yathra*. For those interested in textiles visits to these places, in addition to Thimphu's new Textile Academy Museum will provide an invaluable insight into Bhutan's cultural identity.

Unlike *thangka* painting, which has very precise religious rules, weaving provides the weaver with an opportunity to express herself. Designs, colours, sizes and even the finish have always reflected the materials available and the changes in technology and fashion. Bhutan's weavers specialise in working additional decorative warps and wefts into the 'ground' fabric. The most elaborate weavings are usually for the traditional *kira* and *gho* and these garments may take up to a year to weave in silk.

Legend states that weaving was introduced to Bhutan by the wife of Songtsen Gampo. Each region has its own weaving traditions and designs, with that of Lhuentse, the ancestral home of the royal family, being the most renowned. The weavers in Lhuentse specialise in decorating *kira* and other textiles with intricate patterns that resemble embroidery. Other parts of eastern Bhutan are famous for their distinctive striped garments woven from raw silk. Bumthang weavers produce another popular fabric – *yathra,* hand-woven strips of woollen cloth, stitched into blankets, jackets, cushion covers and even car seats.

Though *yathra* was traditionally produced on back-strap looms, pedal looms were introduced from Tibet in the mid-20th century, while Indian spinning wheels are faster than the drop spindle. Today, all these technologies can be seen being used by weavers in their homes.

More recently, with assistance from the government, new items such as bags, decorations and even bed and table linen have been developed both for the local and international markets.

> Most weaving in Bhutan is done on a simple back-strap loom, similar to looms found throughout Southeast Asia and Tibet. The loom is easily transported and is ideal for setting up in a warm kitchen, on the porch of a house or beside a tent.

Literature

The development of *jo yig,* the cursive Bhutanese script, as distinct from a Tibetan script, is credited to a monk by the name of Lotsawa Denma Tsemang. However, the Bhutanese script is based on the Tibetan script introduced by Tonmi Sambhota during the reign of the Tibetan king, Songtsen Gampo. For the most part, the literary culture of Bhutan has been dominated by Buddhism; first as a means of translating Buddhist scriptures from Sanskrit, and second as local scholars began to emerge, as a means of developing Himalayan Buddhist thought.

Wood-block printing has been used for centuries and is still the most common form of printing in the monasteries. Blocks are carved in mirror-image, then the printers working in pairs place strips of handmade paper over the inked blocks and a roller passes over the paper. The printed strip is then set aside to dry. The printed books are placed between two boards and wrapped in cloth. There is an excellent exhibition in the National Library, Thimphu, showing the printing process as well as examples of rare texts.

> Bhutan is not immune to the charms of reality TV. In 2010 the winning singer of Druk Star (a local form of *Pop/American Idol*) polled over 240,000 votes to win a Maruti car and three flights to Bangkok.

Music

There are four main traditional instruments in Bhutan, beyond the ritual instruments used in religious ceremonies: the ornate *draymen* or Bhutanese lute, the *pchewang,* with only two strings, *lyem* (bamboo flute) and the *yangchen* (zither) made from hollow wood, with 72 strings which are struck lightly with two thin bamboo sticks.

There are various performers who specialise in folk or religious songs, like Am Thinlay. Jigme Drukpa *(Folk Songs from Bhutan)* performs a wide selection of the two main styles of folk singing: *zhungdra,* which developed in Bhutan in the 17th century and *boedra,* influenced by Tibetan folk music.

There is a series of four CDs from the Monasteries of Bhutan, with the misleading title *Tibetan Buddhist Rites* (John Levy, Lyrichord). This collection includes a wide range of sacred and folk music, including a hauntingly beautiful recording of a *manip* (an itinerant ascetic) recit-

> *Zangtho Pelri* (Tashi Nyencha, 2000), available in Bhutan, has a good selection of traditional songs.

ing a song recollecting the Zhabdrung Ngawang Namgyal's arrival in Bhutan.

Theatre & Dance

The main form of dance is the *cham*, performed at the tsechus and other festivals held throughout Bhutan. Festivals are not quaint re-inventions staged for tourists, but are living manifestations of a long tradition and national faith. For a list of dates of Bhutan's major festivals see p19.

Usually the tsechus are performed in the dzong courtyards. The tsechu is a social event, drawing people from the surrounding districts, and it's also an opportunity to be immersed in Buddhist teachings. The Bhutanese believe that they will create merit by attending the tsechu and watching the performances of ritual dances. Tsechus are not solemn occasions, but are marked by a holiday atmosphere as people put on their finest clothing and jewellery, share their food and exchange news with friends and relatives.

Tsechus are based on a series of dances performed in honour of Guru Rinpoche. The dates and duration of the tsechus vary from one district to another and always take place on or around the 10th day of the Bhutanese calendar, which is dedicated to Guru Rinpoche.

There are three broad categories of dance; the main dances performed are described here.

For a blend of traditional and modern music, look out for the beautiful recording of chants by Lama Gyurme and Jean-Philippe Rykiel, *The Lama's Chants – Songs of Awakening* (Sony, 1994) and *Rain of Blessings* (Real World Records, 2000).

Pacham (Dance of the Heroes)

An energetic dance based on a vision by Pema Linga and is thought to lead believers directly to the presence of Guru Rinpoche.

Shawa Shachi (Dance of the Stag & Hunter)

Based on the story of Milarepa's conversion of the hunter Gonpo Dorji to Buddhism, the dance is split into two parts. The first part is comic, with the hunter preparing to set out on a hunting expedition and his servants joking very irreverently with him. The second part is more serious. The hunter and his dog are in pursuit of a deer when the deer seeks shelter with the yogi Milarepa, identifiable by his white cotton robe, who sings a song that converts all three to Buddhism. The conversion is symbolised by a rope that both the dog and hunter must jump over.

Folk dances are often performed during breaks in the main tsechu performances. The dancers form a circle or a line and move in an intricate series of steps accompanied by graceful arm movements. One person may lead the singing, with the other dancers picking up the song or answering with a refrain.

Dranyeo Cham (Dance with the Dranyen)

This dance celebrates the diffusion of the Drukpa lineage in Bhutan by the Zhabdrung Ngawang Namgyal. The dancers carry swords and wear a circular headdress, felt boots and heavy woollen clothes. One dancer carries a *dranyen*, a string instrument similar to a guitar.

TSECHU & YOU

During the tsechu dances *atsara* (clowns) mimic the dances and perform comic routines wearing masks with long red noses. While entertaining the onlookers, they also help to keep order and have developed the habit of harassing tourists for money. Take it as a good-natured game. If you contribute you may even receive a blessing from the wooden phallus they carry.

Wherever there is dancing you should be willing to take part. Traditionally, everybody, including visitors, enthusiastically takes part in the final dance (*Tashi Lebey*), which concludes all festivities or dance performances. Don't feel shy, just follow the person in front of you and smile!

Sha Na Cham (Black Hat Dance)

This dance, on one level, commemorates the killing of the anti-Buddhist Tibetan king, Langdarma in 842 by the Buddhist monk, Pelkyi Dorji. It also represents the transformation of the dancers into powerful tantric yogis, who take possession of the dancing area and drive out all evil spirits as they stamp the ground.

Pholay Molay (Dance of the Noblemen & Ladies)

This is less a dance than a crude play about the two princesses left with an old couple by two princes who leave for war. The two princesses and an old woman are corrupted by some *atsaras* (clowns). On their return, the princes are furious and punish the women by cutting off their noses. Eventually, everybody is reconciled and the princes marry the princesses.

In Thimphu, the Royal Academy for the Performing Arts (RAPA) trains young Bhutanese dancers and musicians in religious and folk dances. The quality of the dancing is exceptional and the program they offer is breathtaking in its colour and vitality.

Drametsi Nga Cham (Dance of the Drametsi Drummers)

Based on a vision by Kunga Gyeltshen, the son of Pema Lingpa, this dance depicts 100 peaceful and wrathful deities. The dancers wear animal masks and knee-length yellow skirts, and carry a large hand drum in their left hand and a drumstick in their right.

Dungtam (Dance of the Wrathful Deities)

In this dance, the deities are the entourage of one of the eight manifestations of Guru Rinpoche, Dorji Drolo. Dorji Drolo and his entourage are armed with *phurba* (special daggers) that execute and thereby redeem an evil spirit (represented by a small mannequin). This represents Buddhist teachings on the liberation of consciousness from the body.

Raksha Mangcham (Dance of the Rakshas & the Judgement of the Dead)

This is one of the highlights of the tsechu. It represents a spiritual drama as two newly deceased men are brought before the Lord of the Underworld, represented by a large mannequin surrounded by an entourage of *rakshas* (a figure or spirit of the underworld). The first to be judged is a sinner, dressed in black. After hearing from Black Demon and White God, the prosecution and defence, his sins outweigh his good actions and he is dragged to the hell realms. The second figure is dressed in white; again the Lord of the Underworld hears about his good and bad actions, and he is found to be virtuous. After a brief attempt by Black Demon to grab the virtuous man, he is led to the pure lands.

Dzongsar Jamyang Khyentse, a celebrated Bhutanese rinpoche, is the director of the films *The Cup* and *Travellers & Magicians*.

Guru Tshengay (The Eight Manifestations of Guru Rinpoche)

The eight manifestations are different forms of Guru Rinpoche, who is accompanied by his two consorts, Yeshe Tshogyel (on his right) and Mandarava (on his left). This is both a dance and a drama and starts with Dorji Drolo entering the dance area, followed by a long procession with the eight manifestations. For more on the eight manifestations, see p186.

Chhoeshey (Religious Song)

This commemorates the opening of the eastern gate to the pilgrimage site at Tsari in Tibet by Tsangpa Gyarey, the founder of the Drukpa Kagyu.

Architecture

Bhutanese architecture is one of the most striking features of the country. Massive dzongs (fort-monasteries), remote goembas (monasteries) and lhakhangs (temples), as well as the traditional houses all subscribe to a characteristic Bhutanese style. The lack of written plans, however, means there are many variations and very few structures sharing the same design. There are also regional variations dictated by local topography and available building materials.

Houses

The style of Bhutanese houses varies depending on the location, particularly the elevation. Thatched bamboo houses predominate in the lower altitudes in the south of the country, whereas at very high altitudes most homes are simple stone structures or even yak-hair tents. Houses in the inner-Himalayan zone, such as those around Paro and Thimphu, are built in a characteristic Bhutanese style oddly reminiscent of Swiss chalets.

A typical Bhutanese house is two storeys high with a large, airy attic used for storage. In rural areas the ground floor is always used as a barn and the upper floor as the living quarters. In most houses, one elaborately decorated room called a *choesum* serves as a chapel.

Bhutanese long-drop toilets hang precariously off the side of the upper story of old houses and goembas.

In central and eastern Bhutan the walls are usually made of stone. In the west the walls are made of compacted earth, an extremely strong and durable structure.

On the lower floor, an opening for a door, and perhaps some windows, is left in the earth wall that forms the front of the house, which traditionally faces south. The upper floor is supported by wooden beams that fit into holes in the mud wall. Central columns support the beams, because it is difficult to find a single piece of timber to span the entire width of the house. The earthen walls for the upper floor

Magnificent Monasteries

» Taktshang (Tiger's Nest) Goemba

» Tango and Cheri goembas

» Kyichu Lhakhang

» Chimi Lhakhang

» Kurjey Lhakhang

POUNDING THE WALLS

The massive compacted earth walls of typical western Bhutanese houses are 80cm to 100cm thick. To build these walls, a wooden frame is constructed then filled with mud. The mud is compacted by being pounded with wooden poles to which a flat ram is attached. When the wall reaches the top of the frame, the frame is shifted upwards and the process begins again.

The pounders are usually teams of women, who sing and dance as they beat the walls. Although Bhutanese women are usually shy and modest with outsiders, they traditionally loosen their inhibitions and exchange ribald comments with men as they perform the pounding, which can take several weeks for a large house. Once the mud wall is finished, it is either left in its natural colour or is whitewashed.

Typical Bhutanese House

Shingled roof weighed down with stones

Wooden phallus tied under the eaves

Elaborate wooden cornice

Top storey – living quarters

Bottom storey – often used to store grain and house livestock

Prayer flag (goendhar)

Airy attic used for storage and drying chillis

Traditional ornate wooden windows

Garuda (jachung) with snake in its teeth

Phallus decoration

Many houses are decorated with carved wooden phalluses, often crossed by a sword, which are hung at the four corners of the roof or over the door to ward off evil.

form only the rear wall and back half of the two side exterior walls. The front portion of the living area is always built of timber, which is sometimes elaborately decorated, with large divided windows facing south. The wooden portion of the house extends out over the front and side earthen walls.

In older houses the windows are sliding wooden panels, not glass. Above all, windows in Bhutan comprise a cut-out of a curved trefoil motif, called a *horzhing*. In Bhutan there are often several explanations for everything, and this motif is said to be either of Persian influence or simply a practical design that allows a person to look out of the window while the smoke blows out through the opening above their head.

An elaborate wooden cornice is usually built along the top of the wall directly under the roof of the house. Traditional roofs are pitched and covered with wooden shingles (often weighed down by large stones as safeguards from the wind), but shingles need to be replaced frequently and many people now choose corrugated sheet metal for their roofs. A feature missing in tradition Bhutanese architecture is a gutter – unless a retro-fitted plastic gutter has been installed, expect a soaking when you enter or leave a house during rain.

The internal walls, and often parts of the external walls, are built with a timber frame that is filled in with woven bamboo and plastered with mud. This construction is called *shaddam* (weave-mud).

The heavy wooden doors are made from several planks held firmly together using a tongue-and-groove technique. This technique is used to fit together all the woodwork, and not a single nail is used in a traditional structure. The door hinge is a pair of wooden pegs that fit into round holes above and below the doorframe.

A large space is left below the roof. This serves as a place for storing hay or for drying animal skins and chillies. In winter the hay helps insulate the house. Sometimes woven bamboo mats seal the attic, but often it is simply left open-sided.

Stairways to the upper floors and attic are often crude ladders made by carving steps into a whole tree trunk. If you find yourself climbing one of these ladders, reach around behind the right edge and you may find a groove cut there to serve as a handrail.

After a house is built, the all-important decoration begins. Wooden surfaces are painted with various designs, each with a special significance. Swastikas, floral patterns representing the lotus, cloud whirls and the *tashi tagye* (eight auspicious symbols) are the most common. Beside the front door are larger paintings, often of mythical animals such as the *garuda,* or large red phalluses. The phallus is not a fertility symbol; it is associated with the Lama Drukpa Kunley (see p92) and believed to ward off evil. A prayer flag called a *goendhar* is erected on the centre of the roof of all Buddhist homes.

Dzongs

Bhutan's dzongs are perhaps the most visibly striking architectural aspect of the kingdom. They are outstanding examples of grand design and construction. These huge, white citadels dominate the major towns and serve as the administrative headquarters of all 20 *dzongkhags* (districts) and the focus of secular and religious authority in each.

As well as the large, active district dzongs, there are a few dzongs that have been destroyed or abandoned, or are now used for other purposes, such as Simtokha Dzong (p68), south of Thimphu, and Dobji

Don't-Miss Dzongs

» Punakha Dzong (p91)

» Paro Dzong (p73)

» Trongsa Dzong (p110)

» Trashi Chhoe Dzong, Thimphu (p45)

» Wangdue Phodrang Dzong (p87)

Dzong

Fortress-temple building shared between administrative offices and monastic quarters

Main courtyard (*dochey*)

Temples (lhakhangs) & monks' quarters

Government offices

Central tower (*utse*)

DEFENDING THE DZONG

During the time of Zhabdrung Ngawang Namgyal (1594–1651), the dzongs served their primary function – as fortresses – well, and each was the stronghold of a *penlop* (regional governor). Many of the feuds and battles for control during the 17th to 20th centuries were waged by *penlops* whose troops attacked neighbouring dzongs. The key to success in these battles was to capture the dzong of the opposing *penlop*, thereby gaining control of that district. Dzongs often feature defensive windows with firing positions and usually have only one massive door, which leads into a small passage that makes two right-angle turns before it enters the main courtyard. This is a design feature to obstruct invaders from storming the dzong.

According to tradition, no woman can be in a dzong between sunset and sunrise. This tradition has only been broken once, when the former Indian prime minister, Indira Gandhi, stayed in Trashi Chhoe Dzong, in Thimphu, after receiving special permission from the Je Khenpo.

Dzong, south of Chhuzom. Not all dzongs are ancient monuments; for example, a new dzong was built in Trashi Yangtse in eastern Bhutan in 1997.

Many dzongs had a *ta dzong* (watchtower), which was either part of the building, as in Jakar Dzong (p114), or a separate structure, as in Paro (p73) and Trongsa Dzongs (p110). This structure was also used as an ammunition store and dungeon. Many dzongs were accessed by cantilever bridges as an additional protective measure. Most dzongs have inward-sloping walls, an architectural feature known as battered walls, which can fool the eye and make the building look imposing and larger than its actual dimensions.

Bhutan's dzongs were built of stone or pounded mud, and a considerable amount of timber, including massive beams and wooden shingle roofs. This, combined with the large number of butter lamps used in temples, has caused fires in almost all dzongs. All important dzongs have been (or are being) rebuilt using traditional construction methods, though in many places corrugated-iron roofs have replaced wooden shingles.

Bhutanese proclaim proudly that no nails are used to construct dzongs. Furthermore, dzong architects don't prepare any plans or drawings. They rely only on a mental concept of what is to be built, and this was how Thimphu's Trashi Chhoe Dzong was reconstructed in 1966.

Each dzong has unique details, but most follow the same general design principles. Most dzongs are divided into two wings: one containing temples and monks' quarters and one for government offices. The monastic wing of many dzongs actually serves as a monastery, with the resident monk body called a *rabdey*. In early days, most dzongs had a *rabdey,* but today only the dzongs of Thimphu, Punakha, Paro, Mongar, Trongsa, Jakar and Trashigang serve as monasteries. The *dratshang* (central monk body) maintains monastic schools in the dzongs of Punakha, Trongsa and Paro. Punakha Dzong is the seat of the Chief Abbot, His Holiness the Je Khenpo.

SIEGE

Because dzongs were usually placed on ridges, a tunnel was often constructed to the nearest water supply so that those in the dzong could survive a long siege.

The main courtyard of the dzong is the *dochey,* which is paved with large flagstones. Along the outer walls of the dzong are several storeys of rooms and galleries overlooking the paved courtyard; these rooms are the monks' quarters and classrooms. Because the monastic wing of the dzong is physically separate from the secular wing, many dzongs have two *docheys,* the second being surrounded by administrative offices.

The central structure of the dzong is the towerlike building called the *utse.* In most dzongs, the *utse* has a series of chapels, one on each floor. On the ground floor of the *utse* is the lhakhang.

Goembas & Lhakhangs

In Dzongkha, a monastery is called a goemba, and the word is pronounced quite differently from the corresponding Tibetan word, *gompa*. A primary reason for selecting the location of a monastery is to have a remote location where the monks can find peace and solitude. This is particularly evident in Bhutan where goembas are built atop rocky crags or on remote hillsides.

Several goembas in Bhutan were built at sacred caves that had previously been places of meditation. Taktshang in Paro (p82) and Kurjey in Bumthang (p121) are two famous examples that were built around caves where Guru Rinpoche meditated for extended periods.

All Bhutanese goembas are different, but they all possess certain common features. They are self-contained communities, with a central lhakhang and separate quarters for sleeping. The lhakhang is at the centre of a *dochey,* similar to that of the dzongs, which is used as a dance arena during festivals.

On all religious buildings in Bhutan, and on dzongs too, a painted red band called a *khemar* runs just below the roof. One or more circular brass plates or mirrors representing the *nima* (sun) are often placed on the *khemar*.

A typical lhakhang has a cupola and a gilded bell-shaped ornament, called a *serto,* on the roof. Most have a paved *kora* path around the circumference of the building. On the outside wall are racks of prayer wheels, which monks and devotees spin as they circumambulate the building.

The entrance to the lhakhang is through the *gorikha* (porch), which is covered with murals, usually depicting the Guardians of the Four Directions or a wheel of life. Entry is via a large painted wooden door that is often protected by a heavy cloth or yak-hair curtain. The door

One way that lhakhangs in Bhutan differ from those in Tibet is that they feature a pair of elephant tusks alongside the altar to symbolise good. Buddhists revere the elephant because when the Buddha was born, his mother had a vision of a white elephant.

ARCHITECTURE GOEMBAS & LHAKHANGS

Goemba

Self-contained monastery community, with a central temple (lhakhang) and separate living quarters

Painted red band called a *khemar* with circular brass plates representing the sun

Entry vestibule where you'll find murals of the four guardian kings, symbols of longevity and a wheel of life

Pilgrims walk around the monastery clockwise, turning prayer wheels

Prayer wheels on the outer walls

Paintings or statues of the Guardians (or Kings), of the Four Directions appear on the *gorikha* (veranda) to guard the entrance to most lhakhangs. The guardians have an origin in ancient Mongolian tradition, and each one holds a different object. They are warriors who guard the world against demons and earthly threats.

Chenmizang, the red king of the west, holds a chorten and a snake, and is the lord of the *nagas* (serpents).

Yulkhorsung, the white king of the east, plays the lute and is the lord of celestial musicians.

Namthose, the gold king of the north, holds a mongoose and a banner of victory. He is a god of wealth and prosperity.

Phagchepo, the blue king of the south, holds a sword in his right hand.

opens to a *tshokhang* (assembly hall), also called a *dukhang* or *kunre*. The hall is usually so large that it has rows of pillars to hold up the roof, and the walls are storyboards of Buddhist paintings.

The following are often depicted at the entrance to goembas:

» The Wheel of Life, which is held and turned by Yama, Lord of Death; it is a representation of the cycle of samsara, separating loved ones and leading to rebirth.

» The inner circle depicts a cockerel (representing desire or attachment) biting a pig (ignorance or delusion) biting a snake (hatred or anger). Surrounding this is a band of figures ascending and descending according to their karma. Outside this are six segments, each depicting the six realms of samsara or rebirth. And outside this are the 12 segments that depict the 12 links of dependant origination representing the processes by which we all live, die and are reborn.

» The Six Symbols of Longevity (Tshering Samdrup) are of Chinese origin and include an old man, peach tree, conch-shell-shaped rock, river, cranes (usually a pair) and a deer.

» The geometric poem set in a grid of squares is dedicated to the Zhabdrung.

To prevent potentially destructive fires in monasteries and lhakhangs, arrays of ritual butter lamps are often burned in a separate small building. All lhakhangs now have smoke detectors; listen for the beeps.

At the far end of the *tshokhang* is an elaborately decorated altar *(choesum)* that can be part of the main room or else be housed in a separate room or lhakhang. The two-tiered *choesum*, with its large gilded statue, is a focal point of the lhakhang, and depending on when and why the lhakhang was built, the statue may be of Sakyamuni, Guru Rinpoche or another figure. Jampa is the central figure in many lhakhangs built before Guru Rinpoche's visits to Bhutan.

On a monastery or chapel altar, you'd see sacred rocks with self-arisen (Rangjung) hand or footprints; a ewer of holy water with a peacock feather in it; a mandala-shaped offering of seeds; a pair of dice used to divine the future; dried seeds; plus elephant tusks and seven bowls of water, referring to the seven first footsteps of Buddha or the first seven ordained monks at Samye in Tibet. On the altar you will also see delicately carved and usually garishly coloured *torma*, made from sugar, butter and flour.

The halls often have cymbals, conch shell *(dungkhar)*, oboes *(jaling)*, and long telescopic trumpets known as *dungchen*. The altar often has the bell (drilbu) and thunderbolt *(dorji)*, Tantric implements that symbolise wisdom and compassion. Plus libraries of traditional texts.

In most lhakhangs, often on the upper floor, is a chapel called a *goenkhang*, which is devoted to the protective deities (see p223). The statues in these rooms are usually covered except when rituals are per-

FIRES

formed. Weapons are stored in this room and may include old muskets, armour, and round shields made from rhinoceros hide. Teams of archers sometimes sleep in a *goenkhang* before a major match, but women are never allowed to enter and the monks are often reluctant to allow entry to any visitors.

Chortens

A chorten is literally a receptacle for offerings, and in Bhutan all chortens contain religious relics. Chortens are often situated in locations considered inauspicious – river junctions, crossroads, mountain passes and bridges – to ward off evil. The classical chorten shape is based on the ancient Indian form of a stupa. Each of the chorten's five architectural elements has a symbolic meaning. The square or rectangular base symbolises earth. The hemispherical dome symbolises water. The conical or pyramidal spire symbolises fire (the spire has 13 steplike segments that symbolise the 13 steps leading to Buddhahood). On top is a crescent moon and a sun, symbolising air, and a vertical spike symbolising ether or the sacred light of the Buddha. Inside is placed a carved wooden pole called a *sokshing*, which is the life-spirit of the chorten.

Some chortens, such as the National Memorial Chorten in Thimphu (p48), are built in memory of an individual. Others commemorate the visit of a saint or contain sacred books or the bodies of saints or great lamas. Bhutan has three basic styles of chorten, usually characterised as Bhutanese, Tibetan and Nepali.

The Nepali-style chorten is based on the classical stupa. On Nepali chortens the four sides of the tower are painted with a pair of eyes, the all-seeing eyes of Buddha. The prototypes for the Nepali chortens in

Wooden roofing shingles typically last about three years before they need replacing, hence the practical and ecological, but not necessarily aesthetic, shift to corrugated-iron roofing.

Chorten

Originally built to house relics of the Buddha, chortens now often contain sacred texts, relics and sometimes even mummified bodies

Pinnacle (symbolising enlightenment)

Spire (symbolising fire with 13 steps which also represent the 13 steps leading to Buddhahood)

Hemispherical dome (symbolising water)

Crescent moon and sun

Square base (symbolising earth)

Bhutan are Swayambhunath and Bodhnath in Kathmandu. The large Chorten Kora (p142) in Trashi Yangtse and Chendebji Chorten (p108) near Trongsa are two examples of the Nepali style of chorten.

The Tibetan-style chorten has a shape similar to the stupa, but the rounded part flares outward instead of being a dome shape. Thimphu's National Memorial Chorten is an excellent example of this style.

When approaching a chorten or *mani* wall, always walk to the left.

The Bhutanese design comprises a square stone pillar with a *khemar* near the top. The exact origin of this style is not known, but is believed to be a reduced form of the classical stupa, with only the pinnacle and square base. Some Bhutanese chortens have a ball and crescent representing the moon and sun on top.

Several other types of chorten are also found in Bhutan. The *khonying* (two legs) is an archway that forms a gate over a trail. Travellers earn merit by passing through the structure, which is decorated with interior wall paintings and a mandala on the roof. The *mani chukor* is shaped like a Bhutanese chorten but is hollow and contains a large prayer wheel. It is often built over or near a stream so that the water turns a wooden turbine below the structure, which then turns the prayer wheel.

Mountains & Valleys

Bhutan occupies a fascinating corner of the globe. Scientists have long considered the eastern Himalaya to be an area critically important in terms of global biological diversity. Add to this the legacy of isolation, the sheer inaccessibility of much of the country, low human population and a traditional reverence for nature, and you have the ingredients for a singular showcase of nature conservation within a region increasingly impacted by overpopulation and indiscriminate development.

The Lie of the Land

Bhutan is a landlocked country about 300km long and 150km wide, encompassing 46,500 sq km. It is bounded on the northwest and north by Tibet, and the remainder by India: on the east by the state of Arunachal Pradesh; on the south by Assam and West Bengal; and on the west by Sikkim. Tibet's Chumbi valley, the old trade and expedition route from India to Lhasa, lies between the northern parts of Bhutan and Sikkim.

Virtually the entire country is mountainous, and ranges in elevation from 100m to the 7541m Gangkhar Puensum peak on the Tibetan border. It can be divided into three major geographic regions: the high or Greater Himalaya of the north; the hills and valleys of the Inner Himalaya; and the foothills and plains of the south.

Greater Himalaya

A range of high Himalayan peaks forms much of the northern and western borders of Bhutan. These are the thrones of the gods; almost none has been climbed, many are virtually unexplored and some are not even named. There are several high mountain passes that cross the Himalaya, but for the most part it remains an impenetrable snow-clad barrier (20% of the country is under perpetual snow). The Himalayan range extends from Jhomolhari (7314m) in the west to Kulha Gangri (7554m), near the centre point of the northern border. A chain of lower peaks extends eastwards to the Indian state of Arunachal Pradesh.

The Lunana region, just south of the midpoint of Bhutan's border with Tibet, is an area of glacial peaks and high valleys that are snowbound during the winter. A range of high peaks forms the southern boundary of Lunana, isolating it from the rest of the country.

Inner Himalaya

South of the high peaks is an area of broad and deep valleys and steep forested hills ranging from 1100m to 3500m in elevation. This is the largest region of Bhutan and all the major towns, including Thimphu, are here. This region is a labyrinth of deep ravines formed by fast-

The Bhutan Trust Fund for Environmental Conservation (www .bhutantrust fund.bt) uses its investment revenue to finance conservation activities and environmental awareness and management.

Geology of the Bhutan Himalaya by Augusto Gansser is a large-format book that comprehensively describes Bhutan's geology.

flowing rivers. The hillsides are generally too steep for farming, and so most have remained covered in virgin forest.

The greater part of Bhutan's western border is formed by the Himalayan range, including the peaks of Jhomolhari and Jichu Drakye (6989m). Several forested ridges extend eastwards from this range, and these define the large valleys of Thimphu, Paro, Haa and Samtse. Between Punakha and Thimphu lies a well-defined ridge that forms the watershed between Thimphu's Wang Chhu and Punakha's Puna Tsang Chhu. The east–west road crosses this ridge through a 3050m pass, the Dochu La.

A range called the Black Mountains lies to the east of the Puna Tsang Chhu watershed, forming the major barrier between eastern and western Bhutan. Pele La (3500m) is the most important pass across the Black Mountains.

A north–south range of hills separates the Trongsa and Bumthang valley systems. The road crosses this ridge via Yotong La (3425m). Further east, the Donga range of hills follows the border that separates the Bumthang and Lhuentse districts, with Thrumshing La (3780m) as the crossing point for the road. Eastern Bhutan, which encompasses most of the Manas Chhu watershed, lies to the east of this range.

Millions of years ago the space Bhutan now occupies was an open expanse of water, part of the shallow Tethys Sea. The Tibetan plateau, or 'roof of the world', was beachfront property.

Mighty Rivers

Rivers, or *chhus,* play an important role in Bhutan's geography, and their enormous potential for hydroelectric power has helped shape the economy. Flowing south, they have created deep valleys, making all east–west travel a tedious process of steep winding descent followed by an equally steep, equally winding climb to the next ridge. There are four major river systems in Bhutan, most known by several names as they flow through the country.

Most of the rivers have their headwaters in the high mountains of Bhutan, but the Himalaya range is not a continental divide, and there are three rivers that actually flow through the mountains into the country. The Amo Chhu flows from Tibet's Chumbi valley across the southwestern corner of Bhutan, where it becomes the Torsa Chhu, and exits at Phuentsholing. Two tributaries of the Manas, in eastern Bhutan, originate outside the country. The Kuri Chhu has its headwaters in Tibet (where it is known as the Lhobrak Chhu) and crosses into Bhutan at an elevation of only 1200m; the other tributary, the Gamri Chhu, rises in India's Arunachal Pradesh.

THE DUARS

The southern foothills rapidly drop down to the great plain of India, and with the great rivers flowing from the north they comprise a region of lush fertile valleys known as the *duars. Duar* is a Sanskrit word meaning 'passes' or 'gates', and is the origin of the English 'door'. Before the British annexed Bhutan's southern regions each *duar* was under the control of a Bhutanese *dzongpen* (lord of the dzong), but as they were malaria-infested they were largely unoccupied by the Bhutanese, who stayed in the northern hills.

Each *duar* is named after a river valley that leads out of Bhutan, though the *duar* itself is actually the land between two rivers. The land ranges from an elevation of about 100m to almost sea level at the Brahmaputra River, and the slope is barely perceptible.

Seven of the *duars* abut the border of Assam between the Dhansiri (Durlah) and Manas Rivers. The remaining 11, from the Manas River to the Teesta River in the east, border on the state of West Bengal.

THE BLUE POPPY

The blue poppy, Bhutan's national flower, is a delicate blue- or purple-tinged bloom with a white filament. In Dzongkha it is known by the name *euitgel metog hoem*. It grows to nearly 1m tall, on the rocky mountain terrain found above the treeline (3500m to 4500m). The flowering season occurs during the early monsoon, from late May to July, and the seeds yield oil. Adding to its mystery, fascination and appeal with plant lovers is its strange flowering behaviour. It takes several years to grow, then it eventually flowers for the first and last time, produces seeds, and dies. Poppies can be found atop some high passes from the far eastern parts of the country all the way across to the west.

At one time the blue poppy was considered to be a Himalayan myth, along with the yeti. In 1933 a British botanist, George Sherriff, who was in Bhutan studying Himalayan flora, found the plant in the remote mountain region of Sakten in eastern Bhutan. Despite this proof that the flower exists, few people have seen one; a mystique surrounds the species in the same way it does the snow leopard.

The Thimphu Chhu, known in its lower reaches as the Wang Chhu, powers the Chhukha and Tala hydroelectric projects and eventually becomes the Raidak River in India. The Pho Chhu and Mo Chhu join at Punakha to form the Puna Tsang Chhu, which drains the area between the Dochu La and the Black Mountains. This river is known as the Sankosh when it reaches India. The Manas is Bhutan's largest river, draining about two-thirds of the country; in its upper reaches it is known as the Drangme Chhu. The Mangde Chhu flows from Trongsa and joins the Manas Chhu just before it flows into India.

All of Bhutan's rivers eventually flow through the *duar*s to become part of the Brahmaputra, which is known in Tibet as the Yarlung Tsampo, with a source near Mt Kailash in the far west.

Because the central Himalaya of Bhutan receives the full brunt of the monsoon, Bhutan's rivers are larger and have created much broader valleys than rivers further to the west in Nepal and India. In their upper reaches, most Bhutanese rivers have created large fertile valleys such as those of Paro, Punakha, Thimphu, Haa and Bumthang. As the rivers pass through the centre of Bhutan, the valleys become steeper and narrower, and roads have to climb high on the hillside. In eastern Bhutan the Manas valley is generally broader, and some roads run alongside the river itself.

When they reach the plains, the rivers drop much of the glacial silt they have collected and follow a meandering course over gravel streambeds. There are several oxbow lakes in the plains where rivers have changed their course over the years.

You can easily distinguish the chir pine from its relative, the blue pine, because the needles of the chir pine are in groups of three and those of the blue pine are shorter and in groups of five.

Bhutan's Green Vault

An astonishing array of plants grows in Bhutan: over 5000 species, including more than 600 species of orchid, 300 species of medicinal plants and about 46 species of spectacular rhododendrons. Few countries could boast the variety of habitats from tropical jungle to alpine tundra in such a compact area. Because glaciation had no impact on the lower reaches of the Himalaya, these foothills remain repositories of plants whose origins can be traced back before the ice age. This area is home to some of the most ancient species of vegetation on earth.

Trees and Shrubs of Nepal and the Himalayas by Adrian and Jimmie Storrs is the best field guide to the forests of Bhutan.

Forests are found up to 4500m and serve not only as a source of fuel, timber and herbs, but also as a cultural resource, as they form the basis of many folk songs and ritual offerings. Though the government policy is to maintain at least 60% of the land as forest, the present ratio is higher, with about 65% of the country covered in forests of conifers and mixed broadleaf species.

Warm & Wet Tropics

Tropical evergreen forests growing below 800m are unique repositories of biodiversity, but much of the rich vegetation at these lower elevations has been cleared for pasture and terraced farmland. In the next vegetation zone (900m to 1800m) are the subtropical grasslands, including the fragrant lemon grass, and forests of chir pine, oak, walnut and sal. Above groves of bamboo, numerous varieties of orchid and fern grace the branches of forest giants.

Between March and May the hill-sides are ablaze with the deep red flowers of the *etho metho*, the country's most famous rhodo-dendron. Ranging from small shrubs to 20m trees, 46 species of rhododendron occur throughout the country.

Deep & Dark Forests

The tropical vegetation of the lower altitudes gives way to the diverse, dense and dark forests of oak, birch, maple, magnolia and laurel of the temperate zone (1800m to 3500m). On most hills, the sunny south side is takes on many shades of green with a variety of broadleaf species. The damp, shady north side displays a more ominous appearance with blue pine and soaring deodars and firs festooned with old man's beard. Spring is the time to see the magnificent red- or cream-flowering rhodo-dendrons of Bhutan that feature particularly on the mountain passes of Dochu La, Pele La and Yotung La. In the autumn you will see the mauve or pinkish blooms of the Himalayan wild cherry.

Alpine Flower Meadows

Between the treeline and the snowline at about 5500m are found low shrubs, dwarf rhododendrons and flowering herbs. Junipers are also found in a dwarfed form at altitudes over 4000m. Their distinctive foliage, short prickly needles and fleshy, berrylike fruit, is unmistakable.

Wild Rhododendrons of Bhutan by Rebecca Pradhan is a beautiful guide to Bhutan's rhododendrons, with photographs of all 46 species.

As the snows begin to melt at the end of the long winter, the high-altitude grazing lands are carpeted with a kaleidoscope of wildflowers, which remain in bloom until early summer. After the onset of the monsoon, in July, a second and even more vibrant flowering occurs, which extends until late August. Some of the magnificent blooms found at these higher elevations include anemones, forget-me-nots, dwarf irises, primulas, delphiniums and ranunculus.

Environmental Challenges

Bhutan emerged into the 20th century with much of its forests and eco-systems intact. But now, with an increasing population, improved and expanding roads and limited farming land, a major effort is required to protect the country's natural heritage.

POACHING IN SHANGRI LA

While the Bhutanese generally observe their own conservation policies, the open southern and northern borders offer opportunities for poaching of both plant and animal life. Many species are sought for their alleged medicinal or other valuable properties. Killing and poaching are unacceptable in Buddhist tradition, but the high prices that wildlife products such as rhino horn, tiger bone, musk and caterpillar fungus (see p246) command outside Bhutan present major challenges to conservationists.

The Department of Forestry Services (DFS) operates effective antipoaching programs designed to protect endangered plants and animals, enforce forestry rules and control trade in wildlife parts and products. A national network of foresters regulates timber harvesting, and road checkpoints are operated throughout the country to monitor the transportation of forest products.

Growing awareness of environmental issues has prompted appropriate conservation measures. Among these are requirements for environmental assessments for all new public or private investment projects, and nationwide bans on the commercial export of raw timber and the use of plastic bags. Bhutan has consciously decided to forego immediate economic gain from exploitation of its natural resources in order to preserve its environment for long-term sustainable benefits.

Firewood

Wood is used as fuel in rural areas and in most monasteries (in urban areas cooking gas or kerosene is used) and Bhutan's per capita consumption of firewood is one of the highest in the world. It was probably only Bhutan's low population that spared the forests before conservation planning was introduced. Managing firewood harvesting is a major problem in the remote regions, and while wood accounts for almost 80% of energy consumption, the government is actively promoting and providing electricity as an alternative source of energy.

Grazing & Farming

Conservation issues centre on human–wildlife conflicts, such as crop and livestock depredation by wild predators, and the deterioration of high-altitude wildlife habitat from grazing pressure. There are government and NGO programs under way to balance the needs of traditional herders and farmers with wildlife protection.

A significant amount of shifting cultivation ('slash and burn', called *tseri* in Dzongkha) is practised in Bhutan, particularly in the east. The practice is officially banned and several methods, including education and fertiliser supply, are being implemented to change this practice.

In the international market *Cordyceps sinensis* (caterpillar fungus) can fetch up to US$10,000 a kilogram!

Wildlife & Sanctuaries

Wildlife

Bhutan features a tremendous diversity of plants and animals living in a range of ecosystems from subtropical jungle barely above sea level to snowbound mountains above 7500m. The country's various habitats are believed to contain close to 200 species of mammals and over 600 species of birds.

Mammals & Birds

Large mammals abound in the wilds of Bhutan, but unless you are trekking or until Royal Manas National Park is opened up you will be very lucky to see more than a few examples. The neighbourhood of Royal Manas is home to a large variety of well-known south Asian game species: water buffalo, gaur, serow, wild pig and several species of deer: sambar, muntjac, chital, and hog. It is also the best place to see Asian elephants and the very rare greater one-horned rhinoceros.

While trekking on the high trails you may well be lucky enough to spot herds of blue sheep, or bharal. Blue sheep are goat-antelopes, taxonomically somewhere between goats and sheep, that turn a bluish grey in winter and are found from 1800m to 4300m. Other mammals that prefer the high life include wolves, yaks and the diminutive, unusual musk deer. The male's musk gland is a highly valued perfume ingredient and this secretive deer is a target for indiscriminate poaching. Fat marmots whistle as you pass their burrows in the high alpine pastures and the curious takins (see p247) can be seen in northwestern and far northeastern Bhutan. However, the most likely place to see a takin is in the Motithang Takin Preserve in Thimphu (see p53).

Monkeys

Several species of monkey are found in Bhutan and some of these are active throughout the day and may be seen not far from villages or a main road – so keep an eye on the roadside trees on those long drives. Most common are the Assamese macaques: reddish-brown, stumpy-tailed monkeys travelling on the ground in troops of 10 to 50 individuals. They are found throughout Bhutan up to 2900m. Rhesus macaques are similar and are the dominant monkey of the Indian plains. In Bhutan the bold rhesus is confined to the southern foothills.

Langurs are elegant, arboreal monkeys with graceful limbs and extraordinarily long tails and a charismatic presence. Three species of langur make a home in Bhutan's forests – up to 3600m in altitude, and usually high up in the forest canopy. The common grey or Hanuman langur is found west of Pele La; the capped langur is found east of the

Best Places to Spot Wildlife

» Bomdeling – capped langurs

» Jhomolhari trek – blue sheep

» Kori La – hornbills, barbets and more

» Phobjikha valley– black-necked cranes

» Zhemgang – golden langurs

The most authoritative and complete guide to Bhutan's mammals, their identification, behaviour and distribution is *A Field Guide to the Mammals of Bhutan* by Tashi Wangchuk.

The reason for selecting the takin as the national animal is based both on its uniqueness and its strong association with the country's religious history and mythology. When the great saint Lama Drukpa Kunley, the Divine Madman, visited Bhutan in the 15th century, a large congregation of devotees gathered from around the country to witness his magical powers. The people urged the lama to perform a miracle.

However, the saint, in his usual unorthodox and outrageous way (see p92), demanded that he first be served a whole cow and a goat for lunch. He devoured these with relish and left only the bones. After letting out a large and satisfied burp, he took the goat's head and stuck it onto the bones of the cow. And then with a snap of his fingers he commanded the strange beast to rise up and graze on the mountainside. To the astonishment of the people the animal arose and ran up to the meadows to graze. This animal came to be known as the *dong gyem tsey* (takin) and to this day these clumsy-looking animals can be seen grazing on the mountainsides of Bhutan.

The takin continues to befuddle taxonomists. The famous biologist George Schaller called it a 'beestung moose'. In summer, takins migrate to subalpine forests and alpine meadows above 3700m to graze on luxuriant grasses, herbs and shrubs. By migrating they escape the leeches, mosquitoes, horseflies and other parasites of the monsoon-swept lower valleys. This is also the time when the alpine vegetation is richest in nutrition and takins gain weight easily: some males become massive, weighing as much as 1 tonne or more. Summer is also the time when takins mate. The gestation period is between seven and eight months, and young – usually a single calf – are born between December and February. Sometimes the Himalayan black bear will follow a pregnant takin and immediately after she has given birth, chase her away and eat the calf.

In late August takins start their slow descent to the lower valleys where the herds begin to break up. They arrive at the winter grazing grounds in temperate broadleaf forests between 2000m and 3000m by late October.

Hunting is banned by law and poaching is limited since there is no high economic value placed on the body parts of the takin. In traditional medicine, however, the horn of the takin, consumed in minute amounts, is supposed to help women during a difficult childbirth.

The major threats that the takin faces are competition with domestic yaks for grazing in the alpine meadows and the loss of habitat in the temperate forests.

Manas Chhu in eastern Bhutan, while the famous golden langur is only found from the Puna Tsang Chhu in the west to the Manas Chhu in the east. Keep an eye out for troupes of them on the drive from Trongsa to Zhemgang. This beautiful primate's existence was not even known to the scientific community until the 20th century. Not surprisingly, its distinctive feature is its lustrous golden coat.

The grey, golden and capped langurs have a specially adapted stomach for digesting forest leaves and are not an agricultural pest.

Bhutanese Tales of the Yeti by Kunzang Choden describes Bhutanese beliefs about where and how this mysterious creature may live.

Big Cats

Several species of cat, ranging from the moggy-sized jungle cat to the powerful tiger, prowl the forests, valleys and mountains of Bhutan. The other cats are the Asiatic golden cat, marbled cat, pallas cat, leopard cat, fishing cat, lynx, clouded leopard, common leopard and the enigmatic snow leopard.

Several tiger-conservation measures have been implemented in Bhutan and, coupled with the strong protected-areas system, has provided a favourable environment for the animal. It is believed the protected regions of Bhutan and India provide sufficient habitat to sustain viable breeding populations.

YETI

WILDLIFE & SANCTUARIES WILDLIFE

Wangchuck Centennial Park
Size 3763 sq km
Bhutan's newest and second-largest national park was inaugurated in 2008. This high-altitude park links Jigme Dorji National Park with Bomdeling Wildlife Sanctuary and protects the headwaters of four major rivers as well as snow-leopard and takin habitat.

Jigme Dorji National Park
Size 4329 sq km
The largest protected area in Bhutan with habitats ranging from subtropical (1400m) to alpine (7000m), it protects several endangered species, including takins, snow leopards, and tigers. Villagers farm and harvest indigenous plants in the park.

Torsa Strict Nature Reserve
Size 644 sq km
Torsa Reserve is located where the Torsa River enters from Tibet. The reserve was set aside to protect the temperate forests and alpine meadows and is the only protected area with no resident human population.

Thanza

Gasa

Punakha

THIMPHU

Trongsa

Paro

Wangdue Phodrang

Haa

Chhukha

Dagana

Sibsu

Chengmari

Damphu

Lamidranga

Samtse

Phuentsholing

Sarpang

Gelephu

Kalikhola

Jigme Singye Wangchuck National Park
Size 1400 sq km
Protecting the Black Mountains that separate eastern and western Bhutan, it harbours tigers, Himalayan black bears, red pandas and golden langurs. An amazing 450 species of birds have been catalogued. The Phobjikha valley, wintering place of black-necked cranes, is included in the park.

I N D I A
(A S S A M)

Phibsoo Wildlife Sanctuary
Size 278 sq km
On the southern border of Bhutan, it was established to protect the only remaining natural sal forest in Bhutan. Several protected species thrive here, including chital deer, elephants, gaurs, tigers, golden langurs and hornbills.

Protected Areas

Biological Corridors

WILDLIFE & SANCTUARIES WILDLIFE

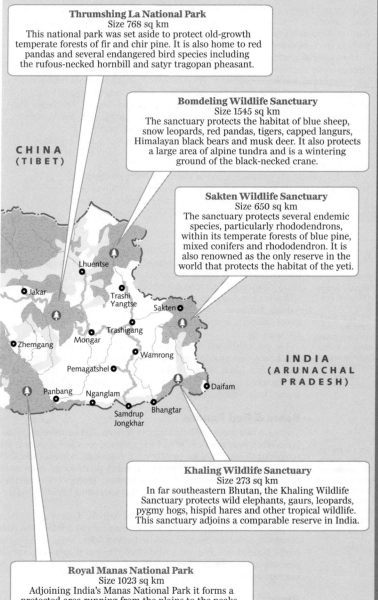

Thrumshing La National Park
Size 768 sq km
This national park was set aside to protect old-growth
temperate forests of fir and chir pine. It is also home to red
pandas and several endangered bird species including
the rufous-necked hornbill and satyr tragopan pheasant.

Bomdeling Wildlife Sanctuary
Size 1545 sq km
The sanctuary protects the habitat of blue sheep,
snow leopards, red pandas, tigers, capped langurs,
Himalayan black bears and musk deer. It also protects
a large area of alpine tundra and is a wintering
ground of the black-necked crane.

Sakten Wildlife Sanctuary
Size 650 sq km
The sanctuary protects several endemic
species, particularly rhododendrons,
within its temperate forests of blue pine,
mixed conifers and rhododendron. It is
also renowned as the only reserve in the
world that protects the habitat of the yeti.

CHINA
(TIBET)

Lhuentse

Jakar

Trashi
Yangtse

Sakten

Trashigang

Mongar

Zhemgang

Wamrong

Pemagatshel

INDIA
(ARUNACHAL
PRADESH)

Panbang

Nganglam

Daifam

Samdrup
Jongkhar

Bhangtar

Khaling Wildlife Sanctuary
Size 273 sq km
In far southeastern Bhutan, the Khaling Wildlife
Sanctuary protects wild elephants, gaurs, leopards,
pygmy hogs, hispid hares and other tropical wildlife.
This sanctuary adjoins a comparable reserve in India.

Royal Manas National Park
Size 1023 sq km
Adjoining India's Manas National Park it forms a
protected area running from the plains to the peaks.
It is the home of rhinos, buffalos, tigers, leopards, bears
and elephants. It is also home to rare species, including
the golden langur, capped langur and hispid hare.

THE BLACK-NECKED CRANE

The rare and endangered black-necked crane occupies a special place in Bhutanese hearts and folklore. Its arrival every autumn from Tibet inspires songs and dances; it usually heralds the end of the harvesting season and also the time when farming families start migrating to warmer climates.

Many legends and myths exist about the bird, which the Bhutanese call *thrung thrung karmo*. Wetlands of the high mountain valleys of Phobjikha, Bomdeling and Gaytsa serve as the winter habitat for up to 500 birds. Like other cranes, these have an elaborate mating ritual, a dance in which pairs bow, leap into the air and toss vegetation about while uttering loud bugling calls. It can be difficult to distinguish the sexes because the coloration is so similar, but the females are slightly smaller. The crane's preferred delicacies include fallen grain, tubers and insects.

The world's entire population of 5600 to 6000 black-necked cranes breeds in Tibet and Ladakh. As well as in Bhutan, they winter in south-central Tibet and northeastern Yunan province in China.

The **Royal Society for Protection of Nature** (RSPN; www.rspnbhutan.org), which is involved in conservation, education and inspiring the Bhutanese populace, annually monitors the endangered black-necked cranes in the Phobjikha and Bomdeling valleys and has produced videos of the cranes.

With its extraordinarily beautiful dappled silver coat, the snow leopard has been hunted relentlessly throughout its range (for more on this, see p251) and is in danger of extinction. This elusive cat is almost entirely solitary, largely because a single animal's hunting territory is so vast and its prey is so scarce throughout its high-altitude habitat. However, when its favourite prey, the blue sheep, migrates to lower valleys in winter, the snow leopard follows them. It is then that the sexes meet.

The essentially solitary tiger is a symbol of great reverence in Bhutan. It numbers probably around 100 animals, mostly concentrated in and around Royal Manas National Park, though tigers may be found throughout Bhutan, even at high altitudes (4100m), and as far north as Jigme Dorji National Park.

> The musk deer is a primitive deer that has no antlers; both sexes have oversized protruding canine teeth, up to 7cm long in males and used in territorial battles.

Bears & Red Pandas

There are two species of bear found in Bhutan. The omnivorous Himalayan black bear is a bane to farmers growing corn and fruit near the temperate forests (1200m to 3500m) it frequents, whereas the sloth bear is principally a termite eater and honey pirate found at lower altitudes. Bears do occasionally attack humans, probably because their poor eyesight leads them to interpret that a standing person is making a threatening gesture.

The red panda is known in Bhutan as *aamchu donkha* and is most commonly found near Pele La, Thrumshing La and parts of the Gasa district. It is bright-chestnut coloured, about 50cm long, including its bushy, banded tail, and has a white face. The red panda is nocturnal, sleeping in trees during the day and coming to the ground to forage on bamboo and raid birds' nests at night.

> *Birds of Bhutan* by Carol Inskipp, Tim Inskipp and Richard Grimmett is a comprehensive, illustrated guide to Bhutan's avian treasures.

Birds

Each year Bhutan's extensive bird list grows longer, a consequence of Bhutan's rich biodiversity and the small amount of systematic birding that has been done in the kingdom. Nevertheless, over 600 species have been recorded and bird-watching tours are extremely popular.

Bhutan is rightly famous for its wintering populations of the vulnerable black-necked crane (see p250). Less well known are the winter populations, mainly as solitary individuals, of the endangered white-bellied heron, listed as one of the 50 rarest birds in the world. This graceful bird may – with luck – be seen from the road in the vicinity of Punakha, Wangdue Phodrang and Zhemgang, especially along the Mangde Chhu valley.

Some bird species are even more transient, migrating through Bhutan between Tibet and northern India in autumn and spring. Pailas' fish eagle, which is considered rare, is regularly seen migrating up the Punak Chhu near Wangdue Phodrang in spring. It is often in the company of ospreys, a wide range of ducks, waders such as the pied avocet, and other birds that breed in Tibet.

The raven is the national bird of Bhutan. A raven guided the Zhabdrung to Bhutan in 1616, and it gives its name to the raven-shaped crown worn by the kings of Bhutan.

Winter brings numerous species down to lower altitudes, including accentors, rosefinches, grosbeaks, snow pigeons and pheasants such as the satyr tragopan, the Himalayan monal and the blood pheasant. Observant early morning walkers can often find these on the mountains and passes around Thimphu. In summer many lowland species move to higher altitudes to breed; these species include the exotic-looking hoopoe, various species of minivets, cuckoos (one can commonly hear at least five different species calling), barbets, warblers, sunbirds, fulvettas and yuhinas.

Given the density of forest cover and the steep vertical descents, the road is often the best place from which to spot birds. Recommended stretches include the road down from Dochu La to Wangdue Phodrang (the adventurous can take the old trail, which is even better), from Wangdue Phodrang to Nobding (on the way to Pele La), and before Trongsa. For those who go east, the 2000m descent between Sengor and Lingmethang is spectacular: the rufous-necked hornbill and Ward's trogon have been recorded in this area.

Trekking will provide you with a greater chance of seeing high-altitude birds, including the lammergeyer, the Himalayan griffon, the raven, the unique high-altitude wader – the ibisbill – and several colourful pheasants.

For more on cranes, including a downloadable field guide, visit the International Crane Foundation (www.savingcranes.org).

The global conservation organisation WWF (www.wwfbhutan.org.bt) has a branch in Thimphu where it funds, manages and communicates with several conservation projects in Bhutan.

CATERPILLARS, FUNGUS & SNOW LEOPARDS

A tragedy is being played out in and beyond the mountains of Bhutan, featuring an exotic cast, high-stakes fashion and a plot that defies imagination. Some Chinese swimming coaches and practitioners of traditional Chinese medicine have talked up the value of Bhutan's *yartsa goenbub* (winter-worm summer-plant), also known as caterpillar fungus, *Cordyceps sinensis,* associating this peculiar fungus that parasitises then kills its caterpillar host, with powers matched only by rhino horns, elephant tusks and tiger penises. Tibetan yak herders wandering in and out of Bhutan traditionally scooped up the fungus to augment their meagre living, but the increased demand for *Cordyceps* in China has brought sudden wealth.

The knock-on effect has been felt most keenly by the big cats of Asia. Increasing numbers of new-money Tibetans with a hankering for traditional garb are providing a growing market for cat skins, particularly tiger and snow leopard, which adorn their *chuba* (cloaks). Bhutanese rangers in Jigme Dorje National Park are faced with increasing numbers of fungus gatherers; meanwhile, already endangered big cats across south Asia are enduring a wave of poaching activity.

National Parks & Protected Areas

Conservation International's website on biodiversity (www .biodiversity hotspots.org) includes facts for the Himalaya, including Bhutan. Hotspots occupy 2.5% of the earth's surface, yet are home to 50% of the world's plant species and 42% of its vertebrates.

There are five national parks, four wildlife sanctuaries and one nature reserve, which together constitute about 35% of the country, or 14,521 sq km. In 1999 an additional 3800 sq km was designated as a network of biological corridors linking all nine protected areas.

All but three of the protected areas encompass regions in which there is a resident human population. Preserving the culture and fostering local tradition is part of the mandate of Bhutan's national-park system. The government has developed an integrated conservation and development program to allow people living within a protected area to continue to farm, graze animals, collect plants and cut firewood.

Bhutan established its national-park system to protect important ecosystems, and for the most part they have not been developed as tourist attractions. Apart from one or two exceptions, you won't find the kind of facilities you may normally associate with national parks, such as entrance stations, camping grounds and visitors centres. In many cases you won't even be aware that you are entering or leaving a national park.

For details on individual national parks and protected reserves, see the map, p248.

Survival Guide

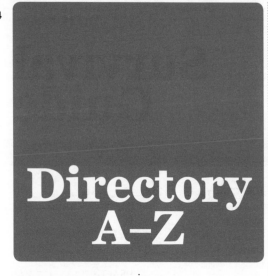

Directory A–Z

Accommodation

Tour operators should book you into hotels approved by the Tourism Council of Bhutan (TCB). Since most visitors effectively pay the same rate whether staying in a budget or midrange hotel, it makes sense to ask for the best when you make your travel arrangements. The TCB plans to introduce a star rating for hotels and will require that agents book tourists in places with a minimum of three stars.

The prices in this book are for a standard double room at the normal foreign-tourist rates and do not include the usual 10% tax and 10% service charge. Ranges are defined as:

$	less than Nu 1500
$$	Nu 1500 to Nu 3500
$$$	more than Nu 3500

Hotels

Accommodation in Bhutan ranges from simple mountain huts to five-star luxury resorts, though most tourists will stay in comfortable midrange tourist hotels equipped with electricity, telephone, TV, private bathroom and hot water. Every hotel has a restaurant that serves buffet meals when a group is in residence and offers à la carte dining at other times. Several hotels advertise IDD, but this can mean that the phones simply connect to the front desk and the hotel operator will then dial the international number.

Many hotels offer standard, deluxe and suite accommodation, although the difference between standard and deluxe in most hotels is minimal. When you book a trip, you may specify which hotel you wish, but your agent may have a list of hotels with whom they have contracts or relationships. Changes and cancellations will be much simpler in these hotels and upgrades more likely. You'll find that smaller agencies often have a hard time getting guaranteed rooms at hotels owned by BTCL or other tour companies. During the off-season (December to February, June to August), hotels often discount their rooms by 30% so you may be able to negotiate an upgrade during these months.

During tsechu time, tourist hotels add a surcharge (which the agent pays) but still get booked up and you may well find yourself 'bumped' into budget digs or even a private home. These can still be comfortable, though the toilet facilities may not be what you're used to.

A confirmed hotel reservation does not always guarantee a booking in hotels as small as those in Bhutan. A large tour group can exert a powerful influence and you may discover that there is an extended negotiation taking place between your guide and the desk clerk when you check in. Don't worry; *something* will be arranged.

Bhutan has several luxury options, including the Uma, Amankora, Zhiwa Ling and Termalinca resorts. For these you will have to pay a substantial supplement on top of the standard tourist tariff. These hotels are marked as 'luxury' in this guidebook. For these luxury hotels you should get at least a 30% discount off the full rate during the off-season.

Winter is cold in Bhutan and central heating is rare. In Thimphu and Paro there are small electric heaters, and in Bumthang many hotel rooms are heated by a wood stove called a *bukhari,* which often has a pile of rocks on the top to retain the heat. Unless you are trekking, you

BOOK YOUR STAY ONLINE

For more accommodation reviews by Lonely Planet authors, check out hotels.lonelyplanet.com/Bhutan. You'll find independent reviews, as well as recommendations on the best places to stay. Best of all, you can book online.

HOT-STONE BATHS

Most hotels offer a *dotsho* (traditional hot-stone bath), a simple coffin-like wooden box containing water warmed with fire-heated rocks. The red-hot rocks tumble and sizzle into the water behind a grill that protects the bather's skin. More traditional places add natural herbs such as Artemisia. You'll need to book a couple of hours in advance for the rocks to heat up; expect to pay around Nu 600 for the experience, double this in top-end places. Bring a towel and soap in cheaper places.

won't need to carry bedding or a sleeping bag, but be aware that hotel pillows tend to be extra firm and mattresses on the thin side.

If there is an electric water heater (called a geyser) in the room, check that it's turned on when you check in. The better hotels supply bottled drinking water in the rooms, but if you come across an open water flask in your room, don't drink from it.

Indian travellers and resident foreigners often get an automatic 20% or 30% discount on hotel room rates, while Bhutanese often get 50%.

Activities

There are plenty of possible day hikes in Bhutan, particularly in Thimphu, Paro and Bumthang, and these are described in the relevant destination chapters. For more serious treks, ranging from three to 25 days, see the Treks chapter (p147). Horse riding is available in Paro and on some treks.

Bird-Watching

Bhutan is rightly celebrated for its wintering populations of the vulnerable black-necked crane, but with over 600 recorded bird species and a spectacular range of habitats (see p250), this tiny country is a bird-watchers' paradise.

Although these companies specialise in bird-watching

tours, Bhutan's plentiful mature forests and lack of hunting makes any travel a bird-spotting opportunity.

Bhutan Birding and Heritage Travels (www.bhutanheritage.com)
Sunbird Tours (www.sunbirdtours.co.uk)
Wings (www.wingsbirds.com)

Wildlife viewing at Royal Manas National Park on the southern border with India's Assam state will be spectacular once park facilities have been built and the park has been opened to foreigners. Plans are afoot but with some dangers still posed by separatist groups in India, it could take a couple of years.

Fishing

Fishing with lure or fly for brown trout is possible in many rivers, though it is frowned upon by many Bhutanese for religious reasons. A licence (Nu 500 per day) is required (ask your tour agency) and fishing is prohibited within 1km of a monastery, temple, dzong or *shedra* (religious college). A closed season applies from October to December and fishing is banned on many religious days throughout the year. The most popular lure is the Tasmanian Devil, available in general shops in Thimphu.

Yangphel Adventure Travel (www.yangphel.com) operates fly-fishing tours and encourages a 'catch and release' approach.

Golf

The international-standard golf course in Thimphu is open to nonmembers and is particularly popular with Japanese golfers. For details, see p54.

Cycling

Mountain biking is rapidly gaining popularity with Bhutanese and expats alike. The **Bhutan Bicycle Club** (☑02-321905; www.bhutanmtb.com) can advise on routes (the best contact is Rinzin) and has mountain bikes for hire (see p54). The normal daily tariff fee applies if you bring your own bike, otherwise local mountain bike hire costs an extra US$30 to US$50 per day. Some adventure-travel companies organise trips that allow bikers to bring their own cycles and travel throughout Bhutan accompanied by a support vehicle. **Bhutan Wilderness Travel** (www.bhutanbiking.com) in particular has experience with mountain bike trips.

Long journeys are challenging because there's a lot of uphill peddling and approaching vehicles roar around corners, not expecting cyclists. Local cycling excursions in the Paro, Thimphu and Bumthang valleys offer a safer and less strenuous mountain-biking experience. Suggested places include:

Cheli La For a wild ride, get dropped off at the top of this pass and ride 35km nonstop, downhill, either on the main road or on logging roads via Gorina.

Paro valley The paved road to Drukgyel Dzong and the return trip along the unpaved western farm road from Satsam make this a 30km day trip.

Phobjikha Bike trails here are part of the local ecotourism initiative, and there are also new opportunities to follow graded logging roads along the Gangte trek route to Tsele La and overnight to Tikke Zampa.

PRACTICALITIES

» **Newspapers** *Kuensel* (www.kuenselonline.com) is the biweekly national newspaper of Bhutan. *Bhutan Today* (www.bhutantoday.bt) is the only daily newspaper. *Bhutan Times* (www.bhutantimes.com) and *Bhutan Observer* (www.bhutanobserver.bt)) are privately owned newspapers published every Friday and Sunday respectively. *Business Bhutan* (www.businessbhutan.bt) is a business-orientated weekly.

» **Magazines** *Faces of Bhutan* is a glossy quarterly on Buddhism and Bhutanese culture; the monthly news magazine is *Drukpa* (www.drukpa.bt); and *Yeewong* (www.yeewongmagazine.bt) is aimed at Bhutanese women

» **Radio** Bhutan Broadcasting Service (www.bbs.com.bt) broadcasts English news at 11am and 2pm on FM 96. Kuzoo FM 105 (www.kuzoo.net) is a private English- and Dzongkha-language station with a mix of music and chat, or try Radio Valley at FM 99.9.

» **TV** BBS TV broadcast evening news in English. Satellite channels such as BBC World and CNN are widespread.

» **Weights & Measures** The metric system is used throughout the country. In villages, rice is sometimes measured in a round measure called a *gasekhorlo*. There is a scale called a *sang* that is used for butter and meat.

Punakha Offering several dedicated mountain bike trails; for more information, see p94.

Tango and Cheri A fine day trip north of Thimphu, combining biking and hiking.

Thimphu to Paro An interesting ride, though traffic can be heavy as far as Chhuzom (the turn to Phuentsholing).

Rafting & Kayaking

Though rafting in Bhutan is in its infancy, those who have scouted the rivers feel that it has the potential for some of the best rafting on earth.

From small alpine runs such as the Paro Chhu to the big-water Puna Tsang Chhu, the white water of Bhutan is as diverse as its topography. Since 1997 small groups of paddlers have been exploring 14 rivers and over 22 different runs that vary from class II (beginner with moderate rapids) to class V (expert only). Unless you are a seasoned river rat, there are essentially two day trips on offer, both in the Punakha valley:

Pho Chhu Combines a hike up the side of the river through forest and farmland to the put-in at Samdinka. The raft trip has a couple of class III rapids and ends in a bang with the 'Wrathful Buddha' rapid next to the Punakha Dzong.

Mo Chhu A very easy scenic float, suitable for all abilities and a good introduction for novices. The run starts about 6km above the Punakha Dzong at the Khamsum Yuelley Namgyal Chorten. As the river meanders through the wide valley, you float past one of the queen's winter residences, the king's weekend retreat and some beautiful farmland before taking out just below the dzong.

Most companies can book you on either of these trips for around US$75 per person in a group of five. The fees for longer river rafting are the same as cultural tours and trekking, though there are extra charges for hiring equipment. The following companies run rafting and kayaking trips.

Needmore Adventures (www.needmoreadventures.com) US-based operator.

Lotus Adventures (www.bhutanlotusadventures.com)

Xplore Bhutan (www.xplorebhutan.com)

Business Hours

Reviews in this book mention business hours only if different from these standards.

Government offices 9am to 1pm, 2pm to 5pm in summer, until 4pm in winter, Monday to Friday

Banks 9am to 1pm Monday to Friday, 9am to 11am Saturday

Shops 8am to 8pm or 9pm. In Phuentsholing shops are open on Saturday and Sunday, but closed Tuesday

Nightclubs and discos Open till the early morning on Wednesday, Friday and Saturday

Bars Closed Tuesday – the national 'dry' day

Children

Children aged under 12 are exempt from the minimum daily tariff, so it needn't break the bank if you bring kids along. Kids may become bored with long, monotonous drives, limited availability to TV and little other 'entertainment' available. On the other hand, they will be immediately accepted by local kids and their families, and they could

Climate

Thimphu

Phuentsholing

Electricity

230v/50hz

230v/50hz

make many new friends. Lonely Planet's *Travel with Children* has lots of useful advice and suggestions.

Bhutan Land of the Thunder Dragon, by Freda Ferne, is a children's book on Bhutan; see www.bhutan-an-introduction.co.uk if you want more info or wish to buy.

Customs Regulations

You will receive a baggage declaration form to complete when you arrive in Bhutan. For tourists, the main purpose of this form is to ensure that you re-export anything you bring into the country. List any expensive equipment that you are carrying, such as cameras and laptops. Don't lose the form as you must return it when you leave the country.

Duty-free allowances include 2L of liquor. You can bring in only one carton (200) of cigarettes and these attract a 200% duty upon arrival. A packet or two is nor-

mally allowed in gratis. There are no restrictions on other personal effects, including trekking gear, brought into the country.

Departure formalities are straightforward, but you'll need to produce the form that you completed on arrival and may need to show all of the items listed on it. A lost form means complications and delays. If you lose the form, let your guide know as soon as possible so that special arrangements can be made to avoid any inconvenience.

The export of antiques and wildlife products is prohibited. If you wish to purchase a souvenir that looks old, have your guide clear it as a nonantique item with the **Division of Cultural Properties** (☑02-322694), part of the Department of Culture inside the Ministry of Home and Cultural Affairs. Customs authorities pay special attention to religious statues. It would be prudent to have any such statue cleared, old or not.

Embassies & Consulates

Visas are not available from Bhutanese embassies abroad. All tourist visas must be channelled through a tour company and the Tourism Council of Bhutan in Thimphu, and from there through the Ministry of Foreign Affairs.

Embassies & Consulates in Bhutan

Only a handful of foreign countries have an official presence in Bhutan. Bhutan's relations with other countries are handled through its embassies in Delhi and Dhaka.

Bangladesh (☎02-322362; fax 322629; Thori Lam, Thimphu)

India Phuentsholing (☎05-252635) Thimphu (☎02-322280; www.eoithimphu .org; India House, Zhung Lam; ◎9.30am-1pm, 2-5.30pm, Mon-Fri, closed Indian holidays)

Thailand (☎02-323978; royalthaiconsulate@druknet.bt; Changangkha, Thimphu)

Food

Since most travel in Bhutan is via an all-inclusive package, most of your meals will be in the shape of a hotel or trekking-camp buffet, with a mix of continental, Indian, Chinese and Bhutanese dishes, plus vegetarian options and rice. The food is fine but is specifically created to not offend anyone, so it can be pretty bland. Small groups can often order from the menu, though the buffet meals offer a wider selection. Unexpected items include a surprising amount of baked beans, the result of a British-style boarding-school education in Darjeeling. If you find the tourist food bland, request some of what your guide is eating. It will be much tastier, if you can take the heat.

On long day drives or hikes you will not return to your hotel for lunch, and most tour operators arrange either uninspiring packed lunches or a much better hot lunch packed inside a series of metal containers.

The food in hotels is often the best in town, but if you want to sample local restaurants, especially in Thimphu or Paro, your guide can arrange it. Your tour operator should pay for your restaurant meals, with the exception of a few upper-end restaurants in Thimphu. In almost all restaurants it's a good idea to order an hour or more in advance, or expect to wait forever. If you are ordering from a menu, don't be surprised if many of the offerings are not available.

Due to the unique nature of travel in Bhutan, restaurant opening hours have little meaning. Almost all tourists will have breakfast in their hotel and guides will prearrange lunch and dinner in restaurants or hotels, which will normally offer a buffet or set meal at whatever time your guide determines. We have listed opening hours where they are fixed, or useful, as in the case of bakeries and private restaurants, but for the most part this guide assumes that restaurants are open for lunch and dinner, with exceptions noted. The price ranges for restaurants in this book are defined as the price of a main dish. Ranges are defined as follows:

$	under Nu 100
$$	Nu 100 to Nu 300
$$$	over Nu 300

Staples & Specialities

The Bhutanese love chillies, so much in fact that some dishes consist entirely of chillies, accompanied by chilli-infused condiments. The mouth-scorching meals will bring tears of joy to the eyes of chilli lovers, and tears of pain to everyone else! Although chillies are ubiquitous, don't expect the aromatically spiced dishes typical of the subcontinent. These can only be found in the Nepali-influenced south of Bhutan or in an Indian restaurant.

Bhutan's national dish is *ema datse,* large green (sometimes red, but always very hot) chillies, prepared as a vegetable, not as a seasoning, in a cheese sauce. The second-most popular dish is *phak sha laphu* (stewed pork with radish). Other typical dishes, always served with chillies, are *no sha huentseu* (stewed beef with spinach), *phak sha phin tshoem* (pork with rice noodles) and *bja sha maroo* (chicken in garlic and butter sauce).

Hotel and trekking cooks make some excellent non-spicy dishes, such as *kewa datse* (potatoes with cheese sauce) and *shamu datse* (mushrooms with cheese sauce). More seasonal are the delicious asparagus and unusual *nakey* (fern fronds), the latter typically smothered in the ever-present *datse.* One interesting vegetable is *olo choto* (literally 'crow beak'), a hooked-shaped broad bean. Don't eat the seeds. Or try *hogey,* a zesty salad of cucumber, Asian pepper, red chilli, spring onion and tomato.

Beef and fish come from India, often travelling long distances in unrefrigerated trucks. Avoid beef during the monsoon season, and be wary of pork at any time. During the summer you are usually limited to chicken, or a vegetarian diet. Yak meat is available, but only in the winter.

Foremost amongst several Tibetan-influenced snacks are *momos,* small steamed dumplings that may be filled with meat or cheese – delicious when dipped in a chilli sauce. Fried cheese *momos* are a speciality of several Thimphu restaurants. *Barthu* is essentially a Bhutanese version of another typically Tibetan dish, *thukpa* (noodles), which may be fried or served in soup. Village people also eat *tsampa,* the Tibetan-style dish of roasted-barley flour mixed with salt and yak-butter tea and kneaded into a paste. Look for the strings of rock-hard, dried yak cheese, *chugo,* hanging from shop rafters, but be careful of your teeth.

Although there is plenty of white rice, the Bhutanese prefer a locally produced red variety, which has a slightly nutty flavour. At high altitudes wheat and buckwheat are the staples. In Bumthang, *khule* (buckwheat pancakes) and *puta* (buckwheat noodles) replace rice as the foundation of many meals. Common snacks served with tea include *zao* (fried rice) and *sip* (fried, beaten corn).

Drinks

NONALCOHOLIC DRINKS

Avoid drinking tap water anywhere in Bhutan. Bottled mineral water is widely available.

Indian-style sweet milky tea *(ngad-ja)* is widely available and often referred to as either masala tea or 'ready-made' tea. Less satisfying is the tourist equivalent, a tea bag that you only get some flavour from after endless prodding. Bhutanese frequently drink *sud-ja,* Tibetan-style tea with salt and butter, which is more like soup than tea, and surprisingly tasty and warming on a cold day. Filter coffee and espresso is available in the top-end hotels and a few restaurants in Thimphu, but elsewhere, 'coffee' is invariably of the instant variety.

ALCOHOLIC DRINKS

The best beer brewed in Bhutan is the very good Red Panda *weissbier,* a tangy unfiltered wheat beer bottled in Bumthang. Bhutan Brewery produces Druk Lager and the high-alcohol (8%) Druk 11000. Imported beers include Tiger and Singha in cans and several varieties of Indian beer. They all cost between Nu 80 and Nu 120 in bars and hotels.

There are several brands of Bhutanese whisky but the

CHEWING THE NUT

One of the great Bhutanese vices is chewing *doma* nut, also known by its Indian name, *paan*. The nut is mixed with lime powder (the ash, not the fruit), and the whole collection is rolled up in a heart-shaped betel leaf and chewed slowly. It's a bittersweet, mildly intoxicating concoction and it stains the mouth bright red. The blood-like stains you see on Bhutanese pavements are the result of spat out *doma* effluent. Or they're just blood stains....

---

most common local brew is *bang chhang,* a warm beer-like drink made from wheat. The favourite hard drinks are *arra,* a spirit distilled from rice, and *sinchhang,* which is made from millet, wheat or rice.

Drinks, including mineral water, are usually charged as extras, and payment is collected at the end of the meal or the following morning when you check out of the hotel.

Gay & Lesbian Travellers

Like most Asians, the Bhutanese believe that what one does in private is strictly a personal matter, and they would prefer not to discuss such issues. Public displays of affection are not appreciated, though, and everyone, regardless of orientation, should exercise discretion. Officially, male homosexuality is illegal.

Insurance

A travel insurance policy to cover theft, loss and medical problems is always highly recommended. Most policies will cover costs if you are forced to cancel your tour because of flight cancellation, illness, injury or the death of a close relative. This can protect you from major losses due to Bhutan's prepayment conditions and hefty cancellation charges.

Some policies specifically exclude 'dangerous activities', and these can include motorcycling and even trekking. Read your policy carefully to be sure it covers ambulance rides or an emergency helicopter airlift out of a remote region, or an emergency flight home. Many travel-insurance policies include repatriation and evacuation through the worldwide network of International SOS Assistance. Keep in mind that if you can't afford travel insurance, you certainly won't be able to afford to deal with a medical emergency overseas.

You may prefer a policy that pays doctors or hospitals directly rather than your having to pay on the spot and claim later. If you have to claim later make sure you keep all documentation. Some insurance companies ask you to call them (they suggest reversing the charges, an impossibility from Bhutan) at a centre in your home country, where an immediate assessment of your problem is made.

Internet Access

Full international internet service was inaugurated on 2 June 1999, the 25th anniversary of the king's coronation. There are internet cafes in most towns and most tourist hotels offer either an internet-connected public computer or free wi-fi (though this may be limited

LAUNDRY

Most hotels offer a laundry service, for a fee, and larger towns have a laundry or dry-cleaners. During wet weather, smaller hotels may return your laundry damp, or not until the following day. If you are on a tight schedule, ask about the drying facilities before you hand in your laundry.

to the lobby and restaurant and not the rooms).

At the time of research, Bhutan had not yet joined any of the global internet roaming agreements, so a local Druknet account was needed to log in. You can access **Druknet** (www.druknet.bt), Bhutan's internet provider, from any telephone in Bhutan by dialling ☑100 or ☑101.

For a rundown of useful internet resources, see p15.

Language Courses

The **Dzongkha Language Institute** (☑02-333869; dzongkhalanguageinstitute@ yahoo.com; Thimphu) can arrange language classes in Dzongkha for between Nu 4000 and Nu 9000 per month, or private tutors from the Simthoka Language Institute from Nu 300 per hour. Courses last from one to six months.

Legal Matters

Although you will probably notice cannabis growing in any bit of spare dirt, even in the towns, there is not a tradition of use and possession is illegal.

Smoking in public places is prohibited. Bring all the cigarettes you think you'll

need but be prepared to be taxed 200% at customs (see p257). Don't sell any cigarettes brought into the country as this is illegal.

Maps

There is a dearth of maps of Bhutan and a good map can be hard to source outside the country. Bookshops in Kathmandu are the best bet for finding a map. **International Travel Maps** (www.itm.com) produce a 1:380,000 *Bhutan* and Nepa Maps produce two maps: 1:380,000 *Bhutan*, and *Bhutan Trekking Routes*. The laminated Berndtson & Berndtson 1:500,000 *Bhutan Road Map* is hard to find inside Bhutan but available in Kathmandu and (with some difficulty) elsewhere.

In Bhutan, bookshops sell Thimphu and Paro city maps as well as country maps published by the Survey of Bhutan. The Survey publishes a large 1:250,000 satellite country map overlaid with roads and major towns and district boundaries, as well as several specialised maps showing historical places and points of interest. See the Treks chapter (p147) for more on topographical maps and their availability.

Money

The unit of currency is the ngultrum (Nu), which is pegged to the Indian rupee. The ngultrum is further divided into 100 *chetrum*. There are coins to the value of 25 and 50 chetrum and Nu 1 and notes of Nu 1, 5, 10, 20, 50, 100 and 500. The Nu 1 coin depicts the eight auspicious symbols called Tashi Tagye, while each note depicts a different dzong.

Indian rupees may be used freely anywhere in Bhutan (don't be surprised if you get change in rupees), except for 500 and 1000 Indian rupee notes, which

are not accepted due to large amounts of counterfeit notes. Ngultrums cannot be used in India.

It is OK with the Bhutanese if you bring a reasonable amount of Indian currency into Bhutan, though Indian regulations prohibit currency export. See p15 for exchange rates and a run-down on costs.

ATMs

At the time of research, only local customers could use the few existing Bhutan National Bank ATMs, though both this bank and the new joint-venture Druk PNB Bank have plans to introduce ATMS and credit-card facilities for foreign cardholders.

Bargaining

Bargaining is not a Bhutanese tradition, and you won't get very far with your haggling skills here, except with trailside vendors on the hike to Taktshang and in the local handicrafts section of the Thimphu weekend market (p48).

Cash

If you plan to make a major purchase, for example textiles or art, consider bringing US dollars in cash. Most shops will accept this, and it can save you the hassle of exchanging a large quantity of money in advance and then attempting to change it back if you don't find the exact piece you were looking for.

Credit Cards

Cards are accepted at major handicraft stores and some of the larger hotels in Thimphu but you will often be charged a surcharge of around 5% to cover the fees levied by the credit-card companies. An online credit-card payment system was introduced in 2010, so transactions should no longer require a phone call to an authorisation office.

Changing Money

Tourist trips are fully pre-paid, so you could in theory manage in Bhutan without any local money at all, though you'll probably want to change at least US$50 to pay for laundry and drinks, plus whatever you need for souvenirs and tips.

The exchange counters at the airport, larger hotels and the banks in Thimphu and Phuentsholing can change all major currencies, and sometimes Scandinavian currencies. If you are heading to central and eastern Bhutan, you will do better sticking to US dollars. In smaller towns foreign-currency exchange may be an unusual transaction so be prepared for delays. You'll often get a slightly lower rate if changing US$ bills in denominations of US$20 or less.

You may change your unused ngultrums back to foreign currency (though usually only into US dollars) on departure from Thimphu or Paro. Travellers departing via Samdrup Jongkhar don't have this facility at the time of research. You will need to produce your original exchange receipts. Ngultrums are useless outside of Bhutan (except just as a curiosity).

Bhutan has two banks, the **Bank of Bhutan** (www.bob .bt) and the **Bhutan National Bank** (www.bnb.com.bt), each with branches throughout the country. Both change cash with no commission and charge 1% for travellers cheques. The Bank of Bhutan's main branches are generally open 9am to 1pm Monday to Friday and 9am to 11am on Saturday, though the branches in Trongsa, Trashigang and Mongar are open on Sunday and closed Tuesday. It also has a branch in Thimphu that stays open later.

Beware that the Bhutan National Bank currently charges an eye-watering €26 to change Euro travellers cheques, since it has to courier them to Europe.

Tipping & Tax

You will usually be accompanied throughout your visit to Bhutan by the same tour guide and probably the same driver. Though it's against the official TCB policy, these people expect a tip at the end of the trip. Many leaders on group tours take up a collection at the conclusion of the trip and hand it over in one packet. With a large group this can be a substantial amount and the practice has created high expectations on the part of Bhutanese guides.

If you've been trekking, it's appropriate to tip the guide, cook and waiter. Horsemen also expect tips, but this can be minimal if they are the owners of the horses or yaks and are making money by hiring out their animals. The stakes go up, however, if they have been especially helpful with camp chores and on the trail.

If arranging tips yourself, hand them over in individual envelopes the evening before you leave, as things get rushed and easily forgotten on the day of departure.

For those paying their own way, most hotels charge 10% Bhutan Sales Tax (BST) and either 5% or 10% service charge on the rates shown. Most restaurants charge the same, especially if you want a receipt.

Travellers Cheques

You can cash travellers cheques at any bank, most hotels and the foreign-exchange counter at the airport. There are bank charges of 1% for cheque encashment. You should carry only well-known brands such as American Express, Visa, Thomas Cook, Citibank or Barclays. There is no replacement facility for lost travellers cheques in Bhutan.

Photography & Video

Film & Equipment

Memory cards are available in Thimphu and you will have no problem finding an internet cafe in Thimphu or Paro that can burn digital images to a CD. There are colour-printing facilities in Thimphu and Phuentsholing.

Many of the dzongs and mountain peaks are best photographed at a distance with a telephoto lens. Bear in mind also that there will be little or no opportunity for photography inside buildings, therefore you don't need to organise a flash attachment and tripod for that purpose. Be sure to carry spare batteries, as these are hard to find when in rural Bhutan.

Grab a copy of Lonely Planet's *Travel Photography* for more tips and advice.

Photography enthusiasts should check out the expert-guided itineraries of **Rainbow Photo Tours** (☎ in the USA 800-685 9992; www .rainbowphototours.com).

Restrictions

Bhutan is generally liberal about photography by tourists. There are a few places, though, with signs prohibiting photography such as the telecom tower above Thimphu and it would also be prudent to refrain from taking pictures of military installations.

There are no restrictions on photographing the outside of dzongs and goembas, but photography is *strictly* prohibited inside goembas and lhakhangs. There are several reasons for this. One is that in the past tourists have completely disrupted holy places with their picture taking. Another is the fear that photos of treasured statues will become a catalogue of items for art thieves to steal. And thirdly, some early tourists made photographs of religious statues into postcards that were then sold, which is unacceptable to the Bhutanese religious community.

During festivals you can photograph from the dzong courtyard where the dances take place. Remember, however, that this is a religious observance and that you should behave accordingly – use a telephoto lens without a flash. Don't intrude on the dance ground or on the space occupied by local people seated at the edge of the dance area and if you do end up in the front row, please remain seated. Don't photograph a member of the royal family, even if you happen to be at a festival or gathering where they are present.

There is an extensive set of rules and restrictions, including payment of additional royalties, for commercial movie making within Bhutan. The TCB publishes a booklet that details all these rules.

Post

The mail service from Bhutan is reliable, and no special procedures are necessary.

Bhutan Post (www.bhutanpost.com.bt) offers both outgoing and incoming Expedited Mail Service (EMS), which is a reliable and fast international mail delivery facility that is cheaper than courier services. It also has a Local Urgent Mail (LUM) service for delivery within Thimphu.

If you have made a purchase and want to send it home, it's easiest to have the shop make arrangements for you. Keep the receipt and let your guide know what you are doing so they can follow up in case the package does not arrive. Send all parcels by air; sea mail, via Kolkata, takes months.

DHL (see p64) has an office in Thimphu. A 500g package of documents costs US$58 to the USA and UK or US$54 to Australia. A

1kg is package is US$85, or US$64 to Australia. There are several smaller courier companies that specialise in service to India.

Postal Rates

Airmail letter rates Letters up to 20g cost Nu 10 domestic, Nu 15 for Nepal, India and Bangladesh, Nu 20 most foreign countries. **EMS Rates** 500g documents cost Nu 250/700 to India/China, and Nu 820/1215 to Australia/UK.

Public Holidays

Public holidays follow both the Gregorian and lunar calendars and are decided by the **Royal Civil Service Commission** (www.rcsc.gov.bt) **Birthday of Fifth King** Feb 21, 22 & 23 **Birthday of Third King** 2 May **Coronation of Fourth King** 2 June, also marked as 'Social Forest Day' **Coronation of Druk Gyalpo** 1 November **Coronation of Fifth King** 6 Nov **Constitution Day/ Fourth King's Birthday** 11 November **National Day** 17 December, the date of the establishment of the monarchy in 1907

The following holidays are set by the traditional lunar calendar and so vary in Gregorian dates: **Zhabdrung Kuchoe** April/ May (Death of Zhabdrung) **Losar** January/February, New Year **Dashain** October, Hindu celebration **Birthday of Guru Rinpoche** June/July **Buddha Paranirvana/ Saga Dawa** May/June (enlightenment and death of Buddha) **First sermon of Buddha** July

FESTIVAL DATES

Bhutan's festival dates are fixed according to the lunar calendar and so the Western date varies every year. Check www.tourism .gov.bt for the latest dates.

Several major festivals are considered local public holidays including September's Thimphu drubchen and tsechu. Note that dates for festivals can vary by several weeks each year especially if they are adjusted to conform to auspicious dates. Before you schedule a trip around a specific festival, check with a tour operator or the **Tourism Council of Bhutan** (www .tourism.gov.bt) for the correct dates. For a summary of major festivals held in Bhutan see p19.

In the Bhutanese lunar system, months have 30 days, with the full moon on the 15th. The 8th, 15th and 30th days of the month are auspicious and you'll notice increased activity and prayers in monasteries across the country.

Safe Travel

Bhutan is a remarkably safe destination, almost completely devoid of the scams, begging and theft that affects its neighbours. There are couple of things to look out for though.

Altitude It's unlikely you will have any problems with altitude unless you are trekking. Most of the places tourists visit lie below 3000m and the maximum elevation you can reach by road is around 3800m. If you are planning a trek, see p276 for advice about high altitude.

Dogs Those cute dogs that wag their tails for you

during the day turn into barking monsters at night. Bring earplugs. There is little danger of dog bites, but occasional rabies outbreaks occur in rural Bhutan, so be wary of big dogs guarding properties, especially if trekking.

Weather Inclement weather can obscure the mountain views that you made such an effort to see and can affect Druk Air flights. In the monsoon heavy rain can turn trails into a sea of mud and can wash away bridges, while leeches can be a real irritation in the lower valleys.

Carsickness If you venture east of Thimphu, you will spend hours driving on rough, winding roads and carsickness is common. Anti-motion medication such as Dramamine can help but bring the anti-drowsy versions or you'll spend most of the spectacular drives snoring in the back seat.

Crime Theft is still minimal in Bhutan but is growing. A trekking group on the Jhomolhari 2 trek was robbed in 2008 after a gang slit the sides of their tent.

Telephone

There are numerous public call offices (PCOs) throughout the country from which you can make STD (long-distance) calls within Bhutan or to India, or international subscriber dialling (ISD) calls overseas. Most hotels can arrange both local and international calls for a premium, though few have in-room direct-dial facilities.

Local calls cost around Nu 2 per minute, or Nu 4 to Nu 5 per minute long distance. International calls cost Nu 30 to Nu 40 per minute, or Nu 16 to India. To send a fax from a PCO costs Nu 20/40/70 to Bhutan/India/abroad.

Some useful numbers:

☑**140** Domestic directory inquiries

☑**116** International directory inquiries.

☑**117** Trunk calls for international numbers

☑**119** Trunk calls for domestic numbers

☑**118** Trunk calls to India.

Mobile Phones

A B-Mobile SIM card is available at any telecom shop in Thimphu against a copy of your passport, for Nu 95 (which includes talk time worth Nu 50). Further top-ups are available in multiples of Nu 100. Apart from **B-Mobile** (www.druknet.bt), there's also **Tashi Cell** (www.tashicell.com), with similar rates but more limited coverage. India's Airtel network is expected to launch in Bhutan soon.

Local call charges vary between Nu 0.30 to Nu 0.70 per 15 seconds, depending on the time of day and network called. Text messages are Nu 1. ISD charges are Nu 5 per minute for India and between Nu 18 to Nu 45 per minute for the rest of the world.

Time

Bhutan time is GMT/UTC plus six hours; there is only one time zone throughout the country. The time in Bhutan is 30 minutes later than in India, 15 minutes later than Nepal, and one hour earlier than Thailand. When it is noon in Bhutan, standard time is 6am in London, 4pm in Sydney, 1am in New York and 10pm the previous day in San Francisco.

Toilets

Most hotels provide Western toilets and loo paper, though there are some exceptions, particularly in eastern Bhutan. There are very few

public toilets so take full advantage of hotel and restaurant facilities before that long drive. Most public toilets are of the Asian squat variety and toilet paper isn't available, though a container of water may be present.

Tourist Information

The **Tourism Council of Bhutan** (TCB; ☎02-323251; www.tourism.gov.bt) has a comprehensive website and it can refer you to tour operators who can assist with arrangements to visit Bhutan. There is no official government tourist office outside Bhutan.

Most of the big travel companies in Bhutan have good general information on Bhutan on their websites; see p28 for details.

Travellers with Disabilities

A cultural tour in Bhutan is a challenge for a traveller with physical disabilities, but is possible with some planning. The Bhutanese are eager to help, and one could arrange a strong companion to assist with moving about and getting in and out of vehicles. The roads are rough and pavements, where they exist, often have holes and sometimes steps. Hotels and public buildings rarely have wheelchair access or lifts, and only the newest will have bathrooms designed to accommodate wheelchairs.

Visas

Most countries issue visas from their embassies abroad and stamp it in your passport, but not Bhutan. Visas are issued only when you arrive in the country, either at Paro airport or (if entering by road) at Phuentsholing or Samdrup Jongkhar.

INDIAN TRAVELLERS IN BHUTAN

Indian nationals are allowed to travel on their own in Bhutan, with or without the services of a tour operator. If they choose to liaise with an operator, they are currently charged a minimum daily fee of US$135 per person (US$175 for teams of three people or less).

Indians don't require a visa to enter Bhutan, and are given a seven-day entry-cum-stay permit at the border offices upon presentation of a passport or government-issued ID such as a driving licence or voter's registration card. This permit allows travel only within Phuentsholing, Thimphu and Paro, and can be extended at the **Immigration Office** (☑02-323127) in Thimphu for successive periods of three weeks each. Bring at least five passport photos. One can also request a route permit here to travel beyond the three above-mentioned towns. Furthermore, a special permit must be obtained from the **Ministry of Culture** (☑02-322301) at the Trashi Chhoe Dzong for visiting all places of religious or cultural importance within Bhutan.

Indians without stay permits can wander freely in Phuentsholing during the day, but must return to India before 10pm. See p269 for arrival immigration details.

You must apply in advance through a tour operator and receive visa approval before you travel to Bhutan.

All applications for tourist visas must be initialised by a Bhutanese tour operator and are approved by the Ministry of Foreign Affairs in Thimphu. The operator submits an online visa application to TCB in Thimphu. It, in turn, checks that you have completely paid for your trip and then issues an approval letter to the tour operator. With this approval in hand, the tour operator then makes a final application to the Ministry of Foreign Affairs, which takes up to a week to process the visa.

It's not necessary to fill in a special visa application form. Just send a jpeg passport photo and a jpeg scan of your passport information pages. You may also need to provide your permanent address and occupation.

When the visa clearance is issued by the Ministry of Foreign Affairs, it sends a visa confirmation number to the tour operator and to Druk Air. Druk Air will not issue your tickets to Paro until it receives this confirmation number and then rechecks the visa information when you check in for the flight.

The actual visa endorsement is stamped in your passport when you arrive at one of the ports of entry for tourists. You will receive a visa for the exact period you have arranged to be in Bhutan. You will normally pay the visa fee of US$20 directly to your tour company. If some unusual event requires that you obtain a visa extension, your tour operator will arrange it.

It's surprisingly efficient considering all the time, distance and various levels of bureaucracy involved. When you arrive in Bhutan, the visa officer will invariably be able to produce your approval form from the file and the visa will be issued on the spot. It's very helpful to have a printout of the scanned visa authority to aid the immigration officials and Druk Air to find your information quickly.

Visas for Neighbouring Countries

INDIA

Nationals of most countries need a visa to visit India. If you are travelling overland to or from Bhutan via the border post in Phuentsholing or Samdrup Jongkhar, you will need an Indian visa.

The government of India strongly prefers that you obtain your Indian visa in the country that issued your passport. It's usually a simple task to get your Indian visa before you leave home, but it's complicated to get one if overseas. It is possible to obtain a seven-day transit visa overseas if you have confirmed flights in and out of India and can produce the appropriate tickets. Otherwise, you must pay a fee to the overseas embassy to send a fax to the Indian embassy in your own country and wait up to a week for a reply.

Tourist visas are generally issued for six months, are multiple entry, and are valid from the date of issue of the visa, not the date you enter India. This means that if you first enter India five months after the visa was issued, it will be valid for one month.

Re-entry into India has become complicated in the wake of the Mumbai terrorist attacks, as India now demands a two-month gap between visits. If you plan to return to India within this time period you will need to get your visa endorsed, either in your own country or at an Indian consulate. In Bhutan this costs Nu 480. You may also need to register once in India.

NEPAL

Visas for Nepal are available on arrival at Kathmandu airport or at land border crossings, including Kakarbhitta, the road crossing nearest to Bhutan. You will need one passport photo. If you are making a side trip to Bhutan from Kathmandu, be sure to get a double-entry visa the first time you arrive in Nepal. You can also obtain a visa for Nepal in advance from embassies abroad or from the Nepali embassy or consulate in the gateway cities of Bangkok, Delhi, Dhaka or Kolkata.

Travel Permits

RESTRICTED-AREA PERMITS

All of Bhutan outside of the Paro and Thimphu valleys is classified as a restricted area. Tour operators obtain a 'road permit' for the places on your itinerary, and this permit is checked and endorsed by the police at immigration checkpoints strategically located at important road junctions. The tour operator must return the permit to the government at the completion of the tour, and it is scrutinised for major deviations from the authorised program. In general you won't be aware that any of this is going on in the background

There are immigration checkpoints in Hongtsho (east of Thimphu), Chhukha (between Thimphu and Phuentsholing), Rinchending (above Phuentsholing), Wangdue Phodrang, Chazam (near Trashigang), Wamrong (between Trashigang and Samdrup Jongkhar), and in Samdrup Jongkhar. All are open from 5am to 9pm daily.

PERMITS TO ENTER TEMPLES

During times when there aren't festivals, tourists are allowed to visit the courtyards of dzongs and, where feasible, the *tshokhang* (assembly hall) and one designated lhakhang in each dzong, but only when accompanied by a licensed Bhutanese guide. This provision is subject to certain restrictions, including visiting hours, dress standards and other rules that vary by district.

Foreign and Indian tourists need a permit from the Ministry of Home and Cultural Affairs (Division of Cultural Properties) to visit government-run monasteries and dzongs. Dzongs are open to all during the time of a tsechu, when you may visit the courtyard, but not the lhakhangs. Your tour company will deal with all the necessary paperwork so let them know in advance if there are specific goembas or chapels you wish to visit.

The Tourism Council of Bhutan is working on a list of places tourists *cannot* visit, with the assumption that all other places can be visited. When this is introduced the cultural permit will likely be abolished. You can generally visit any lhakhang that is private or village-run.

If you are a practising Buddhist, you may apply for a permit to visit certain dzongs and religious institutions usually off limits. The credibility of your application will be enhanced if you include a letter of reference from a recognised Buddhist organisation in your home country.

Volunteering

Bhutan is selective about the type of projects it wants in the country and so the opportunities for volunteer work in Bhutan are limited. The UN has numerous programmes in Bhutan, all coordinated through the UN Development Programme (UNDP). Different agencies feed into the programme.

Other agencies that operate programmes in Bhutan include ACB (Austria), Danida (Denmark), GTZ (Germany), Helvetas (Switzerland), JOCV & JICA (Japan), Save the Children, SNV (Netherlands) and VSA (New Zealand).

Volunteers are not subject to the normal rules for tourists and the agency employing you will arrange your visa. Volunteers are allowed two visitors a year; the visitors must be close relatives and are not subject to the tourist tariff.

Women Travellers

Women, both foreign and Bhutanese, are not usually subject to harassment and do not need to take any special precautions. Men have a reasonably liberated attitude towards their relations with women. There are several opportunities for misunderstanding if you don't make your intentions clear from the very outset, however. Female travellers should be aware that romantic liaisons between tourists and Bhutanese guides are quite common. You might also be invited to a 'party' at the home of a Bhutanese male, and discover too late that you are the only guest.

Women are generally not allowed the enter the *goenkhang* (protector chapel) of a monastery or lhakhang (temple).

For information on Bhutanese women's groups and the status of Bhutanese women, see p208.

Transport

GETTING THERE & AWAY

The majority of travellers to Bhutan arrive by air at Bhutan's only international airport in Paro. Some travellers enter Bhutan by road at Phuentsholing on the southern border with the Indian state of West Bengal. Travellers to the far east of the country may enter or exit Bhutan at Samdrup Jongkhar, not far from Guwahati in Indian Assam. A new partially opened border crossing at Gelephu currently sees very little tourist traffic but this might change in the coming years.

Tours of Bhutan and rail tickets for India can be booked online at www.lonelyplanet.com/travel_services.

Entering the Country

Entry procedures are generally simple because your tour guide will meet you on arrival. Be sure to carry your visa authorisation form from the Ministry of Foreign Affairs. For arrival overland in Phuentsholing and Samdrup Jongkhar, see p268.

Passport

If your passport has less than six months of validity left, get a new one before setting off, because many countries in this region will not issue visas to persons whose passports are about to expire.

Keep your passport safe. No country other than India has the facility for issuing a replacement passport in Bhutan. If you lose your passport, you must travel 'stateless' to another country to get it replaced. You should carry some additional form of identification and a photocopy of your passport to help in such an event.

Indian and Bangladeshi travellers do not need a passport to visit Bhutan (see the boxed text, p263).

Air

Airports & Airlines

Bhutan has one international airport, **Paro** (PBH; ☎08-271423; ✈) and one national airline, **Druk Air** (www.drukair.com.bt).

Druk Air Paro (Map p74; ☎08-272044; reservation paro@drukair.com.bt; Nemeyzampa, Paro; ⊙9am-1pm, 2-5pm Mon-Fri, 10am-1pm Sat)

Druk Air Thimphu (Map p50; ☎02-323420; drukairthimphu@druknet.bt; Chang Lam Plaza; ⊙9am-1pm, 2-4pm Mon-Fri, 10am-1pm Sat & Sun)

CLIMATE CHANGE & TRAVEL

Every form of transport that relies on carbon-based fuel generates CO_2, the main cause of human-induced climate change. Modern travel is dependent on aeroplanes, which might use less fuel per kilometre per person than most cars but travel much greater distances. The altitude at which aircraft emit gases (including CO_2) and particles also contributes to their climate-change impact.

Many websites offer 'carbon calculators' that allow people to estimate the carbon emissions generated by their journey and, for those who wish to do so, to offset the impact of the greenhouse gases emitted with contributions to portfolios of climate-friendly initiatives throughout the world. Lonely Planet offsets the carbon footprint of all staff and author travel.

DEPART	ARRIVE	FREQUENCY	COST
Paro	Kathmandu	three weekly	US$221
Paro	Bangkok	daily	US$391-397
Paro	Kolkata	five weekly	US$221
Paro	Bagdogra	two weekly	US$125
Paro	New Delhi	two to three weekly	US$359
Paro	Dhaka	twice weekly	US$221

The Druk Air schedule changes by season, but normally there are two or three flights per week from New Delhi (sometimes via Kathmandu) and a daily flight from Bangkok, either direct or via Dhaka, Kolkata or Bagdogra, depending on the day of travel. Future connections are planned to Guwahati and possibly Singapore or Hong Kong. Rumoured connections to Mumbai have been cancelled. Extra flights are put on during the Thimphu *tsechu* (festival) in October and the Paro tsechu in April.

Buddha Air (www.buddha air.com), the private Nepali airline, now flies from Kathmandu to Paro, initially with four flights per week but to rise to daily.

There are only a few aircraft that can operate on a runway that is as short and high as Paro's. All landings and take-offs in Paro are by visual flight rules (VFR), which means that the pilot must be able to see the runway before landing, and see the surrounding hills before take-off. This means that no flights can be operated at night or in poor visibility, so when Paro valley is clouded in, flights are delayed, sometimes for days. When this happens your tour program will have to be changed and everything rebooked. The upside of such a delay is that you can probably add some spontaneity into your schedule in Bhutan and make a few modifications as you go.

» Reconfirm your Druk Air flight before departure and also once in Paro, to ensure that the schedule has not changed.

» Check in early for Druk Air flights as they occasionally depart before the scheduled time, especially if the weather starts to change for the worse.

» Flights are often delayed because of weather and Druk Air recommends that you travel on nonrestricted tickets and allow at least 24 hours' transit time with your connecting flight in order to minimise the complications of delays. It makes sense to budget a couple of days' sightseeing in Kathmandu or Bangkok.

DRUK AIR OFFICES ABROAD

Bangladesh (☏02-891 1066; dhaka@drukair.com.bt; Room 52, Terminal 2, Zia International Airport, Dhaka)

India (Kolkata ☏033-2290 2429, airport office ☏033-2511 9976; reservation@drukairccu .com; 51 Tivoli Court, 1A Ballygunge Circular Rd; New Delhi ☏011-2335 7703, airport office ☏011-2565 3207; sales.delhi@ drukair.com.bt; Ansal Bhawan Bldg, G fl 3, 16KH Marg, Connaught Place)

Nepal (☏01-423 9988, airport office ☏01-447 1712; sales@drukair.danfetravels. com; Danfe Travel Centre, Woodlands Hotel; Durbar Marg, Kathmandu)

Thailand (☏02-237 9202, airport office ☏02-134 3040; drukairbkk@drukair.com.bt; 5th fl, Suite 141/4, Skulthai Surawong Tower, Suriyawong, Bangkok)

DRUK AIR SALES AGENTS ABROAD

DNATA (☏02-883 1804; dnatakb@yahoo.com; Suite D1, House 83, 23 Valentine Castle Rd, Gulshan-1, Dhaka)

Druk Asia (☏6338 9909; www.drukasia.com; 60 Albert St, 12-03, Singapore 189969)

Global Union Transportation (☏852-2868 3231; josephlo@aeroglobal.com .hk; Room 22-24, New Henry House, 10 Ice Street, Central, Hong Kong)

Zen International Tours & Travels (☏0353-251 4403; www.zenitt.com; Hotel Central Plaza Market Complex, Mallaguri, PO Pradhan Nagar, Siliguri, India)

Tickets

Because there is little competition with other airlines for flights to Paro, Druk Air fares are relatively expensive. There are no discounts or student fares except for citizens of Bhutan. Moreover, Druk Air rules say that if fares are increased after the ticket is issued, they may collect the difference when you check in. It is now possible to purchase Druk Air tickets online using a credit card.

It's also possible to have your agent book your Druk Air ticket and email you the e-ticket. In the event of a cancellation you are likely to get a refund quicker this way and your agent should get direct notifications if there are changes to the flight times. Your agent will also email you a scan of your visa clearance from the Department of Immigration and you will need to show a printout of this when you check in with Druk Air.

THE RIDE OF A LIFETIME

The Druk Air flight from Kathmandu to Paro provides the most dramatic view of Himalayan scenery of any scheduled flight (snag a window seat on the left if you can). Look for the impressive Bodhnath stupa to the north as the plane takes off. Soon a continuous chain of peaks appears just off the left wing. The captain usually points out Everest (8850m; a black striated pyramid), Makalu (a grey chair-shaped peak) and Kanchenjunga (a huge massif), but if you have trekked in Nepal and are familiar with the mountains you can pick out many more. The elusive Shishapangma (8013m) is sometimes visible inside Tibet. Other recognisable peaks are Gauri Shankar (7185m), with its notched shape, Cho Oyu (8153m), Nuptse (7906m), with its long ridge, Lhotse (8501m) and Chhamlang (7319m).

When you pass Kanchenjunga, look for the dome-shaped peak on the western skyline. That is Jannu (7710m), which some French climbers have described as a 'peak of terror'; the Nepalis have renamed it Khumbakarna. Once past Kanchenjunga, the peaks are more distant. This is the Sikkim Himalaya; the major peaks, from west to east, are Chomoyummo (6829m), Pauhunri (7125m) and Shudu Tsenpa (7032m).

As the plane approaches Paro you may be able to spot the beautiful snow peak of Jhomolhari (7314m) and the grey ridge-shaped peak of Jichu Drakye (6989m). The plane then descends, often through clouds, banking steeply into the wooded valleys of Bhutan. Depending on the approach pattern that day, you may see Taktshang Goemba and Paro Dzong as you descend. Paro airport is often described as the scariest airstrip in the world but it's really not that bad.

You will need to buy a ticket to and from the place where you will connect to Druk Air. For most travellers this essentially means Delhi, Bangkok or Kathmandu, depending on where you are travelling from and which city you'd rather transit through. Delhi and Bangkok offer the most international connections, but Kathmandu will give you an extra taste of the Himalaya. Other connections via Kolkata or Dhaka are possible, but fewer discounted international air fares are available to these places.

TRANSIT BAGGAGE

Because Druk Air has no interline agreements with other carriers, your ticket to Paro will be separate from your other international

tickets. This means you cannot check your baggage all the way through to Paro via a connecting flight. You will need to reclaim your baggage and recheck it at the Druk Air counter. The only exception to this *might* be Thai Airways.

When you depart from Bhutan, Druk Air claims it can check bags through to your final destination if you give then the flight details during check-in but be aware that this information is hand-written on the baggage tags. Call us travel cynics but we don't fully trust the system.

The significance of not being able to check through your luggage is that you may have to go through immigration at your transfer airport to pick up your luggage in order to check in again. Depending on the country this can create visa problems. Bangkok and Kathmandu transit is relatively easy, requiring either no visa or free transit visas on the spot, but in Delhi you will likely need to find a staff member to get

your bag from the carousel and recheck it in for you as you can't exit the transit area without an Indian visa.

Land

Border Crossings

Phuentsholing The primary border crossing from India into Bhutan, on the border with the Indian state of West Bengal.

Samdrup Jongkhar Much less used but still possible for exit or entry, in the far east on the border with the Indian state of Assam.

Gelephu In 2010 authorities announced that foreigners could also make 'emergency exits' here. Few if any foreigners had crossed here at the time of research but things may change with the construction of a new airport, opening up several potential overland loop routes to central and eastern Bhutan.

For more information, head to shop.lonelyplanet.com to purchase a downloadable

PDF of the Northeast States chapter of Lonely Planet's *India* guidebook.

INDIA

To/From Phuentsholing

If you are travelling to or from Bhutan by land, all roads lead through Siliguri in West Bengal, the major transport hub in northeast India. Heading into India, you can make road connections from Phuentsholing or Jaigaon (just across the border) to the train station in Siliguri (169km, six hours) or the airport in Bagdogra (which has flights to Paro). From Siliguri it's easy to arrange a share-taxi or bus on to the Indian hill stations of Darjeeling (77km), Gangtok (114km) in Sikkim or Kalimpong, and also the Nepal border at Kakarbhitta.

The nearest main-line Indian train station to Phuentsholing is in New Jalpaiguri (near Siliguri). From there it's a 12-hour rail journey to Kolkata or a 33-hour trip to Delhi. You can travel by road direct to New Jalpaiguri from Phuentsholing or drive to Siliguri where you can simply flag down a rickshaw.

If you are headed to Bhutan, several Bhutanese transport companies operate a direct bus service at 8am and 2pm daily between Siliguri and Phuentsholing (Rs80, four hours). In Siliguri, the booking office is on Tenzing Norgay Rd (also known as Hill Cart Rd), opposite the Sher-e-Punjab Hotel. You can sometimes find Bhutanese taxis (yellow-roofed minivans with numberplates beginning with 'BT') looking for a return fare. You can technically buy a seat for Rs300, but might eventually have to charter the whole taxi for about Rs1200. Indian bus companies also operate services between Siliguri and Jaigaon on the Indian side of the Bhutanese border.

Bhutanese vehicles may travel freely in India and a Bhutanese tour operator can easily arrange a vehicle to any of these destinations. There are also taxis and shared hire cars available in both Phuentsholing and Siliguri.

Since Phuentsholing offers decent lodging options, few choose to halt at Jaigaon. If you absolutely must stay, try these hotels offering rooms with air-con:

Hotel Anand (☑03566-263783; M.G. Rd; s/d from Rs400/600) You can get a double with air-con for Rs 1200.

Hotel Kasturi (☑03566-263035; N.S. Rd; s/d from Rs400/600) Next to the immigration checkpoint.

The gate between Phuentsholing and Jaigaon closes at 9pm for vehicles, but people can cross on foot until 10pm.

Foreigners

Don't forget to get your passport stamped when leaving India. If your transport has already deposited you in Bhutan, you can simply walk back across the border to complete the paperwork.

Your guide will meet you at the gate and help you obtain your Bhutanese visa. The visa is issued in Phuentsholing, but the arrival details will be stamped in your passport when you pass the immigration checkpoint at Rinchending, 5km away.

Foreigners may cross back and forth across the border during the day but are required to leave Bhutan by 10pm unless staying in a hotel.

Indian Nationals

To go through immigration at Phuentsholing, Indian nationals are required to submit two passport-size photographs, a copy of their identification document such as passport or voters' identity card, and a filled-in application form at the **Immigration Office** (☑05-253079; Zhung Lam; ⊗6am-1pm & 2-6pm), which sits on the 1st floor of the Regional Revenue and Customs Office, located in front of Hotel Druk. A permit, printed on plain A4 paper, is then handed out by the immigration authorities, which must be stamped in at the check-post in Rinchending, en route to Thimphu.

Please note that these rules are changeable upon short notice, especially during politically sensitive periods or due to unforeseen security issues. For more on paperwork for Indian travellers see p263.

To/From Samdrup Jongkhar

Foreign and Indian tourists are allowed to enter or exit Bhutan at Samdrup Jongkhar. Check on the status of Assamese separatist groups before you decide to travel by land through Assam.

The primary reason you would want to exit this way is to avoid the long drive back over the mountains to Thimphu after visiting eastern Bhutan. From Samdrup Jongkhar, drive down to Guwahati in Assam, from where you can fly to Kolkata, Delhi, Bangkok or Bagdogra, or get a train connection to numerous Indian destinations. Due to security concerns, all Bhutanese vehicles have to travel in a convoy as far as Rangiya (there's no convoy on Thursday or Sunday), 49km from the border. (Indian vehicles face no such restrictions.) Six kilometres from the border is an Indian check-post, open 24 hours, where you must get an entry stamp. From Rangiya, it's best to drive the 80km, 2½-hour stretch to Guwahati, and a further 20km to the airport.

Another alternative is a 400km drive through the Indian Duars to Siliguri. On this route you could visit Kaziranga National Park, 233km east of Guwahati, famous for its rhino population.

Panitanki (aka Raniganj), in northern West Bengal, is opposite the eastern Nepal border town of Kakarbhitta. A long bridge separates the two towns across the Mechi River. Bhutanese tour operators can pick you up or drop you at Panitanki or you can arrange for them to take you to Bhadrapur or Biratnagar to catch a flight to Kathmandu.

Panitanki is only one hour (35km) from Siliguri (India). Buses run regularly on this route (Rs20) and taxis are easy to arrange (Rs400). A cycle-rickshaw across the border to Kakarbhitta costs Rs20. Buses depart Kakarbhitta at 5pm daily for Kathmandu (17 hours, NRs500 – Nepali rupees), a long rough drive via Narayanghat, Mugling and the Trisuli River valley. For further information, head to shop .lonelyplanet.com to purchase a downloadable PDF of the Kathmandu chapter of Lonely Planet's *Nepal* guidebook. Otherwise, see Lonely Planet's *Nepal* for details of what to see and do along this route.

A better option is to take a one-hour bus or taxi ride from Kakarbhitta to Bhadrapur and take a domestic flight to Kathmandu (US$147). There is a larger airport at Biratnagar (US$116), a four-hour drive from the border. Yeti Airlines and Buddha Air are the most reliable airlines. **Jhapa Travel Agency** (⌨977-23-562020) in Kakarbhitta will be able to book a flight.

GETTING AROUND

Because Bhutan has no domestic air service and does not have a centimetre of passenger railway track, the only way to see the country is either by foot or by road, though this looks set to change soon.

There is one main road: the National Highway, a 3.5m-wide stretch of tarmac that winds its way up and down mountains, across clattering bridges, along the side of cliffs and over high mountain passes. Rivers, mudflows and rockfalls present continual hazards, especially when it rains. The road can easily become blocked due to snow or landslides and can take anywhere from an hour to several days to clear. Take plenty of reading material.

Tour operators use buses made in Japan, Toyota Hi-Ace minivans and cars, depending on the size of the group. These vehicles can take you almost anywhere in the country, but for trips to central and eastern Bhutan during winter (December to February) or the monsoon (June to September) a 4WD vehicle is an advantage, and often a necessity.

If you are travelling on a tourist visa, the cost of all transport is included in the price of your trip and you'll have a vehicle available for both short- as well as long-distance travel. You'll only have to rely on public transport if you are an Indian national or if you are working with a project that does not provide you with a vehicle.

Air

Bhutan has ambitious plans for domestic air and helicopter service. New airports are expected in Yongphula (south of Trashigang in the far east) in 2011, at Gelephu (in southern Bhutan, near the border with India) in 2012 and then at Bathpalathang/Jakar (Bumthang, central Bhutan). Questions remain unanswered regarding the reliability of weather at these airports and who exactly will operate the flights. It's likely that helicopter services will start before scheduled flights. Check with your tour company to see the current status.

When opened, the airports in Yongphula and Gelephu in particular could really open up travel to the near inaccessible far east and change travel itineraries in that part of Bhutan.

Bicycle

Some travellers bring their mountain bikes to Bhutan, and several companies can help arrange this kind of tour. See p255 for more on cycling.

Bus

Public buses are crowded and rattly, and Bhutan's winding roads make them doubly uncomfortable. The government's Bhutan Post Express and plenty of other companies operate minibuses and so many passengers suffer from motion sickness that these have earned the nickname 'vomit comets'. Private operators such as Dhug, Metho and Sernya use more comfortable Toyota Coasters at about 50% more than the minibus fare. In eastern Bhutan you might arrive at the bus stop to discover that your bus is actually a truck with seats in the back!

Buses run at least once daily from Thimphu to Phuentsholing, Haa, Paro and Punakha. Long-distance buses run between one and three times a week from Thimphu to Zhemgang, Samtse, Trashi Yangtse, Mongar, Phobjika and Trashigang. Fares are cheap.

A public bus service operates throughout Thimphu from Chang Lam, including to Dechencholing in the north and Simtokha and Babesa to the south. Routes, fares and timetables are available at www.bhutan post.com.bt.

Car & Motorcycle

Since all transport is provided by tour operators, you normally do not have to concern yourself with driving. If for some reason you are arranging your own transport, you are still far better off using the services of a hired car and driver or a taxi. Driving in Bhutan is a harrowing experience. Roads are narrow and trucks roar around hairpin bends, appearing suddenly and forcing oncoming vehicles to the side. Because most roads are only about 3.5m wide, passing any oncoming vehicle involves one, or both, moving onto the verge.

Motorcycle trips in Bhutan can be arranged through **Himalayan Roadrunners** (www.ridehigh.com) and **Saffron Road Motorcycle Tours** (www.saffronroad.com). The local **Black Dragons Motorcycle Club** (www.bhutandragonmsc.com) in Thimphu might be able to offer advice for bikers tackling Bhutan's roads.

Your Own Vehicle

If you drive a vehicle into Bhutan, you can get a 14-day permit at the Phuentsholing border. You will need the help of a tour operator to handle the paperwork. If you are driving a vehicle that is registered overseas, you will need a carnet in order to get through India.

Indian visitors may travel throughout most of Bhutan in their own vehicle, upon getting all relevant documents such as registration papers, insurance policies, emission and fitness certificates and individual driving licences endorsed by the **Road Safety and Transport Authority** (www.rsta.gov.bt) at the border. Traffic regulations are the same as in India and are strictly enforced.

Driving Licence

NGO staff and volunteers who insist on driving in Bhutan should obtain a driving licence issued by the Road Safety and Transport Authority. Bhutanese licences are also valid throughout India.

An International Driving Permit is not valid in Bhutan. An Indian driving licence is valid in Bhutan, and it's possible for Indian nationals to drive in Bhutan; but unless you are an accomplished rally driver or are from a hill station such as Darjeeling and have experience in motoring in the mountains, it's safer with a professional driver.

Road Rules

Traffic keeps to the left and is much more orderly than in most other south Asian countries. Speeds are low in towns and on rural roads; you will be lucky to average more than 30km/h on the roads in the hills.

As is the case throughout Asia, it is important that the police establish who was at fault in any traffic accident. This means that the police must arrive and make the decision before any of the vehicles can be moved, even if the vehicles are blocking a narrow road. A relatively minor fender-bender can block the road for hours while everyone waits patiently for the police to arrive from the nearest town.

Local Transport

Taxi

There are taxis in Phuentsholing and Thimphu. Taxis have meters, but drivers rarely use them. For long-distance trips they operate on a flat rate that is rarely open to negotiation.

You should expect to pay Nu 50 for a local trip within Thimphu, Nu 700 for a full day and Nu 1200 (Maruti) to Nu 2000 (Mahindra Jeep or Bolero) from Thimphu to Phuentsholing. If you are travelling between Thimphu and Phuentsholing, look for a taxi that is from the place to which you want to go (vehicles with BT-2 numberplates are from Phuentsholing and those with BT-1 numberplates are from Thimphu or Paro) – you may be able to negotiate a lower price.

Health

The main health concerns in Bhutan are similar to those in other south Asian destinations: there is a relatively high risk of acquiring traveller's diarrhoea, a respiratory infection, or a more exotic tropical infection. The infectious diseases can interrupt your trip and make you feel miserable, but they are rarely fatal. If you go trekking, there are also risks associated with accidents and altitude sickness. Falling off trails, or having a rock fall on you as you trek, is rare but can happen.

The following advice is a general guide only and does not replace the advice of a doctor trained in travel medicine.

BEFORE YOU GO

Pack medications in their original, clearly labelled containers. A signed and dated letter from your physician describing your medical conditions and medications, including generic names, is also a good idea. If carrying syringes or needles, be sure to have a physician's letter documenting their medical necessity. If you have a heart condition, bring a copy of your ECG taken just prior to travelling.

If you take any regular medication, bring double your needs in case of loss or theft. You can't rely on many medications being available from pharmacies in Bhutan.

Insurance

Even if you are fit and healthy, don't travel without health insurance – accidents do happen. Declare any existing medical conditions you have – the insurance company *will* check if your problem is pre-existing and will not cover you if it is undeclared.

You may also require extra cover for adventure activities such as rock climbing. If your health insurance doesn't cover you for medical expenses abroad, consider getting extra insurance – for more information, check **Lonely Planet** (lonelyplanet.com). If you're uninsured, emergency evacuation is expensive; bills of over US$100,000 are not uncommon.

Find out in advance if your insurance plan will make payments directly to providers or reimburse you later for overseas health expenditures. (In many countries, doctors expect payment in cash.) You may prefer a policy that pays doctors or hospitals directly rather than you having to pay on the spot and claim later. If you have to claim later, make sure you keep all documentation. Some policies ask you to call (reverse charges) a centre in your home country, where an immediate assessment of your problem is made.

Vaccinations

Specialised travel-medicine clinics are your best source of information; they stock all available vaccines and will be able to give specific recommendations for you and your trip. Most vaccines don't produce immunity until at least two weeks after they're given, so visit a doctor four to eight weeks before departure. Ask your doctor for an International Certificate of Vaccination, which will list all the vaccinations you've received.

Recommended Vaccinations

The World Health Organization recommends the following vaccinations for travellers to Bhutan (as well as being up to date with measles, mumps and rubella vaccinations):

Diphtheria and tetanus (for adults) Single booster recommended if none in the previous 10 years. Side effects include sore arm and fever.

Hepatitis A Provides almost 100% protection for up to a year; a booster after 12 months provides at least another 20 years' protection. Mild side effects such as headache and sore arm occur in 5% to 10% of people.

Hepatitis B Now considered routine for most travellers, it is given as three shots over six months. A rapid schedule is also available, as is a combined vaccination with Hepatitis A. Side effects are mild and uncommon, usually headache and sore arm. Lifetime protection occurs in 95% of people.

Polio Bhutan's last case of polio was reported in 1986, but it has been reported more recently in nearby Nepal and India. Only one booster is required as an adult for lifetime protection. Inactivated polio vaccine is safe during pregnancy.

Typhoid The vaccine offers around 70% protection, lasts for two to three years and comes as a single shot. Tablets are also available; however, the injection is usually recommended as it has fewer side effects. Sore arm and fever may occur.

Varicella If you haven't had chickenpox, discuss this vaccination with your doctor.

These immunisations may be recommended for long-term travellers (more than one month) or those at special risk:

Japanese B Encephalitis Three injections in all. Booster recommended after two years. Sore arm and headache are the most common side effects. Rarely, an allergic reaction comprising hives and swelling can occur up to 10 days after any of the three doses.

Meningitis Single injection. There are two types of vaccination: the quadrivalent vaccine gives two to three years' protection; meningitis group C vaccine gives around 10 years' protection. Recommended for long-term backpackers aged under 25.

Rabies Three injections in all. A booster after one year will then provide 10 years' protection. Side effects are rare – occasionally headache and sore arm.

Tuberculosis A complex issue. Adult long-term travellers are usually recommended to have a TB skin test before and after travel, rather than vaccination. Only one vaccine given in a lifetime.

Required Vaccinations

The only vaccine required by international regulations is yellow fever. Proof of vaccination will only be required if you have visited a country in the yellow-fever zone within the six days prior to entering Bhutan. If you are travelling to Bhutan from Africa or South America, you should check to see if you require proof of vaccination.

Medical Checklist

Recommended items for a personal medical kit:

» Antifungal cream, eg Clotrimazole
» Antibacterial cream, eg Muciprocin
» Antibiotic for skin infections, eg Amoxicillin/Clavulanate or Cephalexin
» Antibiotics for diarrhoea, eg Norfloxacin or Ciprofloxacin for bacterial diarrhoea; Tinidazole for giardiasis or amoebic dysentery
» Antihistamine, eg Cetrizine for daytime and Promethazine for night
» Antiseptic, eg Betadine
» Antispasmodic for stomach cramps, eg Buscopan
» Contraceptives
» Decongestant, eg Pseudoephedrine
» DEET-based insect repellent
» Diarrhoea treatment – an oral rehydration solution (eg Gastrolyte), diarrhoea 'stopper' (eg Loperamide), and antinausea medication (eg Prochlorperazine)
» First-aid items such as scissors, bandages, gauze, thermometer, sterile needles and syringes, safety pins and tweezers
» Ibuprofen or other anti-inflammatory
» Iodine tablets (unless you are pregnant or have a thyroid problem) to purify water
» Laxative, eg Coloxyl
» Paracetamol
» Permethrin to impregnate clothing and mosquito nets
» Steroid cream for allergic/itchy rashes, eg 1% to 2% hydrocortisone
» Sunscreen
» Throat lozenges
» Thrush (vaginal yeast infection) treatment, eg Clotrimazole pessaries
» Ural or equivalent if you're prone to urine infections

Internet Resources

There is a wealth of travel health advice on the internet. For further information, **Lonely Planet** (lonelyplanet .com) is a good place to start. The **World Health Organization** (WHO; www.who.int/ith/) publishes a superb book called *International Travel & Health,* which is revised annually and is available free online. Another website of general interest is **MD Travel Health** (www .mdtravelhealth.com), which provides complete travel health recommendations for every country and is updated daily. The **Centers for Disease Control and Prevention** (CDC; www.cdc .gov) website also has good general information.

Further Reading

Lonely Planet's *Healthy Travel – Asia & India* is a handy pocket-sized book that is packed with useful information including pretrip planning, emergency first aid, immunisation and disease information and what to do if you get sick on the road. Other recommended

DRINKING WATER

» Never drink tap water

» Bottled water is generally safe – check the seal is intact at purchase

» Avoid ice

» Avoid fresh juices – they may have been watered down

» Boil water – this is the most efficient method of purifying it; let it boil a bit longer at higher altitudes

» Purify water – the best chemical purifier is iodine but this should not be used by pregnant women or those with thyroid problems

» Use water filters – should also filter out viruses; ensure your filter has a chemical barrier such as iodine and a small pore size, eg less than four microns

references include *Traveller's Health* by Dr Richard Dawood and *Travelling Well* by Dr Deborah Mills – check out the website www.travellingwell.com.au.

IN BHUTAN

Availability of Health Care

There are no private health clinics or physicians in Bhutan, but all district headquarters towns have a hospital, and will accept travellers in need of medical attention. The best facility is the **Jigme Dorji Wangchuk National Referral Hospital** in Thimphu. It has general physicians and several specialists, labs and operating rooms. Treatment is free, even for tourists. If you are seriously ill or injured you should consider evacuation to the excellent medical facilities in Bangkok. It is difficult to find reliable medical care in rural areas. Your embassy and insurance company are good contacts.

Self-treatment may be appropriate if your problem is minor (eg traveller's diarrhoea), you are carrying the appropriate medication and you cannot attend a

recommended clinic. If you think you may have a serious disease, especially malaria, do not waste time – travel to the nearest quality facility to receive attention. It is always better to be assessed by a doctor than to rely on self-treatment.

In most large towns there are shops that sell medicines. Most of the medical supplies mentioned in this section are available without a prescription.

Infectious Diseases

Coughs, Colds & Chest Infections

Respiratory infections usually start as a virus and are exacerbated by urban pollution, or cold and altitude in the mountains. Commonly, a secondary bacterial infection will intervene – marked by fever, chest pain and coughing up discoloured or blood-tinged sputum. If you have the symptoms of an infection seek medical advice or commence a general antibiotic.

Dengue Fever

This mosquito-borne disease is becomingly increasingly problematic throughout the tropical world, especially in

the cities. As there is no vaccine available it can only be prevented by avoiding mosquito bites. The mosquito that carries dengue bites day and night, so use insect avoidance measures at all times. Symptoms include high fever, severe headache and body ache. Some people develop a rash and experience diarrhoea. There is no specific treatment, just rest and paracetamol – do not take aspirin though as it increases the likelihood of haemorrhaging. See a doctor to be diagnosed and monitored.

Hepatitis A

A problem throughout the region, this food- and waterborne virus infects the liver, causing jaundice (yellow skin and eyes), nausea and lethargy. There is no specific treatment for hepatitis A – you just need to allow time for the liver to heal. All travellers to Bhutan should be vaccinated against hepatitis A.

Hepatitis B

The only sexually transmitted disease that can be prevented by vaccination, hepatitis B is spread by body fluids, including in sexual contact. The long-term consequences can include liver cancer and cirrhosis.

Hepatitis E

Hepatitis E is transmitted through contaminated food and water and has similar symptoms to hepatitis A, but is far less common. It is a severe problem for pregnant women and can result in the death of both mother and baby. There is currently no vaccine, and prevention is by following safe eating and drinking guidelines.

HIV

HIV is spread via contaminated body fluids. Avoid unsafe sex, unsterile needles (including in medical facilities) and procedures such as tattoos.

Influenza

Present year-round in the tropics, influenza (flu) symptoms include high fever, muscle aches, runny nose, cough and sore throat. It can be very severe in people over the age of 65 or in those with underlying medical conditions such as heart disease or diabetes; vaccination is recommended for these individuals. There is no specific treatment, just rest and paracetamol.

Japanese B Encephalitis

This viral disease is transmitted by mosquitoes and is rare in travellers. Like most mosquito-borne diseases it is becoming a more common problem in affected countries. Most cases occur in rural areas and vaccination is recommended for travellers spending more than one month outside cities. There is no treatment, and a third of infected people will die, while another third will suffer permanent brain damage.

To avoid contact with mosquitoes as much as possible, see the text to the right.

Malaria

For such a serious and potentially deadly disease, there is an enormous amount of misinformation concerning malaria. You must get expert advice as to whether your trip actually puts you at risk. For most rural areas, the risk of contracting malaria far outweighs the risk of any tablet side effects. Before you travel, seek medical advice on the right medication and dosage for you.

Malaria is caused by a parasite transmitted by the bite of an infected mosquito. The most important symptom of malaria is fever, but general symptoms such as headache, diarrhoea, cough or chills may also occur. Diagnosis can only be made by taking a blood sample.

Two strategies should be combined to prevent malaria; mosquito avoidance and antimalaria medications. Most people who catch malaria are taking inadequate or no antimalarial medication.

Travellers are advised to prevent mosquito bites by taking these steps:

» Use a DEET-containing insect repellent on exposed skin. Wash this off at night, as long as you are sleeping under a mosquito net. Natural repellents such as citronella can be effective, but must be applied more frequently than products containing DEET

» Sleep under a mosquito net impregnated with pyrethrin

» Choose accommodation with screens and fans (if not air-conditioned)

» Impregnate clothing with pyrethrin in high-risk areas

» Wear long sleeves and trousers in light colours

» Use mosquito coils

» Spray your room with insect repellent before going out for your evening meal

There are a variety of medications available. The effectiveness of the **Chloroquine and Paludrine** combination is now limited in many parts of South Asia. Common side effects include nausea (40% of people) and mouth ulcers.

The daily tablet **Doxycycline** is a broad-spectrum antibiotic that has the added benefit of helping to prevent a variety of tropical diseases, including leptospirosis, tickborne disease and typhus. The potential side effects include photosensitivity, thrush, indigestion, heartburn, nausea and interference with the contraceptive pill. More serious side effects include ulceration of the oesophagus – you can help prevent this by taking your tablet with a meal, and never lying down within 30 minutes of taking it. It must contiue to be taken for four weeks after leaving the risk area.

Lariam (Mefloquine) is a weekly tablet. Serious side effects are rare but include depression, anxiety, psychosis and having fits. Anyone with a history of depression, anxiety, another psychological disorder, or epilepsy should not take Lariam. It is considered safe in the second and third trimesters of pregnancy. Tablets must be taken for four weeks after leaving the risk area.

Malarone is a combination of Atovaquone and Proguanil. Side effects are uncommon and mild, most commonly nausea and headache. It is the best tablet for those on short trips to high-risk areas. It must be taken for one week after leaving the risk area.

Rabies

Rabies is considered to be endemic in Bhutan. This uniformly fatal disease is spread by the bite or lick of an infected animal – most commonly a dog or monkey. You should seek medical advice immediately after any animal bite and commence post-exposure treatment. Having a pre-travel vaccination means the post-bite treatment is greatly simplified. If an animal bites you, gently wash the wound with soap and water, and apply iodine based antiseptic. If you are not pre-vaccinated you will need to receive rabies immunoglobulin as soon as possible.

STDs

Sexually transmitted diseases most common in south Asia include herpes, warts, syphilis, gonorrhoea and chlamydia. People carrying these diseases often have no signs of infection. Condoms will prevent gonorrhoea and chlamydia but not warts or herpes. If after a sexual encounter you develop any rash, lumps, discharge or pain when passing urine, seek immediate medical attention. If you have been

TRAVELLER'S DIARRHOEA

Traveller's diarrhoea is by far the most common problem affecting travellers – between 30% and 50% of people will suffer from it within two weeks of starting their trip. In over 80% of cases, traveller's diarrhoea is caused by a bacteria, and therefore responds promptly to treatment with antibiotics, such as Norfloxacin. Keep in mind, though, that a couple of loose stools are little cause for concern.

Loperamide is just a 'stopper' and doesn't get to the cause of the problem. It can be helpful, for example, if you have to go on a long bus ride. Don't take Loperamide if you have a fever, or blood in your stools and seek medical attention quickly if you do not respond to an appropriate antibiotic.

Amoebic dysentery is very rare in travellers but is often misdiagnosed. Symptoms are similar to bacterial diarrhoea, ie fever, bloody diarrhoea and generally feeling unwell. You should always seek reliable medical care if you have blood in your diarrhoea. Treatment involves two drugs: Tinidazole or Metronidazole to kill the parasite in your gut followed by a second drug to kill the cysts.

Giardia lamblia is a parasite that is relatively common in travellers. Symptoms include nausea, bloating, excess gas, fatigue and intermittent diarrhoea. The parasite will eventually go away if left untreated but this can take months. The treatment of choice is Tinidazole.

sexually active during your travels, have an STD check on your return home.

Tuberculosis

While rare in travellers, medical and aid workers, and long-term travellers who have significant contact with the local population should take precautions. Vaccination is usually given only to children under the age of five, but adults at risk are recommended to have pre- and post-travel tuberculosis testing. The main symptoms are fever, cough, weight loss, night sweats and tiredness.

Typhoid

This serious bacterial infection is spread via food and water. It gives a high and slowly progressive fever, headache and may be accompanied by a dry cough and stomach pain. It is diagnosed by blood tests and treated with antibiotics. Vaccination is recommended for all travellers spending more than a week in Bhutan. Be aware that vaccination is not 100% effective so you must still be careful with what you eat and drink.

Environmental Hazards

Food

Eating in restaurants is the biggest risk factor for contracting traveller's diarrhoea. Ways to avoid it include eating only freshly cooked food, and avoiding shellfish and food that has been sitting around in buffets. Peel all fruit, cook vegetables and soak salads in iodine water for at least 20 minutes.

High Altitude

If you are going to altitudes above 3000m you should get information on preventing, recognising and treating Acute Mountain Sickness (AMS). AMS is a notoriously fickle affliction and can also affect trekkers and walkers accustomed to walking at high altitudes. AMS has been fatal at 3000m, although 3500m to 4500m is the usual range.

SYMPTOMS

Mild symptoms of AMS are very common in travellers visiting high altitudes, and usually develop during the first 24 hours at altitude. These will generally disappear through acclimatisation in several hours to several days.

Symptoms tend to be worse at night and include headache, dizziness, lethargy, loss of appetite, nausea, breathlessness and irritability. Difficulty sleeping is another common symptom.

AMS may become more serious without warning and can be fatal. Symptoms are caused by the accumulation of fluid in the lungs and brain, and include breathlessness at rest, a dry irritative cough (which may progress to the production of pink, frothy sputum), severe headache, lack of coordination (typically leading to a 'drunken walk'), confusion, irrational behaviour, vomiting and eventually unconsciousness.

The symptoms of AMS, however mild, are a warning – be sure to take them seriously! Trekkers should keep an eye on each other as those experiencing symptoms, especially severe symptoms, may not be in a position to recognise them. One thing to note is that while the symptoms of mild AMS often precede those of severe AMS, this is not always the case. Severe AMS can strike with little or no warning.

ACCLIMATISATION

With an increase in altitude, the human body needs time to develop physiological mechanisms to cope with the decreased oxygen. This process of acclimatisation is still not fully understood, but is known to involve modifications in breathing patterns and heart rate, and an increase in the blood's oxygen-carrying capabilities. These compensatory mechanisms usually take about one to three days to develop at a particular altitude. Once you are acclimatised to a given height you are unlikely to get AMS at that height, but you can still get ill when you travel higher. If the ascent is too high and too fast, these compensatory reactions may not kick into gear fast enough.

PREVENTION

To prevent acute mountain sickness:

» Ascend slowly. Have frequent rest days, spending two to three nights at each rise of 1000m.

» Trekkers should bear in mind the climber's adage 'Climb high, sleep low'. It is always wise to sleep at a lower altitude than the greatest height reached during the day. High day climbs followed by a descent back to lower altitudes for the night are good preparation for trekking at high altitude. Also, once above 3000m, care should be taken not to increase the sleeping altitude by more than 400m per day. If the terrain won't allow for less than 400m of elevation gain, be ready to take an extra day off before tackling the climb.

» Drink extra fluids. The mountain air is dry and cold, and moisture is lost as you breathe and sweat which may result in dehydration.

» Eat light, high-carbohydrate meals for more energy.

» Avoid alcohol as it may increase the risk of dehydration, and don't smoke.

» Avoid sedatives.

» When trekking, take a day off to rest and acclimatise if feeling over-tired. If you or anyone else in your party is having a tough time, make allowances for unscheduled stops.

» Don't push yourself when climbing up to passes; rather, take plenty of breaks. Given the complexity and unknown variables involved with AMS and acclimatisation, trekkers should always err on the side of caution and ascend mountains slowly.

TREATMENT

Treat mild symptoms by resting at the same or lower altitude until recovery, usually in a day or two. Take paracetamol or aspirin for headaches. If symptoms persist or become worse, however, *immediate descent* is necessary – even 500m can help.

The most effective treatment for severe AMS is to get down to a lower altitude as quickly as possible. In less severe cases the victim will be able to stagger down with some support; in other cases they may need to be carried down. Whatever the case, do not delay, as any delay could be fatal.

AMS victims may need to be flown out of Bhutan as quickly as possible – make sure you have adequate travel insurance.

The drugs acetazolamide (Diamox) and dexamethasone are recommended by some doctors for the prevention of AMS. However, you should be aware that their use is controversial. They can reduce the symptoms, but they may also mask warning signs; severe and fatal AMS has occurred in people taking these drugs. Drug treatments should never be used to avoid descent or to enable further ascent.

Bedbugs and fleas don't carry disease but their bites are very itchy. You can treat the itch with an antihistamine. Lice can also inhabit various parts of your body but most commonly your head and pubic area. Transmission is via close contact with an infected person. They can be difficult to treat and you may need numerous applications of an antilice shampoo.

Ticks are contracted after walking in rural areas. Ticks are commonly found behind the ears, on the belly and in armpits. If you have had a tick bite and experience symptoms such as a rash at the site of the bite or elsewhere, fever, or muscle aches you should see a doctor. Doxycycline prevents tick-borne diseases.

Leeches are found in humid rainforest areas. They do not transmit any disease but their bites are often intensely itchy for weeks afterwards and can easily become infected. Apply an iodine-based antiseptic to any leech bite to help prevent infection.

Bee and wasp stings mainly cause problems for people who are allergic to them. Anyone with a serious bee or wasp allergy should carry an injection of adrenaline (eg an EpiPen) for emergency treatment. For others, pain is the main problem – apply ice to the sting and take painkillers.

Skin Problems

Fungal rashes are common in humid climates. There are two common fungal rashes that affect travellers. The first occurs in moist areas that get less air such as the groin, armpits and between the toes. It starts as a red patch that slowly spreads and is usually itchy. Treatment involves keeping the skin dry, avoiding chafing and using an antifungal cream such as Clotrimazole or Lamisil. *Tinea versicolor* is also common – this fungus causes small, light-coloured patches, most commonly on the back, chest and shoulders. Consult a doctor.

Cuts and scratches become easily infected in humid climates. Take meticulous care of any cuts and scratches to prevent complications such as abscesses. Immediately wash all wounds in clean water and apply antiseptic. If you develop signs of infection (increasing pain and redness), see a doctor.

Sunburn

Even on a cloudy day, sunburn can occur rapidly. Always use a strong sunscreen (at least factor 30), and always wear a wide-brimmed hat and sunglasses outdoors. If you become sunburnt, stay out of the sun until you have recovered, apply cool compresses and take painkillers for the discomfort. One per cent hydrocortisone cream applied twice daily is also helpful.

Women's Health

In the urban areas of Bhutan, supplies of sanitary products are readily available. Birth-control options may be limited so bring adequate supplies of your own form of contraception. Heat, humidity and antibiotics can all contribute to thrush. Treatment is with antifungal creams and pessaries such as Clotrimazole. A practical alternative is a single tablet of Fluconazole (Diflucan). Urinary tract infections can be precipitated by dehydration or long bus journeys without toilet stops; bring suitable antibiotics.

Pregnant women should receive specialised advice before travelling. The ideal time to travel is in the second trimester (between 16 and 28 weeks), when the risk of pregnancy-related problems are at their lowest and pregnant women generally feel at their best.

During the first trimester there is a risk of miscarriage and in the third trimester complications such as premature labour and high blood pressure are possible. It's also wise to travel with a companion. Always carry a list of quality medical facilities available at your destination and ensure you continue your standard antenatal care at these facilities. Avoid rural travel in areas with poor transportation and medical facilities. Most of all, ensure travel insurance covers all pregnancy-related possibilities, including premature labour.

Malaria is a high-risk disease during pregnancy. WHO recommends that pregnant women do *not* travel to areas that have Chloroquine-resistant malaria. None of the more effective antimalarial drugs is completely safe during pregnancy.

Traveller's diarrhoea can quickly lead to dehydration and result in inadequate blood flow to the placenta. Many of the drugs used to treat various diarrhoea bugs are not recommended in pregnancy. Azithromycin is considered safe.

Although not much is known about the possible adverse effects of altitude on a developing foetus, many authorities recommend not travelling above 4000m while pregnant.

Language

The official language of Bhutan is Dzongkha. While Dzongkha uses the same script as Tibetan – and the two languages are closely related – Dzongkha is sufficiently different that Tibetans can't understand it. English is the medium of instruction in schools, so most educated people can speak it fluently. There are English signboards, books and menus throughout the country. Road signs and government documents are all written in both English and Dzongkha. The national newspaper, *Kuensel,* is published in three languages: English, Dzongkha and Nepali. In the monastic schools Choekey, the classical Tibetan language, is taught.

As a result of the isolation of many parts of the country, a number of other languages survive, and it's common for regional minorities to have their own language. Some are so different that people from different parts of the country can't understand each other. In eastern Bhutan most people speak Sharchop (meaning 'language of the east'), which is totally different from Dzongkha. In the south, most people speak Nepali. Bumthangkha is a language of the Bumthang region. Also spoken are Khengkha from Zhamgang, Kurtoep from Lhuentshe, Mangdep from Trongsa and Dzala from Trashi Yangtse.

PRONUNCIATION
The simplified pronunciation system used in this chapter is based on the official Romanisation system (used for writing Dzongkha in Roman script), so if you read our coloured pronunciation guides as if they were English, you'll be understood.

There are three accent marks: the apostrophe represents a high tone (eg 'ne) or a 'soft' consonant (eg g'), the circumflex accent (eg ê) represents long vowels, and the diaeresis (eg ö) alters the pronunciation of some vowels, namely ä (as the 'a' in 'hat'), ö as the 'ir' in 'dirt' (without the 'r' sound), and ü (like saying 'i' with the lips stretched back).

An h after the consonants c, d, g, l, p and t indicates that they are 'aspirated' (released with a slight puff of air) – listen to the 'p' sounds in 'pip'; the first is aspirated, the second is not.

Practise pronouncing the ng sound (as in 'sing') at the beginning of a word, eg *ngawang* (a name). The 'dental' consonants, t and th, are pronounced with the tongue tip against the teeth. Note also that c is pronounced as the 'ch' in 'church', and zh as the 's' in 'measure'.

BASICS

Hello.	kuzuzangbo la
Goodbye.	
(by person leaving)	läzhimbe jön
(by person staying)	läzhimbe zhû
Good luck.	trashi dele
Thank you.	kadriche
Yes.	ing/yö
No.	mê
Maybe.	im ong
How are you?	chö gadebe yö?
I'm fine.	nga läzhimbe ra yö
What's your name?	chö meng gaci mo?

Trekking & Country Life

alpine hut	bjobi gâ
alpine pasture	la nogi tsamjo
bridge	zam
cold (weather)	sîtraktra
hills	ri
house	chim
lake	tsho
mountain	gangri
mountain pass	la
mule track	ta lam
plain or meadow	thang
prayer flag	dâshi
river	chhu/tsangchhu
steep downhill	lam khamâ zâdra
steep uphill	khagen gâdra
stone carved with prayers	dogi mani
tired	udû/thangche
trail	lam/kanglam
village	ù
warm (weather)	drotokto/tshatokto

Which trail goes to ...?	... josi lam gâti mo?
Is the trail steep?	lam zâdra yö-ga?
Where is my tent?	ngê gû di gâti in-na?
What's the name of this village?	ani ûgi meng gaci zeu mo?
Let's go.	jogey-la

bird/chicken	bja
cow	ba
dog	rochi/chi
horse	ta
pig	phap
water buffalo	mahe
yak (male/female)	yâ/jim

barley	nâ
buckwheat	bjô
corn (maize)	gâza/gesasip
husked rice	chum
millet	membja
standing rice	bjâ
wheat	kâ

My name is ...	ngê meng ... ing
Where are you from?	chö gâti lä mo?
I'm from ...	nga ... lä ing
Where are you going?	chö gâti jou mo?
I'm staying at ...	nga ... döp ing
I know.	nga shê
I don't know.	nga mi shê
Can I take a photo?	pâ tabney chokar la?
May I take your photo?	chögi pâ ci tapge mä?
That's OK.	di tupbä
It's cold today.	dari jâm-mä
It's raining.	châp cap dowä

daughter	bum
elder brother	phôgem
elder sister	azhim
father	apa
friend	totsha/châro
mother	ama
son	bu
younger brother	nucu
younger sister	num/sîm

hers	mogi
his	khogi
mine	ngêgi
yours	chögi

big	bôm
cheap	khetokto
clean	tsangtokto
dirty	khamlôsisi
enough	tupbä/lâmmä
expensive	gong bôm
good	läzhim
happy	gatokto
heavy	jice
not good	läzhim mindu
small	chungku
that	aphidi
this	di

DIRECTIONS & TRANSPORT

What time does the bus leave?	drülkhor chutshö gademci kha jou inna?
I want to get off here.	nga nâ dögobe

How far is the ...?	... gadeci tha ringsa mo?
Is it near?	bolokha in-na?
Is it far?	tha ringsa in-na?
Go straight ahead.	thrangdi song
behind	japkha
here	nâ/nâlu
left	öm
in front of	dongkha
next to	bolokha
opposite	dongko/dongte
right	yäp
there	phâ/phâlu
where	gâti
north	bjang
south	lho
east	shâ
west	nup

EATING & DRINKING

Where is a ...?	... gâti mo?
local bar	changkha
restaurant	zakha
Do you have food now?	chö dato to za-wigang in-na?
I don't eat meat.	nga sha miza
I don't like food with chillies.	nga zhêgo êma dacikha miga
This is too spicy.	di khatshi dû
This is delicious.	di zhim-mä
Please give me a cup of tea.	ngalu ja phôp gang nang
It's enough.	digi lâm-mä

Key Words

food	zhêgo/to
hot (spicy)	khatshi yömi
hot (warm)	tshatom
slices	pa
tasty	zhimtoto

Meat & Vegetables

cabbage	banda kopi
cauliflower	meto kopi
chicken	bja sha

Numbers	
1	ci
2	nyî
3	sum
4	zhi
5	nga
6	drû
7	dûn
8	gâ
9	gu
10	cuthâm
11	cûci
12	cunyî
13	cûsu
14	cûzhi
15	cänga
16	cûdru
17	cupdü
18	côpgä
19	cügu
20	nyishu/khächi
30	sumcu/khä pcheda nyî
40	zhipcu/khänyî
50	ngapcu/khä pcheda sum
60	drukcu/khäsum
70	düncu/khä pcheda zhi
80	gepcu/khäzhi
90	gupcu/khä pcheda nga
100	cikja/khänga
1000	ciktong/tongthra ci
10,000	cikthri
100,000	cikbum/bum
1,000,000	saya ci

cooked vegetable	tshöse tsotsou
fish	ngasha
meat	ha
potatoes	kewa
radish	laphu
turnips	öndo
vegetable	tshöse

Other Foods

cheese	datse
chilli	êma
corn (maize)	gäza/gesasip
egg	gongdo

mushroom	shamu
mustard	päga
noodles	bathu/thukpa
rice (cooked)	to
salad	ezay

Drinks

beer (local)	bang chhang
boiled water	chhu kököu
cold water	chhu khöm
hot water	chhu tshatom
tea	ja
water	chhu
whisky (local)	ârra

HEALTH & EMERGENCIES

I'm ill.	nga nau mä
I feel nauseous.	nga cûni zum beu mä
I feel weak.	nga thangchep mä
I keep vomiting.	nga cûp cûsara döp mä
I feel dizzy.	nga guyu khôu mä
I'm having trouble breathing.	nga bung tang mit shubä

doctor	drungtsho
fever	jangshu
pain	nazu

SHOPPING & SERVICES

The word *khang* means building; in many cases it's only necessary to add the word for the type of building.

Where is a ...?	... gâti mo?
bank	ngükhang
bookshop	pekhang
cinema	loknyen
hospital	menkhang
market	thromkhang
monastery	goemba
police station	thrimsung gakpi mâkhang
post office	dremkhang
public telephone	manggi jüthrin tangsi
shop	tshongkhang
temple	lhakhang
toilet	chapsa

I want to see ...	nga ... tagobe
I'm looking for ...	nga ... tau ing
What time does it open?	chutshö gademci lu go pchiu mo?
What time does it close?	chutshö gademci lu go dam mo?
Is it still open?	datoya pchidi ong ga?
What is this?	di gaci mo?
I want to change money.	nga tiru sôgobä
How much is it?	dilu gadeci mo?
That's too much.	gong bôm mä
I'll give you no more than ...	ngâgi ... anemci lä trö mitshube
What's your best price?	gong gademcibe bjinni?

TIME & DATES

What is the time?	chutshö gademci mo?
(Five) o'clock.	chutshö (nga)

afternoon	pchiru
day	nyim/za
day after tomorrow	nâtshe
morning	drôba
night	numu
sometime	retshe kap
today	dari
tomorrow	nâba
yesterday	khatsha

Sunday	za dau
Monday	za mîma
Tuesday	za lhap
Wednesday	za phup
Thursday	za pâsa
Friday	za pêm
Saturday	za nyim

> **Politeness**
> To be polite, you can add -la to the end of almost anything you say in Dzongkha, and even to English words you might use in Bhutan. So when talking to a government minister, a lama or someone older than you, you can say eg 'yes-la' or 'okay-la', and you'll be showing respect.

For other useful words and phrases, see p279.

ABTO – Association of Bhutanese Tour Operators

anim – Buddhist nun

anim goemba – nunnery

arra – home-made spirit distilled from barley, wheat or rice

atrasa – masked clown that badgers the crowd at a *tsechu*

bangchung – round bamboo basket with a tight-fitting cover

BHU – Basic Health Unit

bodhisattva – a being who has the capacity of gaining Buddhahood in this life but who refuses it in order to be reincarnated in the world to help other beings

Bon – ancient, pre-Buddhist, animistic religion of Tibet; its practitioners are called Bon-po

Brokpa – minority group in eastern Bhutan

bukhari – wood-burning stove

bumpa – vase, usually used to contain holy water in *goembas*

carom – a game similar to snooker or pool played on a small wooden board using checkers instead of billiard balls

cham – ritual religious dance

chang – north

chhang – beer made from rice, corn or millet, pronounced 'chung'

chhu – river, also water

chilip – foreigner

Choekey – classical Tibetan (the language of religion)

choeshum – altar or shrine room

choesum – chapel

chorten – stone Buddhist monument, often containing relics

chugo – hard, dried yak cheese

dal – lentil soup

Dantak – Indian Border Roads Task Force

datho – astrological calendar

datse – traditional archery

desi – secular ruler of Bhutan

dharma – Buddhist teachings

dharma raja – British name for the Zhabdrung, the religious ruler, during the period 1652–1907

dochey – inner courtyard of a *dzong*

dotsho – hot-stone bath

doma – betel nut, also known by its Indian name, *paan*

dorji – a stylised thunderbolt used in rituals; *vajra* in Sanskrit

drak – cave or hermitage

dratshang – central monk body

driglam chhoesum – code of etiquette

driglam namzha – traditional values and etiquette

drubda – meditation centre for monks

Druk Gyalpo – the King of Bhutan

Drukpa Kagyu – the official religion of Bhutan, a school of tantric *Mahayana* Buddhism

drungkhag – subdistrict

dukhang – assembly hall in a *goemba;* also called a *tshokhang*

dungpa – head of a subdistrict

dzong – fort-monastery shared between government offices and monks' quarters

dzongdag – district administrator

Dzongkha – national language of Bhutan

dzongkhag – district

dzongpen – old term for the lord of the *dzong*

gakpa – police

gangri – snow mountain

gho – traditional dress for men

goemba – a *Mahayana* Buddhist monastery

goenkhang – chapel devoted to protective and terrifying deities, usually *Mahakala*

gomchen – lay or married monk

gorikha – porch of a *lhakhang,* literally 'mouth of the door'

GSI – Geological Survey of India

gup – elected village leader

Guru Rinpoche – the common name of Padmasambhava, the founder of *Mahayana* Buddhism

gyalpo – ruler or king

himal – Sanskrit word for mountain

IMTRAT – Indian Military Training Team

Je Khenpo – Chief Abbot of Bhutan

jogyig – Bhutanese script

kabney – scarf worn over the shoulder on formal occasions

khandroma – a female celestial being; *dakini* in Sanskrit

khenpo – abbot

khonying – archway chorten

kira – traditional dress for women

kora – circumambulation

kuru – a game played with large darts thrown 20m to a small target

la – mountain pass

lam – path or road

lama – *Mahayana* Buddhist teacher or priest

lha – god or deity

lhakhang – temple, literally 'god house'

lho – south

Lhotshampa – southern Bhutanese people, mainly Nepali-speaking

Losar – Bhutanese and Tibetan New Year

lopon – senior monk or teacher

lu – serpent deities, called *naga* in Sanskrit

Mahakala – Yeshe Goenpo, the guardian god of Bhutan, who manifests himself as a raven

Mahayana – school of Buddhism, literally 'great vehicle'

mandala – cosmic diagram; *kyilkhor* in *Dzongkha*

mani stone – stone carved with the Buddhist mantra *om mani peme hum*

mantra – prayer formula or chant

momo – a steamed or fried dumpling

nakey – fiddlehead fern frond

naktshang – temple dedicated to warlord or protective deity, literally 'place of vows'

NCCA – National Commission for Cultural Affairs

ney – sacred site

ngultrum – unit of Bhutanese currency

nup – west

NWAB – National Womens' Association of Bhutan

Nyingma – lineage of Himalayan Buddhism; its practitioners are Nyingmapa

om mani peme hum – sacred Buddhist mantra, roughly translates as 'hail to the jewel in the lotus'

outreach clinic – health posts in remote villages

PCO – Public Call Office

penlop – regional governor, literally lord-teacher

phajo – priest

prayer flag – long strips of cloth printed with prayers that are 'said' whenever the flag flaps in the wind

prayer wheel – cylindrical wheel inscribed with, and containing, prayers

rabdey – district monk body

rachu – shoulder cloth worn by women on formal occasions

RBA – Royal Bhutan Army

RBP – Royal Bhutan Police

rigney – name used for a school for traditional studies

rinpoche – reincarnate lama, usually the abbot of a *goemba*

river left – the left bank of a river when facing downstream

river right – the right bank of a river when facing downstream

RSPN – Royal Society for Protection of Nature

SAARC – South Asia Association for Regional Cooperation. This includes Bangladesh, Bhutan, India, Maldives, Nepal, Pakistan and Sri Lanka.

Sakyamuni – one name for Gautama Buddha, the historical Buddha

shar – east

shedra – Buddhist college

shing – wood

shunglam – highway

sonam – good luck

stupa – hemispherical Buddhist structure from which the *chorten* evolved

terma – texts and artefacts hidden by *Guru Rinpoche*

terton – discoverer of *terma*

thang – plain

thangka – painted or embroidered religious picture

thondrol – huge *thangka* that is unfurled on special occasions, literally 'liberation on sight'

thos – a heap of stones representing the guardians of the four directions

thukpa – noodles, often served in a soup

torma – ritual cake made of *tsampa*, butter and sugar

trulku – a reincarnation; the spiritual head of a *goemba*

Tsa-Wa-Sum – Government, Country and King

tsachhu – hot spring

tsampa – barley flour, a staple food in hill villages

tsechu – religious dance festival

tseri – the practice of shifting cultivation

tshamkhang – small meditation quarters

tsha-tsha – small images moulded in clay

tsho – lake

Tshogdu – National Assembly

tshokhang – assembly hall in a *lhakhang*

tsip – lay monk

utse – the central tower that houses the *lhakhang* in a *dzong*

yathra – strips of woven woollen cloth

yeti – the abominable snowman

Zangto Pelri – the celestial abode or paradise of *Guru Rinpoche*

Zhabdrung, the – title of the reincarnations of the Zhabdrung Ngawang Namgyal

behind the scenes

SEND US YOUR FEEDBACK

We love to hear from travellers – your comments keep us on our toes and help make our books better. Our well-travelled team reads every word on what you loved or loathed about this book. Although we cannot reply individually to postal submissions, we always guarantee that your feedback goes straight to the appropriate authors, in time for the next edition. Each person who sends us information is thanked in the next edition – and the most useful submissions are rewarded with a free book.

Visit **lonelyplanet.com/contact** to submit your updates and suggestions or to ask for help. Our award-winning website also features inspirational travel stories, news and discussions.

Note: We may edit, reproduce and incorporate your comments in Lonely Planet products such as guidebooks, websites and digital products, so let us know if you don't want your comments reproduced or your name acknowledged. For a copy of our privacy policy visit lonelyplanet.com/privacy.

OUR READERS

Many thanks to the travellers who used the last edition and wrote to us with helpful hints, useful advice and interesting anecdotes:

Laerke Aaboe-Jacobsen, Shiriin Barakzai, Stephen Baseman, Bertille, William Bettinelli, Bradley Brin, Georg Burchardi, Marilyn Carroll, Paul Cat, Chris Catton, W Charles Bridges, Joan Ciastkowski, Ghyslaine Côté, Philippe Danneels, Jatin Desai, Vishvesh Desai, Phub Dorji, Paul Enos, Doug Foote, Sally Fri, Daniel Gerster, Sabine Gerull, Dilu Giri, Richard Gosselin, Tashi Gyeltshen, Susan Higginbottom, Russell Huntington, Romin Joseph, Bruno Jousselin, Sandra Kroll, Linda Le, Sonia Levy, Chamberland Marc, Meave O'Connor, Lilly Parker, Dechen Pelden, Fika Perie, Lisa Plag, Nicole Pluss, Audrey Purwana, Ralf, Christopher Robert, Simone Schneider, Tracey Schwartz, Monica Seits, Khetnath Sharma, Jigme Tsering, Jamie Vaughan, Jayanthy Venkataraman, Helga Verhaegh, Tom Waite, Jacques Wells, Garth Willson

AUTHOR THANKS

Bradley Mayhew

Thanks to Karma Gyaltsen, of Bhutan Mountain Holiday, who arranged my entire trip,

answered endless questions and allowed me the flexibility to stop at every monastery and try dozens of local restaurants. My guide Chimi Rinzin was a great help, as was driver and part-time guide Pema Wangchuk, who was the best fixer I could have hoped for. Thanks to Thuji Nadik at the Tourism Council of Bhutan and Tsering Chokyi of the RSPN at Phobjikha, and Marianne, Hendrik and Justin for recommendations. Cheers to Anirban and Lindsay, who took on extra monsoon research at the last minute, and to Suzannah for sending me on a dream gig for a second time.

Lindsay Brown

I am grateful for the guidance of Stan Armington who wrote the first two editions solo. The following also provided invaluable assistance: Rinzin Wangchuk, Robin Pradhan and Chador Wangdi of Yu Druk Tours & Treks; Thuji Dorji Nadik at the Tourism Council of Bhutan; Wangchuk Wangdi of Thunder Dragon Treks; and Fritz and Tshering Maurer at the Swiss Guest House. Special thanks to Tshering Jamdrup for negotiating the mountain passes. Finally, thanks to coauthor Bradley Mayhew, and Jenny, Pat and Sinead.

Anirban Mahapatra

Sincerest thanks to Dago Beda, Tenzin Namgay and guide Sharap Dorji at Etho Metho Tours & Treks for their invaluable help. To officials Chhimi Pem, Garab Dorji Namgyel and Palden Dorji at TCB, who generously let me explore their trekking databases. To mountaineer Robin Pradhan Joshi, for uncomplainingly sitting through my queries and helping me piece my text together. To Lonely Planet author Stan Armington, for bequeathing me a fantastic chapter to work on. To the immigration officials at Phuentsholing and the Indian embassy in Thimphu, for their kind cooperation. Above all, thanks to Suzannah Shwer, senior authors Bradley Mayhew and Lindsay Brown and the team at Lonely Planet.

Acknowledgments

Climate map data adapted from Peel MC, Finlayson BL & McMahon TA (2007) 'Updated World Map of the Köppen-Geiger Climate Classification', Hydrology and Earth System Sciences, 11, 163344.

Cover photograph: Young Buddhist monk with flower at Dechen Phodrang monastery, Thimphu/Gavin Gough, LPI. Many of the images in this guide are available for licensing from Lonely Planet Images: www.lonely planetimages.com.

THIS BOOK

The 1st and 2nd editions of Bhutan were researched and written by Stan Armington. The 3rd edition was researched and written by Lindsay Brown and Bradley Mayhew. Stan updated the Trekking chapter and Richard Whitecross wrote the Buddhism in Bhutan and The Culture chapters. This 4th edition was coordinated by Bradley Mayhew, and written and researched by Bradley, Lindsay Brown and Anirban Mahapatra.

This guidebook was commissioned in Lonely Planet's Melbourne office, and produced by the following:

Commissioning Editor Suzannah Shwer

Coordinating Editors Elizabeth Anglin, Evan Jones

Coordinating Cartographer Julie Dodkins

Coordinating Layout Designer Jessica Rose

Managing Editor Brigitte Ellemor

Senior Editor Katie Lynch

Managing Cartographer Shahara Ahmed

Managing Layout Designer Celia Wood

Assisting Editors Monique Choy, Jackey Coyle, Laura Gibb, Amy Karafin

Cover Research Naomi Parker

Illustrator Michael Ruff

Internal Image Research Sabrina Dalbesio, Jane Hart

Language Content Annelies Mertens, Branislava Vladisavljevic

Thanks to Mark Adams, Imogen Bannister, David Connolly, Melanie Dankel, Stefanie Di Trocchio, Janine Eberle, Joshua Geoghegan, Mark Germanchis, Michelle Glynn, Lauren Hunt, Laura Jane, David Kemp, Indra Kilfoyle, Lisa Knights, Nic Lehman, John Mazzocchi, Wayne Murphy, Adrian Persoglia, Piers Pickard, Lachlan Ross, Julie Sheridan, Laura Stansfeld, John Taufa, Sam Trafford, Gina Tsarouhas, Juan Winata, Emily Wolman, Nick Wood

index

how to use this book

These symbols will help you find the listings you want:

👁	Sights	🎊	Festivals & Events	☆	Entertainment
🏃	Activities	🛏	Sleeping	🔒	Shopping
🍴	Courses	🍴	Eating	ℹ	Information/Transport
👉	Tours	🍷	Drinking		

These symbols give you the vital information for each listing:

🕽	Telephone Numbers	📶	Wi-Fi Access	🚌	Bus
🕐	Opening Hours	🏊	Swimming Pool	⛴	Ferry
P	Parking	🥗	Vegetarian Selection	M	Metro
⊖	Nonsmoking	📖	English-Language Menu	S	Subway
✳	Air-Conditioning	👪	Family-Friendly	⊖	London Tube
@	Internet Access	🐾	Pet-Friendly	🚋	Tram
				🚆	Train

Reviews are organised by author preference.

Look out for these icons:

TOP CHOICE	Our author's recommendation
FREE	No payment required
🌿	A green or sustainable option

Our authors have nominated these places as demonstrating a strong commitment to sustainability – for example by supporting local communities and producers, operating in an environmentally friendly way, or supporting conservation projects.

Map Legend

Sights
- 🟤 Beach
- 🔵 Buddhist
- 🔵 Castle
- 🔵 Christian
- 🔵 Hindu
- 🔵 Islamic
- 🔵 Jewish
- 🔵 Monument
- 🔵 Museum/Gallery
- 🔵 Ruin
- 🔵 Winery/Vineyard
- 🔵 Zoo
- 🔵 Other Sight

Activities, Courses & Tours
- 🔵 Diving/Snorkelling
- 🔵 Canoeing/Kayaking
- 🔵 Skiing
- 🔵 Surfing
- 🔵 Swimming/Pool
- 🔵 Walking
- 🔵 Windsurfing
- • Other Activity/Course/Tour

Sleeping
- 🔵 Sleeping
- 🔵 Camping

Eating
- 🔵 Eating

Drinking
- 🔵 Drinking
- 🔵 Cafe

Entertainment
- 🔵 Entertainment

Shopping
- 🔵 Shopping

Information
- 🔵 Bank
- 🔵 Embassy/Consulate
- 🔵 Hospital/Medical
- 🔵 Internet
- 🔵 Police
- 🔵 Post Office
- 🔵 Telephone
- 🔵 Toilet
- 🔵 Tourist Information
- • Other Information

Transport
- 🔵 Airport
- 🔵 Border Crossing
- 🔵 Bus
- ++🔵++ Cable Car/Funicular
- ·-🔵-· Cycling
- - - 🔵 - - Ferry
- 🔵 Metro
- ═🔵═ Monorail
- P Parking
- 🔵 Petrol Station
- 🔵 Taxi
- +🔵+ Train/Railway
- ═🔵═ Tram
- • Other Transport

Routes
- Tollway
- Freeway
- Primary
- Secondary
- Tertiary
- Lane
- Unsealed Road
- Steps
- Tunnel
- Pedestrian Overpass
- Walking Tour
- Walking Tour Detour
- – – – Path

Geographic
- 🔵 Hut/Shelter
- 🔵 Lighthouse
- 🔵 Lookout
- ▲ Mountain/Volcano
- 🔵 Oasis
- 🔵 Park
-)(Pass
- 🔵 Picnic Area
- 🔵 Waterfall

Population
- 🔵 Capital (National)
- ◉ Capital (State/Province)
- 🔵 City/Large Town
- ○ Town/Village

Boundaries
- – – – International
- – – – – State/Province
- – – – Disputed
- – – – Regional/Suburb
- Marine Park
- Cliff
- Wall

Hydrography
- River, Creek
- Intermittent River
- Swamp/Mangrove
- Reef
- Canal
- Water
- Dry/Salt/Intermittent Lake
- Glacier

Areas
- Beach/Desert
- + + + Cemetery (Christian)
- × × × Cemetery (Other)
- Park/Forest
- Sportsground
- Sight (Building)
- Top Sight (Building)

OUR STORY

A beat-up old car, a few dollars in the pocket and a sense of adventure. In 1972 that's all Tony and Maureen Wheeler needed for the trip of a lifetime – across Europe and Asia overland to Australia. It took several months, and at the end – broke but inspired – they sat at their kitchen table writing and stapling together their first travel guide, *Across Asia on the Cheap*. Within a week they'd sold 1500 copies. Lonely Planet was born.

Today, Lonely Planet has offices in Melbourne, London and Oakland, with more than 600 staff and writers. We share Tony's belief that 'a great guidebook should do three things: inform, educate and amuse'.

OUR WRITERS

Bradley Mayhew

Coordinating Author, Thimphu, Western Bhutan A self-professed mountain junkie, Bradley has been trekking in the Himalaya for over 15 years now, spending extended periods of time in Nepal, Bhutan, Ladakh and Tibet. After crossing Bhutan from west to east for the last edition of this guide, Bradley concentrated on the west for this edition, exploring such lesser-visited destinations as the hike to Kila Nunnery and little-visited Dzongdrakha Goemba, as well as walking the Druk Path Trek. Bradley is the coauthor of the Lonely Planet guides *Tibet*, *Bhutan*, *Nepal* and *Trekking in the Nepal Himalaya*, as well as a dozen other titles. He was recently the subject of an Arte documentary retracing the route of Marco Polo. Find him at www.bradleymayhew.blogspot.com. Bradley also wrote most Plan Your Trip chapters, the Druk Path Trek, Directory and Transport.

Read more about Bradley at:
lonelyplanet.com/members/Nepalibrad

Lindsay Brown

Central Bhutan, Eastern Bhutan Summer in central Bhutan is surprisingly pleasant and relaxed with ample opportunity for interacting with the locals, observing traditional agriculture and tasting the produce. While tackling the roads of eastern Bhutan in summer has its challenges, the raging waterfalls, spectacular birdlife and the intense and varied shades of green make for an amazing adventure. A former conservation biologist and Publishing Manager at Lonely Planet, Lindsay has trekked, jeeped, ridden and stumbled across many a mountain pass and contributed to Lonely Planet's *South India, India, Rajasthan, Delhi & Agra, Nepal* and *Pakistan & the Karakoram Highway* guides, among others. Bradley also wrote Top 20 Experiences, Welcome to Bhutan, Understand chapters and Health.

Anirban Mahapatra

Treks Ever since he enrolled in a Darjeeling school at the age of eight, Anirban has conducted numerous sorties along the Himalaya from Bhutan to Kashmir, trekking down mountain paths, sipping on *chhang* (beer) and meditating in atmospheric Buddhist monasteries. A journalist and travel writer, Anirban has extensively researched Bhutanese culture and society, all the while acquiring a taste for the fiery *ema datse* (chillies). The vertigo-inducing road journey from Phuentsholing to Thimphu remains one of his all-time favourite Himalaya experiences (despite missing a bottomless gorge by a whisker this time around). A Lonely Planet author since 2007, Anirban lives in Kolkata and Delhi. Anirban also wrote Planning Your Trek and part of the Western Bhutan chapter.

Read more about Anirban at:
lonelyplanet.com/members/anirbanmahapatra

Published by Lonely Planet Publications Pty Ltd
ABN 36 005 607 983
4th edition – March 2011
ISBN 978 1 74104 919 0
© Lonely Planet 2011   Photographs © as indicated 2011
10 9 8 7 6 5 4 3 2 1
Printed in Singapore